New Masters of Flash

Volume 3

OLA BERGNER
BILLY BUSSEY
BRENDAN DAWES
ANTHONY EDEN
DANNY FRANZREB
KRISTIN HENRY
NATHALIE LAWHEAD
SIMONE LEGNO
TODD MARKS
SHANE MIELKE
KEITH PETERS
ADAM PHILLIPS
OLIVER SHAW
JARED TARBELL

friendsof

DESIGNER TO DESIGNER™

an Apress® company

New Masters of Flash: Volume 3

ISBN (pbk): 1-59059-314-6

Printed and bound in China 10987654321

Trademarked names may appear in this book. Rather than use a trademark symbol with every occurrence of a trademarked name, we use the names only in an editorial fashion and to the benefit of the trademark owner, with no intention of infringement of the trademark.

Distributed to the book trade in the United States by Springer-Verlag New York, Inc., 175 Fifth Avenue, New York, NY 10010 and outside the United States by Springer-Verlag GmbH & Co. KG, Tiergartenstr. 17, 69112 Heidelberg, Germany.

In the United States: phone 1-800-SPRINGER, e-mail orders@springer-ny.com, or visit http://www.springer-ny.com. Outside the United States: fax +49 6221 345229, e-mail orders@springer.de, or visit http://www.springer.de.

For information on translations, please contact Apress directly at 2560 Ninth Street, Suite 219, Berkeley, CA 94710. Phone 510-549-5930, fax 510-549-5939, e-mail info@apress.com, or visit http://www.apress.com.

The information in this book is distributed on an "as is" basis, without warranty. Although every precaution has been taken in the preparation of this work, neither the author(s) nor Apress shall have any liability to any person or entity with respect to any loss or damage caused or alleged to be caused directly or indirectly by the information contained in this work.

Commissioning Editor:
Steve Rycroft

Graphic Designer and Compositor:
Katy Freer

Technical Editors:
Matthew Knight
Steve Rycroft

Consulting Editor:
Sham Bhangal

Editorial Board:
Steve Anglin, Dan Appleman,
Ewan Buckingham, Gary Cornell,
Tony Davis, John Franklin,
Jason Gilmore, Chris Mills,
Steve Rycroft, Dominic Shakeshaft,
Jim Sumser, Karen Watterson,
Gavin Wray, John Zukowski

Project Manager:
Beckie Stones

Copy Edit Manager:
Nicole LeClerc

Copy Editors:
Nicole LeClerc
Rebecca Rider

Production Manager:
Kari Brooks

Production Editor and Proofreader:
Katie Stence

CD Design:
Pete Aylward

Copyright Research:
Beckie Stones

Indexer:
Kevin Broccoli

Cover Design:
Danny Franzreb, Katy Freer, and Kurt Krames

Manufacturing Manager:
Tom Debolski

CONTENTS

People and ideas, code and design—the *New Masters of Flash*:

Design deconstruction.

ActionScript louder than words.

The original *New Masters of Flash* was the first book friends of ED ever published. And it became more than just a book, it came to define the way we work and the kind of books we aim to create. It outlined our belief in the ability of the visionary designers, New Masters, to create a new form.

We've published almost a hundred books since the moment we drank something fizzy from paper cups to celebrate overtaking Danielle Steel in the Amazon rankings with our first book. And Flash has continued to evolve steadily. It might be possible to get nostalgic about the previous volumes of *New Masters of Flash* if it weren't for the fact that—incredibly—the creativity, scope, and pure talent of the New Masters has kept pace with the software. This book contains by far the greatest breadth of the series, from the maximum-byte design ethos of Billy Bussey's 3D transitions, to the carefully structured scientific illustrations of Kristin Henry's learning applications.

We love how great ideas evolve. Believe in what you see. Pour your heart and soul into your work. Be brave, be passionate, be inspired—and go on to inspire others.

Think you're good enough for the next volume of New Masters of Flash? Prove it:
newmasters@friendsofed.com

Be happy and play nice,
friendsofED.gotoAndPlay()

People and ideas, code and design—the *New Masters of Flash*:

Design deconstruction.

ActionScript louder than words.

The original *New Masters of Flash* was the first book friends of ED ever published. And it became more than just a book, it came to define the way we work and the kind of books we aim to create. It outlined our belief in the ability of the visionary designers, New Masters, to create a new form.

We've published almost a hundred books since the moment we drank something fizzy from paper cups to celebrate overtaking Danielle Steel in the Amazon rankings with our first book. And Flash has continued to evolve steadily. It might be possible to get nostalgic about the previous volumes of *New Masters of Flash* if it weren't for the fact that—incredibly—the creativity, scope, and pure talent of the New Masters has kept pace with the software. This book contains by far the greatest breadth of the series, from the maximum-byte design ethos of Billy Bussey's 3D transitions, to the carefully structured scientific illustrations of Kristin Henry's learning applications.

We love how great ideas evolve. Believe in what you see. Pour your heart and soul into your work. Be brave, be passionate, be inspired—and go on to inspire others.

Think you're good enough for the next volume of New Masters of Flash? Prove it:
newmasters@friendsofed.com

Be happy and play nice,
friendsofED.gotoAndPlay()

Browse and read this book in any order you like, but here follows a quick summary of the dazzling delights on show. If you read something that you didn't expect to, you may well end up creating something that you didn't expect to. . .

Interaction

We'll start with what we can loosely call interaction design. First off, Brendan Dawes shares his thoughts on the state of the art and why we should all delete the term *Flash Designer* from our résumés. Brendan encourages us all to get outside and look beyond the screen for our inspiration. Billy Bussey will show you that "more is more," and how being drunk at a party in 1999 led to some dramatic and intense Flash transitions that are "slightly over the top." Simone Legno will justify his belief in heroes and sketchbooks by showing you the kawaii characters that are responsible for "so many sleepless nights," and Oliver Shaw will tell you about slapsies, Flashturbation, and how "being a master of Flash is more than just knowing how to code cool toys." Danny Franzreb shows how mixing skateboarding, trigonometry, restless passion, and Sven Väth can create some great interactive sound, while Shane Mielke talks about his conversion to design and the process of conceiving and creating immersive Flash environments.

Animation

Moving on to animation and motion graphics, ever-popular topics that define the origins of Flash, Ola Berger will show you what he can do when he combines the amazing images that he encounters on journeys into his own mind with a love of storytelling and an ability to "think 3D." Adam Phillips will introduce you to the life of a lightbulb, and demonstrate why lighting effects are "kind of sneaky." You should see the size of this guy's hands! Finally, Nathalie Lawhead journeys from threatening white sparks, hissing, crackling, and the molten aftermath to a detailed animation "as random as life itself" by way of some haiku and ActionScript.

Generative design

ActionScript is a good link into the next group, where the designers engage in some generative ActionScript programming. Anthony Eden asks "how cool is it that you can eat four ice creams and take the remaining sticks to form a stable structure without the need for glue?" He then tells the story of how he moved on from a "shed full of rusty old crap" to create some programmatic environments in Flash, which harness the same math concepts that impressed Pythagoras to sacrifice 100 oxen in awe. Keith Peters admits to becoming the very first spammer, to being scared of programming anything more than his VCR for a while, and to the ingestion of some questionably healthy takeaway food en route to showing you his crazy particle madness. Jared Tarbell introduces us to his fantastic attraction to complete irregularity by showing us the "great complexity in the instantiation of the indefinite" by way of recursion, chaos, completeness, and emergence. Yikes!

Learning

In the interests of learning, Todd Marks introduces you to his XML-driven Sidekick and Kristin Henry shows how Tetris with organic chemistry symbols, electron microscopy, and jellyfish inspired her to use Flash to communicate science.

Shane Mielke says it best in his chapter: it's people like these who can break apart our mental barriers and lead us to create new concepts. And we whole-heartedly agree.

ABOUT THE AUTHORS

BRENDAN DAWES

Brendan is Creative Director with interactive agency magneticNorth, based in the UK. His portfolio of work includes projects for Disney, Golden Wonder, Benetton, Club 18-30, Volvic, Fox Kids, Kellogg's, Coca-Cola Schweppes, and Channel 4.

As well as commercial work, Bren also has personal projects including the highly acclaimed Saul Bass website, and its quirky offshoot, Psycho Studio, an application built entirely in Flash that allows you to edit your own version of the Psycho shower scene!

Over the years Brendan's work has been featured in many industry publications including *Cre@te Online*, *Graphics International*, and *Creative Review*, and he has received various awards including three Shockwave Sites of the Day, a nomination in the New York Flashforward Film Festival, and a nomination in the 2001 Webby Awards in San Francisco.

He also writes Dreamweaver extensions and wrote the official QuickTime extension in conjunction with Apple and Macromedia. Bren is also heavily involved with product development at Macromedia in San Francisco as part of the alpha and beta testing teams for many of their products.

Before becoming an interactive designer, Brendan dabbled in the music industry landing a record contract with Liverpool dance label 3 Beat Music. Before that, he worked as a photographer for the national newspapers in the UK. Both disciplines have helped him understand sound design and visual composition in interactive design.

He's a regular speaker at design seminars across the world including Flashforward in New York and San Francisco, Macromedia Web World in Seattle, Internet World in Los Angeles, and the New Media Age Congress in London. He was a coauthor of the ground breaking first volume of *New Masters Of Flash* from friends of ED, and in 2001, he published his first solo book for New Riders, *Flash ActionScript for Designers: Drag, Slide, Fade*. Brendan's work has also appeared in a book by Californian design house Juxt Interactive as one of the ten featured creatives.

ADAM PHILLIPS

Adam Phillips has been working in traditional 2D animation for Disney since early 1993, with eight of those years spent in special effects. With all his free time, he writes and animates short stories for his personal website and online gallery, www.biteycastle.com.

Most recently, Adam convinced US band, Ween, to let him animate the video for their single "Transdermal Celebration." All involved were happy with the result, and an optimized QuickTime version of the video can be found on this book's CD.

Adam is quite small, but has big hands.

BILLY BUSSEY

Billy Bussey is best known for his digital portfolio located at www.billybussey.com and for his unique 3D Flash animations. Since 1999, Billy has focused on developing innovative ways to blend Flash, video, and 3D to form a new style of multimedia. His expertise in both vector and raster 3D has brought much attention to his work and enabled him to speak at many Flash conferences. Billy has created designs and animations for many well-known companies and individuals including Sprite, Fox, General Electric, Merck & Co., Tommy Boy Music, Hyundai, Smirnoff Ice, Coolio, and Michael Jordan.

ANTHONY EDEN

From an early age, Anthony developed a love for interacting with mathematics and computational languages. Along the way, he gained an appreciation for any given natural environment and developed the ability to transform his environment into a digital construct. Inspiration for his latest project, www.arseiam.com (essentially an ActionScript anthology of his Flash work), is a testament to this philosophy. For Anthony, the last decade has included commercial roles with Microsoft, Disney, Toyota, and Adobe, opportunities that have provided him with a sound framework in which to explore and diversify his technical skills and style. Spare time? If he's not thinking about it, he's doing it!

OLIVER SHAW

Oliver has been dabbling with Flash for a number of years now. He earns his keep working as a Lead Flash Developer for London-based design agency NOWWASHYOURHANDS (www.nowwashyourhands.com). Before this, his work hats included interaction design, information architecture, and being an experience designer. He likes cheese, the outdoor life, and the color blue.

Shane is best known for his personal portfolio site located at www.pixelranger.com and for his work as an Art Director for 2Advanced Studios (www.2advanced.com). Throughout his career, Shane has designed solutions for notable companies including Allergan, AOL, Elektra Records, Ford Motor Company, Lexus, Mazda USA, Pittsburgh Penguins, Qualcomm, Sony, Toshiba, and Toyota. With every professional project, Shane strives to combine the client's vision and goals with his own unique mixture of passion, experience, and creative expression. His greatest personal achievements include finding his wife Jolene, playing college football, traveling abroad while working in Switzerland, and having every close friendship that has influenced his life. When not reclining in front of the computer, Shane enjoys spending time with his wife, working out, coaching high school football, going on photography outings, and getting minimal hours of sleep.

"I would be remiss if I didn't mention some of the influential and inspirational people in my life who have helped, shaped, and guided me as an artist, developer, and individual. My wife Jolene, Douglas Arthur (www.douglasarthur.com), Yasuto Suga (www.rayoflight.net), Eric Jordan (www.2advanced.com, www.chemicalheart.com), Mark Wisniowski (www.probe3.com), Ken Donnellan (www.platinumspade.com), Ricardo Luevanos (www.rilumedia.com), Jim Hartigan, and Michael Harris are my foundation. Additional support always comes from the rest of the hard working crew at 2Advanced Studios along with Patrick Miko, Brad Jackson, and the rest of the mods at Ultrashock.com."

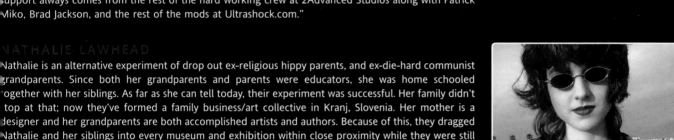

NATHALIE LAWHEAD

Nathalie is an alternative experiment of drop out ex-religious hippy parents, and ex-die-hard communist grandparents. Since both her grandparents and parents were educators, she was home schooled together with her siblings. As far as she can tell today, their experiment was successful. Her family didn't stop at that; now they've formed a family business/art collective in Kranj, Slovenia. Her mother is a designer and her grandparents are both accomplished artists and authors. Because of this, they dragged Nathalie and her siblings into every museum and exhibition within close proximity while they were still in their baby strollers. Since she was born in Minneapolis, Minnesota, and lived for many years in Cologne, Germany, and in Los Angeles, California, Nathalie grew up with a deep appreciation for cultural diversity, critical thinking, and art. This has profoundly influenced how she views the world and expresses herself.

JARED TARBELL

Jared Tarbell was born in 1973 to William and Suzon Davis Tarbell in the high-altitude desert city of Albuquerque, New Mexico. First introduced to personal computers in 1987, Jared's interest in computation has grown in direct proportion to the processing power of these machines.

Jared holds a Bachelor of Science degree in Computer Science from New Mexico State University. He sits on the Board of the Austin Museum of Digital Art (amoda.org) where he helps promote and encourage appreciation of the arts within the global community.

Jared is most interested in the visualization of large data sets, and the emergent, life-like properties of complex computational systems. Jared has recently returned to Albuquerque to work closer to friends and family while enjoying the unique aspects of desert living.

Additional work from Jared Tarbell can be found at levitated.net and complexification.net

OLA BERGNER

Born in Täby, Stockholm, in 1972, Ola realized his passion for illustration around the age of 15—he would draw caricatures of his teachers and fellow students, and he continued to draw, in his books, on school benches, everywhere, until his teachers became mad and his parents lost hope. He had found his way of life, but he was the only one who knew it. After discovering Flash in 1999, he went on to achieve critical acclaim with his animated film, *The Gooberstory*, a huge project that was a year in the making. Since *The Gooberstory*, Ola has created various new worlds in his Flash work. His work relies heavily on moods and the experiences of tranquility and calm.

TODD MARKS

Todd Marks is an avid developer, designer, instructor, and author of information display technologies. In 2000, Todd moved from teaching Mathematics and Computer Science in the public sector to becoming a Vice President of Research and Development at digitalorganism. In 2002, Todd founded Mindgrub Technologies and established a web technologies portal (www.mindgrub.net). In 2003, Todd joined Pope de Flash as the Head of Technology to form The Unity Project (www.theunityproject.com). Todd currently works as a Product Engineer for the mediaEdge division of Exceptional Software Strategies Inc. (www.media-edge.com).

Todd is a Macromedia Certified Developer, Designer, and Subject Matter Expert. His efforts have earned him three Flash Film Festival nominations, a Macromedia Site of the Day award, two Addy Awards, and several educational partnerships. Todd has written and contributed to several books including *Macromedia Flash MX Video*, *Foundation Dreamweaver MX*, *Beginning Dreamweaver MX 2004*, *Advanced PHP for Flash*, *Macromedia Flash MX Components Most Wanted*, and *Macromedia Flash MX 2004 Magic*.

KRISTIN HENRY

Maybe she's inherited the pioneer spirit of her ancestors, but Kristin Henry loves a challenge and working out on the frontier. Some of the best advice she ever got was from her first editor, who told her to study something to write about, not how to write. That's how she approaches Flash —as a way to communicate science and mathematics. Kristin is founder and president of GalaxyGoo (galaxygoo.org), a nonprofit organization dedicated to exploring expressions of science and math with online technologies.

ABOUT THE AUTHORS

KEITH PETERS

Keith Peters lives in the vicinity of Boston, MA, in the US with his wife, Kazumi, and their daughter, Kristine. He has been working with Flash since 1999, and has coauthored many books for friends of ED, including the groundbreaking volumes, *Flash Math Creativity* and *Extending Flash MX 2004: Complete Guide and Reference to JavaScript Flash*. In 2001, Keith started the experimental Flash site www.bit-101.com on which he regularly posts new, cutting-edge, open source experiments. The site recently won an award at the Flashforward 2003 Flash Film Festival in the Experimental category. In addition to the experiments on this site, Keith has produced several highly regarded Flash tutorials that have been translated into many languages and are now posted on websites throughout the world. Keith is currently working full time on Flash development and various writing projects.

ABOUT THE TECHNICAL EDITOR

MATT KNIGHT

After taking a degree in History/English and a tentative stab at a career in journalism, Matt's first exposure to Flash took place when he joined a fledgling publishing company yet to publish a book. The company was called friends of ED, and their first book was *New Masters of Flash*. Over the next two and a half years, Matt fulfilled a variety of editorial roles and watched Flash grow from a promising but awkward adolescent into a well-rounded individual.

Matt has recently returned to his native Wales and now works for the Church in Wales, where he pursues a variety of video, web, and CD-based projects. One day he hopes to do something interesting with www.countlessscreamingargonauts.com, but he's been saying that for ages.

Let me start at the beginning. I first met the folks at friends of ED after applying for a web design position.

I fancied that rosy future. I sent them a short e-mail that read

Hi, I don't have a Fine Arts degree, but I am a graduate, and I do have my own teeth and hair. I also have some URLs you might want to look at. Give me a bell and we can have a chat.

and ended the e-mail with a short list of URLs to some Flash 4 pieces. Don't ask me where the teeth and hair bit came from, but it got me the interview.

As part of that interview, they let it slip that it wasn't actually a web design position at all. They were not really sure *what* the job was when questioned, but anyway, they asked me to think about it.

Richard Collins, the Strategy Manager at the time, had a well-worn old biker's jacket on when he appeared at my interview, and he went on to become very animated when he spoke about the creative possibilities of the Web (rather than just the technical or commercial potential that was the more obvious angle back then). I thought both of these facts, the laid-back appearance and the genuine enthusiasm, were just right for the manager of a new start-up. So that was enough thinking for me, I took the job.

That's not so much an introduction of how I got to meet friends of ED, it's more of a summary of the way they worked. The whole company had attitude, but they were also committed professionals with real aptitude. That same mix of attitude and aptitude went into the first *New Masters of Flash* book. Informed chaos, blended with professionalism.

Anyway, I started by doing some consulting and Flash web design for them, but I ended up working on a Flash book to help out in other areas. That book did rather well, so I did more.

At the time (mid 2000), computer books were pretty much a known quantity. They were either written by programmers, or they were based on lecture notes. Design-oriented Photoshop books were all over the place, of course, but the computer book world didn't want to have anything to do with it. That is probably an oversimplification that will get me in trouble, but I don't think it's that far off. Of course, right now computer books that address design are the big growth area. But back then, there were no glossy computer books styled like fashion magazine layouts, and certainly none that would look good resting on expensive coffee tables.

Nobody had really done this "mixing code and design" gig, so there were all sorts of problems . . . .

We wanted to fill the book with innovators from the Flash under-ground rather than the first dozen or so cool sites we saw, and we didn't want to use corporate sites. So choosing the contributors took a serious amount of time.

Some of the contributors had never written before.

The book was very expensive to make, so costing was problematic.

The printing press didn't understand the fact that this book required heavy paper, so they used a cheaper binding appropriate for a normal computer book, but of a lower quality than friends of ED had specified. The pages very occasionally fell out. We pulped the entire first print run because it didn't meet our expectations of quality.

The book stores were not sure what we were trying to do; they just looked at us and said "Huh, code *and* design?"

Finally, *New Masters of Flash* was published.

Soon, all the big Flash conferences were adding the New Masters authors to their most wanted speaker list.

Other publishers were using the same list of authors as a poaching checklist.

New Masters of Flash peaked well within the top 10 on the Amazon all-book chart.

Because we'd used such mad layouts that totally covered the pages in color, one reviewer complained about the *smell* of all that ink. We laughed.

New Masters of Flash took the Computer Book of the Year Award. A competitor was worried enough to have an intern write bad reviews about us first thing every Monday morning.

We kept running out of stock and reprinting.

Things were looking rosy.

Fast forward. . . A few months ago, Gary Cornell gave me a call. He owns Apress, and now also friends of ED. He wanted to know what my suggestions would be for future friends of ED books. I said that friends of ED is a design imprint. Even when they're writing about programming, ED should always be design-oriented. I said we need to do a third *New Masters of Flash* book as a priority.

Gary told me it was a difficult book, and people might not "get it" in the new post dot-boom publishing industry. He said it was risky, but deep down I think he knew that the New Masters series lay at the heart of friends of ED. The ED in friends of ED is supposed to mean whatever you want it to mean, but it mostly means Every Designer. Sure, ED needs to know the standard principles and techniques of design, but they also need to know what other designers are doing out on the edge, away from the normal path.

You know the rest. Gary published the book. You're holding it.

I know what will happen. We'll still see some people just not getting the *why* of it. They'll bang on about this not being a proper computer book, nor a proper design book, or how <insert name> is missing from it, especially because they work for so-and-so studio, and they've got a great big blog.

Here's my *why*. Design and programming go hand in hand. A book on Flash that doesn't include both is a book that is stuck in the days of publications created from lecture notes. This book isn't coming from there.

The contributors in this book are just like the book itself: they have the attitude and aptitude. They make their own rules and set their own agendas. Nobody showed them the right way—they just did it, and wondered why later.

They're already famous, or about to get famous because of their attitude to their art. And they're worth reading about because of their aptitude.

They're the future of Flash. And it's looking rosy.

Sham Bhangal
April 2004, England

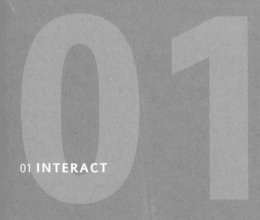

01 **INTERACT**

"PUSHING IDEAS TO THE LIMIT, SEEING WHAT WE CAN MAKE, DOING GREAT WORK, DOING BAD WORK. THAT'S HOW THINGS GET INVENTED: PLAYING WITH THE TECHNOLOGY. EXPLORING . . ."

BRENDAN DAWES
WWW.BRENDANDAWES.COM

It was nearly four years ago that I was lucky enough to appear in the first volume of *New Masters of Flash*. In those four years, Flash, and the web design industry itself, has seen a lot of changes. When I look back on it now, the year 2000 was the beginning of the end of the "balls out" new media party. Like many other people, I had grown up with a web design company that had embraced this technology called Flash. Let's face it, Flash brought with it stuff like full screen animation, whereas before, you had to make do with animated GIFs. Now we could let rip and really show off. And show off we did . . . .

The first thing anyone ever did in Flash was make a circle and then make it bigger over time. Back in 1997 this was a big deal on the Web—honest! And so I became a Grand Master of Tweened Circles. No matter what I needed to communicate, I would always employ a circle. Users? Screw 'em. Why wouldn't people want to see my slick tweened intro epics?

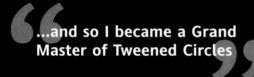

> **"...and so I became a Grand Master of Tweened Circles"**

All this "Flashturbation" eventually manifested itself in a site that, now that I look back on it, represented everything that was wrong about the use of Flash. This was a site for a well-known British holiday company that specialized in hedonistic holidays for, well, let's just say, people between specific ages. These holidays were all about excess and having a good time, so what better way to show that than to create a website that would be the Flash equivalent!

We just went to town on the whole plug-in thing: I think we ended up using five different plug-ins, including Flash. After all, *we* had the plug-ins in the studio, so surely people out there would have them too! And we went on to bamboozle the user into submission with the technobabble that we were well versed in.

WARNING: This is an advanced website, using the latest web technology. Because of this Internet Explorer 3 will not work with this site due to it's limited Javascript support. Please read the technical details before proceeding any further.

Just what the user needed when they were trying to book a holiday—a warning about browsers and limited JavaScript support. Read the technical details? Sod that, I just wanna have a drink and get a sun tan! And it's odds on that they haven't got a clue what JavaScript support is anyway. Nor should they . . . .

This arrogance wasn't just exclusive to the user—we extended it to the client too. The fact is, this client didn't even have Flash on his machine due to the paranoia about plug-ins that existed back then from the typical *Dilbert* tie-wearing IT managers. So every time the client had to approve something on the site, he had to drive up the M6 from London to the deepest part of Lancashire in the northwest of England. After all this, he still loved the site!

It's kinda funny, but the excesses of the dot com era were matched onscreen with the excesses of gratuitous use of Flash. And personally, I think that was good. It had to happen. Pushing ideas to the limit, seeing what we can make, doing great work, doing bad work. That's how things get invented: playing with the technology. Exploring . . . .

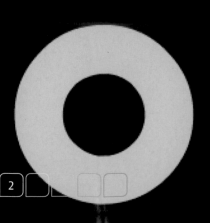

People and ideas

The problem was that we were starting to lose sight of one thing—**ideas**. They're the lifeblood of creativity. Unfortunately the industry started to be led by the tools rather than by the people creating with the tools. The plumbers were taking over. And a terrible term was coined that only compounded the problem: **Flash Designer**.

This industry has become obsessed, seduced even, by the technology itself—so much so that we describe designers by the type of tool they use.

Take this as an example: I recently had an e-mail from the editor of a well known digital graphics magazine; in it, he asked me if I would be up for writing a tutorial on some new area of Flash MX 2004. I sent a message back, rather sharpish, saying that I really didn't want to do it. I'm now doing lots of things, not just Flash, and I really wouldn't consider myself qualified to talk about new stuff in the latest version. I got a message back from him, and he was obviously a little surprised—apparently I am regarded by some as one of the UK's foremost authorities on Flash. After all, I'm a Flash designer, aren't I? A bloody Flash designer. Yes, that's right, all I do for a living is design those lightning strike flashes on car mud flaps and sneakers. Isn't that what a Flash designer is?

Yet we don't call architects concrete designers. Or sculptors clay molders. So let's never use the term Flash Designer ever again. Maybe then we can start to think about interaction design in its wider sense. Maybe then we can stop looking at other people's work on all those design portals that rot our brains and stop us from creating our own work. What a crazy idea: making your own work rather than blindly following other people's. With such recursive inspiration, you'll always be looking at a limited horizon, rather than the infinite possibilities that are waiting for you in the real world.

> **Go outside. Look beyond your monitor.**

For me, things like design portals make life a bit too easy. It's design for a fast food generation. Of course, we need to look for inspiration in all sorts of places—and design portals can be a good place to start—but it can also make people very, very lazy. It fast becomes the only place they go for inspiration. And laziness, above all else, is the cancer of creativity. It slowly eats away at you until you're happy glued permanently in place in front of your Mac, never going out, never looking up. Never interacting with anyone or anything. I've got to be honest with you—I hardly ever visit design portals. In fact, I hardly surf the Web that much. But I do look and listen to a bucket load of disparate stuff.

> **Screw design portals.**

So why bring up my feelings about design portals when I'm writing an intro to a book about Flash? Well, I think a generation of designers have grown up with them. Instead of looking at the wider world around them to be inspired, they've simply emulated or copied what's gone before. Like our town centers, many designers' portfolios have become bland and unoriginal. They're all clones of one another, all desperate to be accepted by the design community, and it's easier to "get in" if you're wearing the right clothes, so to speak. I'm not saying this is true for all—there's some breathtaking talent out there—but it just worries me that many of the résumés I receive all look the same. We've had conversations at work about why no one seems to be breaking things any more. Surely that's where the fun is?

But being original takes hard work. And we like things to be easy. We like the commonplace. We like to feel comfortable. Take our towns and cities. Go to practically any town in the UK and you could be *anywhere* in the UK. You've got the same shops, the same bars, the same places to eat out. It's all the same. But we feel safe. We're not challenged. It's all just *OK*. We're comfortable. But nothing good ever came out of feeling comfortable. Look at Elvis. As soon as he had it all, it was down hill creatively—not to mention for his waistline.

What's your point of difference?

The thing you have to ask yourself constantly is "what's my point of difference?" Why is *your* stuff more memorable than anyone else's? That's something we ask ourselves here at magneticNorth all the time—especially in a pitch situation. In fact, that's the time you really need to be remembered. And I'm not just talking about the design work itself—how you present your work in that scenario is equally important.

We recently pitched for a job where we ended up being 3 hours late for the pitch meeting due to our flight being cancelled. The potential new client was great about it though, very understanding. Eventually, we turned up, but rather than just fire up the iBook and get to it, I announced that we would need an extra plug socket for our speakers. "Speakers?" they asked. "Oh, you have sound!" Straight away we knew that nobody else had used sound in their pitch. But then, rather than just pull out a set of standard portable speakers, we pulled out a set of inflatable speakers, and spent the next 5 minutes blowing them up. Well that was immediately a talking point and it was a massive point of difference from everyone else they had seen that day. Luckily, our work was mighty fine too, and we ended up winning the job.

We pulled out a set of inflatable speakers, and spent the next 5 minutes blowing them up.

Now every time we go back and see them, I get asked about the inflatable speakers! Yeah, it was gimmicky, but along with the work, it gave them a reason to remember us, on top of the millions of other things they're thinking about in their busy schedules.

Being different and being original is what it's all about. Take Thelonious Monk. Along with other like-minded Jazz musicians, Monk was responsible for a new form of Jazz—bebop. If you've ever listened to a Thelonious Monk record, you'll know that his style of playing the piano is, well, odd, to say the least. He takes notes and puts them in places they're not supposed to be, but somehow he makes it work. What I love about this is that he took the rules of music and then bent them, twisted them to try something new. He didn't use any newfangled machine to do this. He simply used a standard piano. After all, the piano is just a contraption made of wires and wood. But add some original talent, and you get something incredible.

Follow your instincts.

Monk didn't worry about what the establishment thought of him. He didn't worry about the critics. He just loved what he did and followed his instincts. Now there's something we definitely need more of—people who following their instincts. I recently read that Walter Murch, legendary film and sound editor on such movies as *Cold Mountain* and *Apocalypse Now*, often stands up when he edits a film. It's almost like a cowboy stance—he makes cuts in an instinctive, natural way rather than sitting down and chin rubbing for hours on end.

These days, though, we seem to be obsessed with running things by groups of people rather than going with the creative impulses of an individual. That's the problem with a democracy—it has to involve the general public. And when you're trying to innovate, sometimes the general public doesn't always know what's good for them. Because they like comfort.

On the flipside of this, a designer obviously shouldn't work in isolation, wrapped in a cozy bubble of super smugness. What we need is balance. I see far too much work, particularly created with Flash, that is just done to impress other people who use Flash. That's total bollocks. It's just like saying, "Look at the size of my massive New Media balls!" You know what, mate? I couldn't give a damn about the size of your balls. You design for the people that are going to use your stuff, and invariably, that's *not* other designers, but actually real people—like my mum, for instance. When the mums of the world start to use this stuff, that's when we'll have a seismic shift in the perception of interaction. The designers are already using it, but the mums of this world—now that's what we need more of!

> **If my mum can't use it, you don't get paid.**

The big thing I'd like to see happen now is for Flash to completely disappear . . . for it to vanish from the whole user experience. What I mean is that you, the designer would still... still be using Flash, of course, but the everyday user wouldn't know it and, more to the point, wouldn't even care. It's an irony that the more things become commonplace, the less you notice them. Nobody actually thinks about electricity and how amazing it is. It's just there, doing its job, silently and effortlessly. I think this is really starting to happen with Flash now, and that can only be a good thing.

Beyond Flash

As for myself, I'm now working with lots of different technologies to explore this concept we call interaction design. Flash has helped me explore new territories, and now I'm bringing other things into the mix, like video cameras, sound, Java, PHP, DVDs, and even, well, err, snow globes.

The Snow Globe Memories project was born out of the idea of using the simple physical shaking motion of a snow globe as a "user interface." After all, everyone knows how to use a snow globe—pick it up, shake it. That's it! So as far as usability goes, it's the bee's knees. I got hold of a Basic Stamp microcontroller and then spent a Saturday morning connecting it to my computer and integrating it with a Flash piece. I knew it was possible to send information from a vibration sensor to Flash via Director, so after several hours, I got it all working. And that was something that just started out as a crazy idea because I'd seen a snow globe and just thought, "I wonder if . . . ."

You can view this project online at www.brendandawes.com/sketches/snowglobe/.

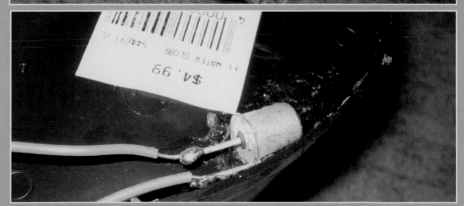

"Creativity starts with an idea"

Over the 4 years since the first *New Masters* book, Flash has clearly changed, matured, and evolved. It's no longer just a tool for creating brand experiences, experimental interfaces, or animation, but it is now being touted as the ideal software for creating Rich Internet Applications (RIAs). Let's face it, it's cross-platform, it's pretty easy to get into, and more than anything, it has a massive development community and a large existing user base. And indeed, the RIA and development side of the coin is helping to make Flash become invisible to the end user. One of the best uses of Flash I've seen in a long time is at www.interflora.co.uk. I've used this site many times over the years and it has always been fine; a bit clunky maybe, but it did the job. But on a recent visit, I found that the whole user experience was vastly improved—and it was because they've now got a fabulous Flash application that handles the whole business of ordering flowers. Imagine that—the phrase "user experience" and "Flash" in the same sentence. No longer do I get frustrating pop-up windows when I want to get an address from my stored address book. No longer does the whole page change when I click Order. It's all there on one page because of some beautiful, intelligent, and most importantly, *invisible* Flash design work.

Of course, producing highly functional designs like that of the Interflora site is just one use of Flash. And to be honest, that isn't really what this book is about either—*New Masters* is about *people and ideas*. Flash is a fabulous creative tool that allows you to really pour your thoughts and imagination into it. I think it's the openness of Flash as a tool—art combined with code —that really appeals to such a wide cross section of people. It fuses the so-called right brain with the left brain. Go to any Flash conference and you'll find hardcore coders standing next too traditional animators. Anything that allows such a diverse range of skills to interact within the same space is bound to make for very exciting possibilities creatively. We've always got to remember that creativity starts with an idea rather than with the tool you use to make it. People and ideas: that's why we're here.

"I see more of what's going on because I'm not concerned with finding a parking space."

—New York cab driver

02

02 ENLIGHTEN

Inspirations

Growing up in a small Australian country town gave me a real appreciation and love of natural environments. Although the region where I lived as a kid is a dry, flat farming community, I enjoyed exploring and walking for hours in my spare time. Quite often I would walk far out of town along the road at night, usually alone but other times with my brother and a couple of friends.

Living in that hot and dry environment had a profound effect on my dreams and goals. As a result, I've always wanted to live where there is plenty of water and greenery, in a place where rain falls often and streams and rivers are always running. Even now, living close to the city in Sydney, whenever I hear the rain I go outside and stand in it for a while. Occasionally, I'll put on my shoes, grab an umbrella, and go for a walk. In the years since I left my dusty hometown, I've taken great pleasure in spending time in forests, mountain parks, or open fields, preferably with as few people as possible. As a result of all this, you can see that water, nature, open space, and full-moon nights are dominant themes in my personal work.

All my life I've liked to hear stories and tell stories as well, and thanks to my animation career at Disney I suppose that it was a natural progression from spoken and written stories to animated ones.

The art of Simon Bisley

The turning point of my life came in 1990. While I was working in a steel factory on Queensland's Gold Coast, my left arm was dragged into a machine and my forearm was broken twice near the wrist. From that moment, my direction in life changed.

Six months of fully paid disability leave followed the accident. I was 19 and lived alone in a trailer on the beach, so my days were spent sleeping and my nights were spent wandering, thinking, inventing, and drawing.

While I've always been deeply inspired by music, dreams, and folktales, most of my artistic inspiration at the time came from reading DC's *Lobo* comics and studying Simon Bisley's work. That guy can **draw**! Not only his construction of people and environments, but also his knowledge and application of lighting effects made a deep impression on me. The volume, depth, and moods he created with black ink on white paper are still among my greatest inspirations.

I left the Gold Coast in 1991 to work as a farmhand back in my hometown. There I continued drawing in my free time and working on an idea for a comic book about a thief who sleeps all day and burgles castles at night. I sent two pages of that comic as part of my application submission to Disney back in 1992, which eventually landed me a job as an inbetween artist with the company. From there I progressed to character animator, and then I moved on to effects animator, where I've settled.

Lobo: The Last Czarnian™ and © 1991 DC Comics
All Rights Reserved. Used with Permission.

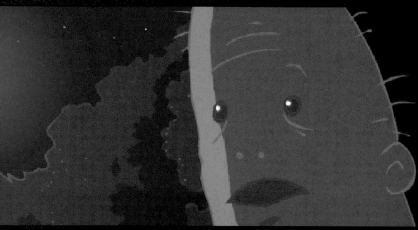

Traditional animation and Flash

Working in a traditional animation studio for the past 10 years has undoubtedly given me high production values, and working in the effects department for the past 7 years or so has definitely been a major influence on the look and feel of my Flash work.

Up until around 4 years ago, I'd been searching for a storytelling outlet. Something finally dawned on me: I had some good traditional animation experience under my belt, I had the desire to tell stories, and now I had the perfect program to bring the two together. Suddenly Flash really began to interest me.

For years and years up until that point, I'd been tossing a few big ideas around inside my head, thinking that if I could get a good pitch document together I could maybe get some funding to help me get my stories made into short films. In Flash I saw a medium in which I could animate a professional-looking movie in my own home without expensive, specialized camera equipment, reams and reams of paper, and lots of money. I soon found that the advantage of being a Flash user is that I can exhibit the movies I create to a global audience from my own online gallery.

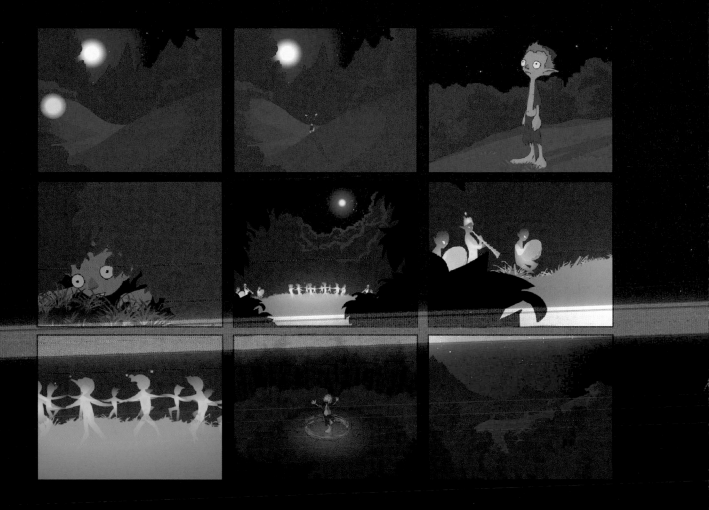

I bought a Wacom tablet and threw myself into Flash animation. I was beginning to feel comfortable with Flash, and soon enough not only was I using the entire toolbox, but also I found myself testing the program, pushing it to see how far it could go in certain areas, in addition to working out Flash equivalents of traditional animation techniques.

Although owning a tablet is, of course, not necessary to go through the exercises in this chapter, I personally find a Wacom tablet extremely helpful with my method of Flash animation. That said, I know only a handful of animators who, like me, draw directly into Flash with their graphics tablets. Most other Flash animation techniques involve scanning or importing images, or simply working with the mouse. There is no right or wrong way—it all comes down to how you're comfortable working.

Being that Flash is a limited animation tool, the early techniques of traditional camera and animation translate perfectly, especially in the area of lighting effects. I managed to re-create some of those techniques with some stunning results, and I now use those techniques regularly in my movies. I'll talk more about them later in the "Animated light effects" section of this chapter.

Anyway, a few months after learning Flash, I had made one or two movies and started to build a website when I began to experiment with gradients. Up to that point, I was afraid to use them, because I'd heard they were heavy on bandwidth and demanded extra processing power. I was delighted to discover, though, that with some confident use of gradients, alpha paint, and lighting effects, I could apply some really nice realism. I also began to imagine the possibilities of Flash being used just for illustration (i.e., static artwork), something that hadn't occurred to me at that early stage.

I find Flash perfect not only for my animation, but also for static images like illustrations for print as well as my online artwork gallery.

As I developed a style, one day it occurred to me that lighting is at the forefront in my work, and my art direction incorporates the use of light and shadow to the fullest. Gradients featured more and more heavily in my work, and I began making sacrifices in other areas to allow for more atmosphere. In my full-time job as a special-effects animator for Disney, I'm reminded constantly that light and shadow really do make all the difference, so in my personal work, effects have come to dominate my style.

The music of Ween

Many visual artists are inspired by music, which I guess could be one reason animation and music go hand in hand. Almost every piece of music I hear brings images and scenarios to my head. If you know the group Ween at all, you may know that many of their songs are character driven. Their lyrics range from hilarious to nightmarish, as does their music itself, and I don't think any other music brings such vivid thoughts to my mind.

For about 5 years I've only been what you'd call a casual fan. Sure, Ween is one of my favorite bands, but I didn't wear the T-shirt or own the coffee mug. When I bought the group's latest album, *Quebec*, I listened to it in the car on the way home and scenes and images began to flow through my head. It prompted me to visit the Ween website, where I found a merchandise page and a member forum, among other things.

The shirts looked great, so I bought a couple (thereby becoming a **real** fan!), and then I checked out the forum. The first thread I noticed there was one titled Transdermal Video: Looking for ideas. The band was actually asking their fans for visual ideas for their new single, *Transdermal Celebration*.

I e-mailed Ween's manager, Greg Frey, who told me to get a pitch to them as soon as I could. Based on my interpretation of the song's lyrics, I came up with a story and submitted it along with some concept artwork, but Ween eventually decided to go with a live video instead. I really wanted the job, however, so I told them that I'd do it free of charge if they could assure me it would be used.

They agreed to let me go ahead. Aaron Freeman (a.k.a Gene Ween), the singer/songwriter of *Transdermal Celebration*, e-mailed me with all the meaning and inspiration behind the lyrics, which I was very pleased to see worked nicely with the scenario I'd already written. I reworked my original story here and there to accommodate Aaron's ideas, but the basic premise stayed the same.

The face of the creature that you see flickering on and off throughout the video for *Transdermal Celebration* appears on almost every Ween album cover since their earliest days. It's the image of Ween's demon god **Boognish**, so I thought it would be perfect to create alien terrorists with this as a basis. I came up with the design and concept of the **Boognish Wrongens** (see the following concept image). Greg said it was a great idea, but we didn't tell Ween at that stage.

My first concept sketch of the Boognish Wrongen.

Even though I was making this animated video, I was told the band would be doing a live video as well. They probably thought it would be wise to have a video to fall back on, should mine fail. I couldn't blame them—the deadline for the video was just a little over three weeks away, and everyone knows that animation is a long and tedious process.

I knew I needed to make the animation as good as I possibly could in that short length of time. This would mean full-time dedication, so I took two weeks off work. Every day I animated two lines of the song, and at the end I was slightly ahead of schedule and pretty happy with the result.

Transdermal Celebration
by Ween

Director: Adam Phillips

Aaron was delighted with it and sent me an e-mail telling me it would be the official *Transdermal Celebration* video. This also meant that I'd be signing ownership over to Ween and that they'd be paying me for the work (which was a very nice surprise!).

So why am I telling you all this? Well, I'll be referring to the *Transdermal Celebration* video here and there throughout this chapter, as much of it showcases the lighting effects I'll be talking about. Being my most recent work, it's full of lighting techniques that I've been refining over the last couple of years. I'm eternally grateful to Ween for granting permission to put the video on the CD accompanying this book. You can find the full-length video in QuickTime format in this chapter's folder. It's of very small dimensions and optimized quality, but you can find the full DVD-quality version on the double-DVD set of Ween shows in Chicago. For more details on the DVD set, visit Ween's official website, www.ween.com.

Why use lighting effects?

The most frequently used effects in traditional animation are lighting effects. While explosions, water splashes, fire, smoke clouds, and magic effects steal the scene, it's the more subtle lighting effects that will give the entire movie a real sparkle throughout.

Lighting effects, as I'll show you in this chapter, are kind of sneaky. As in the preceding image, they don't—and never should—steal the scene. They should help tell the story or portray a mood without being too noticeable. In my experience, this often causes viewers to say "Wow, really nice atmosphere!" without them realizing exactly why.

Do you need lighting effects?

Effects in animation help give the characters and environment depth and volume. Basically, they make that 2D world just a little bit more real and believable. When an animated ball flies across the screen, bounces, and rolls to a stop, the shadow moving over the background makes not just the ball, but the whole scene a little deeper and more convincing. With a seemingly insignificant dark blob moving in a realistic way, you can subtly tell the audience that the ball is real, the light source is real, and the ground is real. In the process, viewers are drawn into the scene.

Check out `ballTreeShadow.swf` on the CD to see a short piece of animation in which the ground plane is illustrated using shadows alone.

Pros and cons of lighting effects

There are pros and cons to be considered if you want to add lighting effects to your movies. To me, there are many more lighting effects pros than cons, which, after all, is the reason I'm writing this chapter. Let me put it this way: to really grab an audience by the face, you need to make sure each and every frame of the movie is worth looking at.

The more obvious cons of using light in Flash raise questions of playability and file size, as well as the practical issues of workload and schedule, and knowledge and experience.

Playability and file size

The issues of playability and file size are exclusive to the world of computers. If you're making a television show, a DVD, or a video, then playability and file size aren't concerns. I go all out in these instances, tweaking and fine-tuning the effects as far as my schedule will allow. These issues only arise if your movie will be viewed on somebody's computer and things like high detail and gradients threaten to slow down the playback or the download. For me, there's little more horrifying than finishing a movie that plays fine on my own computer, only to watch it play like a slide show on somebody else's. When I'm worried about how a scene might play, I usually test it on a slow machine to see whether or not I can go ahead with those types of effects in that scene for the remainder of the movie.

Don't lose any sleep over this—if you'll be making movies for the Internet, it's usually just something to keep in the back of your mind. The biggest downside to using effects is that if you're not careful, they can sometimes reduce playability. The best indication of how your movie will perform is to frequently Test Scene (on a PC press CTRL+ALT+ENTER, and on a Mac press CMD+ALT+ENTER).

A frame from Auld Sage, one of the movies on my website. Check it out to see some effects in action. The waterfall plays fine on my machine, but it slows down on low-spec computers. The duplicated waterfall for the reflection also increases the load.

As with anything else in the movie, extra-lovely means extra file size. You may have dreams of amazing photorealistic backgrounds in your head, but be careful you don't add effects for the sake of adding effects or overload the scene with detail unnecessarily. Remember, those elements are there to add atmosphere and depth but, above all, they're there to play their own little part in telling the story.

The following image shows a background gone terribly wrong. I didn't plan anything; I just kept adding more and more effects, until finally the scene became unusable.

Sure it looks great, but it crawled along at around 3 fps, the level of detail was overkill, and the file size ended up near 600KB. What a ridiculous download for an opening shot—and that's without any characters! It's now up for download as desktop wallpaper in the artwork section of my site.

Workload and schedule

If you have a schedule to work within, try to factor in your lighting effects at the start. I could polish any scene until the cows come home, but I have to be clever about it if the deadline is looming. On those occasions when I find myself slightly ahead of schedule, I use the time to tweak the animation and see where there may be any lack of depth or atmosphere. The following is the schedule I kept under my Wacom sheet while I was working on the Ween video. As each day's work was completed, I'd tick it off. You can see where I've added extra things to be done, should I gain a little extra time.

☑	TC - start	Friday	14	
☑	TCa - Intro	Saturday	15	
☑	TCa -12	Sunday	16	
☑	TCa - 34	Monday	17	
☑	TCa - 56	Tuesday	18	→ Add FG crowd
☑	TCb -12	Wednesday	19	
☑	TCb - 34	Thursday	20	
☑	TCb - 56	Friday	21	
☑	TCba - 12	Saturday	22	
☑	TCba - 34	Sunday	23	
☑	TCba - Instr	Monday	24	→ Cam moves?. Fix Wrangen
☑	TCc - 12	Tuesday	25	→ Hilites on land,
☑	TCc - 34	Wednesday	26	
☑	TCc - 56	Thursday	27	→ Add jet trails overhead
☑	TCca - 12	Friday	28	
☑	TCca - 34	Saturday	29	
☑	TCc out	Sunday	30	

My schedule for the Transdermal Celebration video was 17 days.

Knowledge and experience

The knowledge of effects comes from observing, and then re-creating what you see. The more you observe what goes on in the real world, and the more you think about what you've seen, the better you'll be equipped to re-create those observations in animation and effects. Several people I know in effects animation often return from a holiday with stories of how they noticed the way flames leaped from the campfire or how water moved over the rocks. Their digital cameras inevitably hold footage of ripples or reflections or dancing flames. This kind of observation and commitment to learning effects is why these people are among the best. The same goes for a dedicated character animator who sits in a park or mall and watches people, noting what makes each individual unique in the way the person's body moves, and often sketching what he or she sees.

A live-action reference is very helpful when you're trying to work through a piece of animation. Recently, I needed to know how a bush might move when somebody brushes past it, so I took my digital camera out and shot some footage of a small shrub as I brushed my hand through it. You can find that piece of footage, `shrubRef.swf`, on the CD. When you open the movie you can see where I've begun to animate some of the leaves to try to get a feel for how things like this will work in Flash.

Habitual observation and constant practice will give you the confidence to go ahead, knowing that it's right because you've seen it working in the real world.

Types of lighting

If you decide that your movie could use some light effects, you'll soon find that different scenes or sequences within your movie will require various types of lighting. The specific lighting effects I'll cover later may belong to one or more of some broader type categories, a few of which I'll talk about in this section:

- Static lighting

- Animated lighting

- Mood lighting

- Theatrical lighting

Later I'll discuss the specific effects in these categories, and you'll put some of them into practice in a short exercise or two.

Static lighting

The effects in this category are fairly straightforward, and their rules are easy to follow. The reason for this is that the light source is stationary, so the effect doesn't change or move.

An example of static lighting is sunlight. Going back to the simple example of the bouncing ball, you can imagine how the tone (shadowy side) and the highlight stays in the same place on the ball, regardless of how high or at what angle it bounces, or how fast it moves. These are static light effects. The shadow, however, is an animated effect, which is next on the list.

In the Ween video, take a look at the second scene in the movie, the street scene. The moonlight, streetlights, and shadows here aren't moving around; they're static effects.

Animated lighting

This is where things start getting tricky. Animated lighting and the effects cast by an animated light source are much more difficult to master, because now you're truly animating the effect. With each new position of the light source in every frame, you need to plot the shadows, so there's a lot of drawing involved. That's what animation is about, right?

There are many good examples of animated lighting effects. This category includes animated tones and shadows (such as those cast by firelight), animated character shadows, reflections on a water surface, sparks, flashes, glints, and magic effects.

In addition to the everyday shadows, the *Transdermal Celebration* video has moonlight and sunlight reflections on all the water surfaces, which are animated light effects.

Mood lighting

This category overlaps some others, as it often encompasses many specific types of effects such as those in the static and animated categories. I think mood lighting deserves its own category, though, because lighting is often one of the most powerful visual tools available to convey atmosphere and emotion.

Candlelight and firelight are prime examples of mood lighting, as they're often associated with romance. There's more to mood lighting than firelight, however—you need only imagine various light colors. For example, a scene lit with a lot of red can suggest warmth and comfort. Blue light, on the other hand, may convey coldness or emptiness. In the past, green has been used to hint at evil. Various other colors are open to experimentation and interpretation. For example, who knows what a scene lit predominantly with purple might convey?

To me, it conjures otherworldly or dreamlike scenarios, but to others it could perhaps suggest melancholy. What color scheme would you use to convey a nightmarish terror?

Color isn't the only thing to consider with mood lighting. In many big-budget animated features, mood lighting features shadows that are shaped or animated in a specific way. In Disney's *The Lion King*, for example, as the villain Scar sings a song, he's underlit by green with lots of steam and long, sharp shadows (pointy means bad) throughout the sequence, and the scene is punctuated by ranks of marching hyenas reminiscent of a military rally. The mood here is very successfully set by the effects in the scene, which are consistent and well directed throughout. Thanks in large part to the effects, Scar is set up as an unmistakably evil character. This is just one great example of how effects and light can be used to tell a story and set the mood.

The teddy bear is identical in each frame, but in each the mood is set with light direction, color, tones, and highlights.

Theatrical lighting

This is a case where the rules are thrown out the window. Sometimes a scene or mood may be set by deliberately disobeying the rules and going against what should realistically happen. The perfect example of this is the underlight, which makes an instant bad guy. So when the bad guy walks into the scene, why is there suddenly a light under him? Who cares? The guy is pure **evil**—just look at the light on that chin!

Sometimes a character may need to be framed by shadows to make him the center of the scene. This is similar to a stage spotlight, which highlights the area on which the director wants the audience to focus. Another good example of this, which I'm sure everyone has seen in at least one movie, is where a character's eyes are lit by a band of light. This leads the audience to focus on the emotion in the character's eyes.

The little flashlight he carries makes him look even more evil.

Essential tools for light in Flash

OK, I've done a lot of yapping over the last few pages, and I'm sure you're dying to see what the fuss is all about, so I'll talk about Flash now. Three essential tools for lighting effects in Flash are:

- Alpha paint
- Gradient fills
- Masking

Alpha paint

I call this tool **alpha paint**, because by adjusting the alpha level of your colors and gradients, you can add an entirely new dimension to your images. Probably the most useful tool for lighting effects is the alpha gradient, which grades from a solid color to a transparent one. This is great for effects such as highlights and shadows, and glowing things like fireflies, sparks, and lights.

I usually use alpha paint for shadows. Simply create your shadows using black paint with a low alpha setting (anything lower than 40% is fine), and background detail will be visible through the shadow.

There are two main types of shadow in animation. The first is the **cast shadow**, which is usually a well-defined shadow that is cast in a particular direction. Animated cast shadows are fairly difficult to create, as you're basically drawing the character or object's outline on the ground. One way to cut down on this workload is to duplicate the character, and then flip, scale, and distort him to make the shadow, as shown in the following illustrations.

The second type of shadow is much easier to create and just as effective. On a day when the weather is overcast, take a look at people's shadows. The shadows have no definition at all; they're just fuzzy patches of darkness. In animation, this type of shadow is called the **contact shadow**.

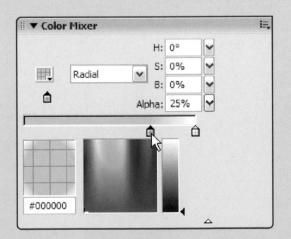

It's very simple to make a contact shadow like this one in Flash. Create a radial gradient that grades from black paint with 25% alpha to black paint 0% alpha, as shown in the following image.

With the Oval tool, make sure the No Color icon for the Line/Stroke is selected.

Then draw a circle on the stage filled with this paint. Convert that circle to a graphic symbol, and there's your cast shadow, waiting to be dragged out of the Library and used all over the place.

> *In the following scene from the* Transdermal Celebration *video, you can see some very subtle contact shadows on the wall behind the character. There's a cast shadow off to the left, and the contact shadows make the character's hands and lower back appear to be touching the wall.*

Gradient fills

How you choose to use gradients can determine the look of your movie, for better or worse. The main limitation of a Flash gradient is the choice of shape you're presented with. Linear or radial—there are your options. However, if you split your scene into smaller elements, you can apply various gradient styles, shapes, and shades to each element, and when used together with the Fill Transform tool, these tricks, tools, and techniques can produce amazing depth in the scene.

Gradients make 2D objects look 3D; that's the idea behind them. For example, you can make a circle into a sphere by applying a radial gradient. A linear gradient can turn a square into a cylinder and a triangle into a cone. It will come as no surprise to you, then, that gradients can make a flat 2D tree appear to possess volume.

Using the Fill Transform tool to fine-tune your gradient gives you complete control over the final look of your object, and when you apply the gradient with some basic awareness of lighting rules in mind, your movie or scene will ooze style.

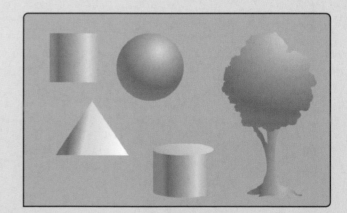

Masking

Masks are handy when you're working with effects, both static and animated. As mentioned earlier, Flash translates very well from traditional animation-camera techniques, and many of these may be emulated using masks.

One noteworthy example of a traditional camera technique applied to Flash that uses a mask as the primary device is the **scribble cel**. As you'll learn later in the "Animated light effects" section, this old and simple technique gives any animated water surface a remarkably realistic quality.

Other applications for masked effects include the **rimlight** and the **tone** shown in the following images.

In the images below, the human character in the left figure has an offset rimlight, which is the brighter area closest to the Boognish character. The kid in the right image has an offset tone, which is the area of darkness on his body, to give him a little bit of form.

How and where to start

You now have a little bit of introductory knowledge and a few facts in front of you, and you might have even started playing around with some of the techniques I've discussed. You may be wondering how you should start. Well, first of all, it will pay to think a bit about whether or not your scene needs lighting effects and, if so, what effects they should be.

What your scene needs

Not every character scene needs animation. Likewise, not every scene in your movie will require lighting effects. Before you add effects to a scene, you need to ask yourself some important questions.

Suppose you've just completed the following scene, which shows a close shot of a character's face in a dark environment. Somewhere in the story of this movie, the character falls into a hole, and this is the first shot viewers see of him as he gets to his feet. He stares up at the opening to see if there's a way out.

Ask yourself the questions addressed in the following sections one by one.

What effects are required in this scene?

Being in such a small, dark environment, this scene will need only one light source: the opening through which the character has just fallen. It will need some tones on the character and some highlights in the character's eyes. Some rays of light with floaty particles in them will set a certain claustrophobic, dusty atmosphere.

Are the effects necessary to help tell the story?

For the effects just listed, the answer is yes. Without these added touches, the character would be in a less-than-realistic environment.

Are the effects necessary to help set the mood or atmosphere?

Again, yes. These effects will play a big part in setting up the character's emotional response, therefore helping the audience empathize with him.

Will the effects distract from the story or character?

The only effects here that may distract the audience are the floating dust particles in the light rays. If you want the audience to watch the character's reaction or expression, you'll need to downplay those particles by making them fairly subdued. Keeping them all behind the character will also ensure that he is the focus of the scene.

With those questions answered, and having a fairly solid idea of how the scene should look, you can go about adding the lighting effects.

Nailing the light source

Part of the construction of each scene should involve some kind of light source icon, which will show the position and direction of the light in the frame. This is hardly more complicated than adding a small hand-drawn arrow on your rough background sketch. If your light source is in shot, then the rays may be traced straight from it (more on that in the sections "Raytracing" and "Perspective").

For now, here's a work-in-progress sketch of the previous scenario:

Note the red arrow, which shows the offscreen light source, indicating both position and direction of the rays. This ensures the effects are accurately placed in the scene.

Constructing scene lighting

Now that you have a better idea of how and what the effects should be doing in this scene, you can begin to construct them. Two important aspects of this construction process are **perspective** and **raytracing**.

The lighting in the example scene is quite simple. There are no shadows to be cast on the floor or walls, only rays of light through the dusty air. At this point I'll need to go over some lighting construction fundamentals, so let's leave the example scene here and come back to it soon.

Perspective

While things start to get complex when you're working with perspective, it truly adds another dimension to your work. You'll probably only ever need to know the basics of perspective when working in Flash. Check out `perspectiveTut.swf` for an animated demonstration of some simple perspective.

I'm not quite a perspective guru, so when people ask me about perspective, I recommend that they buy a book on perspective drawing to learn what they can. Because the rules of perspective are timeless, the oldest books are as good as the latest, so you should be able to pick up something quite cheap that will show you all you'll need to know.

I'll assume you have basic knowledge of one- or two-point perspective, but if you're an artist who isn't familiar with these rules, I suggest you do a little online learning before continuing. The most easy-to-understand and complete online resource I've come across for learning perspective basics can be found at www2.evansville.edu/studiochalkboard/draw.html. I've bookmarked that site, and I visit it often. There's even a small section on lighting.

Raytracing

Raytracing at first glance appears complicated, but in fact it's a very simple procedure that's used to roughly construct a light effect or shadow outline. It involves simply drawing straight lines from the light source, which radiate out until they touch an element in the scene, such as background elements, props, or characters.

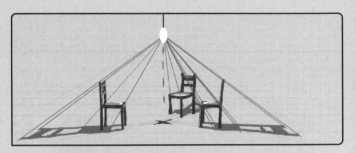

This image shows basic raytracing for parallel light rays (sunlight).

If there's a very faraway light source in the scene, such as the sun or moon, then the shadow root will be on the horizon, directly under the light source.

I've prepared an animated tutorial which is on the CD, `boxShadow_Construction.swf`, to give you visual guidance on how this is done. The very first part of the animation shows the red dotted line dropping from the light source onto the ground, from where the blue lines fan out. This is the construction of the shadow direction. On your ground plane, you should mark the spot directly underneath the light source, which I call the **shadow root** (marked in the following image with a red **X**), and from that point all shadows will radiate.

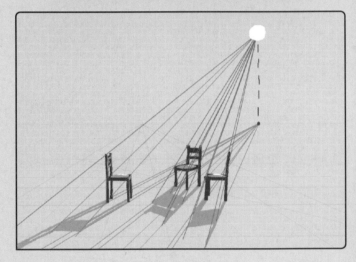

Once you have a feel for raytracing, you'll have little need to construct each scene so accurately. With some practice, you'll soon be capable of placing simple shadows like these without any construction. Instead, you'll be able to draw freehand effects while simply bearing the basic rules in mind.

Construction

Before I talk more about the construction of scene lighting, have a look at `boxShadow.swf` from the CD. The box in the first frame has a **contact shadow**, which is just a patch of diffused darkness to "ground" the box into the scene. Click the various lights in the room to see some different types of cast shadows. You can also toggle the raytrace toggle button to see how the shadows are constructed in each of those frames.

Finally, click the window to see how the box casts a diffused shadow from a large ambient light source, such as a window. You can view the raytracing construction here also, by toggling the raytrace toggle button.

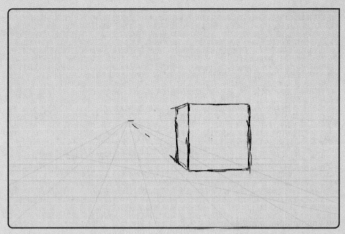

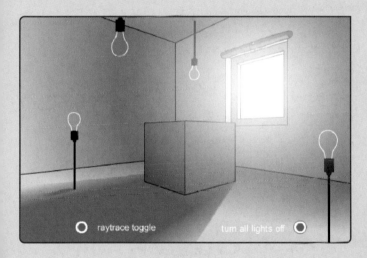

Raytracing exercise

Let's construct some lighting. The simplest object to start with is a featureless box on a flat ground plane.

1. Open `boxCastShd.fla` from the CD, and you'll see a ground plane with a few rough indications of perspective and a box sitting on that plane.

For the sake of this exercise, you'll want to see the whole shadow, so cast it toward camera slightly. To do this, imagine that the light is at the back of the scene pointing in the direction of the camera. You need to decide in which direction you want the shadow to fall, and here's where you need to start thinking in 3D.

2. I always sketch a 3D light-source icon for this, so as shown in the following image, add a light source icon to the scene.

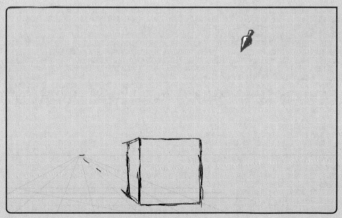

The light source icon shows only the x,y position and direction of the light source. You also need to think in terms of the z position and direction (depth).

3. As indicated in `boxShadowConstruction.swf`, draw a vertical line down from the light source and decide at which point on the ground plane the shadow root should be.

Note that wherever you choose to put the light source, your shadow root must always be on the ground plane directly below it. The following images show two examples of light placement.

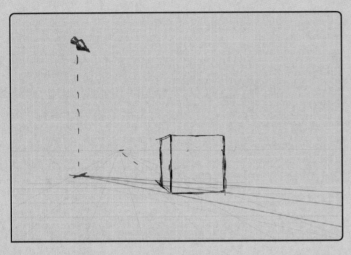

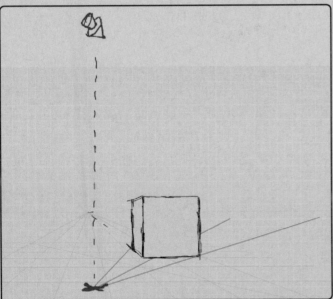

Now back to the exercise:

4. Place an X where you'd like your shadow root, and begin drawing lines to and beyond the base of the box, as shown in blue here:

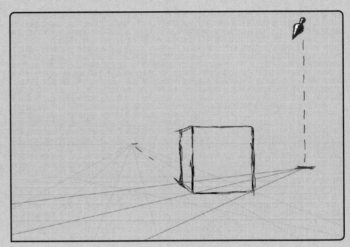

5. Do this for each corner of the box, and you'll soon see that you've mapped the shape of the box onto the ground plane.

6. On the shadow layer, draw in the complete shadow outline by connecting the points. Fill it with color and there's your shadow. Quite simple, isn't it?

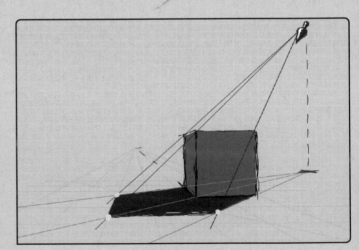

As your experience with raytracing develops, you can start working with more intricate objects and more complicated surfaces.

Despite the complexity of any given scene, the principles of raytracing and light direction are always fairly straightforward.

In `boxShadow.swf`, with the raytrace toggle button toggled, you can see how rays are traced from the light source to the objects n the room. When you're raytracing, you're projecting the image of that object in straight lines from the light source to the walls and floor.

To see some more complex raytracing with animated shadows and a bouncing cube, check out `shadowBoxing.swf`. This is a scene I made in Swift 3D, in which, once I had set up the scene with the animation and the light, all the shadows and raytracing were animated for me automatically. I think the only problem with this scene is that the shadow is a bit too realistic and can appear distracting or confusing.

That's a whole other issue with animation. The most realistic scene isn't always the most visually appealing, so an animator usually has to take some creative license. I've hand-animated a simpler version of the dancing box scene, where the shadows are less accurate but a bit more appealing and much less distracting. It's on the CD and it's called `handAnim_shadowBoxing.fla`.

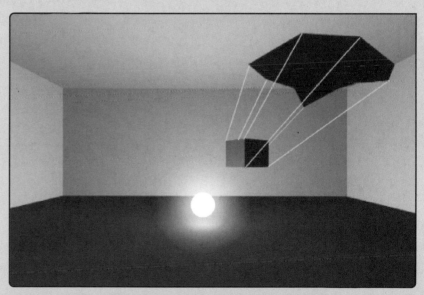

Mathematical perfection doesn't necessarily make an image aesthetically pleasing.

Light color

When working with light effects, you're likely to find that the default color swatches aren't enough to suit your needs. The best way to mix the right color for your light effect is to take existing colors from the scene and adjust them. This is often a process of trial and error, as you'll see in the following example.

Finally we're back to the simple example scene! Open `moonlight.fla` from the CD and you'll see the guy in the hole again. I've colored him with moonlight colors, but he's still quite flat and toony. You'll give him some volume and form by applying a very simple light and shadow effect using a gradient.

Mixing colors

The ghostly pallor of the character's skin at the moment tells you he's either very sick or he's lit in a certain way. The effects you're about to add will tell the audience much more about the scene. You'll add some simple tones to the character by mixing and applying a new gradient. The character's existing colors are as good a place as any to start, and from this moonlit skin color you can base the new gradient.

Step through the following exercise to mix a radial gradient that grades from the moonlit skin color to a darker version of the same.

Tone color exercise

1. Start by opening the Color Mixer panel. Choose Radial from the color type drop-down list, and then in the panel menu choose HSB.

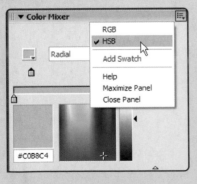

2. Select the moonlit skin color for both colors on the gradient ramp. If you like, you can simply enter the hexadecimal value as shown in the previous screenshot.

3. You'll make the right color slightly darker now, so make sure the right color-pointer is selected. Drag the brightness slider (B) down slightly to darken the color. Again, the quicker way here would be to type in the hexadecimal value of the darker version, as shown in the following screenshot.

    This darker color on the gradient will be the shadowy part, or the tone effect, on the character's skin.

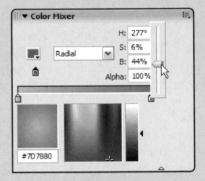

4. Before you apply the gradient, make sure the transition between the colors isn't too gradual. Drag the two pointers on the gradient ramp a bit closer together, so the color transition is a little more sudden.

5. Paint the character's skin with the new gradient. Then with the Fill Transform tool, adjust the gradient's scale and rotation until you have something that shows the character's form.

You can go ahead and mix gradients for his eyes and clothing if you like, and to finish him off add some highlights to his eyes. Because he's looking directly at the light source, the highlights should be right on his pupils. You'll find the complete image as shown in the following image on frame 7 of `images.fla` on the CD. Feel free to explore the gradients.

Note how the curve of the radial gradient accentuates the roundness of the character's head. Here I've also filled his shirt with a gradient.

Here's the image I prepared earlier. The completed scene with character lighting, dust particles, and moonbeam is quite a bit different from the toony one, isn't it?

Use of contrast

Lighting effects really stand out when you use them in the context of a dark environment. A perfect example of this is a nightscape, which can be mostly blackness punctuated by well-defined lighting effects such as glints and flares. Using lighting effects to contrast sharply with the surrounding darkness is a simple yet powerfully evocative technique, so it makes for a highly immersive viewer experience. Highlighting a character with a bright spotlight, for example, draws the audience's focus toward that character.

Here the eye is drawn to the brightest object, because it stands out against the dark environment.

If you've seen a good sampling of my work, you can probably tell that I favor nightscapes in which contrast plays an important part. A lot of what I try to achieve in my nightscape atmospheres is inspired by childhood memories of dark nights and moonlit countryside scenes.

This nightscape shows a bright, moonlit hillside framed by a dark forest and mountains.

Static light effects

Within the 2D family of light effects, the basic three are shadows, tones, and highlights. A trainee effects animator usually starts with these.

In Flash, static lighting effects require a lot less work than their animated counterparts, and you can often incorporate them into the background drawing. The atmosphere in a shot can be done with the background alone. In this section I discuss a number of static light effect–related techniques and methods to help you set up some moods in your scene.

Shadows

The perspective in a scene determines how any shadows should be placed, even the simple ones like contact shadows. When you need shadows in your movie, make sure you have some perspective guidelines drawn in so your shadows don't disagree with the ground plane.

Making shadows realistic has nothing to do with their complexity. If you adhere to the rules of construction and keep your shadows consistent, your shadows can be as simple as you need them to be. One excellent way of simplifying character shadows is to cast a simple contact shadow for each major volume of the character, as follows:

Key volumes of the character (that is, head, torso, and legs), each casting a simple shadow, come together to form a very effective cast shadow.

These images are from animVolShadow.fla, which you'll use later to construct some animated shadows.

How shadows fall

Suppose you were a lightbulb on the ceiling in the center of a room. Pretty boring life, but hey, at least you'd get to look down on everyone. Your typical view of a person standing in the room would be something like this.

To demonstrate raytracing, I created this image in Swift 3D. Shadows and raytracing are performed automatically by the program, so it's all mathematically correct.

Think about how the rays are traced. If you're the only light source, it makes sense that you won't see any shadows in the room. Therefore, on the other side of the person, hidden from your view, the shadow is an exact silhouette of that person.

Project that silhouette on the floor, and then look at it from a slightly different angle. Note how the shape of the shadow on the floor is identical to the shape of the character in that first frame.

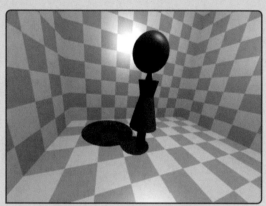

*By definition, a **shadow** is a projection of the silhouette of an object onto a surface, from the angle as seen from the light source.*

Ugh, what a mouthful! It's probably easier to memorize it visually. Take a look at animSilh.swf *and* animSilh2.swf *to see a visual demonstration. In the first frame of each, the camera occupies the same space as the light source. By using the* move camera *button, you can shift the camera away from the light so you can view the shadows from a different angle.*

Tones

Once again, if you're the light source, you don't see shadows. This also means that you'd never see **tones** (that is, the shadowy side of objects). For yet another example, if you lived on the sun, you'd only ever see a full moon (that is, if you weren't too busy slapping at flames and screaming!). Therefore, try to visualize your 2D character or object with volume, and which parts of that volume will be out of the light's reach.

In Flash, as with any 2D medium, you're faking 3D by illustrating volume on an otherwise featureless object. You can use tones to describe whatever volume or shape you like, but this is also a reason to be careful with them. Applying tones carelessly or in the wrong way can mean the difference between a cute character and an ugly one.

The "ugly" image below has tones that are drawn and constructed correctly, but this illustrates how drastically small changes in tones can affect the character's appearance. They can describe fat cheeks or hollow cheeks, bugged eyes or hooded eyes, a button nose or a broken nose.

You should observe the rules of light direction when using tones, even simple ones. Once again, if you choose lighting effects, take some time to learn their rules, use them properly, and you'll be ahead of most others out there.

Highlights

Without a doubt, **highlights** raise the sparkle of a scene almost by themselves. They add to the final atmosphere immensely, and they're probably the easiest lighting effect to create.

Highlights are the reflection of the light source. You can imagine all surfaces as being mirrors of varying reflectivity. An eyeball, for instance, is highly reflective because it's wet. The highlight in this instance is small, sharp, and bright.

This eyeball highlight example shows that wet things and glossy things have high reflectivity.

A tennis ball, on the other hand, is fuzzy and dry, so its reflectivity is very low, resulting in a matte finish. The highlight still exists, but it's soft and broad.

You can use highlights to add gloss or moisture, but more often you'll use it to add depth and volume.

This tennis ball example shows that dry things and rough things have low reflectivity.

Using gradients for depth

The background is a 2D rendering, but in Flash you can fake depth with gradients. To the human eye, color and detail are gradually diluted as distance increases. That's part of the way we perceive great distance. To re-create depth as perceived by the human eye, you can use a gradient that moves from an ordinary saturated color to a washed-out form of the same.

Desaturating objects helps to make them appear further from the camera, which emulates what happens to images reaching the eye from a great distance. To achieve this effect in Flash, you adjust the saturation slider (S) on the HSB menu set, which is exactly what I did to the mountains in the previous image.

The Fill Transform tool is also a handy lighting device, and when you have your light source icon in the scene, you can use the Fill Transform tool to decide how to place and transform your gradients. The following image shows a number of spheres, all filled with a simple gradient, to show how light affects them all from one source.

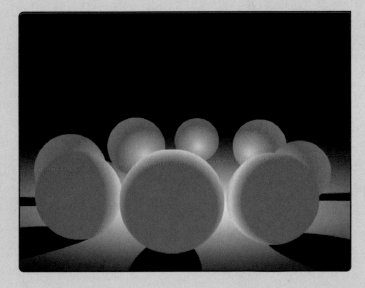

Animated light effects

This is it! Things really start to get exciting when you begin to animate your lighting effects. This is also where things get challenging. The static stuff teaches you the basics, which are core skills required for the complicated work. So my advice is to start simple, get comfortable with the basics, and build up to the heavy gear–animated light effects.

The best effects to begin animating with are the basic three: shadows, tones, and highlights. If you have experience in making static character shadows, then you can apply the same rules and construction techniques to the animated ones. Likewise, if you know how to construct and draw a static character tone, then learning to animate it will be fairly easy.

Here's an example of animated rays. Note how the rays lead to the light source.

Animated shadows

In the file `animVolShadow.fla` on the CD, you'll find an animated character on a featureless ground plane. Also in the scene is all the lighting construction you'll need. This file has been provided for you to add the character's shadow.

When you open the movie, unhide the lightingGuide guide layer. You'll see that I've done the raytracing in the scene, and in the Library you'll find a contact shadow. Also you'll notice there are three empty layers: headVolShadow, torsoVolShadow, and legVolShadow.

Place a single contact shadow for each major volume of the character: one for his head, one for his torso, and one for his legs. To do this, simply drag the shadow from the Library, and then position, scale, and squash it using the green construction sketches as a guide.

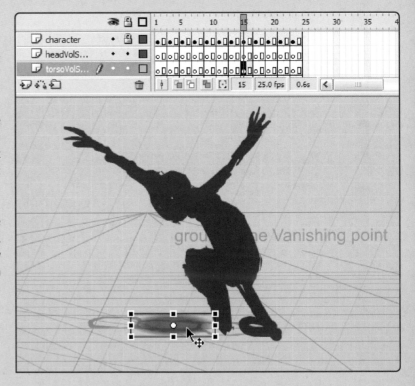

In `animVolShadow_Complete.fla`, you'll see there are three green circles on the ground to guide you in the placement of each cast shadow. These rough circles on the ground are approximately where the shadows for each major volume should fall. If you'd like to see the finished shadow animation, take a look at `animVolShadow_Complete.swf` from the CD, and toggle the raytracing and construction with the button. You can pause the playback by pressing CTRL+ENTER (CMD+ENTER), and then step through the frames by using CTRL/CMD and the left arrow and right arrow keys.

The character animation is quite snappy, so you don't need to be dead accurate with the shadows. Because all the construction is done, it should be quite simple for you to finish the scene.

Animated tones

Fire casts dancing shadows, and this is the perfect place to put simple animated tones into practice. When the light source is changing position and direction slightly from frame to frame, the objects in the scene are going to be illuminated differently in each frame. In Flash and any other limited animation, a cycle for this effect is efficient and helpful.

> A **cycle** in traditional animation terminology basically denotes a looping clip of animation. It could also be called a "loop," but to avoid confusion with ActionScript loops, I'll stick with the term "cycle" here.

When the character is still, you can often get away with a three- or four-drawing cycle. You'll probably soon find out for yourself that short cycles can be distracting. In a long scene, a four-frame cycle will appear to pulsate in a mechanical way. To combat this, you could put a lot more drawings in the cycle, but there's an easier way. Before I show you that way, open `animToneCycle_5.swf` from the CD and watch the animation.

There are only five drawings in this cycle, so the tones pulsate. Japanese anime uses this technique a lot, which I guess originally must have come about from the need to limit the workload and speed up production. Now these short cycles and pulsating effects are a "look" and a design choice.

I prefer longer cycles, but I'd still rather not have to do too many drawings. That's fine because a few drawings can be made into a longer cycle. Open `animToneCycle_15.fla`, go to the Library, and double-click the `mc_animTone` movie clip. Inside the movie clip, you can scrub the timeline and make note of how the tone moves. See if you can identify a pattern in the animation. You can't, because even though there are only five drawings here, they're held for two frames each and placed in such a way that when the movie is played, the animation actually cycles every 54 frames.

While still in the `mc_animTone` timeline, you can press CTRL+ALT+ENTER (CMD+ALT+ENTER) to watch the clip cycle. It appears to be much more random than the pulsating tone you saw earlier.

As you've seen, the five-frame cycle pulsates, so the trick as illustrated in the following image is to place those five drawings in random repeating order over a greater number of frames. This makes a much longer cycle, with only five drawings. Clever, huh? If you can turn five drawings into a 54-frame cycle, imagine what you could do with ten drawings! The idea here is to get the maximum effect from the minimum effort. It's up to you how much work you put into it and how you want it to look.

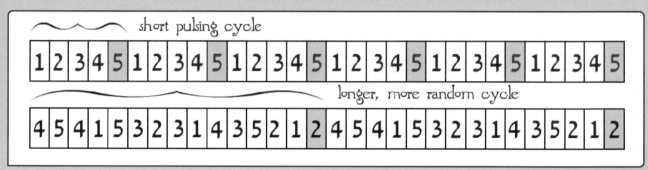

Using five drawings to make a 15-frame cycle

Another type of animated tone that I think is worth mentioning happens when a character moves in and out of shadow. It involves more construction and drawing practice, but it really shines in the moment.

Suppose you have a character in the dark, and he emerges into the light. There's one such scene in the *Transdermal Celebration* video. Even though it happens quite quickly at normal playback speed, it gives the impression that the character has real volume. His head comes into the light, one slice at a time, and the rest of his body follows, one slice at a time.

Practice first on a simple object (a sphere, for instance), and then try your hand at more complicated objects. I've animated a ghostlike object moving through an archway, emerging from darkness into light. The file on the CD is called `animTone.swf`.

If you have a 3D program, such as Swift 3D, 3D Studio MAX, LightWave, or Maya, it can be very helpful to move various objects through a translucent plane and watch how the plane cuts the object.

Think of the line that divides light from shadow as a plane through which the ghost glides, almost like it's emerging through a sheet of water.

Animated highlights

As previously mentioned, highlights are some of the most dazzling lighting effects you can put into a scene. They make water look wet, they make leaves appear glossy, and they can even define the surface texture of your scene objects.

Animated highlights, therefore, are extra special. From bright, wobbly dots in a pair of sad eyes to the intricate reflection of the moon on the water, these effects breathe magic into a scene.

In a fairly static medium like Flash, it's important to keep the image alive. Sometimes you don't want the character to be throwing her arms around and jumping up and down. Sometimes you just want to make her subtly show her emotion, and the aforementioned wobbly dots allow you to hold on a still image of her face, yet keep the image alive by showing her wet eyes quivering.

A wobbly white dot puts life into this character's eye.

Well that's easy stuff, so let me show you something more interesting. The technique I use for animated water-surface reflections in my movies is quite effective, but incredibly simple. It's all thanks to a camera technique I learned from working in early 2D animation. It's called the **scribble cel**, and this is how it works.

Imagine a black card with pinholes punched in it. Underneath the black card, you shine a bright light through, and this happens:

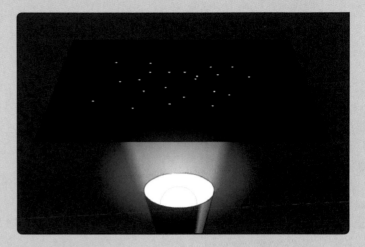

Now, take a clear sheet of acetate (cel) with random black scribble on it and move it slowly between the black card and the light. Open `scribbleDemo.swf` and drag the acetate cel around under the black card. Note how the scribble on the acetate cel blocks the light coming through the holes in what appears to be a random order.

Drag the acetate cel to see how the light is affected.

This is how highlights on a water surface were animated in the days of the traditional animation camera. Only two drawings required: the water surface glints (the holes in the card) and the random scribble.

The way to do this in Flash is with masking. Using the `scribbleDemo.swf` file as a guide, try it for yourself. Simply draw your water surface glints (the "holes") on the Mask layer, and then tween the scribble cel as the masked layer. After you play around with the scribble cel a bit, you can refine the technique (the scribble design, motion, and speed) to come up with something that you're completely happy with. I love this technique, and you can see it in action throughout the Ween video.

In Flash, there are scores of applications for masked effects, many of which can make a quick piece of work look incredible. Open `magicLight.swf` from the CD and see if you can figure out how it was done. Come on, you can do it! Give up? OK, leave me a message on the www.friendsofed.com forum and I'll send you the FLA.

Tricks of the effects animator's trade

Over the last 10 years I've picked up a few little tricks, like the scribble cel, that have been in use since the earliest days of 2D animation. As time goes by, however, I'm increasingly surprised at the fact that these tried-and-true skills aren't taught to new animators. I've met certain effects animators, some with 5 or 6 years' effects animation experience, who have never heard of these techniques. Why should stuff like this be forgotten? How can anyone allow these techniques to fade away? They are proven, fundamental principles that may be applied to a broad range of effects animation—not only 2D but 3D . . . and probably every other D!

Well, enough of my ranting, I'll talk about a couple of these essentials now and how they relate to Flash.

Impact flicker

One particular animation timing trick that I learned early in my effects career impressed me greatly. It's used in effects where you'd like to show visual impact, such as explosions, flashes, impact effects, and even popping bubbles. The technique is effective, yet remarkably simple to achieve, and it tricks the viewer's eye in a very subtle but physical way. I've seen the occasional classy intro on the Web that uses the technique, but I've never seen it used before in Flash cartoon animation, so I guess I'm about to spill a bit of a secret.

I'll illustrate this technique with a few effects, starting with a standard light-flash, such as a camera flash. The following images show how a frame sequence, when played at speed, can flick at the viewer's eye.

The effect is all about contrast and opposites. It starts with a medium flash, then sucks back in to a small one (as if imploding), and then immediately blows out to fill the screen and finish the effect. At speed, this effect is great for showing impact. Memorize the sequence: medium, small, large. You can apply it to many other types of effects that could benefit from visual impact.

Just like a strobe light that causes fits, I suppose this technique must momentarily confuse the brain, making the effect truly physical. Don't worry, though—this three- to four-frame sequence at 25 fps isn't going to drop anyone.

Here's the same technique used with an explosion, which you can see in action, along with various other effects when you open `impact.swf` from the CD:

This sequence shows impact by flicking from one extreme to another in the first few frames of the effect: black to white, large to small, and so on.

Offset rimlights

A rimlight (or **rim** for short) is the lit edge of a character, prop, or background element. A rimlight appears when the light source is behind the character or object, and you see that sharp bright edge. You have several ways to create this effect in Flash, the best of which is to hand draw the rimlight. This gives you unlimited control, but it's obviously a lot trickier than the examples that we'll look at here. Here's a scene in which I've used hand-drawn rimlights.

I'll demonstrate two much easier ways to create a rimlight. Use these techniques carefully, as both are quite crude and playback may slow down if there is too much of rimlight elements onscreen at the same time.

Hand-drawn rimlights offer precise control and are very effective.

Offset rims, method A

1. Duplicate your character on a layer underneath it, and turn its brightness up to 100%. You won't be able to see this layer yet, because it's underneath the character.

2. Slightly offset the rimlight layer by selecting it then pressing the up arrow key once or twice. You'll see the sharp, white highlight peek out from behind the character, which you can position further by using the arrow keys or simply moving it with the Arrow tool.

Because the light source is behind this character, I've given him some offset rims using method A.

This method is also well suited to text.

Offset rims, method B

Method B isn't for everyone. The following example is for use with a character that will require a radial gradient. Using this procedure on props with straight edges should require a linear gradient, but there are many shapes and objects for which radial and linear gradients won't work.

Macromedia FreeHand MXa has some nice gradients, one of which is the Contour gradient. This is the perfect effect for offset rims, and while bringing them into Flash may be a bit fiddly, you might find it suits your needs.

This offset rim was made in Macromedia Freehand MX using the Contour gradient.

As far as the look is concerned, the Contour gradient is actually the best vector equivalent of traditional offset rims that I know of. While Contour gradients are currently unavailable for Flash, here's how to do something similar.

Create a radial gradient that grades from white 0% alpha to white 70% alpha. Place the color pointers fairly close together on the right side of the ramp so the transition is fairly short and the gradient leaves a wide, transparent hole, as shown here:

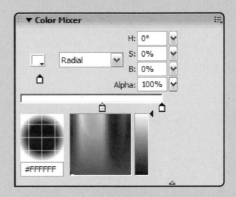

Now you'll draw a circle on the stage, so select the Oval tool. With no stroke selected and the new gradient selected as the fill, hold down SHIFT and drag an area on the stage to create a circle.

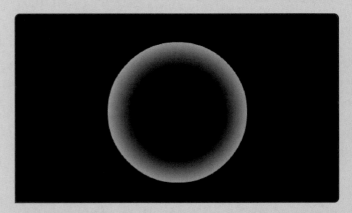

Convert the circle to a graphic symbol, resize it, and reposition it so it appears to be the lightened area of the character.

Now you can mask off the excess by duplicating the character and using him as the mask layer.

This is a masked offset rim. It's crude but often effective.

Summary

There's much you can do with lighting effects in Flash. If you'd like to take them on, it's a matter of studying the real-world rules, building on these principles, and even inventing your own types of lighting effects. The possibilities are limitless, and I for one intend to keep working on new and better ways to animate these effects in Flash.

In this chapter you've seen how lighting effects can boost the visual quality and appeal of any scene, even the most mundane. With some understanding of the real-world rules of light and shadow, you can apply these lighting effects to Flash and indeed any other visual medium.

Again, the *Transdermal Celebration* video is on the CD for you to watch and see almost everything I've discussed in this chapter in action. You won't find any character tones in video, but there are simpler equivalents here and there, such as tone gradients and masked offset rims.

As you watch the video and as you practice the effects you learned about in the chapter, I'm sure you'll agree that lighting is effective in conveying depth, mood, and atmosphere, and with Flash it's also quite straightforward.

"PEOPLE OFTEN ASK ME WHERE MY INSPIRATION COMES FROM, AND I CAN HONESTLY SAY THAT MY MAIN SOURCE OF INSPIRATION IS SHEER BOREDOM."

BILLY BUSSEY
WWW.BILLYBUSSEY.COM

I'm pretty much a computer nerd, a Flash loser, if you will. And if you're reading this chapter, you're probably an even bigger nerd than I am. I basically have no life outside of my computer, and like most Flash developers, I spend 12 hours a day making Flash sites. Even in my spare time, I like to make Flash sites. People often ask me where my inspiration comes from, and I can honestly say that my main source of inspiration is sheer boredom. I often find myself staring at my computer screen and after 20 minutes thinking, "Well, I might as well try to make something cool." The next 16 hours of my day are then spent trying to make some 3D animation work perfectly in Flash.

Out of all the "how I got started in Flash" stories, mine seems to be the strangest. I was drunk at a party in 1999 at my best friend's house. I was looking through a stack of CDs for some music to put on when I found a CD labeled "Flash 3." I had heard of Flash before but had no idea what it really was. I asked my friend if it was his CD, he said no, so I took it. Now, mind you, I had been using computers for only about a year and had never done any sort of design. I installed Flash 3 (it was a fully legitimate copy) with no idea what it was for, but I tried making some animations anyway.

Now here is the weird part. Three days later, another friend called and asked how much I knew about Flash. I lied and said plenty. He immediately hired me to make a full Flash site. I spent the next 3 months making that site (which ended up being terrible) and have been in love with Flash ever since.

I originally studied television production in school and planned to create TV shows for the rest of my life. After college, I created a small video production house and concentrated on small digital video projects. During this time, I learned how to use a few programs such as Adobe Premiere and Photoshop. I quickly became frustrated with the production side of things. Not only is it boring to videotape other people, but it's also difficult to handle the many real-world variables involved, such as weather, lighting, actors, and equipment. I realized I enjoyed only the graphics portion of video, and after a year of making far too many wedding and training videos, I finally found Flash.

Although I would never go back to video production, the one thing I think I would have liked to have tried out is creating movie trailers. I'd like to make trailers for movies that don't even exist. Trailers take the essence of any feature-length film and pack it all into 60 seconds. Lately, it seems like everything I make in Flash looks and feels like a trailer: dramatic, climactic, and intense. I'm never satisfied with things unless they're slightly over the top.

BBV2.5
COMING SOON

IN THE MEANTIME
PEEP THIS!

V2 WATCH INTRO
ENTER SITE
BB FORUM

A BILLY BUSSEY CREATION
HTTP://WWW.BILLYBUSSEY.COM
ME@BILLYBUSSEY.COM
COPYRIGHT 2003-2004

Get QuickTime
Free Download

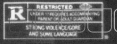
R RESTRICTED
UNDER 17 REQUIRES ACCOMPANYING
PARENT OR ADULT GUARDIAN
STRONG VIOLENCE/GORE
AND SOME LANGUAGE

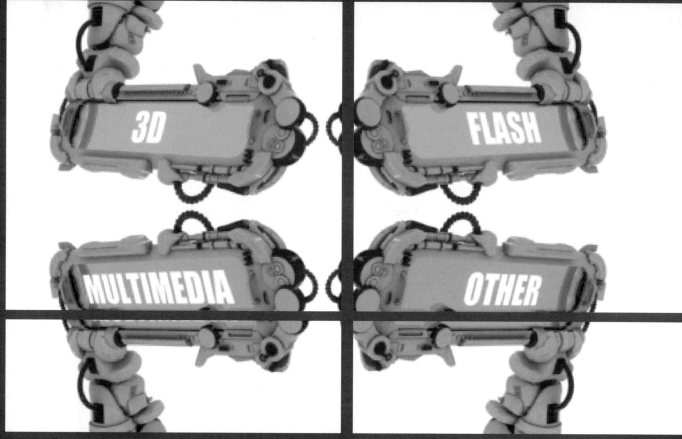

It's fairly obvious to anyone who has seen my work that I'm greatly influenced by science fiction and anime, for example, *Star Wars*, *The Matrix*, *Transformers*, and *Robotech*. I love the whole futuristic look and feel of robots and machinery. There are no real rules or boundaries to how they look, feel, or move. They appear to have a physical functionality, when in actuality, they're purely aesthetic. I guess I enjoy the irony of that concept. When I'm creating something, whether it be a 3D model or a Flash intro, I simply keep adding as much as possible, focusing on as many details as my mind can handle. Which sums up my most important philosophy: more is more.

"My goal is always to please the eye, but never confuse the brain."

Now don't get me wrong, I don't always think it's appropriate to just add and add to every element of every project that I work on. There are some situations, of course, where simplicity really is the best rule. In any situation where confusion may arise due to the complexity of a navigational system or the layout of a page, you should avoid the "more is more" philosophy. My goal is always to please the eye, but never confuse the brain. For this reason, I try to keep all my sites under six pages. I find that sites with too many pages automatically intimidate most users. I personally like things right on the edge of being too complex, while remaining comprehensible. I find that for the most part, many things that seem simple are secretly complicated. When I created www.billybussey.com/coolio I wanted the transitions to work and feel flawless, which required a large amount of complex ActionScript.

The resulting transitions feel simple when you're moving from page to page, but that "simplicity" required a lot of preparation and testing.

In addition to making things appear simple, transitions can function as a sort of guide through a more complex set of destinations. While a user is moving through a site, traveling from page to page, the more the user can associate his or her current location with a physical position, the more likely he or she is not to be confused by the navigation. I often use transitions to serve as a connection to make the pages seem less "separate." A site without transitions may be five pages of content, with each page isolated from the others, whereas the same site with transitions will feel more like a coherent timeline with five distinct points of interest.

tran·si·tion n 1 : passage from one form, state, style, or place to another

Inside billybussey.com's navigation

I'm often asked how my site's navigation is set up, and although it seems fairly straightforward, there actually are a few tricks behind how it all works. If you've ever visited my site and you have a broadband connection (or a lot of patience), then you've experienced its navigation. My goal in creating this navigation was to develop a unique way of showing off an interesting 3D model and at the same time emphasize a large amount of motion. My training and experience with video editing and compositing has greatly influenced my Flash work, and you can see this throughout my site. Because I do 3D animation as well as Flash, I felt it was necessary to use photorealistic images as opposed to vector 3D. Performance and file size are greatly affected by this, of course, but quality was most important to me and was more than worth it.

My main movie is a very large SWF file that contains only one scene. That scene contains one long bitmap sequence that serves as the entire animation sequence for the main movie. I have five page destinations in my site and therefore five keyframes within the timeline. Every sixtieth frame is a stop frame that serves as a gateway to the actual content, whether it's a loaded SWF, an image, or even text contained within that frame. Whenever users click a page, they are taken to that respective position on the timeline. If users click the first page's "home" button, they are taken to frame 60. If they click the second button, they are taken to frame 120; if they click the third button, they go to frame 180; and so on.

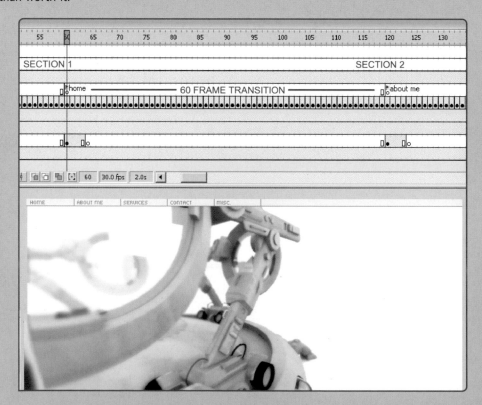

Essentially, there are 60 frames between each section where the "transition" lives. In a 30 fps file, like most of my sites, that would result in 2 seconds of playback between each page, or 60 frames played between any two pages.

Now here's the tricky part. Users aren't always going to look at all five pages in order. So I can't simply play the timeline, stopping at each of the five keyframes as users get to them. Therefore, I have to use some ActionScript coding to be able to jump around from page to page, playing each transition respectively. Of course, I don't want the timeline to jump to the right frame right away—I want it to play the transition first.

I also need to be able to do more than just play the animations forward; I need to be able to go backward within the timeline. So if a user was currently on page 2 and clicked the page 1 button, the transition between pages 1 and 2 would be played backward. Or if a user were to jump from page 1 to page 4, I would need to quickly play the transitions from 1 to 2, 2 to 3, and 3 to 4. When the timeline is taken to any one of the page destinations, a movie clip is embedded within that frame and contains the content for that frame. Within my own site that content serves as a preview for the actual section the user is about to see.

When the user clicks proceed, the user is taken to a preloader page where the section he or she is about to see can be loaded. I keep an empty movie clip in the top-left corner of my site at (0,0) that I'm able to load my external SWFs into. Since my site has five sections, I have five external SWFs that are loaded into the main movie to cut down on the initial file size. I recommend loading external SWFs into a movie clip rather than a layer because it's easier to position that loaded SWF and to have other Flash elements on top of it. It's also just as easy to replace that loaded SWF by loading another one into the same movie clip.

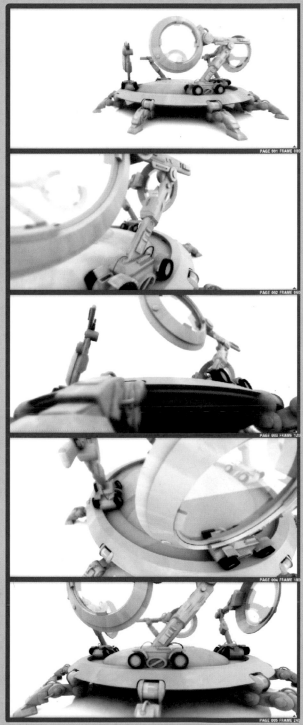

Building better buttons

To create my bitmap sequence, I simply exported all 21 frames out of 3ds max as separate files that could be imported into Flash. This particular file has two sets of bitmap sequences: one for the top button and one for the bottom button. Flash recognizes that the images are named in a numerical order and imports them to the stage, placing one image in each frame starting with frame 1, and filling each frame until all the bitmaps are imported. In this tutorial, you'll concentrate on the top bitmap sequence only.

I don't like the standard use of the normal three state buttons —up, over, and down—in Flash. And neither does anyone else who makes cool buttons. If you want any sort of animation of your buttons to be smooth, you're going to have to use movie clips controlled by an invisible button (or a movie clip now, since the latest version of Flash allows you to give movie clips "button" properties). I basically have an in and out animation for every button. So if a user were to roll over a button and quickly roll out, the changing state of the button would be smooth rather than instantaneous.

If you plan to use a bitmap sequence (which is what this tutorial covers), you'll need to create it in some program other than Flash. In this example, I've used a bitmap sequence rendered in Discreet's 3ds max (www.discreet.com/3dsmax/). It's a basic set of two 3D buttons, one on top of the other. The animation is just the two buttons going up and down independent of each other.

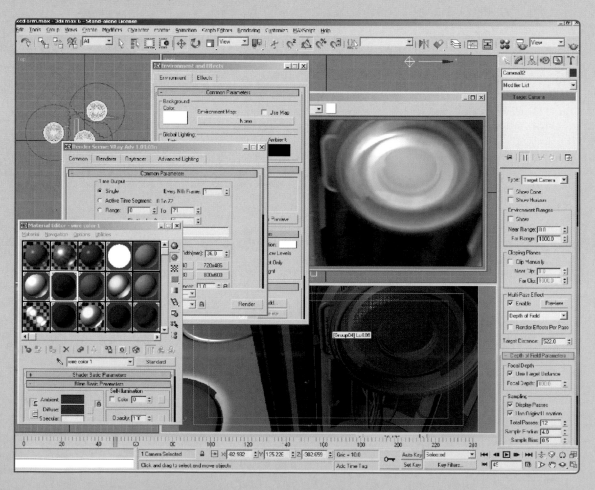

Most of my work starts in 3ds max and eventually finds its way into Flash. I'm by no means a professional 3D modeler, but I do have a good understanding of 3ds max. Like my Flash files, my max files end up being very large and complex, and usually cause my graphics card to practically ignite. My process for modeling is to get a basic concept in my head of a final product, something like a blue magnifying glass that spins around on a track. I'll then make a simple version by just throwing stuff together—a sphere here, a cylinder there, and so on. After it starts to take shape I slowly add details. I mainly use box modeling with editable polygons and a whole bunch of modifiers.

I tend to focus on this part of the process too much. I can recall spending 40 hours on a 3D model that I never even used. It literally took a full week to render the 120-frame animation used in the main timeline of my site. To get a realistic look, I had to dabble with the lighting forever, which meant playing with all the settings for global illumination and ray-traced shadows. The actual models are somewhat simple and are mainly composed of basic primitives. On an earlier version of my site, a similar animation took 144 hours to render, and about 120 hours into it my hard drive crashed and I lost the entire thing. I seriously felt like crying.

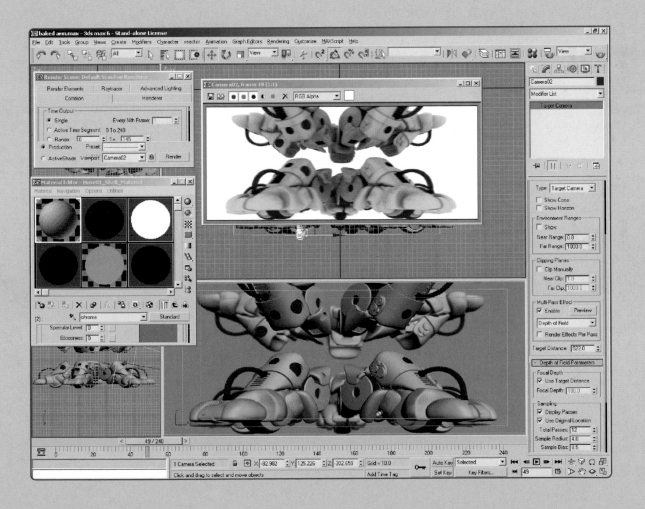

You can use any program you like that is able to export bitmap sequences. I also use programs such as Adobe Premiere, Adobe After Effects, and Electric Rain's Swift 3D. I primarily use After Effects for traditional video footage, Swift 3D for vector 3D, and 3ds max for all my realistic 3D needs. I find it's easiest to create the entire look and feel of any animation within the 3D program itself, and then as a final process actually import the images into Flash. You're usually able to export a sequence in any format you like. I tend to stick to BMP and PNG for quality reasons. You can also use JPG or GIF if they're required.

Using bitmap sequences within a Flash button

Let's get started with this first tutorial. Note that the ActionScript you'll be using here may not be the most fantastic and optimized available, but it gets the job done. My philosophy is that if your finished design is stunning enough, the intended audience shouldn't really worry about what's under the hood. Feel free to skip ahead and have a peek at what you're going to create (open `navigation_button_complete.swf` from the CD to see the finished product).

1. Open Flash and create a new file.

2. Go to Modify ➤ Document and change the dimensions to 320 pixels wide and 320 pixels high. Change the document background color to #4D5268. Change the frame rate to 60 fps and click OK.

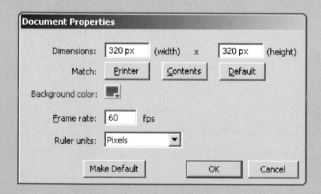

3. In the Library create a movie clip named `button top`.

4. Go into that movie clip, choose File ➤ Import, and select the first bitmap from whatever bitmap sequence you've created. Choose yes when it asks if you would like to import the entire sequence, and import it to the stage. If you don't want to create your own bitmap sequence, refer to the Library of the file `navigation_button_start.fla` from the CD, into which I've already imported the relevant PNG files. You can just drag them from this FLA to your own working movie.

5. Rename the only existing layer within your movie clip as bitmaps and create a second layer named button above it.

6. Create a shape that will become the hit area for your button, and place it in the button layer. In my file, I created a semicircle that matched the shape of the button in the bitmap sequence. After you create that shape, highlight it and press F8 to call up the Convert to Symbol dialog box. Choose Button as the symbol type, and name it button 1.

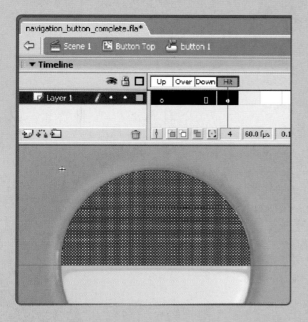

7. Now double-click the newly made button and you'll be taken to the button's timeline. Move the keyframe in frame 1 to frame 4, so that the first three frames (button states) are empty and the last has your button shape. This creates an invisible button that will allow you to control the animation when the user runs his or her mouse over it.

8. Go back to the button top timeline. You'll see that your button has become green and is transparent. Give it an instance name of top_btn.

9. Add a new layer, call it actions, highlight it, and add the following actions to the first frame:

```
// button actions
top_btn.onRollOver = function() {
  play();
  backcontrol.gotoAndStop(1);
};
top_btn.onRollOut = function() {
  backcontrol.gotoAndPlay(2);
};
```

10. Don't worry about the references to backcontrol —you're going to make this now. Create two more layers above the other two in the button top timeline. Name the top layer commands and the layer underneath that one controller.

11. Create a new movie clip and call it follow control. Give it three blank keyframes, and attach the following actions to each of the keyframes:

```
// Frame 1 actions
stop();
```

```
// Frame 2 actions
_parent.gotoAndStop(_parent._currentframe
➡ - 1);
```

```
// Frame 3 actions
gotoAndPlay(2);
```

12. Return to the button top timeline and drag an instance of the follow control movie clip out of the Library and into the controller layer, in the top-left corner. Give it an instance name of backcontrol.

This movie clip will serve as the controller for the backward-playing animation. As you can see, if you look back to the earlier button script, putting your mouse over the button will send the backcontrol movie clip to frame 1, where there is a stop action, and the animation will play forward. As soon as you move your mouse out of the button, the backcontrol movie clip is sent to the second frame, and it will start looping between the second and third frame, running the timeline backward.

13. If you test now, you might get some strange results! To make sure that the backcontrol movie clip stops trying to go backward when it hits the first frame, add the following code to the first frame of the commands layer:

```
// Frame 1 actions
stop();
backcontrol.gotoAndStop(1);
```

14. To prevent the animation from looping, create a keyframe on the commands layer in frame 21 and add the following code:

```
//Last frame actions
stop();
```

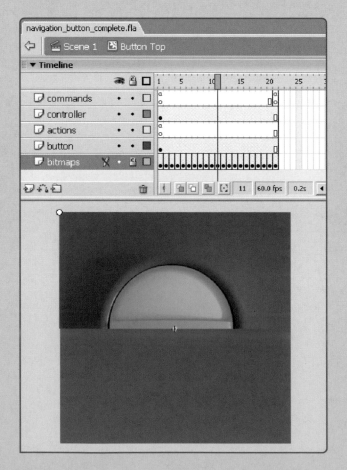

15. Return to the main timeline and drag your button top movie clip from the Library to the stage. Be sure to save your file and test your movie. If everything was done correctly, you should be able to mouse over your button and see it animate. When you roll out, the animation should play backward and go to the original up state.

16. If you used the supplied images from navigation_button_start.fla, you'll notice that the button is in two halves. To create the bottom half, simply start the exercise again at step 3, using the bottom_button01.png through bottom_button21.png files. You can reuse your invisible button and backcontrol movie clip—just change the instance name and actions for the button from top_btn to bottom_btn.

If you'd like to see the final version of my file, refer to navigation_button_complete.fla on this book's accompanying CD. You can add as many buttons to one movie as you like —just be aware of performance issues. My file has its frame rate set to 60 fps. If you notice playback issues, try changing to a lower frame rate (such as 30 or 24).

Making tremendous transitions

Everyone loves a good transition. Transitions are one of those things in life that you don't notice until someone points them out, and once you see them, you wonder how you never noticed them before. My favorite examples of transitions are the different sets of "wipes" George Lucas used in the *Star Wars* series. Simple circular wipes, or even blurry corner-to-corner wipes, seemed to fit perfectly with the story and also helped viewers better understand the films' timelines. In Flash, transitions can serve a similar purpose. Instead of displaying the passage of time or a change of scenery, as they did in *Star Wars*, transitions in Flash can represent a change in style or content.

If your only goal is to deliver content to a user, then any sort of transitions used within a site are probably unnecessary. I, however, create sites that also try to convey a feeling. Transitions aren't intended to add to the content information; they merely serve as the "in-between."

Transitions fill in the gaps within content and make sites feel more like the rest of the world, rather than just page after page of information.

Situations in which you shouldn't use transitions may seem fairly obvious. For example, of course the search engine Google shouldn't have lengthy transitions because all Google users care about is getting to the information they're searching for. It would be annoying for them to have to wait for a transition to finish playing to get to each page. But if you're making a site for a sci-fi blockbuster, you almost have to use transitions because over-the-top special effects and fancy graphics are what the movie is about.

Using bitmap sequences to form a navigational system

Before you start this tutorial, take a sneak peek at the finished piece on the CD: `navigation_transitions_complete.swf`.

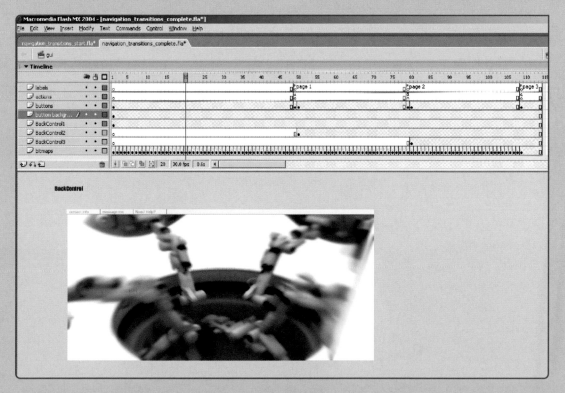

If you plan to use a bitmap sequence of your own for this tutorial, I suggest you create one with a similar number of frames to the one you'll find in my example file, which is 120 frames long. You can make your bitmap sequence any size you want, but I suggest you not make it any larger than mine or you're likely to run into performance issues.

This particular tutorial takes a slightly simpler approach than the billybussey.com navigation I talked about earlier, with three possible destinations rather than five (I'll leave you to load in your own external SWFs). It also requires a fairly fast computer. I suggest you attempt to complete this tutorial only if you're working on a Pentium 4 1.8 GHz computer or higher, and you have at least 512MB of RAM. If this isn't the case, don't be surprised if the "blue screen of death" hits you.

1. Open Flash and create a new file. Go to Modify ➤ Document and change the dimensions to 650 pixels wide and 320 pixels high. Use the default document background color (#FFFFFF), but change the frame rate to 30 fps. Click OK.

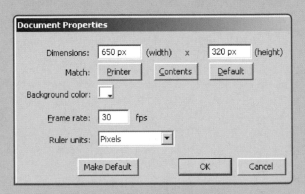

2. Go to File ➤ Import ➤ Import to Stage and choose the first frame from your bitmap sequence. Click yes when asked if you would like to import all the files. If you choose not to create your own bitmap sequence, then refer to file navigation_transition_start.fla on the attached CD and complete this tutorial using my example file.

3. Rename the only existing layer as bitmaps. Now create five additional layers above that layer called labels, actions, buttons, button background, and back mc.

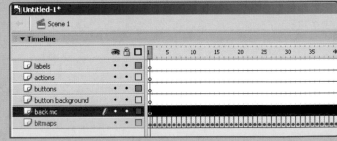

4. You'll now split your animation into three parts, and you'll call each part a "page." Essentially, you'll have three destination frames for the entire file. If you're following my example, then in the labels layer, add a label of page1 to the first frame. Next, add keyframes to frames 50 and 80, and give these labels of page2 and page3.

5. The first 49 frames of my file are the opening to the animation, which will serve as an aesthetic transition that leads up to the first frame of the page and allows me to start from a blank white screen. I personally feel an intro is the perfect opportunity to show off a little, and no one seems to notice you're showing off. In order to stop this and the other animations from looping endlessly, add a keyframe to frames 49, 79, and 109, and add stop() actions to each of these frames.

6. Now that you have a fully functional timeline with stop() actions in all the right places, it's time to add some buttons. In the buttons layer, create three buttons and name them as you want. You can create any buttons that you want, but you'll find that they need to be fairly small so as not to get in the way of the actual animation.

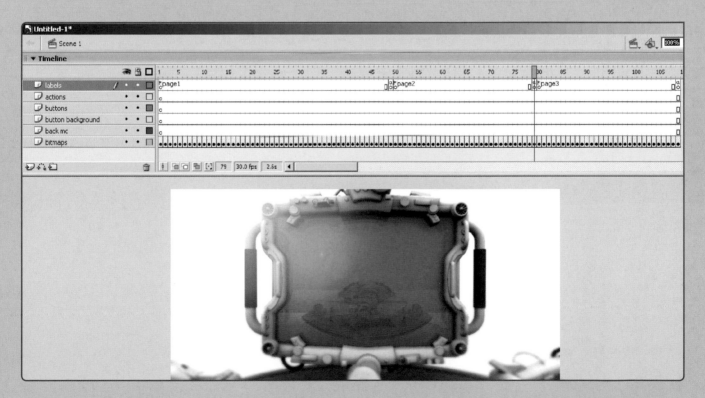

7. In my version of the file, I've also added a background to the buttons that goes across the top of the stage. Add this in the button background layer if you want the same effect.

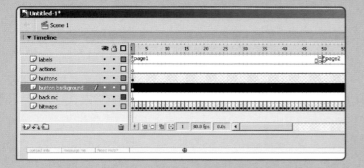

8. Now you want to add exactly the same ability to play the timeline backward as you created in step 11 of the previous exercise, so open navigation_button_complete (or whatever you named your file) and drag an instance of the follow control movie clip into the first frame of the back mc layer. Put it somewhere just offstage—I've used the top-left corner again—and give it an instance name of controller.

9. All you have left to do is write some ActionScript to run your timeline. Start by giving the three buttons instance names. I've used contact_btn, mesg_btn, and help_btn, but you can change these to something more meaningful for your version if you want.

10. Select the first frame of the actions layer. Start by declaring a variable to remember which "page" you're on:

```
frame = "page1"
```

11. Add functions for each button. You'll add instructions into these in a moment.

```
contact_btn.onPress = function() {

};
```

```
mesg_btn.onPress = function() {

};
```

```
help_btn.onPress = function() {

};
```

12. Each button, when clicked, should take you to the respective page, so you need to set your frame variable to the new page by adding the lines in bold:

```
contact_btn.onPress = function() {
    frame = "page1"
    };
```

```
mesg_btn.onPress = function() {
    frame = "page2"
};
```

```
help_btn.onPress = function() {
    frame = "page3"
};
```

13. Here's the meat of the code. Each button can be clicked when the timeline is at page1, page2, or page3. Let's start with the last button, help_btn. If this is clicked when the viewer is looking at page3, then you're already where you want to be and can stop. If it's clicked when the viewer is looking at page2, then you can do a simple gotoAndPlay ("page3"):

```
help_btn.onPress = function() {
    if (frame == "page3") {
        stop() }
    else if (frame == "page2") {
        gotoAndPlay("page3");
        }
```

14. If, however, the button is clicked when the viewer is looking at page1, then you need to play your way through the page2 animation and proceed to page3. This is a bit difficult when you have a stop() action at the end of the page2 sequence. To do this, you have to make that stop() action function only in certain circumstances. Select the stop() action in frame 79 of the labels layer and change it as follows:

```
if (middlestop == "1") {
  gotoAndPlay("page3")
}
else {
  stop();
}
```

15. The timeline will now ignore this stop() action and proceed to page3 if the middlestop variable is 1, but it will stop if middlestop has any other value. By default, you want it to stop, so return to the script in the actions layer and add middlestop = "0" to the top of the script, next to the frame variable declaration.

16. You can now add the final possibility to your help_btn: setting the middlestop variable to 1 to hurdle the stop() action.

```
help_btn.onPress = function() {
  if (frame == "page3") {
    stop() }
  else if (frame == "page2") {
    gotoAndPlay("page3");
    }
  else {
    middlestop = "1"
    gotoAndPlay("page2");
  }
  frame = "page3"
};
```

17. There's one last bit of tidying up to do here. If the user does jump from page1 to page3, then you need to set middlestop back to 0 in case the user then wants to go and visit page2 again. Select the stop() action on frame 109 of the labels layer and add middlestop = "0"; on the line before it.

18. Next, you'll deal with your first button, contact_btn. If people want to view the first page, then you're going to have to go backward with your controller:

```
contact_btn.onPress = function() {
  if (frame == "page2") {
    controller.play(2)
  }
  else if (frame == "page3") {
    controller.play(2)
  }
  frame = "page1"
};
```

19. The controller is running on a separate movie clip time-line, so to stop it add this line underneath the stop() action on frame 49 of the labels layer:

```
controller.gotoAndStop(1);
```

20. Finally, you come to your middle button, mesg_btn. If the user is on page2, then he or she is already there, and you can stop where you are. If the user is on page1, you can simply move up the timeline with a gotoAndPlay ("page2") action:

```
mesg_btn.onPress = function() {
  if (frame == "page2") {
    stop();
  }
  else {
    gotoAndPlay("page2");
  }
  frame = "page2"
};
```

21. Moving from page3 to page2 is a little bit more difficult, as you've already set up your timeline to deal with moving from page3 to page1. You'll have to run backward, but find a way of stopping your controller movie clip timeline at the end of the page2 animation *only* if the user has clicked the mesg_btn. You can do this by using your trusty middlestop variable:

```
mesg_btn.onPress = function() {
  if (frame == "page2") {
    stop();
  }
  else if (frame == "page3") {
    controller.play(2)
    middlestop = "3"
  }
  else {
    gotoAndPlay("page2");
  }
  frame = "page2"
};
```

22. Now you can add a conditional stop of the controller movie clip's timeline based on whether or not middlestop is equal to 3. Add this to the script on frame 79, between the existing if and else actions:

```
if (middlestop == "1") {
  gotoAndPlay("page3")
}
else if (middlestop == "3") {
  controller.gotoAndStop(1);
}
else {
  stop();
}
```

23. Test your file and watch it go. Of course, you could also design an exit button to run back to frame 1 from whichever page you're on, but I'll leave that up to you. If you have any problems, take a look at navigation_transitions_complete.fla on the CD. Pay particular attention to ensuring that your timeline labels and button and controller movie clip instances are correctly named.

Optimization and refinement of animations within a navigational system

Whenever you're combining an ActionScript-controlled timeline with Flash graphics and bitmap sequences, you're bound to run into performance issues. And to be honest, sites like my own can be viewed only on high-end computers. The best advice is to always test your sites on as many computers as possible, and to make sure you get a variety of people, connections, and machines to test on. There are ways, however, to make your site work as well as it can by optimizing your code, graphics, and images. The following techniques should help.

- Set your **frame rate** as low as possible. For a Pentium II 233, 60 fps is far too much to handle. If you can use 24 fps (which is around the same as film), then do it. In the button tutorial earlier in this chapter, I used 60 fps because the movie consists solely of a button. My normal fps is set to 30 (around the same as video), but I feel it's important that you experiment with the fps for each site you make. Lower fps means better playback performance.

- Determine your **target audience**. When I created my own site, I didn't worry too much about my audience. I pretty much made whatever I wanted and hoped that the audience would be able to view it. The point of my site was to *really* impress a specific group of people, not to *sort of* impress a lot of people. I assumed most of my visitors would be Internet-savvy people with decent machines, therefore I was able to be a little more daring with my content. I've received a large amount of feedback about the site, and although most of it is positive, I do get complaints about usability and long download times. It's important to realize who your target audience is, and to do your best to accommodate their computers and Internet connections.

- When creating any transition with a large number of moving graphics, you'll want to **avoid gradients** as much as possible because graphics cards can handle only so many colors at once. Although vector animations download quickly, they're processor intensive. Since transitions are brief, there's no sense in putting too many graphics into any one transition. Let's face it, if your transition plays slower than it's supposed to, it's actually having the opposite of its intended effect on the user.

- Keep your **bitmap sequences** to as few frames as possible. Bitmaps can quickly fill up RAM and, although they look great and have unlimited uses, Flash can handle only so many of them. I've encountered several errors in Flash due to an overwhelming number of bitmaps contained in the FLA itself. I've had files that wouldn't open after being saved, images that suddenly turned red, and bitmaps that just vanished from the Library altogether.

- The **resolution** of each bitmap is also a factor to be aware of. Anything larger than 640x480 is definitely out of the question. I suggest using images more along the lines of 320 pixels high or wide. If you intend to use a bitmap as a background item or stationary image, then resolution isn't as big of a factor. Only when you intend to tween large images or use a bitmap sequence containing large images will resolution become a problem. In some circumstances, you're able to not worry about resolution and frame count as much (that is, presentations that will be run locally from a hard drive or even a CD).

- **JPG compression** is the key to successfully using any bitmap sequence. The philosophy is simple: use as much compression as you possibly can while still maintaining the image quality you require. Smaller, more compressed images will load more quickly and be used by the Flash player more easily. A technique I use to minimize file size and boost performance playback within a bitmap sequence is to manually control the compression settings for each bitmap. For example, in my site I have a 240-frame animation. Five of those frames are keyframes. Since the user moves between those five frames and never actually stops on any of the other frames, I make the bitmaps within those frames have very little compression. Since the rest of the frames in the animation are only shown briefly during any transition, those images can be highly compressed. Therefore the images found in frames 1, 60, 120, 180, and 240 could all have their JPG compression levels set to 90, whereas all the in-between frames could be set to 45 or lower. In my site's circumstance, I noticed quite a jump when a user reached keyframes in the timeline. To remedy this, I raised the compression level of the images found in the frames adjacent to my keyframes. Basically, I use less compression in frames 2, 59, 61, 119, 121, and so on.

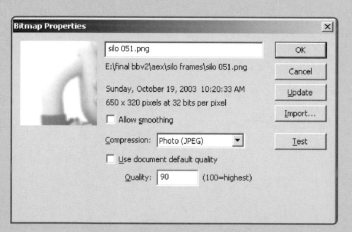

- Occasionally, you may feel the need to incorporate **animated bitmaps**, via ActionScript or tweening. I recommend doing this as little as possible. For some reason, Flash doesn't animate bitmaps well, especially when tweening. However, if you do have to tween, it's best for the bitmap to lie on a whole integer coordinate such as (0,0) as opposed to (.5, 2.5). It also helps the animation to move whole integer steps. If you're moving a bitmap from left to right 200 pixels, I suggest that the animation's length be a factor of 200. If the animation is 50 frames long, and you're moving 200 pixels, that's 4 pixels per frame. This will result in much smoother animations than if you were to move 3.3 pixels per frame. If at all possible, I suggest you avoid easing in or out of any keyframe, as this causes the bitmap to move in fractions of pixels. If you know anything about ActionScript (which is more than I know), you can also use this to move a bitmap. This will result in an even better performance than any tween could, especially if you follow this whole integer rule. All of the preceding rules apply for any sort of change you make to a bitmap, from rotation, to scaling, to color, to x- and y-coordinates.

- As far as **graphics formats** go, it's best to know which one works in each situation. Certain images work well in some circumstances; others work poorly in most situations.

  - **PNG**: If you ever need to use any sort of image with a high-quality transparency (alpha channel) in it, your first choice should be PNG.

  - **BMP**: If all you need is a standard image with no transparency, BMPs are acceptable. They look great and compress well, although they make your FLA much larger. If you ever have a site, like I do, that contains hundreds of BMPs, you can quickly find yourself with a 300MB FLA.

  - **JPG**: I recommend that you avoid using JPGs as much as possible. Flash recompresses them and you end up losing image quality.

- **GIF**: I've occasionally used GIFs in projects, but you'll rarely need them for anything besides small buttons or icons. Their transparency is either on or off, so PNGs are more useful than GIFs.

- As a final (although slightly off-topic) thought, it's worth considering **video** in Flash. I've experimented with the new video capabilities of Flash MX 2004 and have had mixed results. Mixing video files with a site's content or navigation is risky, and I've discovered that small bitmap sequences have better playback performance than video files. I feel that video files should be used only to show videos. I would avoid using video for buttons, looping animations, or transitions. I suggest using video only to show an actual video, such as a news clip or TV commercial. Although video compression has gotten much better recently, and Sorensen Squeeze has its own Flash compression tools, video files still tend to be large and low quality. However, I do think that with each new version of Flash, video will become a more commonly used element within Flash sites. If you have to use video within a site, I recommend using the QuickTime format with the Sorenson codec.

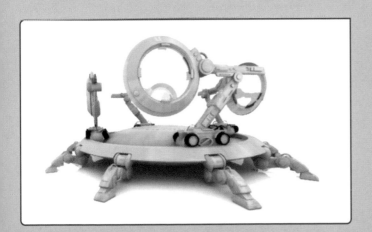

Summary

Now that you've learned several different techniques for creating nontraditional Flash elements, you can find out for yourself what's best for you. In this chapter, you covered the following topics:

- Using bitmap sequences appropriately

- Optimizing and refining Flash animations for better performance

- Creating smoothly animated Flash buttons

- Determining the best image formats to use in various situations

- Understanding the pros and cons of video usage

- Moving within a timeline to control transitions

You can use your newfound knowledge to enhance your own work. Let these techniques serve as a base of knowledge for you to do something creative with the space between one page and another, and to use Flash to do more than just create quick-loading content. Your transitions certainly deserve a little more thought in future.

Of course, you must be realistic when attempting to create sites like these. Flash wasn't intended for uses I've described. When you push the bounds of Flash and the Flash player, you have to realize that there will be many bugs, and some computers may even crash. I recommend you use these techniques in moderation. If you decide to use them as I've described, do be prepared to get flack from the more conventional Flash community. I feel that as Flash advances, broadband connections become faster, and high-end computers become more common, sites like my own will become more accepted.

For further information, please refer to my developer forum at www.billybussey.com/forum.

04 NATURE

"JUST AS NATURE OFFERS A TAPESTRY OF AMAZING
TEXTURES, STRUCTURES, AND PATTERNS,
TECHNOLOGIES SUCH AS FLASH ALLOW US TO
CREATE AND EXPLORE OUR OWN INTERPRETATIONS
OF THEM AND IN A WAY GIVE US A SMALL TASTE OF
WHAT IT MIGHT BE LIKE TO BE A GOD."

ANTHONY EDEN
WWW.ARSEIAM.COM

The recipe of me

Ingredients:
1 x love of mathematics
1 x love of physics
1 x appreciation of nature
2 x amazing parents
1 x hunger for life
Mixed thoughts

To flavor:

Fun, laughter, and chicken. A pinch of sarcasm (or the devil's advocate when sarcasm is unavailable).

Utensils:

1 laptop with Flash and a set of well-balanced scales.

Preparation:

Have parents commit to cleaning up any mess while giving unconditional support. Add an equal portion of mathematics and physics (and any spare emotions) into a large bowl. Add a fistful of mixed thoughts and blend well. Make sure to pause occasionally and appreciate. Add as much fun and laughter as the bowl will accommodate and a pinch of sarcasm to taste.

Cooking:

Bake frequently on high. Engage in conversation with chicken.

Serves:

Those that consciously respect themselves and others.

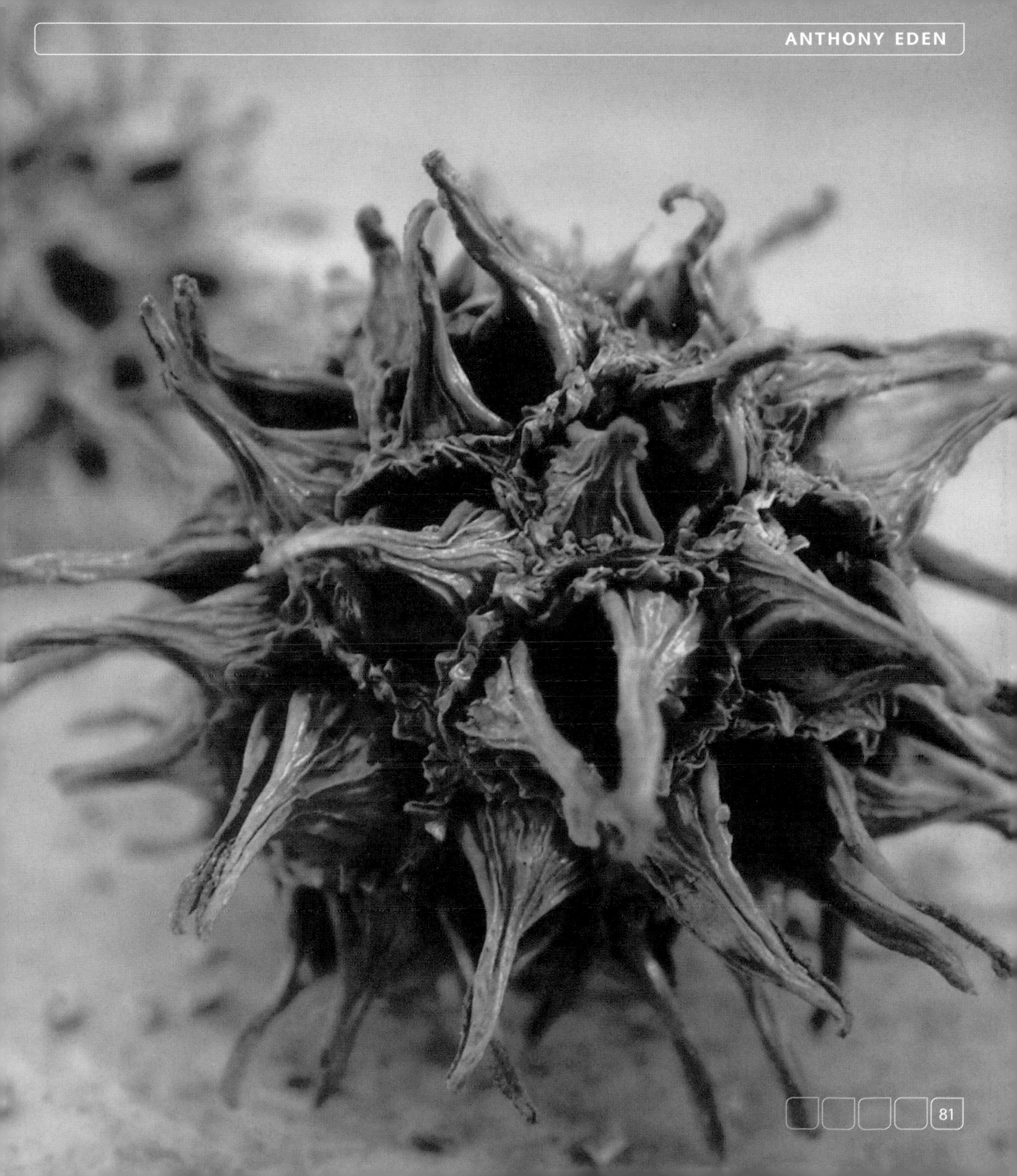

Observe, replicate, evolve

When I was first asked to submit a chapter for this latest volume in the *New Masters of Flash* series, I was a little concerned that I may not have the time or energy to work on it. You see, I had just finished developing a large Flash-based application and had decided to destress by spending the next 3 months traveling through Europe (being from Australia, this doesn't happen all that often). I really wanted to travel, but I also wanted to write this chapter very much. After some thought, I decided not only to do both, but also to use my travel as inspiration for the chapter. Thus, most of this chapter was written from different locations (and different living conditions) throughout England, Wales, France, and Sweden (with a bit of Australia and Japan thrown in for good measure!). Also, all the images used in this chapter are of my crafting. To make my little egocentric universe even more complete, I've formed this chapter around my love of mathematics, life, and nature, and the patterns that emerge from them.

To me, "patterns in nature" transcend the physical realm and are prevalent in all aspects of life. The basic principals of object-oriented programming hold similarities to the structure of permaculture or the anatomy of a bee. The sciences that study the human psyche do so by examining patterns in thought and behavior. From molecules to our DNA and even the universe itself, all things are underpinned by a rigid structure and patterns that we use to try to understand them.

> The basic principals of object-oriented programming hold similarities to the structure of permaculture or the anatomy of a bee.

observe

replicate

evolve

I was always fascinated with structure, whether it belonged to formally scored music, architecture, the art of M.C. Escher (www.mcescher.com), or something as fundamental as clumps of grass . . . not that I ever really understood it.

As a child, I had a naive appreciation of how things were formed and how they stayed formed. Why is it that tree branches grow in such a way that they seem to occupy a space in the most efficient way possible without overlapping or blocking light from the branches underneath? How is it that rules can be applied to a progression of musical chords so that when played in a sequence they form harmony? How cool is it that you can eat four Popsicles and then use the remaining sticks to form a stable boomerang shape without the need for glue?

I guess my wonderment was an attempt to remove myself from the practical (and sometimes completely impractical) things that they were trying to teach me at school. Over years of obsessions, the folds of naivety slowly peeled away as I educated myself in the wonderful worlds of engineering, physics, and mathematics. The only inhibiting factor in my progress was a desire to focus on the aesthetic while generally ignoring the possibility of function.

I dabbled with all sorts of mediums. Pencils, oils, acrylics, airbrush, wood, and metal all suffered from my inability to create anything I was actually happy with. I avoided doing anything practical or too meaningful, mostly through the process of collecting masses of junk with the knowledge that one day it would all have a context and fit neatly into my ideals of maturity and the meaning of being adult and being an artist.

M.C. Escher's "The Borger Oak" (1919, linoleum cut)

It was about 10 years ago when a software engineer passed me a book titled *On Growth and Form* by D'Arcy Thompson, and my love for mathematics and nature was finally bridged. I had discovered what it was that was meaningful in my life! And I was left with a shed full of rusty old crap.

I don't read very often, and when I do, I seem to always stick with the genre that lies somewhere between science fiction and science fact. I'm hopeless at reading and retaining information, except for little anecdotal facts that rarely serve any other purpose than passing amusement. For instance, I learned Flash mostly through trial and error and experimentation. I don't think this "style" of learning suits all people, but it certainly suited me. The process of discovery lends itself to a deeper understanding of your subject matter. If you start from the inside and work your way out, then you end up with a deeper understanding of the whole.

Simulating physics in Flash, for example, I learned by experimenting with some basic constructs until I had created something that appeared to work like it should in the real world. I had, in a sense, discovered for myself some of the fundamentals of Newtonian mechanics and was left with a deeper understanding of physics than I would have had if I just read about it.

Anyway, reading is good for you. I should read more and so should everyone else.

Of the few books I have read, some have had a significant impact on the way I think about my life and all the life around me. The first book I read that warranted any meaningful reaction was Lyall Watson's *Supernature: A Natural History of the Supernatural*. And I don't mean just any old "Wow"—it was more of a "Zut alors, le poulet est à la fenêtre!" kind of reaction and awakening. Man, this book has everything you would ever want to know about the natural environment that most people spend their entire life ignoring. Watson talks about everyday topics in everyday terms, only in a depth that simply stuns you. Did you know that with a small piece of glass tubing and the careful removal of a cockroach's brain you can make a double-decker cockroach that functions as a single entity merely by sharing body fluid? For this reason alone, I truly think that *Supernature* should be required reading and even part of the school curriculum. Needless to say, *Supernature* changed my life in a significant way. Should you read this book (and you should), you might also want to check out Lyall Watson's other books, *Beyond Supernature*, *Dark Nature*, *Gifts of Unknown Things*, *The Romeo Error*, and *Jacobson's Organ*, all of which are wonderful adventures through science (see www.lyallwatson.com for further details).

I should also mention that at the time of reading these books, I was living with my parents on a partially forested acreage and was surrounded by plants and animals. And though I was also exploring programming for the first time on Commodore 64 and Amstrad computers, the concept of using computers to replicate natural phenomenon had not yet hit me. The seed, however, had been planted. I was 16 then, I'm 31 now, and Lyall really got me started.

By the time I hit my early twenties and had experienced everything you should experience while attending university (except for actually passing any classes), I had moved onto bigger and better books. *Gödel, Escher, Bach: An Eternal Golden Braid* by Douglas R. Hofstadter took me a lifetime and a day to read, but it was well worth it. It was my first introduction to how the same patterns and structure can be seen in different schools of thought. Hofstadter manages to make obscure mathematical subjects understandable and entertaining, all the while drawing surprising points of contact between the music of Bach, the artwork of Escher, and the mathematics of Gödel.

Metamagical Themas: Questing for the Essence of Mind and Pattern, also by Douglas R. Hofstadter, is a compilation of short essays written originally for *Scientific American* magazine. The essays focus on Hofstadter's main areas of work: consciousness, patterns, music, language, and computer systems. Once again, Hofstadter drove me to deepen my understanding of mathematics and patterns, and continues to do so.

I guess it's fairly safe to conclude that, in the past, I've drawn inspiration from both books and nature, and they themselves offer a wonderful symbiosis in that nature drives me to learn and books educate me about nature.

The golden ratio

In more recent times, I've been inspired by the number **phi** (also known as the **golden ratio**, the **golden section**, and the **golden mean**). Salvador Dali's *Sacrament of the Last Supper* is almost a tribute to phi, as the number reoccurs in the background geometry and throughout the different objects (such as the rose), and even the aspect ratio of the framing is equal to phi.

For those uninitiated into the wonderful world of 1.61083399, phi is best described by Euclid:

"A straight line is said to have been cut in extreme and mean ratio [phi] when, as the whole line is to the greater segment, so is the greater to the less."

A   B   C

In other words, the ratio of the length of AC to BC is the same as the ratio to the length BC to AB.

The amazing thing about this innocent-looking line division is the way in which it has impacted the study of mathematics and various other schools of thoughts throughout history. Botanists have discovered countless examples of phi in nature, astronomers note it as a recurring theme in the structure of galaxies, it appears consistently in the relics of ancient societies, and artists have, at times, relied on it to achieve aesthetic perfection. Phi had such an impact on Pythagoras's worldview that he sacrificed 100 oxen in awe of this number. In a lot of ways, phi seems to underpin all aspects of physical reality. Some people believe phi is such an intrinsic element to life that it's the closest thing to God and, being an atheist, it's not a struggle for me to appreciate that concept.

The thing that captures me most about phi is that it's very giving. It potentially offers us a greater understanding of mathematics and nature, as well as supplying the building blocks for structure and aesthetics.

Apart from books, nature, and the odd special number, I draw a lot of inspiration from the world of computing and those who actively participate in it. For a long time now, I've been experimenting with generative patterns and shapes. It has only been in the last couple of years that I've tried to re-create living systems with any serious level of realism. The first major study that resulted in some success and facilitated the first—but essential—surge of momentum was my study on the movement of flagellates (www.arseiam.com/fx/28.htm).

After watching a documentary and learning that flagellates are small organisms that move by whipping their tails (euglena, for example), I decided that I could reduce their movement to a simple algorithm. While the algorithm turned out to be rather more complex than I'd first imagined, the process of creating my first virtual life-form had an impact that was, in contrast, very simple. I realized that Flash allows me to put my love of math and physics into practice in a way that enables me to understand old ideas and learn new ones in the same process. Just as Lyall Watson influenced me as a teenager, the flagellate experiment inspired me to continue to explore the idea of simulating life.

There are a large amount of experiments on display at my site (www.arseiam.com). One of the most recent additions is my camel simulator. The camel simulator represents the latest stage of my creative exploits: the desire to simulate objects that simulate real-world things—and, of course, the concept of the ridiculous.

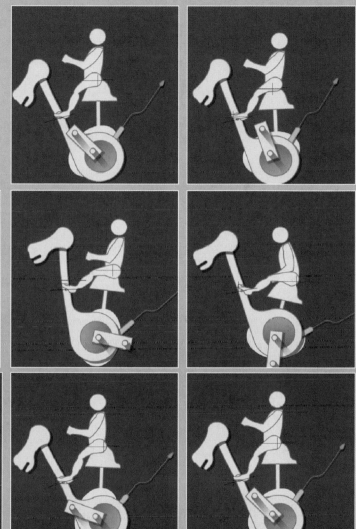

Using Flash for simulations and experiments

The very nature of Macromedia Flash as a technology lends itself to creating interactive nature simulations and self-replicating experiments. Its extensive drawing API and movie clip methods allow you to develop quickly while facilitating a huge scope for further experimentation. Being able to create objects that in themselves are composed of objects makes the creation of organic, interactive objects an easy and enjoyable process. It is these elements of Flash, the drawing API and the movie clip concept, that we'll explore throughout this chapter.

> "THE VERY NATURE OF MACROMEDIA FLASH AS A TECHNOLOGY LENDS ITSELF TO CREATING INTERACTIVE NATURE SIMULATIONS AND SELF-REPLICATING EXPERIMENTS."

Flash isn't particularly good at handling a lot of objects at any given time, however, as it requires a lot of processor resources to function.

One particular issue with the creation of patterns is the combination of too many objects, complex mathematical calculations, or simply too many pixels needing to change every frame, so the intrepid explorer should travel with a little caution.

There are alternatives to Flash for those who want to take their experiments even further. The best alternative I've found so far is Processing (http://processing.org), which is a Java-based authoring environment with a syntax loosely related to ActionScript. Processing offers far superior processing power, allowing you to simultaneously manipulate thousands of objects, but of course it lacks the functionality that the native classes and objects in Flash have to offer, along with its obvious user interface. Processing clearly isn't yet another supposed "Flash killer," but I encourage anyone with a serious interest in programmatic digital art to check it out.

Back to Flash, in this chapter I hope to offer a mere taste of the nature of numbers and the mathematics of nature as I continue on my own exploration and attempt to put my environment into some kind of quantifiable context.

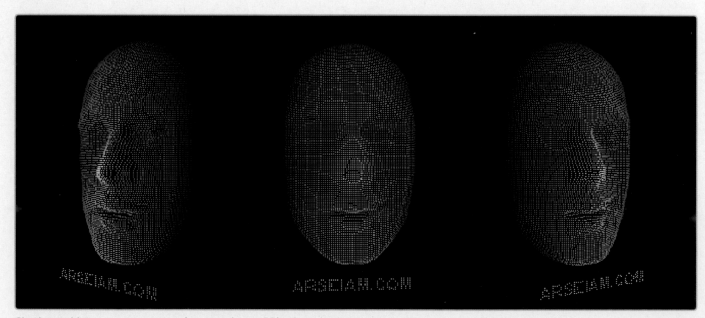

Check out this geezer at www.arseiam.com/proce55ing/man/.

Creating interactive programmatic landscapes

Getting down to the Flash side of things, I would like nothing more than to write about exploring patterns alone, but here I'm hoping to impart something a little more useful and structured. In any case, there are a billion and one snippets of open source ActionScript available online that will demonstrate to you the art of the programmatic pattern.

In this chapter, you're going to build an interactive landscape populated by randomly generated plant life and textures. You're then going to add some programmatic parallax movement to give the environment a 3D feel. You'll also experiment with ways of adding further animation such as branch physics and shading to simulate the time of day.

The chapter and final file is structured in such a way that each landscape element is independent of the others. You'll use a constructor-style system that allows you to simply invoke a function, such as `createTree(vars)`. Keeping your elements modular allows you to easily change the functionality or aesthetic to suit your needs.

Depth structure

To use lots of different objects that, when combined, result in a landscape, you need to be careful in the way you separate these objects along the z-axis (or depth). You'll create a background, a series of slices of land, clouds, trees, and creatures. You'll give each element a priority value for its depth—that is, the higher the number, the closer to the front the object will appear. You'll then place your objects, according to their depth priority, at different depth intervals (in this exercise, they'll all be 100 apart). This allows you to control the order in which items are placed and control the objects that move in and out of varying depths.

Here's the rough plan you'll follow in the next few sections:

1. Set up your file.

2. Create some backgrounds.

3. Play with a couple of methods for making terrain.

4. Explore iterative techniques for making plants.

5. Learn how to integrate your objects into your landscape (including plants and critters).

6. Add depth to the landscape with parallax and dynamic shading.

7. Examine some ways of extending the techniques, such as tree physics.

Setting up your file

1. Before you begin, you'll start with a little file preparation. Create a new movie with frame rate of 21. Change its dimensions to 518x320. You may notice that this aspect ration is approximately equal to phi. I sometimes do this to adhere to the phi aesthetic philosophy—and because cool people like Salvador Dali used to do it.

2. You'll write all the ActionScript into the first frame of _root. You'll create and attach all your movie clips at runtime (using `createEmptyMovieClip` and `attachMovie`), and you'll programmatically define their handlers and variables so there will be no need for stage clips or attached scripts. I prefer to work with my ActionScript spread out over multiple layers (or AS files) with logical names, so create the following layers: global variables, background, plants, ground, creatures, and animation. As you progress, you'll populate the first frame of these layers with the appropriate ActionScript.

3. Create a new folder in your Library labeled runtime assets. You should place all movie clips that you intend to "attach" in this folder. Feel free to establish your own folder structure and nomenclature for any other assets you create.

4. You need to define some variables that will be used by the different objects by placing the following script in the layer global variables. You'll add to these variables as you require them.

```
sw = Stage.width;
sh = Stage.height;
groundZindex = 1; // the depth index for
// land slices
creatureZindex = 1; // the depth index for
// creatures
```

When creating generative landscapes, the best approach is to start from the back and work your way forward, so let's move forward by creating a background (or horizon, depending on the style of landscape you choose to make).

Creating a background

You're about to make your background, and in order to do so, you'll create your first function. As discussed earlier, you'll need to place all code on the _root timeline in the relevant layer. Alternatively, you could just load the file background.fla from the accompanying CD.

1. The following script creates a rectangle and allows you to define gradient colors. You need to place it in the first frame of the background layer:

```
function makeBG(x, y, wd, ht, colors, depth) {
    var hor = this.createEmptyMovieClip
    ➥("horizon", depth);
    alphas = [100, 100];
    ratios = [0, 0xFF];
    matrix = {matrixType:"box", x:x, y:y,
    ➥ w:wd, h:ht, r:Math.PI/2};
    hor.beginGradientFill("linear",
    ➥ colors, alphas, ratios, matrix);
    hor.moveTo(x, y);
    hor.lineTo(x+wd, y);
    hor.lineTo(x+wd, y+ht);
    hor.lineTo(x, y+ht);
    hor.lineTo(x, y);
}
```

2. The function is invoked using the form *makeBG(x, y, width, height, colors, depth)*. For instance, you can create a nice blue sky by placing the following code directly after the preceding makeBG function:

```
makeBG(0, 0, sw, sh, [0x0099CC, 0xBAD6EF],-1);
```

3. Alternatively, comment out the last line and add the following two lines to create a skyline with a horizon:

```
makeBG(0, 0, sw, sh/2, [0x0099CC,
➥ 0xBAD6EF],-1);
makeBG(0, sh/2, sw, sh/2, [0x4FD55F,
➥ 0x009900],-2);
```

For the moment, let's stick with the simple blue sky.

You could add more variables to the makeBG function, such as alpha and matrix variables or a flag that indicates the gradient type as being either linear or radial. The makeBG function is easily extensible, but you already have all the functionality you need for this exercise, so I'll leave any additions to you for now.

Making the terrain

1. You're now going to create a ground texture. Keeping in mind that you're going to add some parallax effects, you'll create the texture using a series of slices. The script that follows (which should reside in the ground layer) uses the drawing API and a bunch of randomness to give the feel of rough textured land:

```
Number.prototype.HEXtoRGB = function() {
    return {red:this >> 16, green:(this >> 8) & 0xff, blue:this & 0xff};
};

function makeGround(slices, x, y, wd, ht, ros, roy, cols, plants) {
    col1 = cols[0].HEXtoRGB();
    col2 = cols[1].HEXtoRGB();
    for (var i = 0; i<slices; i++) {
        var newSlice = this.createEmptyMovieClip(i, i*100+groundZindex);
        var newCol = (col1.red+(col2.red- col1.red)*i/slices) << 16 | (col1.green
  ➥+(col2.green- col1.green)*i/slices) << 8 | (col1.blue+(col2.blue-col1.blue) *i/slices);
        newSlice.beginFill(newCol, 100);
        newSlice.moveTo(x, y-ht);
        for (var j = 0; j<=ros; j++) {
            newSlice.lineTo(x+j*(wd/ros), y- ((slices-i)/slices)*ht+Math.random()* roy- roy/2);
        }
        newSlice.lineTo(x+wd, y-ht);
        newSlice.lineTo(x+wd, y);
        newSlice.lineTo(x, y);
        newSlice.lineTo(x, y-ht);
    }
}

makeGround(10, 0, sh, sw, sh/2, 10, 50, [0x776313, 0xD6AA29],1);
```

Note that, unlike makeBG(), the HEXtoRGB script uses prototype, which allows you to create a function (well, a **method**, to be technical) that's accessible by all objects of a particular type. In this case, all instances of the Math objects have access to the HEXtoRGB method.

Testing the movie (ground.fla on the CD) will result in the creation of a random desert landscape with undulating mounds of graduating color (similar to the landscape on the left). Try playing with the parameters to produce various landscape types.

2. The makeGround function takes the following form:

        makeGround(slices, x, y, wd, ht, ros, roy, cols, plants)

where

        slices = number of slices required
        x = x coordinate for the right edge
        y = y coordinate for the bottom edge
        wd = width
        ht = height
        ros = number of steps of terrain for each slice
        roy = maximum offset for the terrain
        cols = the two colors required (top to bottom)
        plants = number of plants per layer (this is not used until we have covered plant creation)

 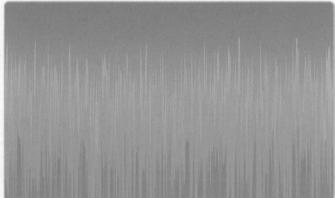

3. While most of the process should be easy enough to follow, three particular sections warrant further explanation. First, these two lines of script use the HEXtoRGB prototype, resulting in col1 and col2 being declared as objects with red, green, and blue values:

```
col1 = cols[0].HEXtoRGB();
col2 = cols[1].HEXtoRGB();
```

To achieve a smooth graduation of color, you need to reduce the required colors into their red, green, and blue components. This is where the HEXtoRGB number prototype comes into it. By passing a hexadecimal color value into the prototype, this method returns an object containing the required red, green, and blue components.

4. The next potentially confusing line is this one:

```
var newCol = (col1.red+(col2.red-col1.red)*i/slices) << 16 | (col1.green+(col2.green-
➡ col1.green)*i/slices) << 8 | (col1.blue+(col2.blue-col1.blue)*i/slices);
```

Here, the creation of newCol is contained with a loop and effectively steps through the colors in equal intervals starting from col1 and ending at col2, taking the following form:

*Start + (end − start) * current step / total steps*

5. This is applied to all three color channels.

6. Finally, the following line:

```
for (var j = 0; j<=ros; j++) {
        newSlice.lineTo(x+j*(wd/ros), y-((slices-i)/slices)*ht+Math.random()*roy-roy/2);
    }
```

is the loop used to create the top of each section.

```
x+j*(wd/ros)
```

The x-coordinate is calculated in a similar way to the color—that is, it's divided into equal steps starting from x and spanning the width:

```
y-((slices-i)/slices)*ht + Math.random()*roy-roy/2
```

The second portion does the same on the y-axis, except it's a calculation of the height of each slice with an additional random factor.

Feel free to check out the file ground.fla should you have any trouble.

Making the terrain, version 2

Another method for creating the slices is to use predrawn assets. Both methods have their pros and cons depending on what you want to achieve. The previous method is good for quick, random landscape generation that requires little effort and results in a small file size. The following method allows you to create theme-specific elements and facilitates more manual control over the random elements.

To continue with this exercise, you'll need to open the file ground2.fla because it contains the movie clips required for this example. Also note that the movie clips have their **linkage identifiers** defined (right-click the symbols in the Library and select Linkage), with Export in first frame checked to allow you to use attachMovie to attach them at runtime.

By the way, the movie clips contained in the Library folders slice1 and slice2 appear to be empty, but they actually contain white shapes (clouds).

1. Have a look at ground2.fla, which contains a bunch of assets that I've already created. By "assets," I mean movie clips in the Library that have a linkage identifier and are available to be exported at runtime.

   You'll also notice that the makeBG function has now changed to this:

   ```
   makeBG(0, 0, sw, sh/2, [0x0099CC, 0xBAD6EF],-1);
   makeBG(0, sh/2, sw, sh/2, [0x996600, 0xff9900],-2);
   ```

2. Likewise, the makeGround function has changed to this:

   ```
   function makeGround(st, x, y, wd, ht, num, assets) {
       for (var i = 0; i<st; i++) {
           var slice = this.createEmptyMovieClip(i, i*100+groundZindex);
           var objects = Math.round(Math.random()*num);
           for (var j = 0; j<objects; j++) {
               var objectNum = Math.ceil(Math.random()*assets);
               newObj = slice.attachMovie("s"+(i+1)+"_"+objectNum, "obj"+j, j);
               newObj._x = Math.random()*wd+x;
           }
           slice._y = y+(ht/st)*i;
       }
   }
   // makeGround(slices, x, y, width, height, number of objects, number of assets available)
   makeGround(9, 0, 115, sw, 200, 5, 5);
   ```

The result is a rocky desert landscape.

Instead of using the drawing API to create the landscape, you're attaching movie clips. The clips are randomly chosen and placed. There are a number of ways to structure the selection and placement of clips, and in the case of this example I've created a list of separate clips that relate specifically to each layer. This gives you the scope to create graphics specific to each layer. For example, you don't want clouds underneath rocks, and so on. It can get a little tricky making sure that clips don't overlap in an unrealistic manner, but a little experimentation will get you there.

Creating plants

I'm now going to discuss ways of programmatically creating trees using attached movie clips. I hadn't seen many examples of branch systems prior to building my first version, though there are now quite a large number of examples online and in books such as *Flash Math Creativity* (friends of ED, 2002). The following example will be sufficient for what I'm demonstrating, but I highly recommend checking out some of the other examples available in books and online. And I'm sure I don't need to encourage you to check out Jared Tarbell's amazing *Complexification* work in this book!

The basic idea is that you attach a branch, and then continue to attach more branches, while randomly deciding if the branch stems into extra branches. You continue this process until one of the branching constraints—branch length, overall branch segments, or a random factor that terminates the branch (creating an increased chance of termination the longer the branch gets)—is met.

You'll use the previous file that uses the drawing API for this exercise, so go ahead and reload the `ground.fla` file if you want to work along with this tutorial (or take a look at `plant.fla` to skip ahead).

1. The first thing you need to do is create some assets that you'll attach at runtime. Only simple graphics are needed for this exercise, so all you need to do is create a vertical line about 20 pixels high. Turn it into a movie clip called `stem` with the linkage identifier `stem`, check Export in first frame in the Convert to Symbol dialog box, and make sure that the graphics are aligned to the bottom edge of the symbol. Make sure to delete any instances of `stem` from the stage before proceeding.

2. Ultimately, you're going to place the trees within each ground slice, but for the moment you'll just work with a single tree in `_root`. To do so, you'll need to comment out the following line of code from the ground layer:

   ```
   // makeGround(10, 0, sh, sw, sh/2, 10, 50, [0x776313, 0xD6AA29],1);
   ```

This effectively *turns off* the ground creation so you can actually see what you're doing.

3. Add the following script to the global variables layer:

   ```
   stemLengthMax = 20; // maximum length of branch
   stemCountMin = 10; // minimum number of segments
   stemAng = 20; // maximum angle of stem rotation
   stemChance = 0.7; // chance of stem splitting
   ```

4. And the following script to the plants layer:

```
MovieClip.prototype.createPlant = function(x, y, scale) {
    var newPlant = this.createEmptyMovieClip("plant"+global_plantCount, depth++);
    newPlant._y = y;
    newPlant._x = x;
    newPlant._xscale = newPlant._yscale=scale;
    newPlant.createStem(0);
    stemCount = 0;
    stemLength = 0;
};

MovieClip.prototype.createStem = function(ang) {
    var newStem = this.attachMovie("stem", "stem", stemCount++);
    var sl = (this.stemLength=this._parent.stemLength+1);
    newStem._y -= 20;
    newStem._rotation = ang;
    newStem.gotoAndStop(sl);
    if (sl<stemLengthMax && sl/stemLengthMax<Math.random() || stemCount<stemCountMin) {
        if (Math.random()>stemChance) {
            newStem.createStem(Math.random()*stemAng-stemAng/2);
        } else {
            newStem.createStem(Math.random()*stemAng);
            newStem.createStem(-Math.random()*stemAng);
        }
    }
};
this.createPlant(sw/2, sh, 100);
```

When you compile the movie, you should see a randomly created tree.

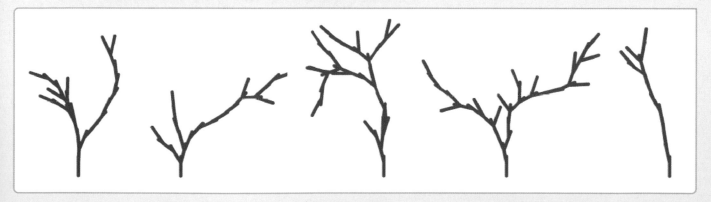

You'll notice that you're invoking the createPlant prototype, which in turn invokes the createStem prototype, which in turn invokes itself until a constraint is reached. The createPlant prototype is used to create a new movie clip, set up some basic variable requirements, and then invoke createStem to set the process into motion.

The createStem prototype contains a number of elements that you'll need to understand, so let's break it down line by line:

```
var newStem = this.attachMovie("stem",
➥ "stem", stemCount++);
```

This creates a new movie clip and increments the variable stemCount, which is used to ensure the plant doesn't have branches of infinite length.

```
var sl = (this.stemLength =
➥ this._parent.stemLength+1);
```

Here you declare variable this.stemLength at the same time as you declare a temporary variable sl, which are both equal to this._parent.stemLength. sl is declared to allow easy reference to this.stemLength. The purpose of this declaration is to pass the length of the current stem up the chain of stems to conform to the stemLengthMax constraint you set earlier in the global variables layer.

```
newStem._y -= 20;
```

This shifts each stem in relation to its _parent and is roughly equal to the height of your original stem asset.

```
newStem._rotation = ang;
```

The preceding line of code rotates the stem according to the value of ang (which is passed through to the prototype when invoked).

```
newStem.gotoAndStop(sl);
```

This action tells the stem to gotoAndStop at a particular frame. As your stem symbol is only one frame, this line has no purpose—yet.

```
if (sl<stemLengthMax && sl/stemLengthMax
➥ <Math.random()|| stemCount<stemCountMin) {
```

These are the conditionals that decide whether to add any more stems to the current stem. The first conditional ensures that the current branch hasn't reached its maximum length, stemLengthMax. The second conditional randomly determines if the stem should continue to grow (as the branch gets longer, the chance of it stemming again decreases as the value of sl/stemLengthMax approaches 1). The use of the || (*or*) in the third conditional ensures that no matter what the outcome of the first two conditionals is, if the plant doesn't have enough stems in total it will keep stemming.

```
if (Math.random()>stemChance) {
    newStem.createStem(Math.random()
    ➥ *stemAng-stemAng/2);
} else {
    newStem.createStem(Math.random()
    ➥ *stemAng);
    newStem.createStem(-Math.random()
    ➥ *stemAng);
}
```

This randomly determines (based on stemChance) whether the stem splits into one or two stems. The new stems' angle is chosen randomly and the createStem prototype is invoked.

Experiment with changing the different variables—particularly the ones set in the global variables layer. If you're having trouble getting the script to work, then open file plant.fla to rule out typos.

5. Hopefully you've played around with the prototype a bit and are now ready to add some more meaningful design such as foliage and branch thickness (see also `plant2.fla`).

Edit the movie clip `stem` and create a keyframe at the frame equal to the value of `stemLengthMax` (in this case, 20). Modify the line on the first keyframe by making it thicker (6 pixels, for example) and add a shape tween between the two keyframes.

Do you remember that little snippet of script containing the `gotoAndPlay()` method? Well, that's what determines which frame the stem is going to (and in this case, it will go to the frame corresponding to how many segments along the branch you are).

Test the movie and you should now see that as the branch gets longer, the stems get subtly thinner, just as might happen with a real tree.

6. Creating the foliage is just as simple, though it requires a bit of trial and error. Start by creating a new layer in the `stem` movie clip. Create a keyframe on the frame where you wish to start your foliage (this will be equal to the number of stem lengths you want in a branch before the foliage starts, for example, frame 10).

Test the movie. Make a note of how the foliage looks on the branches and modify your frames to suit any changes you might require. I ended up making simple foliage consisting of a number of green circles. I then turned the shapes into a movie clip; modified the first keyframe by rotating 105 degrees, scaling (75%), and tinting (45%); and tweened the frames to the end keyframe.

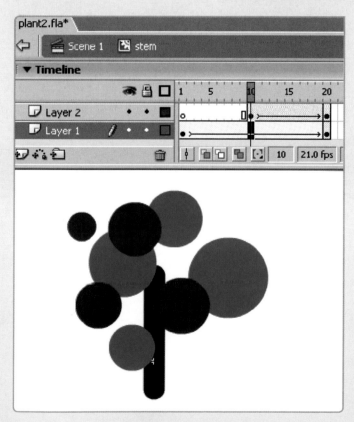

I highly recommend going outside, looking at various plants, and trying to reproduce them using this stem system. You won't be able to reproduce some plants at all, but with a little experimentation, you should be able to make fairly close representations of most of them. Try adding flowers, making shrubs, or even adding complexity to the stems.

7. You'll now take the final step of adding the plants to the ground layer. Start by uncommenting the following line of script in the ground layer (or just load the file plant3.fla):

```
makeGround(10, 0, sh, sw, sh/2, 10, 50,
➡ [0x776313, 0xD6AA29],1);
```

Then *remove* the following line from the plants layer:

```
this.createPlant(sw/2, sh, 100);
```

8. I mentioned previously that the makeGround function has a plants parameter. This is where you'll make use of it. You're going to attach plants to each layer by adding a loop and an attachMovie method to the end of the for loop in the makeGround function like so (note that the function remains the same as before, except an additional for loop has been included toward the end):

```
function makeGround(slices, x, y, wd, ht, ros, roy, cols, plants) {
    col1 = cols[0].HEXtoRGB();
    col2 = cols[1].HEXtoRGB();
    for (var i = 0; i<slices; i++) {
        var newSlice = this.createEmptyMovieClip(i,
        ➥ i*100+groundZindex);
        var newCol = (col1.red+(col2.red-col1.red)*i/slices) << 16
        ➥ | (col1.green+(col2.green- col1.green)*i/slices) << 8
        ➥ | (col1.blue+(col2.blue-col1.blue)*i/slices);
        newSlice.beginFill(newCol, 100);
        newSlice.moveTo(x, y-ht);
        for (var j = 0; j<=ros; j++) {
            newSlice.lineTo(x+j*(wd/ros), y-((slices-
            ➥ i)/slices)*ht+Math.random()*roy-roy/2);
        }
        newSlice.lineTo(x+wd, y-ht);
        newSlice.lineTo(x+wd, y);
        newSlice.lineTo(x, y);
        newSlice.lineTo(x, y-ht);
        for(var j = 0;j <plants;j++) {
            this[i].createPlant(Math.random()*sw, y-((slices-
            ➥ i)/slices)*ht, i*10+20);
        }
    }
}
```

This will loop according to the number of plants required and will attach them.

If you're testing and viewing the movie inside the Flash authoring environment, you'll no doubt notice that the trees sometimes appear outside the stage. This is potentially due to a bug in the Flash authoring environment that causes Stage.width to read differently than the Flash player. In any case, it isn't an issue because you want the trees to render offscreen so that they're only partially shown.

Creating creatures

Next, you'll look at a basic example of how you can control the objects moving in and out of the landscape. You can easily modify this technique to create birds and insects. In this exercise, you'll make some bugs that fly around a little above the ground level.

1. Continue to use the file from the previous exercise or open the file `plants3.fla` (or even `bugs.fla` if you don't want to type anything in!). Begin by drawing a small white circle with no fill that has a diameter of 4 pixels and a red stroke of 1 pixel. Convert it into a movie clip named `bug` and give it a linkage identifier of `bug`.

2. Add the following script to the global variables layer:

```
bugHeight = 100; // distance from top of stage
bugVariance = 60; // variation in x position
bugZvariance = 10; // variation in depth
bugScale = 2; // scale
bugSpeed = 0.05; // speed (0.05 - 0.3)
```

Here, `bugHeight` is the distance that bugs appear in relation to the top of the movie. A smaller number will allow the bugs to fly in the air, whereas a larger number will result in the bugs flying closer to the ground.

> Hint: If the bugs fly lower than the ground, then you won't be able to see them.

`bugVariance` defines the amount of movement along the x-axis, and `bugScale` defines the amount of movement along the y-axis. `bugScale` can be calculated by dividing the ground height by 100, though, so nice depth effects can be achieved by changing this value by small amounts. `bugSpeed` represents the speed of the bug, where 1 is the maximum and a sensible value is between 0.01 and 0.3.

3. Add the following script to the creatures layer:

```
createBugs = function (bugs) {
   for (var i = 0; i<bugs; i++) {
     var newBug = this.attachMovie("bug", "bug"+i, i*100+creatureZindex);
     newBug.tx = newBug.seekX = Math.random()*sw;
     newBug.ty = newBug.seekY = Math.random()*sh;
     newBug.az = newBug.seekZ = Math.random()*100;
     newBug.id = i;
     newBug.onEnterFrame = moveBug;
   }
};
MovieClip.prototype.moveBug = function() {
   // determine seek points
   this.seekX += Math.random()*bugVariance-bugVariance/2;
```

```
        this.seekZ += Math.random()*bugZvariance - bugZvariance/2;
        this.seekY = this.seekZ*bugScale+bugHeight;
        // detects sides
        if(this.seekX > sw) this.seekX -= 100;
        if(this.seekX < 0) this.seekX += 100;
        if(this.seekZ < 0) this.seekZ = 0;
        if(this.seekZ > 100) this.seekZ = 100;
        // smooth move to
        this.tx = this.tx-(this._x-this.seekX)*bugSpeed;
        this.ty = this.ty-(this._y-this.seekY)*bugSpeed;
        this.tz = this.tz-(this.az-this.seekZ)*bugSpeed;
        this._x = this.tx;
        this._y = this.ty;
        this.az = this.tz;
        // scale bugs
        this._xscale = this._yscale = this.az*bugScale +20;
        // effect depth
        this.swapDepths((Math.ceil(this.az/10))*100+creatureZindex+this.id);
    };
    createBugs(10);
```

The createBugs function loops through, attaching movie clips and setting parameters for each bug's x-, y-, and z-coordinates. An id is also set to avoid any conflict when dynamically changing each bug's depth value. The onClipEvent handler is then declared as moveBug.

The moveBug prototype sets seek values for x, y, and z. These values are used in an **ease-to** algorithm (that is, the bugs will constantly be moving toward a new position, which in turn is constantly changing). This gives the effect of smooth, random movement.

The first block of script in moveBug sets these seek values. seekX and seekZ are purely random values based on bugVariance and bugZvariance, respectively. seekY gets its value from seekZ multiplied by bugScale; this is done to represent movement along the z-axis (as the seekZ value increases the bug's movement toward the bottom of the movie). An additional value of bugHeight is used to effectively lift the bug above the ground.

The second block of script restrains the bug's movement along the x-axis and z-axis. The third block calculates the next position of the bug using a basic ease-to algorithm. The x and y scale process is also fairly obvious, except that I've added a value of 20 (which results in the maximum scale of a bug being between 20 and 120, ensuring that it's never too small to be seen).

The final line of the moveBug prototype addresses the z-order, or depth, of the bug. While it may look a little convoluted, it's actually quite simple. The bug is moved to a depth equal to

```
(Math.ceil(this.az/10))*100+creatureZindex +this.id)
```

where this.az is equal to its z-depth, 10 is the number of slices in the ground, Math.ceil is used to ensure that the division results in an integer, 100 is the distance that each slice is apart (I discussed this at the start of the tutorial), creatureZindex is the depth of set in relation to the other object types, and this.id is each bug's unique ID (which ensures no depth conflicts).

In the sample file bugs.fla, I've thickened the plant branches and added more bugs so that the change in depth levels is more obvious.

Using parallax 3D

Now that you've designed and built your environment, let's add some flavor through the use of mouse reactivity and parallax. **Parallax** is a cheap form of 3D in the sense that it doesn't actually involve any real 3D but has a nice 3D-like feel to it. Parallax works on the principle that if an object changes position relative to another object (or even a series of objects), then a sense of perspective or depth is achievable.

To implement the parallax effect you're going to move each ground slice at different speeds relative to its proximity to the foreground (see `parallax.fla`; in fact, this is a fairly complex example, so it's worth taking a peek at `parallax.swf` to see the finished effect in action).

1. To implement parallax, you need to make some modifications to the ground slice. Parallax can get rather complex with dynamically moving objects, so for the sake of this exercise you're going to turn off your bugs by commenting out the following line from the creatures layer:

   ```
   // createBugs(10);
   ```

2. While you're at it, define the `parallaxOffset` variable in the global variables layer:

   ```
   parallaxOffset = 5;
   ```

3. You'll now apply some parallax to the `makeGround` function by first changing the way in which the slices are rendered:

   ```
   function makeGround(slices, x, y, wd, ht, ros, roy, cols, plants) {
     col1 = cols[0].HEXtoRGB();
     col2 = cols[1].HEXtoRGB();
     for (var i = 0; i<slices; i++) {
       var paraWD = wd+wd*(i+parallaxOffset)/slices;
       var paraX = (wd-paraWD)/2;
       var newSlice = this.createEmptyMovieClip(i, i*100+groundZindex);
       var newCol = (col1.red+(col2.red-col1.red)*i/slices) << 16 | (col1.green+(col2.green-
   ➡ col1.green)*i/slices) << 8 | (col1.blue+(col2.blue-col1.blue)*i/slices);
       newSlice.beginFill(newCol, 100);
       newSlice.moveTo(paraX, y-ht);
       for (var j = 0; j<=ros; j++) {
         newSlice.lineTo(paraX+j*(paraWD/ros), y-((slices-i)/slices)*ht+Math.random()*roy-roy/2);
       }
       newSlice.lineTo(paraX+paraWD, y-ht);
       newSlice.lineTo(paraX+paraWD, y);
       newSlice.lineTo(paraX, y);
       newSlice.lineTo(paraX, y-ht);
       for (var j = 0; j<plants; j++) {
         newSlice.createPlant(paraX+Math.random()*paraWD, y-((slices-i)/slices)*ht, i*10+20);
       }
       newSlice.id = i+parallaxOffset;
       newSlice.onEnterFrame = move;
     }
   }
   ```

To facilitate parallax movement, the width and x-coordinate of each layer has to change; that is, they need to increase in size the closer they are to the foreground to accommodate a greater change in position. To maintain the values of variables x and wd, you create two more variables, paraX and paraWD. These variables are derived from x and wd to cater for the parallax requirements.

4. Now to get these suckers moving, you need to add an event handler that calculates the mouse position relative to the center of the movie every frame (you should add this script to the animation layer):

```
this.onEnterFrame = function() {
    _global.mX = (this._xmouse-sw/2);
};
```

5. Finally, to the end of the script on the ground layer, you can add your movement prototype:

```
MovieClip.prototype.moveGround = function() {
    this._x = mX*(this.id)/(sw/100);
};
```

6. If you've invoked the makeGround() function, make sure to comment it out before adding the following:

```
makeGround(10, 0, sh, 518, 200, 10, 30, [0x776313,
➥ 0xD6AA29], 1);
```

You can take this effect a lot further than I've demonstrated, though even this simple implementation can give a nice 3D look and feel to the piece.

Something to keep in mind when you use similar techniques is that generative techniques often facilitate very small file sizes, but this can come at a price. This parallax technique, for example, requires a reasonably robust graphics card to render properly and would need some testing and redevelopment to suit a required minimum configuration machine.

Shading

Another good way to give a sense of depth to your environment is through procedural **shading**.

1. You can continue with your previous file, open the file `parallax.fla` (to follow this exercise), or open the file `shading.fla` (to view the resulting effect).

2. Shading is a relatively easy process that requires some minor changes to the background, ground, and creature constructors. You're going to push all of the objects (ground slices, creatures, and so on) into an array and assign `shadeDepth` values so that each object is affected differently.

   Set up your shade array by adding the following script to the global variables layer:

   shadeObjects = [];

3. Now, to push all the objects into this array, you need to make some modifications. In the `makeBG` function, change this line:

   ```
   var hor = this.createEmptyMovieClip("horizon", depth);
   ```

   to this:

   ```
   shadeObjects.push(hor =
   ➡ this.createEmptyMovieClip("horizon", depth));
   hor.shadeDepth = 1;
   ```

4. Likewise, in the `makeGround` function, change this line:

   ```
   var newSlice = this.createEmptyMovieClip(i,
   ➡ i*100+groundZindex);
   ```

   to this:

   ```
   shadeObjects.push(newSlice =
   ➡ this.createEmptyMovieClip(i,
   ➡ i*100+groundZindex));
       newSlice.shadeDepth = i;
   ```

All your objects now have a unique `shadeDepth` value and can be referenced by the `shadeObjects` array.

5. All you need to do now is create a function that uses each object's `shadeDepth` and tints it accordingly. Add the following script into the animation layer to do this:

```
initShading = function () {
    this.createEmptyMovieClip("shader", -1);
    shader.onEnterFrame = shadeController;
};
shadeController = function () {
    for (var i = 0; i<shadeObjects.length; i++) {
        var col = new Color(shadeObjects[i]);
        var pc = (this._ymouse/sh)*(shadeObjects[i].shadeDepth)*10;
        var trans = new Object();
        trans = {ra:pc, rb:0, ga:pc, gb:0, ba:pc, bb:0, aa:100, ab:100};
        col.setTransform(trans);
    }
};
initShading();
```

6. Testing the movie will result in mouse-reactive shading. You've created a new movie clip and defined its `onEnterFrame` handler (which invokes `shadeController`). `shadeController` loops through all the objects within the `shadeObjects` array and tints them (black) according to their unique `shadeDepth` value. Experiment with the way in which variable `pc` is created for all sorts of different shade and light effects.

Note that shading like this can be processor intensive, depending on the number of objects you want to shade. Experiment with different techniques such as using `onMouseMove` and removing objects that have a dynamic `shadeDepth` value, such as the bugs.

Extending the environment

There are many ways in which you can extend the core functionality to suit your requirements. In this section you'll first look at ways of adding physics to the branch systems, and then I'll briefly discuss some other examples of functionality that you could integrate and their potential uses.

Branch physics

Adding physics to branches so that they bend and fall in a realistic way isn't a particularly easy prospect. For starters, a comprehensive understanding of physics and mathematics is required, as is a computer capable of massive processing speeds. Alternatively, you could look at ways of simulating branch physics without having to deal with all the complications. I stumbled across the following technique almost by accident when I was trying to simulate some of the effects of the real world.

The easiest way of getting some lifelike movement into the branches is to add an event handler to each and every stem. Open the file branch_physics1.fla and test the movie. You'll notice that as you move the mouse from left to right, the branches of the tree bend. The process is relatively simple in that an event handler has been added to the createStem prototype:

```
MovieClip.prototype.createStem = function(ang) {
    var newStem = this.attachMovie("stem", "stem", stemCount++);
    var sl = (this.stemLength = this._parent.stemLength+1);
    newStem._y -= 20;
    newStem._rotation = ang;
    newStem.gotoAndStop(sl);
    this.ang = ang;
    newStem.onEnterFrame = moveStem;
    if (sl<stemLengthMax && sl/stemLengthMax <Math.random()|| stemCount<stemCountMin) {
      if (Math.random()>stemChance) {
        newStem.createStem(Math.random()*stemAng - stemAng/2);
      } else {
        newStem.createStem(Math.random()*stemAng);
        newStem.createStem(-Math.random()*stemAng);
      }
    }
};
```

An additional prototype has also been added:

```
MovieClip.prototype.moveStem = function() {
    this._rotation = ((_root._xmouse-sw/2)/100)*(this.stemLength)+this.ang;
};
```

You invoke the createPlant function like so:

```
createPlant(sw/2, sh);
```

What's happening here, you ask? The rotation of each stem is effected by the _xmouse position relative to the center of the stage. A scaling factor of 100 is used to affect the rotation only slightly, while this.stemLength is used to ensure stem movement increases as the branch gets longer. Finally, the initial rotation value of each stem is added to retain its original angle relative to the other stems.

You're probably thinking that the tree physics looks kind of weird because the branches actually curl up instead of drooping like they would in the real world. Strap yourself in because you're about to enter the world of branch physics! Well, not really, but you're going to make a simple change that has a huge effect on how the branch physics works (refer to `branch_physics2.fla`). To do so, change this line:

```
this._rotation = ((_root._xmouse)/100)*
➥ (this.stemLength)+this.ang;
```

to this:

```
this._rotation = ((this._xmouse)/100)*
➥ (this.stemLength)+this.ang;
```

So what's going on? To be perfectly honest, I don't know. Well, I don't know enough of the actual mathematics to explain it in any accurate sense, but I do know that the individual branches are rotating according to the _xmouse position relative to themselves and not the stage, and that the _xmouse position changes as they rotate. The resulting effect is that the branches rotate toward the mouse until they reach equilibrium, which is a combination of the mouse position relative to their rotation. Yet another reason why I love Flash so much!

Continuous scrolling

Due to space and time constraints, I've been able to demonstrate only a very basic form of parallax movement. A great way to extend these techniques would be to implement continuous scrolling either by continually creating random elements (and destroying them when they leave the screen) or by creating the ground slices in pairs so that they automatically repeat whenever they leave the screen. I think these techniques would be great for a side-scrolling game and would also facilitate slow changes in the environment as the player progresses.

Changing the angle

I'm currently working on a project that requires top-view parallax movement. The process is much the same, only the objects' y-coordinates have a literal value instead of a procedural one.

Time of day

By integrating the date object into the shading, you could directly represent the time of day. Try experimenting with the shading techniques and using date() to control the level of shading.

Sharing environments

Something that I've wanted to develop for some time now is a system that allows users to create their own plant species and environments, and save the information to a database. Given the accumulation of enough data, people could connect, select a region (country, and so on), and interact with a virtual landscape that's somehow representative of the region's flora and time of day.

Audio

Just like a good film, the user is drawn in by images, emotional engagement, and sound. It's amazing how much depth can be added to a piece with the inclusion of an ambient track and some random or event-based sound effects.

Summary

So there you have it. Just as nature offers a tapestry of amazing textures, structures, and patterns, technologies such as Flash allow us to create and explore our own interpretations of them and in a way give us a small taste of what it might be like to be a god.

The techniques I've used throughout this chapter are fairly typical to a lot of the experimental work I undertake.

I haven't used any mind-bending math or complex code—just a bunch of simple ActionScript code that when viewed alone holds no function or relevance, but when combined offers myriad options to explore. It's like anything in life: the *whole* may look complex, but when you break it down into its parts, you'll often find it's made up of simple ideas and decisions.

Now go hug a tree, and if you see Lyall while you're out there, say hi from me.

05 **ENGAGE**

THE INTERACTION DESIGN
PROCESS SHOULD BE
CONSIDERED, CONSISTENT,
AND CONCISE IN ITS
USAGE. MOST IMPORTANT,
IT SHOULD BE CREATIVE
IN ITS DESIGN.

OLIVER SHAW
WWW.PHOTO-GENETIC.COM

The art of interaction design

This chapter covers interaction design theory, with a focus on Flash interfaces and experiences. In this chapter, I'll present practical information for you to use as a guide for creating successful interactive experiences, from planning through production. The art of creating interactive experiences involves not only focusing on the code of interactive elements, but also looking at the "big picture." You can think of creating an interactive project as akin to baking a cake: it's all about getting the right mix and balance of ingredients.

I aim to help you create interactive experiences that will draw users further into your project or show them where to go (within a website environment, for instance) and how to get there with grace and finesse. I'll discuss what to avoid when you create an interactive project, and I'll present ways to ensure that your project's level of interaction is enough to excite and engage your users, but doesn't frustrate them and prevent them from using the project.

In this chapter, you'll discover that being a "**master**" of Flash involves much more than just knowing how to code cool toys and gizmos.

My background in the Flash world

My initial encounter with Flash was when a friend of mine showed me some beta experiments created in Flash 3 that had been released online. Having previously only used JavaScript to create online interaction, I was instantly amazed and captivated. At the time, I was working for a small new-media agency outside of London. I showed my then boss the Flash experiments, and he instantly ordered the currently available version of Flash (Flash 2) and instructed me to learn it. I sat down and started to play with it. By today's standards, the functionality of Flash 2 was quite limited—it was more of an animation tool than anything else. Once Flash 3 and then Flash 4 were released, I was already creating numerous websites at work, and in my spare time I experimented with different approaches to interaction.

I first ventured out of my private Flash experiments at the 2000 Online Flash Film Festival (OFFF). OFFF is held annually in Barcelona and has become a key event for those involved with using Flash. Aside from presentations and workshops, OFFF holds a Flash competition, which is divided into a range of categories. I entered a piece titled *Time Taken vs. Time Spent* in the Experimental/Art category. My film made it through the initial voting and was a finalist in its category.

At the time I created this piece, I was reading a lot about information graphics, and I was experimenting with layering and scrolling via Flash 4's increased coding capabilities. The aim of this piece was to challenge what users expected, but so subtly that they were distracted by the main body of content and didn't notice the layer upon layer of interaction embedded within.

After OFFF, I met a group of like-minded Flash developers on the Flashcoders mailing list (http://chattyfig.figleaf.com). This open mailing list is for anyone with a reasonably high level of Flash coding ability. The list is hosted by Fig Leaf Software and is administered by Branden Hall. Should you wish to join, please be aware that this is a very high-volume mailing list. One of the best things about the list is its online archives, through which you can access all the list messages for the last few years. If you have a Flash code problem, one of the best first places to look for an answer is the Flashcoders archive.

In 2001, some of the developers I met on the Flashcoders list and I got together and produced the book *Macromedia Flash: Super Samurai* (Macromedia Press, 2001). The chapter I wrote for the book focuses on interface design.

why?

Time Taken vs. Time Spent was a 2000 Online Flash Film Festival (OFFF) Finalist.
You can find the design on the CD as nyccab.html.

disfunktional   hide

FILE   EDIT   PROPERTIES   CONTACT   HELP

a-z drop objects
0-9 sets drop colour
<delete> removes last object droped
hold <shift> transparency
toggle <capslock> distort

• to view in image in high quality, hide the panel

| 1 | 2 | 3 | 4 | 5 | 6 | 7 | 8 | 9 | 0 |

g-j-d-f-l-k-g-j-l-d-k-g-j-o-t-t-o-i-r-r-r-t-t-t-t-t-o-y-o-
y-o-y-o-y-i-i-i-i-i-i-i-i-i-i-i-i-y-i-o-u-p-o-i-i-m-m-m-m-
m-m-m-m-x-z-m-m-n-d-k-j-k-f-j-k-d-k-j-h-j-k-l-l-k-j-
h-k-m-n-b-m-n-b-m-c-x-v-d-s-d-w-w-e-c-n-c-n-v-b-n-u-u-
t-y-u-y-n-b-v-c-x-v-c-v-c-x-j-k-f-d-s-f-o-r-e-o-p

timeElapsed[0:2:52]   totalObjects[141

Random Engine was a finalist in the 2002 FlashintheCan Awards.
You can find this piece on the CD as randomengine_v46.exe.

Continuing my personal exploration into interaction, I next created a Flash random engine. When I was creating the engine, numerous other Flash developers were playing with scripted random engines in Flash. I wanted to do something a little different, though. Still fascinated by interaction design, I decided to let the user have control over the random aspects of the engine. The piece I created relies on the user interacting with the keyboard to draw a random picture, with each alphabetical key releasing three objects associated with that key. By holding down more than one key at the same time, the user could randomize the transparency of the object released, while another combination would affect the scaling and rotation.

I worked on this piece for some time, gradually adding more functionality to it. As soon as I added a new feature, I asked some friends to test it. During the testing process, the developer half of me would be looking to see if the feature was working correctly and trying to spot any bug in the code, while the designer half of me would note how much the testers enjoyed the new feature.

One thing that amazed me about this piece was that it appealed to a wide range of people from diverse backgrounds, from members of the Flash community (who you might expect to be used to experimental interaction designs) to friends who used a computer only to check their e-mail.

As I got this piece to a fully functional state, coincidentally the By Designers for Designers (BD4D) group (www.bd4d.com) was preparing to host its first ever event in London. After speaking with the organizers, Ryan Shelton and Ryan Carson, I was asked to present this project in the Three Minute Madness (3MM) section of the event. On the whole, my presentation and project were well received.

After I further developed the project by adding yet more functionality and frequently testing it on my friends and co-workers, I entered it into the first ever FlashintheCan Awards, held in Toronto, Canada, in 2002 (www.flashinthecan.com). I entered *Random Engine* in the Experimental category, where to my surprise it was one of the top three finalists (there were many entries in the competition, and this particular category was one of the most popular).

Personal work

My personal work falls into a range of areas, from my love of photography, to my fascination with motion graphics and animation, to my interest in interaction design and interactive narrative. I find it difficult to make enough time for everything that I enjoy and am interested in, so I try to incorporate aspects of each area into my projects.

Take www.photo-genetic.com, for example. I'm continually taking photographs, which I would normally admire shortly after developing them but then put in boxes, where they would remain indefinitely. After numerous conversations about photography and sharing pictures, my co-worker Simon Brown and I realized that we should group our photos together and produce a site for showcasing some of them instead of hiding them away.

Photo-genetic.com, Issue 2: Nature (2003), showing the Flash and XML-based menu system

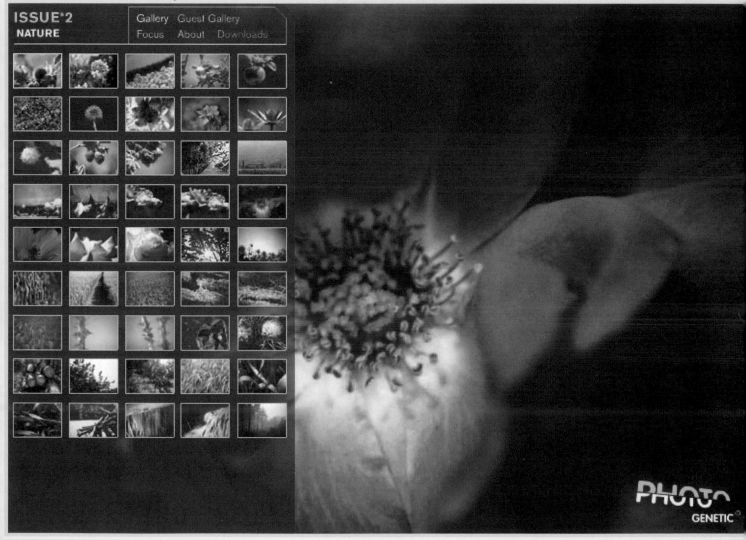

Photo-Genetic 2003© ISSUE2: **NATURE**   Photographer: Oliver Shaw   Location: Suffolk, UK   ◀ 20 / 62 ▶

With the Flash interface shown here (Issue 2: Nature), I was trying to showcase the photography in the best possible way —everything else was secondary to that purpose. I made a discreet navigation menu that could be hidden away, leaving the user to view the photographs in their full glory. In addition, to improve the site's usability, I made use of the cursor keys, enabling the user to scroll through the images in the portfolio with the left and right arrow keys. The other noteworthy feature of this piece is that all the content—images, thumbnails, and body text—is fed into the Flash file through an XML file, creating a photography portfolio engine. This was quite useful when Simon and I were putting images into the engine, as the XML file allowed us to swap out the images and reorder them with ease.

Photo-genetic.com, Issue 2: Nature (2003) is available to view at www.photo-genetic.com/issue2.

LyndaLorraine.com Autumn/Winter 03/04 (2003) is available to view at www.lyndalorraine.com.

In addition to this kind of practical project, from time to time I get the opportunity to take a more experimental approach to a project, which is what I did with this chapter's case study, LyndaLorraine.com, Autumn/Winter 03/04.

Having seen some of my pervious work, Lynda Lorraine, a London-based fashion designer, asked me to create an interactive experience to represent her autumn/winter collection that would work in unison with her portfolio presentation of the collection. After my initial discussions with the client, it was clear that I was free to create a highly experimental project. My only real instruction was to make sure the site was consistent with the look of the printed material associated with the collection.

The biggest obstacle to overcome related to the target audience. There was quite a large gap in experience among the audience members: some weren't very experienced with using the Internet, while others were very familiar with highly interactive sites.

After further discussions with the client, it was decided that the site should be more on the interactive and experimental side.

With this obstacle out of the way, I decided I wanted to explore an interactive narrative through the site's design. This would prove to be more difficult than I initially thought, as it was a site to showcase a collection of garments. In this case, there was little story to accompany them. So I settled on a compromise: I would make it so users would have all the interaction and navigation of an interactive narrative, but the focus would be on the clothes.

Ultimately, I believe the finished piece works well and meets all my hopes and expectations for it. Users are continually focused on the clothes, but they're still free to roam around the landscape, so to speak. The client was happy with the finished piece, and the feedback from users has been extremely positive, so from a project perspective it was a success.

Operation Slaps (2003) is available to play and download at www.operationslaps.com.

Professional work

I work for **NOWWASHYOURHANDS** (www.nowwashyourhands.com), or **NWYH,** a UK design agency, where my role is lead Flash developer. Although I'm mainly focused on Flash, this role enables me to perform a wide variety of tasks, from assisting in the conception and planning of a Flash project, to developing the project and interaction design, to handling testing and quality control of Flash projects. Some of the greatest aspects of my work at NWYH involve the diverse clients I have the opportunity to work with and the types of projects NWYH gets involved in. Projects range from online gambling games, e-learning projects, desktop applications, Flash websites, Flash games, CD-ROMs, and more. NWYH does work for both external commercial clients and internal marketing projects, such as *Operation Slaps*.

Operation Slaps is a self-promotional viral game for NWYH. We based the game on the old English playground game of "slapsies." While we were conceiving the game, we decided to try and make it different from run-of-the-mill, vector-based Flash games, so we went down the photographic route. Although this was, of course, a lot of fun (we spent a day getting into costume for the photographs; I'm the one in the hat and glasses), it added a few more technical challenges to the project's development.

All in all, the project was a huge success. We released the game virally, and by the end of the month, the site had received over 1 million visitors. The choice to incorporate the graphical elements as photos certainly adds something extra to the game, ultimately making it memorable to users.

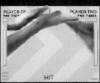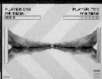

Interaction design

What is **interaction design**? The concept refers to the creation of anything that has been designed and created for users to interact with. This covers a lot of possibilities—it's not confined to computers and the Internet. Interaction design can affect anything from opening a carton of milk to buying movie tickets.

More specifically, Flash interaction design covers interfaces, desktop applications, games, e-learning, storytelling, and many other similar areas. It's anywhere you want to engage users, to encourage them to interact further and take the time to explore your project fully, so that they can learn, experience, or to be entertained by what they've found. It's important to consider that for every request you make of the users, there should be some sort of reward given back to them, so that they're encouraged to continue deeper into your project.

Consider the **action and reward** process involved in video games, for example. The game player works through a level, and at the end of the challenge he or she is rewarded with an animation or video clip. There are, of course, more factors involved than just this, such as a narrative or various game-play items within the game, but action and reward is one of the fundamental premises for many types of games. Likewise, to create a successful interactive experience, you should consider the user's journey: what you're asking the user to do, when the user should do it, how the user should do it, and what the user will get in the end.

Here are some important points to consider when you're producing an interactive project:

- Identify the goals of the project by realizing what you're attempting to achieve. For example, in the interactive fashion site featured in this chapter's case study, the following are some of the goals I wanted to achieve with the menu system (I'll come back to this project in the latter half of this chapter):

- I wanted it to be presented in such a way that the user would have to feel his or her way through the project and explore without the guidance of words. I wanted to remove the distraction of labels as navigation items, and thus focus the user's attention on the representation of the clothes.

- I wanted the user to have to "discover" what a button was. I would, of course, include an indication, but I wanted to make it as subtle as possible for the target audience. Once the user had activated a button, I wanted to send a clear signal back to the user that he or she took the correct action.

- I aimed to include a lot of movement in the menu, so that there was constant feedback or rewards to the user for every action he or she made, both as a direct result and as an indirect result of an action the user had taken. By "indirect result," I mean that the result was nonessential to the project navigation—it was more a general enhancement to the overall user experience.

- Ensure that the interaction is consistent throughout your project. It soon becomes frustrating to the user if after every click he or she needs to learn how to navigate through your project all over again. For example, in the case study project, the user has to click a picture of the fashion model to navigate, and these are the only buttons used in the project. The user soon learns that if he or she sees a picture of a model, it must be a button.

- Ensure that you've chosen the best method or combination of methods to guide the user through your project. You have a number of methods to choose among, so consider using aspects such as sound, animation, text, and so on.

Consider various interaction techniques; don't limit yourself to mouse clicks for user interaction. It's important to challenge and surprise your user, and this aspect can be a very easy method of accomplishing this effect. You have various ways to get the user to interact with your project, and I've listed a few of the main ones here. You might find nothing new to you in this list, but it's always worth carefully considering which method or combination of methods you'll use:

Mouse

- Mouse press
- Mouse press speed
- Mouse hold
- Mouse hold time
- Mouse drag
- Mouse release
- Mouse speed

Keyboard

- Key press
- Key combination
- Key hold
- Key sequence

Sound

- Sound input level
- Sound output level
- Sound pan amount
- Sound on
- Sound off
- Sound change

Animation

- Animation start
- Animation stop
- Animation speed
- Animation change

- Determine what the user should be experiencing when viewing your project. Should the user be entertained, educated, or enlightened? The user will feel something as he or she uses your project, and it's up to you to decide what that feeling should be and to what extent the user should experience it.

- Surprise the user, catch the user off the guard, and intrigue and captivate the user. Your project should deliver above and beyond what the user is expecting from it.

- Ensure that the project works correctly and as you intended. There's nothing worse for a user to experience than an interaction design that breaks unintentionally.

- Consider how you want the user to feel once he or she has finished using your project. At the very least, the user should leave your project feeling that it was an enjoyable experience in which he or she was challenged and entertained.

> *The interaction design process should be* considered, consistent, *and* concise *in its usage.* Most important, it should be creative in its design.

In the next few sections, I'll cover some of the more important interaction design issues in a little more detail.

Avoiding Flashturbation

It's important to be aware of what interaction design **is not**. In other words, you should understand what makes for bad interaction design. Flash has had a reputation for overusing interactive design elements, a process that was famously dubbed "Flashturbation." Recently, however, designers and developers in the Flash community have worked hard to turn this perception around.

Good interaction design isn't about using the latest Flash gizmo or toy that you've just created, downloaded, or seen. You shouldn't try to cram so much interaction into your project that it's overflowing. There's much more to designing an interactive experience than just making something interactive.

Interaction design overuse will have an adverse effect on your user. It will unintentionally alienate the user from the project by frustrating or confusing him or her. In the worst cases of interaction design overuse, it's impossible for the user to navigate through a project or to experience anything after the first mouse click (or whatever the user input method is).

Inconsistent interaction design can have the same effect as too many interactive elements. Although you want to surprise the user and give the user more than he or she is expecting, you don't want to make your project too inconsistent. For example, if at every single click the user is faced with a new method of interaction that contradicts the last, he or she will never learn how to use your project. And in some cases, the user may simply come to the conclusion that your project is faulty and leave it.

> *Interaction design shouldn't overflow with unnecessary interaction and be inconsistent in its methods and actions. It should be well thought out from beginning to end.*

Achieving balance

One of the hardest parts of interaction design is deciding when and where to use the interaction, and use it in greater or lesser quantities as appropriate to the specific project. There are no hard and fast rules to this, as there are in many coding practices. As with everything in life, there's a balance to achieve—a yin and yang, if you will. In the case of Flash interaction design, the balance is between an artistic, experimental experience in which the user explores the screen carefully and feels his or her way around, which leaves the user feeling excited or inspired with a vivid memory of the experience, and an easy experience that offers nothing new and leaves no impression in the user's memory.

It's up to you as the designer and developer to use your best judgment in this area. Ultimately, it's the user who decides whether you've achieved a good balance, but note that there's no one correct way to achieve balance, as projects and users vary. This is why interaction design (as with all design) has to be well thought out, ensuring every thing has meaning and purpose, and leaving little to chance. Use restraint as much as creative flair.

Determining the learning curve

A **learning curve** is the course of a user's progress when learning something. If you aren't familiar with this concept, you may find it easier to understand from the perspective of video games. When you start to play a new game for the first time, you're unfamiliar with the controls used in the game and what effects the controls have on the game. You need to learn how to progress through the game, and it's only as you become familiar with the controls and the controls' effects that you can start to understand, enjoy, and appreciate all the other aspects of the game.

There's some degree of learning with every interactive project, and it's up to you as the design/developer to decide how steep the curve is for users.

Understanding your target audience

I won't go into too much detail on this subject, as it's a very large topic that goes far beyond a project's interaction design. It's important to note, however, that understanding your target audience is key to finding the right balance for your interactive project. Knowing your audience will assist you in your design and help you understand how much you'll need to **pull** the user and how far you can **push** the user. (I'll define the terms "push" and "pull" shortly.)

For example, if you create an experimental interactive interface for an e-learning project, the user could find it difficult to navigate through the content, and this will, in some cases, prevent the user from learning anything at all. Likewise, creating an interactive experience through the use of a game might not be the best way to communicate with elderly users.

Here are some things you should consider about your audience:

- The average age of users

- The users' computer specification and Flash experience

- The amount of time you expect users to use the project

- The degree to which you'll need users to interactively learn as they use the project

- The users' expectations of the project

Simply put, the better you define the target audience for your project, the easier it will be for you to estimate the levels and amount of interaction you should ideally use in it.

Push and pull interaction

As mentioned earlier, knowing how to pull and push your user is one of your greatest tools for creating good interactive experiences. Let's examine these concepts further in the following sections.

Pull

The concept of **pulling** a user involves leading the user down a path or in a direction using signs and signals to guide him or her. Little is left to chance, and you're effectively holding the user's hand as he or she navigates through your project.

This is a weak form of interaction design, as it requires little effort and learning on the user's part. This isn't to say that it's a negative form of interactive design—far from it. Pull interaction is ideal for projects with a specific purpose, such as an e-learning application or any other project in which the user will want to navigate the content efficiently and swiftly.

The most effective form of this interaction design is found in **transparent** interfaces. Transparent interfaces aren't interfaces that can't be seen; rather, they're interfaces that are so simple and easy to use that the user can "transparently" move through the content, doing his or her tasks without being hindered or distracted by the interaction.

The following example of pull interaction design (which you can also find on the CD in this chapter's `PullInteraction` folder) shows how the user's interaction makes navigating the content easier.

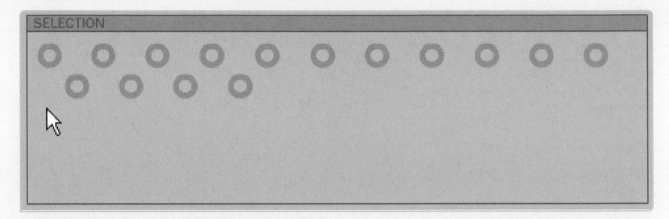

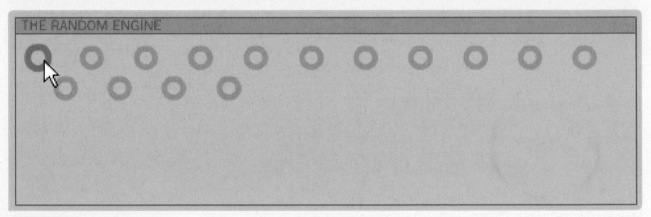

Pull interaction example

The first image shows the navigational buttons and menu interface in their default (inactive) state. As soon as the user moves the mouse over one of the navigational buttons, the menu springs to life. The button changes color and scales up by 10% to focus the user's attention on the button. This lets the user know without a doubt that this element is a button and that it should be clicked. In addition, the label bar above the buttons shows the text label for the button that has been rolled over.

Even the most straightforward navigational menu can be made more interesting and usable by adding a bit of animation or a subtle use of sound.

Push

The concept of **pushing** a user involves making the interactive experience increasingly subtler and perhaps less obvious as to what to do. Thus, it requires some effort on the user's part and it means giving the user more to learn in a shorter space of time. In addition, the user will need reasons for investing effort and time in learning and using the project.

This form of interactivity obviously requires strong interaction design skills from you as the designer, and you need to take into account factors such as what your user should be capable of and how far you can "push" the user in terms of requiring him or her to explore the project in more detail. There are still markers and guides for the user to follow or discover, but these are far less obvious and will often require some challenge or obstacle to work through to progress further.

The most effective forms of this type of interactive design are found in games and interactive stories (or storytelling), in which the user explores and progresses through a multitude of challenges, puzzles, and the like, followed by a reward of some description to tease the user onto the next trail to be completed.

This example of push interaction shows how the user is required to explore the piece by feeling his or her way around. The only goal here is seeing what the user's actions do as the piece reacts accordingly. This alone isn't sufficient as a navigation system, but in combination with a more standard navigational menu, it could be used to enhance a menu interface.

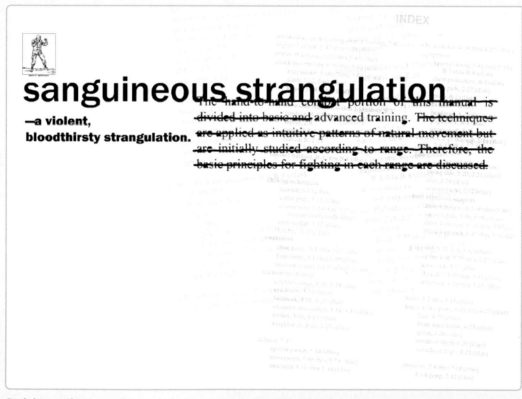

Push interaction example

Case study: LyndaLorraine.com menu system

For the case study in this chapter, I'll dissect the LyndaLorraine.com menu system to demonstrate how it was designed and developed. I'll detail not only the mechanics of how I created the menu system, but also the concepts involved in its creation. Take a look at the files in the \CaseStudy\FinishedProject folder on the accompanying CD to see the finished product.

Before I focus on the technical details, it's worth studying an overview diagram to illustrate exactly how the menu was developed. In the following sections, I'll break down each section of this flow diagram to show how I created this Flash design.

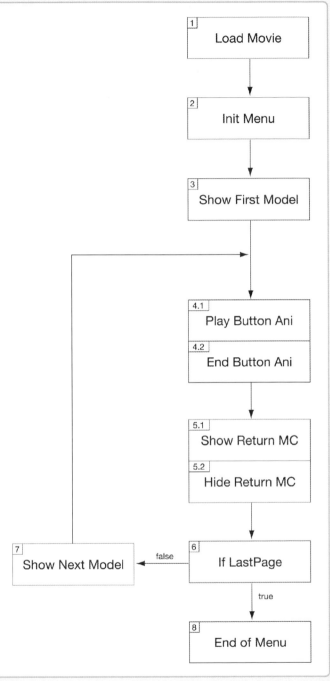

Load Movie

Go ahead and open `CaseStudy.fla` from the CD to follow along with this description. First of all, you'll notice that the preloader for this movie is coded in frame 1 but runs across the timeline to frame 100. Although I'll avoid going into the specific details of what is essentially a pretty standard preloader, it's worth mentioning my reasoning for doing it this way instead of placing all the frames in a movie clip and animating it: I want to use images for each percent marker. If I put all these images into one movie clip in the first frame, Flash would have to load all of them at once before displaying them. This way, each percentage image will load one at a time, and the user won't have to wait too long for the initial image to show up and let him or her know what's going on.

Another point to note here is that I've set the movie to low quality in the ActionScript on frame 1:

```
_quality = "LOW"
```

I prefer to do this using ActionScript, but you can also do it via the File > Publish Settings panel in Flash or by manually changing the quality parameters in your HTML file. The reason I chose to set the movie to low quality is because I'm not using any vector elements—the entire movie is composed of PNG files (you could use JPG or GIF files, but I prefer the quality of PNG), and as such, the Flash movie will run smoothly if it's set to low quality.

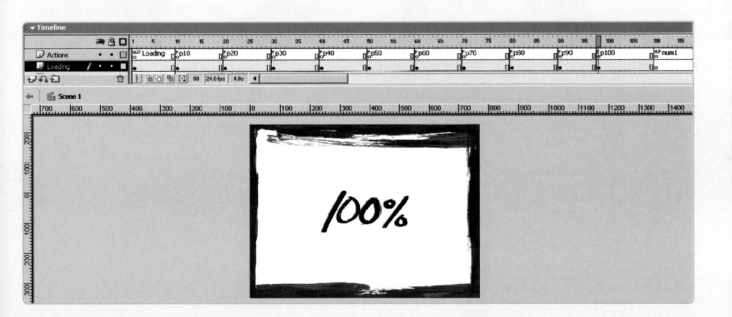

Init Menu

For clarity, I'll split the discussion of this stage into three parts:

- Movie clips used in the menu

- Generic functions used with this interactive design

- Specific code used on the num1 fram

Menu movie clips

Before I get started on the code for setting up the menu, I'll give you an overview of the movie clips used in the menu:

The Foreground *layer, where the associated movie clip instance name is* lorraine

The Midground *layer, where the associated movie clip instance name is* buttonsImg

The Background *layer, where the associated movie clip instance name is* bkImg

The preceding images show the key three layers in the menu system. The Background and Midground layers are primarily aesthetic layers. There are no buttons or navigational controls used in these movie clips, and they're simply scrolled. The movie clip in the Foreground layer, lorraine, however, is the heart of the design—it contains the navigation for the movie. Each image of the model is a button that launches a pop-up window containing further content.

These images also indicate what their associated movie clip instance names are. This is useful to reference as I explain the code used to set up the movie, which is all contained in the num1 frame.

Note the combined effect of the three layers:

The combined Foreground, Midground, *and* Background *layers*

Generic functions

Familiarize yourself with the functions described in the following sections, as they're used throughout the case study. In addition to being used in this project, these functions are coded so that you can use them in any Flash project.

openWindow

To open the new pop-up window, all the JavaScript used to create a custom-sized pop-up is contained within the Flash file, which makes it easy to keep track of and control the code. That is, none of your interactive design code needs to be placed in the HTML file.

```
//open pop-up window
openWindow = function (URL, wWidth, wHeight){
getURL("Javascript:openWin('"+URL+"',
➡ 'scrollbars=no,height="+wHeight+",
➡ width="+wWidth+",left=0,top=0')");
}
```

By passing the new URL, the new window width, and the new window height into this function, it's easy to adjust for future use.

fadeTo and flyTo

Full credit goes to Brendan Dawes (www.brendandawes.com) and Andy Beaumont (www.eviltwin.co.uk) for the creation and development of these functions, both of which are useful for saving time when developing interactive projects.

Both functions work by extending the methods of the MovieClip class, using the ActionScript 1.0 prototype technique. For instance, the fadeTo function allows you to easily control a movie clip's _alpha transparency. This is what it looks like:

```
//Created by Brendan Dawes & Andy Beaumont
MovieClip.prototype.fadeTo =
➡ function(targetA,startSpeed,precision){
  if(this.fadeProto.targetA == null){
    this.createEmptyMovieClip
    ➡ ("fadeProto",this.depthCount + 1);
    ++this.depthCount;
  }
  this.fadeProto.targetA = targetA;
  if(targetA>=99){
    this._visible=1;
  }
  this.fadeProto.startSpeed = startSpeed;
  this.fadeProto.precision = precision;
  this.fadeProto.onEnterFrame =
  ➡ function(){
    if(Math.abs(this._parent._alpha -
    ➡ targetA) < precision){
      this._parent._alpha = targetA;
      if(targetA<=1){
        this._parent._visible=0;
      }
      removeMovieClip(this);
    }
    this._parent._alpha -=
    ➡ (this._parent._alpha - targetA)
    ➡ /startSpeed;
  }
}
```

The fadeTo function is used like this:

```
this.fadeTo(targetA, startSpeed, precision)
```

where targetA is the amount to fade to, startSpeed is the fade speed or duration (the smaller the number, the quicker the speed), and precision is the preciseness of the mathematical cutoff point (the **snap-to** amount), for example:

```
this.fadeTo(10,2.4,1)
```

This line will cause the `this` movie clip to fade to 10%, with a speed of 2.4 and a precision of 1.

The `flyTo` function is much the same as the `fadeTo` function, but instead of controlling a movie clip's `_alpha` transparency, it controls the position on the stage.

```
//Created by Brendan Dawes & Andy Beaumont
MovieClip.prototype.flyTo = function(targetX,targetY,startSpeed,precision){
  if(this.moveProto.targetX == null){
    this.createEmptyMovieClip("moveProto",this.depthCount+1);
    ++this.depthCount;
  }
  this.moveProto.targetX = targetX;
  this.moveProto.targetY = targetY;
  this.moveProto.startSpeed = startSpeed;
  this.moveProto.precision = precision;
  this.moveProto.onEnterFrame = function(){
    if(Math.abs(this._parent._x - targetX) < precision && Math.abs(this._parent._y -
    ➥ targetY) < precision){
      this._parent._x = targetX;
      this._parent._y = targetY;
      removeMovieClip(this);
    }
    this._parent._x -= (this._parent._x - targetX)/startSpeed;
    this._parent._y -= (this._parent._y - targetY)/startSpeed;
  }
}
```

The `flyTo` function is used like this:

```
//this.flyTo(targetX,targetY,startSpeed,
//precision)
this.fadeTo(100,100,2.4,1)
```

To see more examples of dynamic functions similar to these, I recommend you explore http://proto.layer51.com. There, you'll find a large collection of useful code, and a community to discuss and share issues with.

num1 frame code

First off in the num1 frame, I declare the generic functions openWindow, flyTo, and fadeTo, which I've just covered.

Next, I declare the **bespoke** functions, or functions that have been created specifically for this movie:

```
// Bespoke Functions
fullLockFnc=function(what){
  if(!what){
    _root.fullLock=false;
    _root.returnMC.fadeTo(1, 3,1);
    if(!_root.lastPageVar){
      //If returning from any page, but NOT
      //the last page, go to the next num +
      //number on root timeline
      _root.gotoAndStop("num"+
      ➥ _root.lorraine.counter);
    }
  }else{
    _root.fullLock=true
    _root.returnMC.fadeTo(99, 4,1);
  };

};
```

The full lock function, `fullLockFnc`, is used when a user has clicked one of the navigational links. This function sets the full lock variable to `true`, which deactivates any `onEnterFrame` functions that are being used (such as the background scrolling code). Then it fades up `returnMC`, so the user is locked out of the menu until the click to return. This is all done so that the main navigation movie doesn't drain the processor while the user is using one of the Flash movies contained within the pop-up window launched from the main navigation.

If the user has passed `false` to the function, which is done when the user clicks the return to menu button in the `returnMC` movie clip, the full lock variable is released (set to `false`), allowing all the enter frame functions to run. Then the `returnMC` movie clip fades out from the user's view. Finally, if the `lastPage` variable is `false` (this is set to `true` by the last model image button), then the function advances the root timeline to the next section. If the `lastPage` variable is `true`, there's nowhere for the menu to advance, so it does nothing.

`findPercent` is a basic function used to determine the percentage of the movie clip's scroll amount:

```
// Initialize the scrolling
_root.stageW = 770;
findPercent = function (myWidth) {
  return ((myWidth-_root.stageW)/
  ➥ Number(- 100))*((_root.fmouse._x/
  ➥ _root.stageW)*100);
};
```

This function determines the scrolling percentage by working out the width of the movie clip (working on the assumption that the movie clip's width is greater than the stage's width), subtracting the width of the stage (the viewable area), and multiplying the percentage of that by the percentage of the mouse position on the screen. (I cover the creation of the `fmouse` movie clip shortly—for now, just know that it represents the mouse position.)

There may well be a more mathematically efficient and accurate way of doing this equation, but for me interaction design isn't about being a mathematician; it's about making things work the way I want them to. Note also that I simply declare a variable to hold the width of the stage in this case. You could do this using the Stage object, but I prefer to do it this way.

Despite being complex to explain, the action this function performs is quite simple. It returns the position at which the movie clip (whose width was passed to the function) should be in relation to the position of the mouse on the screen. The movie clip is scrolled 0% when the mouse is at the far left of the screen, and it's scrolled 100% when the mouse position is at the far right of the screen.

The remaining bespoke functions are all attached to movie clips, rather than being relevant to the whole movie, so it's easier to explain these separately.

```
// Drag movie clip:
// This creates an invisible mouse follower
// with a bit of friction for a nice smooth
// animation
_root.createEmptyMovieClip("fMouse", 2);
fmouse.onEnterFrame = function() {
    if (!_root.fullLock) {
      this._x += (_root._xmouse-
this._x)/3.4;
    }
};
```

As the comments in the code indicate, drag is a blank (or invisible) movie clip that's assigned to follow the mouse. Why not just use the mouse x and y variables already within Flash, you ask? Well, to make the run a little smoother and, in turn, to make the movement of the scrolling movie clips smoother, I use an additional movie clip that follows the mouse with a slight delay and creates a less harsh effect.

First, I create the movie clip that will follow the mouse. Then I assign an enter frame function to it, which is set to follow the mouse's horizontal movement (x property). Because I only need to scroll horizontally with a slight delay, I'm using 3.4 here, but you can play with these figures to see what works best for you.

As you'll notice, there's an if loop that checks for the full lock variable here. When the full lock variable has been set to true, the enter frame function will stop following the mouse and the scrolling will slow to a stop.

Next, I return to the top of the code and initialize the variables I'll be using throughout this movie:

```
_root.fncLock=false;
_root.fullLock=false;
_root.lastPageVar=false;
_root.returnMC._visible = 0;
```

The fncLock and fullLock variables are used to stop enter frame functions from performing actions, such as stopping the background from scrolling. The lastPageVar variable is used to flag when the user has clicked the last button and there are no more model image navigational buttons to show. The returnMC movie clip is set to invisible because it sits above everything and contains a big button. In Flash, if a movie clip is set to 0% alpha, the user can't see it, but any buttons it contains are still active. If a movie clip is set to invisible, however, the buttons are no longer accessible, which is why I'm setting it to invisible here.

Finally, I declare two variables at the top of the code for the starting position of the lorraine movie clip (Foreground layer):

```
homeX=275;
homeY=134;
```

3 Show First Model

This step continues the code in the num1 frame. I've separated this task into its own section because this code relates to the Foreground, Midground, and Background layers of the movie.

I first initialize the lorraine movie clip (the Foreground layer), using the flyTo function described earlier. The movie clip is animated onto the screen into the homeX and homeY positions:

```
//Set up first model image
lorraine.flyTo(homeX, homeY, 2.4, 1);
```

Then I declare the counter variable, which is used to track the current model image and therefore the navigational button on display. It will be incremented each time a model image button is clicked.

```
lorraine.counter = 1;
```

Next, I set the bkImg movie clip's (Background layer) enter frame function, which enables the movie clip to scroll. This has an if loop to check if the fncLock and fullLock variables are both false. If either variable is set to true, the background won't scroll, which will vastly reduce the processor usage. If both variables are false, the function sets the bkImg movie clip's horizontal position (x property) to the scroll percentage (as described earlier), according to the mouse position.

```
// This is for the background image to
// scroll
bkImg.onEnterFrame = function(){
  if(!_root.fncLock && !_root.fullLock){
    this._x = _root.findPercent
    ➥ (this._width);
  };
};
```

After this, I set the buttonsImg movie clip's (Midground layer) enter frame function, which works in the same way as the bkImg enter frame function. I use an if loop to check the fncLock and fullLock variables as before, and I set the horizontal movement (x property) to the scroll percentage (as described earlier), according to the mouse position.

```
// This is for the buttons image to scroll
buttonsImg.onEnterFrame = function(){
  if(!_root.fncLock && !_root.fullLock){
    this._x = _root.findPercent
    ➥ (this._width);
  };
};
```

Finally, I add a stop command to hold the movie at the num1 frame until the user clicks the navigational button.

```
stop();
```

This concludes the code in the num1 frame.

The menu's foreground

The menu's background

The menu's midground

4.1 Play Button Ani

In this section, I'll explain the model image navigational buttons and how they work. All the buttons work in essentially the same way, but with subtle differences.

This preceding image shows how the button looks in the Flash authoring environment. You can see the invisible button hit area. Notice that the hit area is actually a different shape from the image it covers. This is so that when the mouse is over the image, it displays the rollover image that's also covered by the hit area. If this wasn't the case, the user could roll over the image and then have it automatically roll out, even though the user has the mouse over the image.

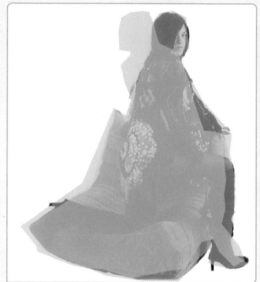

The navigational button in its default state

The navigational button in its default and rollover states

The preceding images illustrate the default and the rollover states of the navigational button, and show you why the button's invisible hit area is shaped the way it is. The code used on the button is as follows:

```
on(rollOver){
  if(!_root.fullLock){
    this.gotoAndStop("active");
  };
}
```

The rollover code has an `if` loop to check if the `fullLock` variable is set to `true`. This is so that if `fullLock` is on when the mouse rolls over the button, nothing happens. If `fullLock` is `false`, then the button will show the rollover image.

The rollout code also works if the user drags the mouse out of the button's hit area. The code has an `if` loop to check if the `fullLock` variable is set to `true`. This is so that if the `fullLock` is on when the mouse rolls out of the button, nothing happens. If `fullLock` is `false`, then the button will return to the default (normal) image.

```
on(rollOut, dragOut){
  if(!_root.fullLock){
    this.gotoAndStop("normal");
  };
}
```

Finally, the release code sets `fncLock` to `true`, stopping any enter frame animations that are happening (such as the Background or Midground scrolling). Then the button code plays the button press/release animation, and finally (before playing the animation) the counter is incremented. As described earlier, this `counter` variable is used when `fullLockFnc` is called (once the user has clicked the return to menu button in `returnMC`), and it sends the root timeline to the next navigational button.

```
on(release){
  _root.fncLock = true;
  this.gotoAndPlay("hold");
  _parent.counter++;
}
```

This image shows how the button movie clip looks in the timeline:

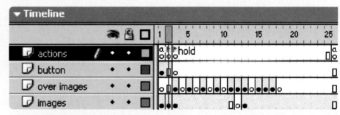

The timeline for the button

- Frame 1 has the frame label `normal` and a contains a `stop()` action. This is the button's default state, and once a user has rolled over and out of a button, the movie clip will return to this position (as shown in the `rollOut` code).

- Frame 2 has the frame label `active` and contains the rollover image.

- Frame 3 has the frame label `hold`, and this is the start of the button animation. When a user releases a navigational button, the button movie clip starts at this frame and animates.

4.2 End Button Ani

At the end of the button animation (frame 26 in the previous image), the remaining release code is called. I put this code at the end of the animation so that the user can see the button. The user rolls over the button and then clicks it. Next the user sees the button's transitional animation, and at the end the pop-up window's content is launched. In this section, I explain the code that's called at the end of the animation.

The fncLock variable, which was set to true in the button's release code, is now reset to false as it was needed only while the button's animation was playing (to ensure that the animation played smoothly and had no interference):

```
_root.fncLock = false
```

Then the fullLockFnc variable is called and passed the value of true, as explained earlier. This will set the fullLock variable to true (preventing any enter frame animations), and it will also fade up returnMC, which covers the menu navigation until the user clicks return to menu.

```
_root.fullLockFnc(true);
```

Next, I use the openWindow function. I call this function here and not on the button release code because I want the user to first see the button's animation. After that, the user can play with the pop-up window's content. Had I done it the other way around, it's possible that the user wouldn't ever see the button animations.

This part of the code is different for each button, so it can open the right content for the right button. I'll explain each button's code in turn. The first button uses this code:

```
_root.openWindow("page1.html",
➡ "LyndaLorraine",980,710);
stop();
```

The second button uses this code:

```
_root.openWindow("page2.html",
➡ "LyndaLorraine",980,710);
stop();
```

The third button uses this code:

```
_root.openWindow("page3.html",
➡ "LyndaLorraine",980,710);
stop();
```

The fourth and final button uses this code:

```
_root.openWindow("lastPage.html",
➡ "LyndaLorraine",980,710);
```

As this is the last button in the menu, the lastPageVar variable is set to true. This is so that when the user clicks return to menu in returnMC, the code won't try and move the root timeline any further.

```
_root.lastPageVar = true;
stop();
```

5.1 Show Return MC

This is the `returnMC` movie clip, which is used to lock out the menu when the user has clicked one of the navigational buttons. When the `fullLockFnc` variable is called and passed a value of `true`, this will fade up `returnMC`.

The menu navigation is now static and waiting for the user to return from the pop-up window's content.

The `returnMC` *movie clip*

5.2 Hide Return MC

Once the user has finished with the pop-up window's content and come back to the menu, the user clicks the button in the middle of the movie clip, the `returnBUT` button. This button unlocks the menu and advances the navigation to the next frame numbers, `num2`, `num3`, and `num4`, unless the `lastPageVar` variable has been set to `true` (as explained earlier).

This is the code for `returnBUT`:

```
on(release){
    _root.fullLockFnc(false);
}
```

This code calls `fullLockFnc` and passes it a value of `false` which, as explained earlier, will fade out `returnMC` and set the `fullLock` variable to `false`.

6 If LastPage

The last page check is in `fullLockFnc`. It simply checks to see if the `lastPageVar` variable has been set to `true`, which occurs in the last model navigational button. If it isn't the last page, the function will move the root timeline to the next frame label (`num1`, `num2`, `num3`, `num4`); if it is the last page, the function will do nothing (as it's the end of the experience).

Show Next Model

At this point I'll explain the code used in frames num2, num3, num4, and num5 (I've already explained what happens in num1, as this is where the menu was initialized).

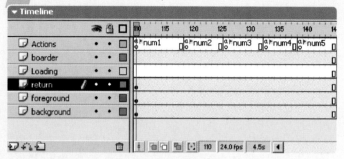

A view of the main part of the menu timeline

num2 code

The code on this frame is as follows:

```
lorraine.flyTo(homeX*Number(-1.5), homeY,
➥ 2.4, 1);
stop();
```

This code moves the lorraine movie clip (on the Foreground layer) to the second model image. This is done by using the flyTo function to animate the movie clip along to a new horizontal position (x property). The position is determined by multiplying the homeX variable value set in the initialization process by a value to get the correct position. The value that it's multiplied by was calculated manually.

num3 code

The num3 code is as follows:

```
lorraine.flyTo(homeX*Number(-4.85),
➥ homeY, 2.4, 1);
stop();
```

As before, this code moves the lorraine movie clip (on the Foreground layer), but this time to the *third* model image. To achieve this, the flyTo function again animates the movie clip along to a new horizontal position. To determine the position, the homeX variable value set in the initialization process is multiplied by a manually calculated value to get the correct position.

num4 code

The code on this frame is a little different from the others: it will display the fourth and final model image navigational button. I've done this because I wanted to signify to users that the experience is coming to an end and hopefully fool some users into thinking that it has already finished. Only their sense of intrigue keeps them going, and they'll explore more of the interface because of what they've learned throughout the menu and additional content in the pop-ups. The effect I was aiming to achieve is that of the menu sliding off to the right as before, but then sliding in from the left to reveal all the model images at the same time.

First I started by redefining the onEnterFrame function on the lorraine movie clip (Foreground layer):

```
lorraine.onEnterFrame = function() {
```

Then, because it's on an onEnterFrame function, I used an if loop to ensure that this command is called only once. I set the lorraine movie clip to move to the horizontal position of −2030, which ensures that it's offscreen and the user can't see any model images.

```
if (firstTime<>false) {
  firstTime = false;
  this.flyTo(Number(-2030.0), homeY,
  ➥ 2.4, 1);
};
```

Next, the `if` loop continually (once every frame, because it's within an `onEnterFrame` function) checks when the `lorraine` movie clip is in a good position to animate back onto the screen.

```
if (this._x<=Number(-2000)) {
```

Once the `lorraine` movie clip is in position, I set the movie clip to frame 2 (labeled `end`). Before this point in the movie, each model image has needed to be far enough apart so the user could see only one model image at a time. Now I want the user to be able to see all four model images side by side. So on this frame (`end`), all the model images are much closer together, which allows the user to see more than one at a time.

```
this.gotoAndStop("end");
```

I then set the root timeline to the frame labeled `num5`:

```
_root.gotoandStop("num5");
```

Finally, once all these tasks are finished, there's no need for the enter frame function anymore, as I'll be redefining it in the next frame:

```
    delete this.onEnterFrame;
  };

};
stop();
```

num5 code

This frame has two uses, one of which I'll explain in the next section. The other use comes into play before the user has clicked the final model image navigational button. The frame will fix the Midground layer (`buttonImg`) and the Background layer (`bkImg`), scrolling only the Foreground layer (`lorraine`) and waiting for the user to click the fourth and final navigational button.

First I set the `fncLock` variable to `true`. This stops the Background and Midground layers from scrolling, but it doesn't affect any other code (such as the button rollovers):

```
_root.fncLock=true;
```

Next, I declare the new `onEnterFrame` function:

```
lorraine.onEnterFrame = function(){
```

I then add an `if` loop to see if the `fullLock` variable is set to true. I do this so that the `lorraine` movie clip stops scrolling when the fourth and final button has been clicked:

```
if(!_root.fullLock){
```

Finally, I set the `lorraine` movie clip (Foreground layer) to follow the mouse, depending on the `if` loop:

```
    lorraine.flyTo(_root.findPercent
  ➥ (this._width), homeY, 8, 1);
  }
};
stop();
```

8 End of Menu

The end of the menu is when the user has clicked the return to menu button in returnMC for the last time. In frame num5 on the main timeline, I set the fncLock variable to true to stop the Background and Midground layers from scrolling. When the user clicks the fourth and final model image navigational button, once the button animation has finished playing, the code will set the fncLock variable to true. This enables the Background and Midground layers to scroll again. The Foreground layer will also scroll.

I've done this so that when the user returns from the last pop-up window, the navigation is finished and the menu interface is much more chaotic, with everything sliding around horizontally in relation to the mouse's location. This indicates to the user in a fun way that the experience has come to an end.

Summary

I hope this chapter has sparked your interest in and increased your understanding of the creation of interactive projects. The best general advice I can give you is to create your own library of code to use, refine it, and make it as flexible as possible. This will make it far quicker and easier to create interactive projects from a development perspective, and it will give you more time to decide on the interaction method or combination of methods that best suits your needs.

That said, sometimes the best method of interactive design is trial and error, plugging interactive gizmos into a project and testing them to see if they work as well as or better than an earlier idea. In my mind, this is treating interactive design much more like an art than a science.

The following list sums up the points presented throughout this chapter and should serve as a guide for when you create interactive projects:

- **Make your interaction consistent**: It's vital to make your interaction consistent within a project. This helps users become familiar with how to navigate through your project.

- **Employ the element of surprise**: Much like when a feature film is all too predictable and moviegoers leave before the film's finale, users will become bored quickly and desert your project if there's little to please or challenge them. It's good to surprise users from time to time within a project to keep them on their toes.

- **Know your audience**: Making sure that a project is always geared toward the right users is important to all aspects of the project.

- **Review your work**: When you're planning, designing, and developing your project, you should frequently review the project as a whole to ensure everything is on track and working correctly.

- **Get outside perspectives**: Once you're familiar with a project, you may miss problems and assume too much, so you should ask others to check it for you from time to time. You should be able to learn or confirm something with every fresh perspective you can get on a project.

- **Challenge and reward the user**: If your project or the interaction within it is meant to challenge users, make sure that there's a good balance of rewards for the tasks you're asking users to carry out.

- **Test, test, test!**: The end product of your project has to work perfectly 100% of the time. Failed or faulty interaction does no one any favors, and users' experience of your project becomes more negative with each fault they encounter.

- **Use restraint**: Don't try to cram too much into a project; strive for a good balance of elements. Just as white space provides benefits in the design world, restraint is a good thing in interaction projects.

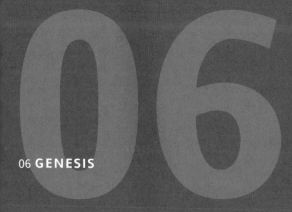

06 GENESIS

Gen·e·sis *n*

1 : an event that is a beginning; a first part, or stage of subsequent events

2 : the first book of the Old Testament

3 : the world-building experiment in *Star Trek II: The Wrath of Khan*.

"IN ALL AREAS OF OUR LIVES, INFLUENTIAL PEOPLE, WEBSITES, SNIPPETS OF CODE, PHOTOGRAPHS, AND NEW IDEAS AND TRENDS HELP BREAK DOWN OUR MENTAL BARRIERS AND SPAWN NEW CONCEPTS INSIDE US."

SHANE SEMINOLE MIELKE
WWW.PIXELRANGER.COM

Inspirations

My belief in creating immersive "environmental" experiences in the projects I work on isn't a revolutionary concept, and the Internet was definitely not the first place to captivate and engage people in such a way. Every time period in history has such media with great examples to point out as being inspirational for artists, creative people, and the general masses of people at that time. For ages, people have been drawn to storytellers, music, fables, legends, and books. For example, think of the impact that Orson Wells's *The War of the Worlds* had back in 1938. Although listeners could experience his storytelling only via the radio (a simple medium by today's standards), it was such an immersive experience for people that its influence is still mentioned in history books.

Immersive experiences come to me in many shapes and sizes, and through many different media and formats. Authors such as Terry Brooks (the *Shannara* series), Piers Anthony (the *Adept*, *Incarnations of Immortality*, and *Bio of a Space Tyrant* series), David Farland (the *Runelords* series), and J.R.R. Tolkien (*The Hobbit*, *The Lord of the Rings*) had a major impact on me growing up on a rural Southern California ranch without a neighbor for miles around. I had nothing to do other than read everything I could get my hands on from the school library or my local bookstore, which was more than 30 minutes away by car. Gracing the covers of many of those books was the amazingly detailed artwork of Darrell K. Sweet, whose fantasy artwork taught and influenced me to sketch and draw from a young age. I was fascinated by his intricate brush strokes and the amount of detail he put into each piece of artwork. On the big screen, immersive movie experiences such as *Dune*, *Star Wars*, the *Indiana Jones* saga, as well as the cartoon versions of the *The Hobbit* and *The Lord of the Rings* amazed me with their absorbing audio and visual experience. Each had many layers of love and detail added to them by their creators.

In the photography realm, the body of work of Ansel Adams captivates me. His photography of Yosemite is especially meaningful to me, and I regularly visit the valley for inspiration.

As computers, graphics, and 3D artists developed, games such as the popular *MYST* series emerged to engage me and many others, and quickly become a worldwide phenomenon.

As the Internet and Flash evolved, sites such as Rayoflight.net by my friend Yasuto Suga (whose work was featured in the original *New Masters of Flash* book) surfaced and began shaping a new generation of developers and artists like myself, who wanted to create and be a part of similar experiences.

In addition to those influences, growing up on a 5-acre ranch at the edge of the Cleveland National Forest played a major part in the development of my nature-oriented style. Drastically different from most of my "urban" friends, I grew up hiking, exploring, fishing, swimming, hunting, and riding all-terrain vehicles (ATVs), all in my own backyard. Consciously or unconsciously, all these extraneous experiences, miracles of nature, and mass-media influences combined to impact my style and me long before I started expressing myself through digital design.

Transformation

I got a very slow start as a digital artist. I attended the University of California, Davis, focused on playing American football and getting my degree in a major that had nothing to do with art or computers. Initially I majored in aeronautical science and engineering, but I found those subjects to be boring and uninspiring. A year later, after interning in the sports department of a local news station, I made a fairly dramatic switch to major in rhetoric and communications and German. My intent was to follow in the footsteps of my cousin, who was a successful sportscaster in Southern California. By the time I finished college, I had gained enough experience in the broadcasting world to know it was not the job or lifestyle I wanted.

As with many people, I finished college even more confused with what I wanted to do in life than when I started. After working in Zürich, Switzerland, at a sporting complex, I returned to Southern California in 1996 and entered into the whole Internet fad, as many others did at the time. I had no real experience, but I knew someone who worked at an Internet company, and I got in at the ground level with a tiny startup. Other than having frequented the computer lab at UC Davis to write papers, send e-mails, play games, or chat on IRC, I was the stereotypical beginner. For those first 2 years, I built some of the worst sites known to humankind and worked 16-hour days as I set up some of my early site-building processes and techniques.

EXPEDITIONARY RECON FORCE
MISSION CODE: 05-12 - LOCATION: N. AMERICA

WWW.3ADVANCED.COM

In the early years I never considered myself an artist or designer. My role in any given company was as an integrator/developer, and I worked closely with my friends who were artists and designers. I took their visions and designs and made them function, live, and breathe. Designs were simply something that I integrated with HTML as I learned the business from the ground up. After you've seen enough designs pass in front of you, certain elements start to stand out as good or bad, and you begin to form opinions and preferences. I started seeing things that were done simply for artistic reasons that served no purpose and that actually impaired the function and message of the sites I was building.

Likewise, I saw applications and sites that were desperately in need of artistic help. Since I didn't have confidence in my own design skills, I felt that I surely wasn't the answer.

I think it was those early experiences combined with the influence and guidance of my good friend and former co-worker Douglas Arthur (www.douglasarthur.com) that inspired me to design. I simply aspired to create cool things, as my friends were doing, but I wanted to have the power to change the things I didn't feel were right.

In 2000, I started to make the mental transition to become an "artist." It took this mental transition because although I always considered myself creative, I felt inferior to those with a formal education in art. In my mind, they knew what was right or wrong according to the principles of art and design. I fell into the hole that many beginners do and questioned everything I did. I always asked for feedback (which is a good thing), but I never had the confidence to say "I know this looks good and is the best solution." I still considered myself a developer/programmer with a regimented, organized, and analytical mind-set; I didn't consider myself creative as well. It wasn't until I started calling myself a designer in my own mind that I was able to relax and feel a creative flow when I worked. It took years, but I slowly began to see the way I wanted things and no longer had to ask others for advice or look to other people's websites for inspiration.

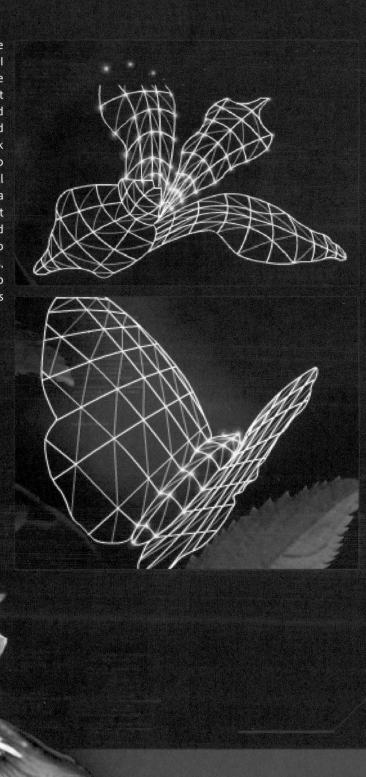

During this transition period I made some mistakes, of course. One example is when I worked on the Mazda USA website in 2000. The design style and branding for that site used curves and swoosh elements to highlight the vehicles and other important information in the site. I remember applying similar design elements in some of my side work at the time, regardless of that particular site's tone, style, or product. A friend pointed out what I was doing, and I quickly learned that while having a distinct artistic style is important, using the exact same elements in different projects won't help me grow. This is something I try to keep in mind with each new project I develop. For example, www.realvast.com looks nothing like www.skyworksinc.com, although both convey my style for setting a tone or mood.

With each mistake and each success, I grew exponentially. In a sense, I reinvented myself and I was no longer just a developer who knew everything about building a site and not much about the pure design or aesthetic side of things. I evolved into someone with balance as both an artist and a developer.

Environmental Flash

My goal for this chapter is to give you some advice on and insight into how to conceive, create, and organize immersive environmental experiences, and at the same time possibly spark some possibilities, ideas, and processes for your next project. This chapter isn't intended as some template, de facto standard, or full tutorial on how to design, program, and build a full Flash site, nor will it provide inquisitive designers with a paradigm-shifting revelation for design or Flash. I merely hope to convey that any project (corporate, commerce, experimental, or personal) has room for the designer and developer to add a little bit of his or her life force and personality. It's never fun to build a lifeless project; likewise, it's boring to visit a site lacking in personality. I hope that by reading this chapter (or any chapter in this book), a new idea, process, or habit may open up alternatives to the way you bring your next project to life.

To simplify things, I'll break the rest of this chapter into five main areas:

1. Concept: Defining your idea

2. Creation: Laying out your idea

3. Organization: Managing your assets

4. Genesis: Techniques to enhance your environment

5. Application: Integrating environmental concepts into client projects

Any project you're involved in, whether it's an intro, a website, an interactive image, or a navigation system, can be grouped into these five phases. Of course, more stages can branch out of these five phases, but I'll work with these five to give you a foundation.

Concept: Defining your idea

Every good project starts with a solid concept. What is it that you want to bring to life in your project? What assets do you have at your disposal for this project that you can work with and draw inspiration from? If there are minimal assets, how do you go about creating a theme, concept, or strategy?

The conception of new ideas, design styles, and solutions for a project is a struggle for all designers at some point in their career. It's much easier to function inside the preexisting habits, limitations, and styles of others. As designers and developers, we struggle with this every day. Change is often hard because there's comfort in knowing that what you're doing looks "normal," works correctly, or follows an accepted standard. Why improve upon a piece of code from a previous project when you already know it works and you can reuse it?

Unfortunately, these barriers all too often confine us in design styles, force us to see only certain options in a project, and hinder our growth as artists and developers. If we choose to let them, these barriers can limit our perceptions of the possibilities, lessen our self-growth and value to a client, and bring our creativity to a halt. To remain competitive, motivated, and happy, continual adaptation is a necessity. No one likes doing the same thing over and over, whether it's using the same design style or programming technique, or just eating the same foods. Taking the initiative to break down these barriers inside of us is important to open up new pathways and approaches we never previously perceived.

I don't mean to build this up as some life-altering event that must occur with each project, nor do I presume that breaking down these barriers is always of our own volition. More often than not, moving forward with our personal style involves small, imperceptible changes in our techniques, styles, processes, and habits learned by simply being perceptive to the influences and inspiration swirling around us. When used in our own distinctive ways, these inspirations can affect how we approach projects and, if they're unique enough, they can in turn influence others, creating a chain reaction.

My initial experience with this genesis of new ideas was the first time I opened up an FLA created by Eric Jordan (www.2advanced.com, www.chemicalheart.com), who was also featured in the original *New Masters of Flash* book. It was our first day working together almost 4 years ago, and Eric nonchalantly passed me an FLA from a previous project so that I could grab a vector map from the Library. As I opened the FLA, I was astonished at the complex patterns formed by the layers, keyframes, tweens, and sounds dancing across the timeline. I analyzed every nuance and effect, amazed that it could all be so easy yet still so hard to piece together. Needless to say, my jaw dropped, synapses fired in my brain, and a door suddenly opened in my mind.

> " MOVING FORWARD WITH OUR PERSONAL STYLE INVOLVES SMALL, IMPERCEPTIBLE CHANGES IN OUR TECHNIQUES, STYLES, PROCESSES, AND HABITS LEARNED BY SIMPLY BEING PERCEPTIVE TO THE INFLUENCES AND INSPIRATION SWIRLING AROUND US. "

Later that day, I proceeded to create for a client an intro that was much more complex than any intro I had previously created. In it, I added many tiny movements and more easing to my tweens, and I integrated small details that I had never thought of adding before that day. After concluding the project, I noticed that my added attention to detail had more than doubled the number of layers in comparison to my previous projects. In addition, the final product was significantly better than I had ever achieved in similar types of projects.

Although intros are now frowned upon and the animations might be simple by today's standards, this was my first major step forward in how I approached projects involving Flash. In all areas of our lives, influential people, websites, snippets of code, photographs, and new ideas and trends help break down our mental barriers and spawn new concepts inside us. I envision it all much like the roots of a developing tree as they dig deeper into the earth.

While I'm on the subject of the evolution of ideas, it's interesting to consider the uses of Flash over the years. Flash had an inauspicious beginning, as it became known primarily as software used solely to create intros and text effects. As more users became bored with intros, experimentation by people with diverse backgrounds and ideas gave rise to new uses for Flash in areas not previously envisioned. I have long considered Flash as the glue that joins different media, technologies skill sets, and visions together. Raster, vector, audio, and video are media that can be integrated in Flash to create and improve visual experiences by designers. Likewise, Flash can be used in conjunction with other technologies, programming languages, and applications to create a more robust, powerful, and visually pleasing environment for many developers. As a result of this marriage of skill sets, technologies, and ideas, more presentations, applications, kiosks, websites, interactive CDs, video game menus, PDA interfaces, and DVD menus are born every day. These advances will continue to grow as more creative individuals and developers work together to push their ideas through Flash.

The core ideas for my personal site (www.pixelranger.com) and the Genesis Project came from my desire to try and gain a small bit of respect among the other artists in the community who studied digital media, when I myself had absolutely no training. Many of the people I observed in the community with fine-arts backgrounds or some type of traditional training had all sorts of amazing abstract experiments or pieces of art in their portfolios. For example, anyone visiting Jens Karlsson's Chapter Three site (www.chapter3.net) is sure to be blown away by the artistic expression in his personal and client work.

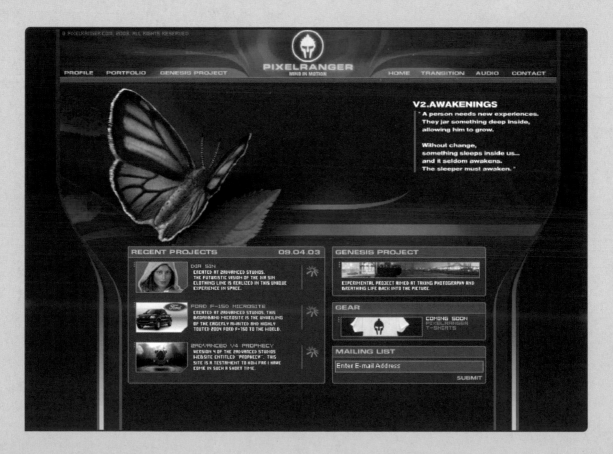

Simply having a list of websites in my portfolio would label me as "just a web designer." I aspire to become something more as I learn and grow as an artist. To help distance myself from the stigma of being "just a web designer," I reached back to the things that influenced me for ideas on something I could do that would be Flash-based and different from other things I had seen on the Web. In the end I devised a concept that was neither a trendy ActionScript experiment nor abstract wallpaper (things that were seen as cool in 2001).

My goal with both my own portfolio site and the Genesis Project was to break away from visually flat web designs by using visual depth and photographic environments to create in viewers an emotional attachment with and an extended stay on the site.

I didn't want to try to do too much, as some of the most beautiful things in design are the simplest. And I wasn't going to attempt to pack in as many extraneous Flash effects as I could (something occurring more and more in those days). Instead, I decided to create an experience based upon sounds and image manipulation that people could experience as if they were actually there. I wanted to create something that any visitor—regardless of experience, occupation, age, or gender—could view, experiment with, and find appealing. Animating everything would be overkill.

Creation: Laying out your idea

With most of the projects I've been involved with, the idea behind a design or concept normally starts with the combination of the goals of the project in addition to whatever product imagery or assets I've created or have access to. Using my site as an example, I felt the pictures integrated into my site needed to be appealing to all audiences; I didn't want to target them toward any single group, clique, or gender. Simple, beautiful objects with vibrant colors and soft edges were important for the atmosphere I wanted visitors to experience. For the Genesis Project, my image selection began with choosing a location to focus on. The location itself wasn't anything unreal, crazy, or terribly surreal. The first Genesis Project scene is a nondescript street in downtown Long Beach, California, at 3:00 a.m. Most people could find such a street or similar location within driving distance of their home.

My initial idea was to find a city street, capture a series of photos, stitch them into a 360-degree panoramic representation, and bring it back to life in Flash. After further consideration of file size and other issues, I settled upon a 180-degree, three-panel format.

At the time of the first two scenes, I was still new to photography. I had an old camera that was given to me by a family member, but I had very little experience with it. To realize my concepts, I enlisted the help of my friend Douglas Arthur to shoot the photos I envisioned. The first scene is a street a few blocks from where he lived in downtown Long Beach, and we captured it on one of our late-night photo expeditions. After having the photos developed and scanning the negatives, I stitched and cleaned up the image by hand in Photoshop.

In that original scene, the things I took out from the pictures included leaves on the ground, reflections in the windows, a car that was driving on the street, and all of the lights and glow that came from the streetlights and stoplights. This was all done with simple experimentation with the Rubber Stamp tool and some intricate airbrushing on my Wacom tablet.

The reason I had to remove the streetlights was that we took the photos late at night, and to capture a night picture, the camera's shutter must be left open for an extended period of time (15 seconds) to soak all the light and color present at the time. This meant that the pictures with streetlights had brilliant bursts of all three lights (red, yellow, and green) in the picture, since the shutter was open as the lights were changing. These light bursts radiated in some cases inches away from the light source and bled into the buildings and objects in the picture. I used Photoshop to erase the light bursts and glare, leaving only bare light frames and the buildings cleaned up behind them. To remedy the problem, I took pictures of the stop and walking symbols from a light down the street from my house and used them to help create the blank lights. From there, I created versions of the lights (red, green, and yellow lights, and blinking hand and crossing symbols) and their reflections on the poles to finish off the scene. This took some time, but it was essential to be able to animate the scene and make it believable. The end result was more than 35 folders in my Photoshop document that when hidden make the scene devoid of any light bursts or colors and free from the previous imperfections. I've included flattened layers of the first scene in the `genesis_lb.psd` document located on the CD. These layers show the progression of the scene from rough scanned and stitched color prints, to cleaned-up and stitched scans from the negatives, to the final scene devoid of any lights.

For the third installment of the Genesis Project (which I'll use for one of my examples in this chapter), I used a single photo taken on the set of the SCI FI Channel's *Frank Herbert's Dune* miniseries. Since I already had an established and developed concept, the next step involved creating and fabricating my scene in Photoshop before animation. Taking the original photo, I doubled its physical width in Photoshop and began brainstorming the things I wanted to add to widen, enhance, and bring to life the scene. Things that came to mind were cables, camera equipment, and a TV monitor that would reflect what the camera pointed at in the scene. I envisioned that the user would also be able to interact with the cables, camera equipment, and lights to modify the scene.

For me, the next part is by far the most gratifying aspect of a project. At this stage the colorization, modification, and creation of everything (in Photoshop) that will be animated begins. This could be the entire layout of a Flash site, or something as simple as a navigation system or header. In every project, I lay out all aspects of the project in Photoshop before I begin any Flash development. This includes items that will eventually be represented as vector shapes in Flash. Nothing is started in Flash until the imagery is created, enhanced, finalized, and laid out in Photoshop. This is important to get all of your ideas laid out in a unified manner, rather than creating each piece as the site is being built.

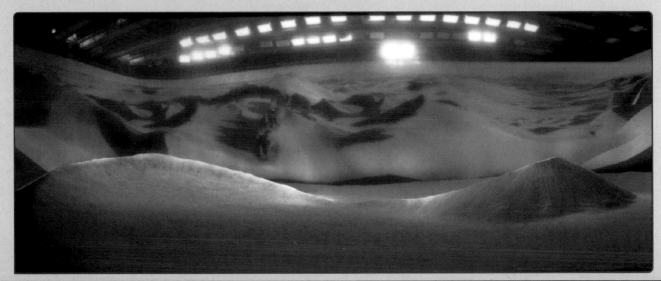

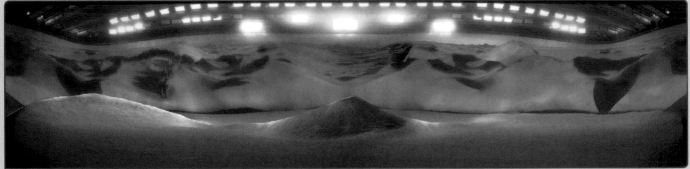

At this stage, it's also valuable to sketch out your ideas on a piece of paper or in Photoshop, or simply make a list of the things you'd like to accomplish with your project. Especially in a website, you want to make sure that the theme and visual assets are consistent throughout the design, rather than a mixture of things you might have been feeling over the time period it took you to develop the site. If you design a site without regard for the overall concept, when you put all of the pieces together you'll find you've built a disjointed site. If possible, plan out everything in Photoshop beforehand rather than designing as you go.

After creating the main background, my next task was creating the camera, lights, and stands I envisioned in the scene. Here are the steps I followed:

1. After doing some Web research using Google, I came across images of various camera paraphernalia, lights, and stands found on movie sets that were similar to what were on the film production set.

2. Using Photoshop, I cut these items out of the original pictures using the Pen and Lasso tools. I filled their selections with black, creating several black silhouettes. I saved these original images and their cutouts, as I would use them again later in the project.

3. I quickly dragged the black silhouettes into my main scene in Photoshop, and resized and laid out everything the way I envisioned it.

4. I finalized this snapshot of the entire scene by adding placeholder cables and shadows under the silhouettes, which I later used as references for the final vector objects.

The point of describing my process for this particular aspect of my project isn't necessarily for you to go and create your own Genesis Project. The intent is more to use this project as an example to describe some of the thoughts and ideas that should occur when commencing any project. Whether you're working a website, DVD, interactive game, screen saver, or just a simple Flash navigation system, your goals should be deciding on imagery, developing concepts, and realizing those combined assets in Photoshop. Once your vision is realized in Photoshop, it's time to proceed to project build-out.

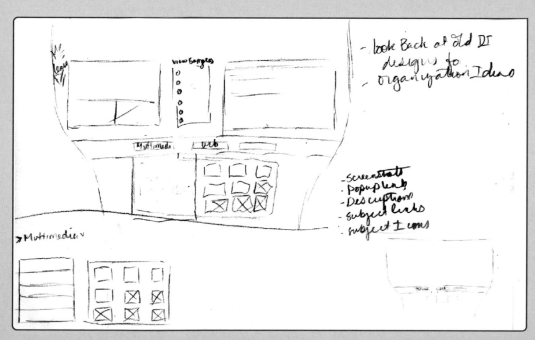

Organization: Managing your assets

By sticking to a regimented, organized process at the beginning of a project, I'm allowed the luxury of doing two things at once. First, I have the freedom to work out any bugs in a clean, pristine environment free of extraneous effects and factors. Second, I allow my mind to wander and explore the possibilities of the project while I'm doing the mundane tasks of exporting and importing graphics. Let's take a moment to look at some organizational techniques.

Exporting from Photoshop

Before I animate anything, I export all the graphics I created in Photoshop (up to that point). Of course, there might be some that I import into Flash at a later time, but I try to use Photoshop create and export as many assets as possible before animation begins. I prefer the PNG format when exporting from Photoshop so that I can import the images into Flash without any compression (I'll explain why shortly).

I always export PNG files from Photoshop with a 2-pixel transparent border around the image. I do this by increasing the height and width of the canvas size by 4 pixels and then saving the image. At first this can seem like a tedious task, but I've found it to be amazingly helpful in reducing the amount of pixel shifting in Flash movies. Some people prefer to use the workaround of changing the opacity of their symbols to 99% or increasing the brightness of the symbols by 1. I've never liked this solution, so I set up a process for handling my images and symbols that doesn't require me to use this particular workaround.

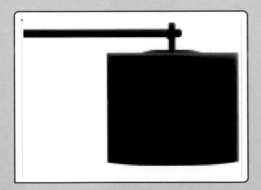

Pixel shifting is the result of an imported bitmap resting in a symbol/movie clip where the registration point of the symbol (that little plus sign [+] designating the center of a symbol) overlaps any part of the physical image. When a bitmap is centered in the symbol, the shifting always happens as a vertical/horizontal imperfection in the image. For those who align a bitmap to a corner without a transparent border, you've probably noticed 1-pixel blurring at the edge of your image that runs along the registration point. For example, when you're saving a circular bitmap with transparency where the pixels are flush with the edge of the image, many times pixel shifting occurs and distorts the image by 1 pixel. By giving the image a border and aligning the registration point over a corner (which is now over the transparent part of the image), you can eliminate any shifting in the image. For the record, it's also worth noting that when publishing for the the Flash Player 7, you can avoid this pixel shift issue entirely if you place the image in the positive quadrant (positive x and y values) of the movie clip.

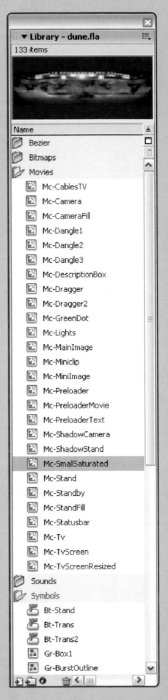

Organizing the assets in layers and the Library

Before importing images and creating symbols, I always make sure my movie settings are set to Snap to Pixel (located under the View menu) so that all of the symbols and text (pixel fonts or not) start on a whole integer when dragged onto or imported into the main timeline. After I import them, all of the symbols and text elements are positioned on different layers in the main timeline, re-creating the design or scene exactly as I have it in Photoshop. One by one, I select each bitmap and press F8 to place all the bitmaps into symbols or movie clips (depending on their purpose). I always take care to align any bitmaps to the corner inside the symbols as mentioned before.

Although it's not the standard Flash naming convention, my symbol-naming system is simple and purposeful: text = Tx, movie clip = Mc, graphic symbol = Gr, and button = Bt (for example, Tx-Pixelranger, Mc-Pixelranger, Gr-Pixelranger, Bt-Pixelranger). I then organize everything into folders sorted by asset and symbol type (Text, Movies, Graphics, and Sounds). Sometimes it's necessary to create folders that group multiple symbol types that work together performing specific functions (for example, Text Scrollers, Animation sequences, and so on). When multiple symbol types are grouped together in one folder, it's much easer to scan the Library when the symbol type has been specified first in the name (for example, Tx_Pixelranger, Mc_Pixelranger rather than Pixelranger_txt). When you're working on projects that have anywhere from 100 to 500 symbols, scrubbing the Library for that elusive asset can only slow you down. A clear naming system is obviously also useful for projects with many team members or projects where the FLA files are given to the client.

After I've imported the images into Flash, placed them into symbols, and organized the timeline, I make sure to give instance names to all movie clips I'll be animating. To do this, I click the movie clip, go to the Properties palette, and give the movie clips instance names reflective of their names in the Library for consistency's sake. Labeling all the movie clips before animating allows me to control them with scripts at the exact point each movie clip enters the timeline. Labeling a movie clip after you've already tweened it is a bad idea, one that leads to unpredictable results and frustration if you have to go back and name every instance of a movie in an animation.

Modifying compression settings

Now that I've positioned everything on the timeline, I open the Library (CTRL+L) and double-click each bitmap to modify its settings in the Bitmap Properties window. By default, Flash checks Allow Smoothing on all imported images. To achieve a crisp look from my bitmaps and to avoid pixel shifting, I uncheck the Allow Smoothing setting in all the bitmaps in the Library. (Smoothing is sometimes the culprit in pixel shifting, and also I prefer to view everything without smoothing so that my images look crisp as they're moved around the design.)

While I have the Bitmap Properties window open, I modify the compression settings of each PNG depending upon its visibility, size, and complexity. I do this in Flash as opposed to saving an image from Photoshop as a JPG file with compression. If I used a JPG that was saved at 60%, for example, but I wanted to change it to 80% at a later time, I would have to go back into Photoshop and resave the image at 80%. On the other hand, if I wanted to increase the compression in Flash, I'm essentially compressing an image twice, which reduces the quality of the image even more. By using the uncompressed PNG format and setting the compression in Flash, I have complete control over the bitmap at any time, and I save the time and hassle of having to go back to Photoshop to resave a JPG at a different compression setting. This technique is also amazingly useful when you change the compression settings of large bitmap sequences in a Flash movie without having to re-export your footage.

Creating prototypes

With all of the setup work out of the way, the next step involves creating working prototypes (with little to no animation) of the project and integrating any special components. This is the stage where I hammer out any possible component bugs and lay the foundation for how the project functions as a whole. This applies to all aspects of the project. If it's a simple text scroller, then create it outside the main project to ensure it works flawlessly in a pristine environment with no outside variables (this also makes it easier to reuse later). If it's a navigation system, then create the navigation system with few animations and maybe some simple content transitions.

Once your logic is bulletproof and the sections load and transition like you want, then it's time to work through your project and add the other components along with layers of complexity and detail to the animations. I call this adding "layers of love" to the project. By doing all of your functionality first and then going back to add the complex animations, you ensure that the site works regardless of how pretty the animations are. Focusing too much time and energy on things like animations or an intro before your functionality is complete is a sure way to make debugging a technical issue later in the project more difficult.

Using an organization checklist

To summarize the previous paragraphs, I adhere to the following checklist when commencing any Flash project. I find the following process to be extremely helpful in setting up my projects as quickly as possible, while also eliminating many of the small surprises or issues that presented themselves in past projects.

1. Create all aspects of the design or scene in Photoshop before opening Flash.

2. Export each bitmap being used in the project as a PNG with a 2-pixel transparent border.

3. Ensure that the movie settings are set to Snap to Pixel (located under the View menu).

4. Import the PNG images into Flash.

5. One by one, place the PNGs into symbols and/or movie clips (depending on their purpose).

6. Take care to align each PNG to a corner inside the symbols and movie clips, and name them appropriately.

7. In the Library, organize all the assets into folders, disable smoothing, and modify the compression settings on those images you want compressed more or less.

8. Re-create your design with the symbols and assets organized onto different layers on the timeline.

9. Give each movie clip on the timeline an instance name before you commence any animation.

10. Create a functional prototype with little to no animation to eliminate logic errors early in the project.

11. Add "layers of love" by going over the project in successive waves adding animation, details, and further functionality until your deadline is reached and you're happy with your work.

Justifying organization

Having a set process before adding any crazy visual effects is vital to ensuring that functionality is set in stone, deadlines are met, and time on a project is maximized. Funky effects are nice, but a project's main priority should be working flawlessly. I've seen designers set visual effects before functionality and lose days brainstorming or playing with animations, techniques, or ideas that may not even make it to launch. Then as deadlines approach, bugs are still being worked out, functionality is still being added, and a mad frenzy to bring everything together ensues.

However, with an appropriate level of organization, and upon completion of the active prototype, I can begin the process of adding "layers of love" with the utmost confidence in the project structure and its operation.

The reality is that the client doesn't know or care how many hours or days you spent fine-tuning an effect. They just care that it works. This being the case, you should make creating a working effect your first priority in any project.

Genesis: Techniques to enhance your environment

Even though you've laid out all aspects of your project in Photoshop, you should still use a good balance of raster and vector assets to enhance the experience of the final project. Creating a Flash movie consisting of only bitmaps will slow down the speed of your movie by taxing the user's computer processor.

If you're lucky, some of your assets will already be in a vector format, ready to be brought into Flash. Adobe Illustrator, Macromedia FreeHand, and even 3D Studio MAX using the Swift 3D plug-in are great tools for creating additional vector assets for your projects. Most of the time, these tools aren't needed and only add production time to a project. The technique for creating vector outlines, fills, and masks of a bitmap or object in a bitmap is simple and one that I use quite often in my daily forays into Flash. I've employed this easy-to-use technique in just about every Flash site I've worked on, from my personal site (www.pixelranger.com) to client work for Ford Motor Company. The technique in question uses the Line tool (N on the keyboard) and the Arrow tool (V or SHIFT) within Flash.

Outlines

Here are the steps you need to follow to use the technique described in the preceding section:

1. Start by importing any graphic element that you would like to have an outline, filled silhouette, or mask of. Make sure to lock the layer containing the bitmap and create a new layer for your outline to go on. To assist you in this tutorial, I've included the `butterfly.fla` file on the CD. It contains the butterfly graphic from my site, which you can use to follow the steps of this process.

2. Go to your stroke color selection tool (located in the Tools palette) and choose an obnoxious color such as bright green. Using bright colors makes it easier to see what has been traced since it's in drastic contrast with the image.

3. Make sure that Snap to Objects is checked (under the View settings). Doing this helps to eliminate problems trying to fill the outline (later in the tutorial) as a result of unconnected lines.

4. Zoom in very close to a corner of your bitmap so you can see its fine details. If things look blurry, make sure you've unchecked the smoothing option in the Library as I described earlier.

5. Using the Line tool (N), begin a small, straight line at any point where the silhouette begins to curve and end the line at a natural peak nearby.

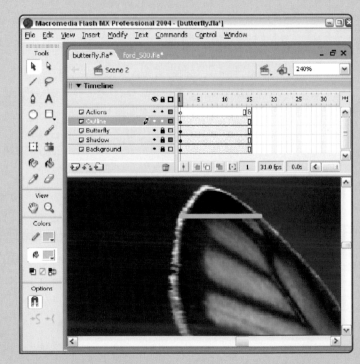

6. Hold down the SHIFT key, (a hot key that toggles you to the Arrow tool) and pull at the middle of the line, curving it in an attempt to match that particular line to the curve of the bitmap edge as closely as possible. Getting the hang of where to pull on the line is easily mastered, and simply toggling the SHIFT key allows you to work quickly between the Line and Arrow tools with little effort.

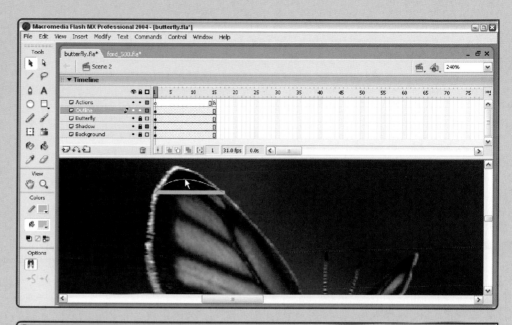

7. Repeat this process, working around the outer edge of the image in addition to any open areas inside of the image itself. The end result is an outline of your object that you can then use in several ways.

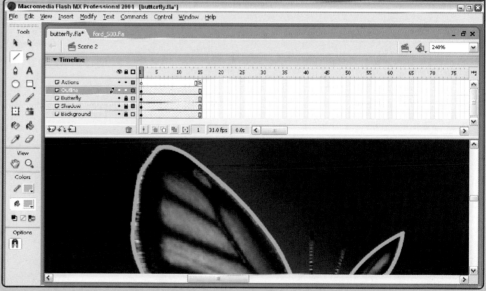

You can use this technique through the Pen tool in Flash, Illustrator, or FreeHand. The concepts are the same, and I can only advise you to use whatever tool you're fastest and most comfortable with. I personally prefer doing it in Flash to save time.

I've found that the more you hop back and forth between programs, additional quirks, importing issues, and extra files are added to your project. This may seem like a tedious process at first, but it's one that ensures the highest quality shapes, outlines, and fills. If you've ever played with the Trace Bitmap feature in Flash, you understand the futility of trying to get a perfect outline or shape. Once you master the technique I describe in this section, you can easily create outlines and shapes in your project in a matter of minutes. The idea here is to learn the technique and then brainstorm about what it can add to your project in the form of vector objects and masks. Although all you've done so far is outline or fill a shape from a bitmap, there are endless applications and possibilities. You're limited only by your imagination and creative use of these new assets.

Frameworks

In my own site, I created simple outlines of objects like the butterfly on the home page. I took the technique a step further by creating additional lines inside the outline's framework to mimic 3D wireframes. I then used masks to reveal the lines to simulate rendering the butterfly layer by layer as if I had created it all in a 3D program.

The most common question I've received regards what program I used to create the 3D wireframes in my site. Of course, the answer is the Pen and Line tools within Flash!

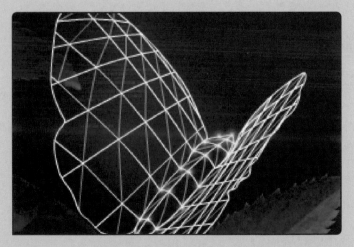

To see the final version of the butterfly outline combined with masks, open the `butterfly_final.fla` file included on the CD.

I used this outlining technique in an intro I created to highlight the Ford Escape Hybrid vehicle. This intro is currently viewable at www.fordvehicles.com/escapehybrid. I created outlines by hand in every phase of the intro as it demos the unique capabilities of this hybrid gas and electric vehicle.

Fills

After outlining an object, you can use the Paint Bucket tool (K) to fill the space with a solid color. You may then use this silhouette on the stage as either a physical asset or as a mask. If for some reason you find that you're unable to fill an outlined object, simply go back and pull at each connection point to ensure that they're all connected.

Using the third installment of the Genesis Project as an example, I created vector assets in the shape of camera equipment and lights by outlining bitmaps. Open `tripodmask.psd` from the CD to see one of the original images I used as reference to outline and fill in Flash.

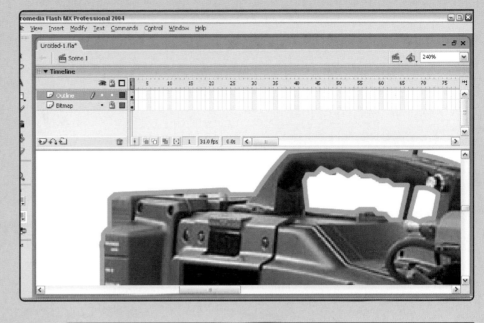

Once I outlined the image, I filled the center to create the various vector pieces of the scene like the camera, stand, lights, and hanging cables. I've included the following FLA files on the CD: `genesis_stand.fla`, `genesis_camera.fla`, and `genesis_light.fla`. Open these files to compare the original imported PNG files in the Library to the final vector fills I created by hand. Practice your technique for creating vector outlines on these FLA files and especially on images in your own projects. As you will see in the FLA files, you'll achieve greater detail when working on larger bitmaps and then shrinking the vectors down to a usable size.

I've also included an early beta build of the third Genesis Project titled `genesis_dune_beta.fla` on the CD. Although it's not a complete version, it shows how vectors and shadows created in Photoshop can be used together to enhance a project.

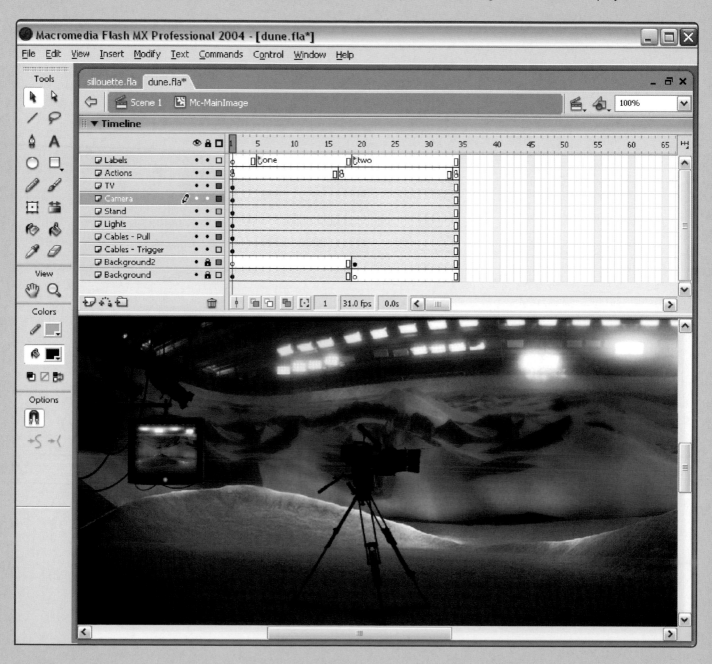

Fills as masks

Filled outlines also make great masks. One thing to remember is to delete an outline after you've filled it using the Paint Bucket tool (K). An example of mask can be found in the subtle effects I created for the Ford Five Hundred intro (www.fordvehicles.com/fivehundred). In this scene, I outlined several buildings and filled them using the technique outlined previously. Then I used a complex series of masks, gradients, and color tweens, which gives the illusion that the buildings are slowly lighting up and shedding light onto the scene.

I included the `Ford_500_final.fla` file on the CD so you can see how it all comes together. When you open the file, you'll immediately notice that there are probably more layers than you would expect. Having each building as a separate layer allowed me to mask and reveal them individually as the scene unravels.

Application: Integrating environmental concepts into client projects

Creating environmental scenes for my own site and the Genesis Project was relaxing and fun, and I received a lot of positive feedback because of them. People enjoy being immersed in a site and feeling that they can almost touch something.

As a result of the positive feedback and without conscious effort, I began mixing similar immersive styles in different pieces of my professional work. I wanted to enhance and heighten the user's experience with a product using an immersive style, as opposed to standard text effects, Flash navigation concepts, or animations you can see in thousands of sites.

This fundamental concept is easily broadened and applied to many other areas of interactive design. Virtually any website, presentation, application, kiosk, interactive CD, video game, DVD menu, PDA, or phone interface can be greatly improved with a little extra planning, attention, and energy. I believe the greatest potential can be realized in the areas of marketing and commerce. Working at 2Advanced Studios, I'm fortunate enough to assist companies both big and small in fulfilling their visions for their products. The following sections present examples of immersive environments I've created to help market specific products.

> " ONLY THROUGH FLASH CAN YOU PUT TOGETHER A PIECE OF MARKETING COLLATERAL THAT ALLOWS USERS TO SELECTIVELY READ ABOUT A PRODUCT, VIEW THE BUILDING PROCESS IN 3D, WATCH A SPOKESPERSON TALK ABOUT THE BENEFITS OF THE PRODUCT, AND INTERACT WITH ALL ASPECTS OF THE WEBSITE AT THE SAME TIME. "

Ford F-150 microsite

The Ford F-150 microsite (www.fordvehicles.com/trucks/f150) was released in September 2003 through 2Advanced Studios. For this site, I used Flash to create a virtual experience that goes above and beyond simple dissemination of textual information. The site combines 3D, video, and information to bring users as close to the product as possible to create a memorable brand impression.

I like to refer to this area of design as "environmental Flash marketing and enterprise." This term doesn't apply to simply using Flash in a company's website for a banner animation or a piece of text. Only through Flash can you put together a piece of marketing collateral that allows users to selectively read about a product, view the building process in 3D, watch a spokesperson talk about the benefits of the product, and interact with all aspects of the website at the same time.

Dia Sin website

The Dia Sin website (www.diasin.com) was released in October 2003 through 2Advanced Studios. The site represents an additional unique environmental experience applied to a marketing/commerce model. This futuristic and progressive vision was the brainchild of the Dia Sin founders and was realized through video, 3D environments, audio soundscape, textual information, and product shots. Using immersive techniques, ideas, and a tone that I initially honed in my Genesis Project experimentations, the site creates a unique environment for discovery of the company's objectives and products.

VAST website

The VAST website (www.realvast.com), published in June 2003, represents another example of success with immersive styling. VAST (which stands for Visual Audio Sensory Theater) is the former Elektra recording artist Jon Crosby. The site uses Flash, photography, and sound to create an immersive visual representation of the style and mood created by Jon's music. The goals of the site were to create a memorable visitor experience, successfully market the release of two "online only" records, and assist Jon in signing with another recording label. The result was the sale of thousands of downloadable online records via the website and VAST signing with 456 Entertainment (founded by Jonathan Rifkind and Carson Daly). The website was a primary catalyst for the opportunities leading to the creation and release of VAST's third album, *Nude*.

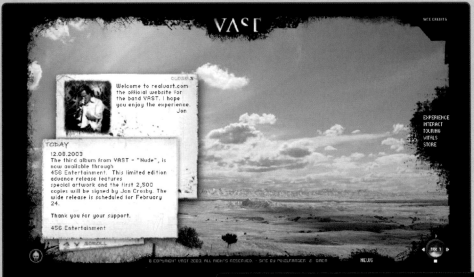

2Advanced Studios website

The 2Advanced Studios v4 Prophecy website (www.2advanced.com), made public in July 2003, represents a unique environmental experience applied to a services model. The theme of the site is a progressive vision of Tokyo in the future. This unique experience was created to market and promote the vision and creative abilities of the 2Advanced Studios team. The site functions as a sales tool that serves as a beacon for companies looking to enhance and position their online presence with a forward-thinking attitude and style.

Summary

I hope this chapter—and the book as a whole, for that matter—has inspired you in some small way, maybe through your creating a new process, idea, or approach to your projects where previously a barrier stood. Oftentimes the barriers before us go unnoticed until someone or something comes along to spin us around and point us in a new direction.

It's important to embrace both the negative and positive influences that we stumble across in our path toward growth. Our successes and failures (and those of others) can be the sparks that infuse us with energy, motivating us to improve in some aspect of our lives. When used properly, every success or mistake in a project can be a lesson learned and a step forward if we allow it to be. The old saying "misery loves company" can mean those who are stagnant will surround themselves with others in a similar situation, so instead surround yourself with people who are positive, motivated, and have intense work ethics and aspirations for success.

There's excitement in coming across people in all areas of our lives—even people we don't know—who are passionate about their own vision and are moving forward in their chosen field in life. There's also motivation to be found by people who are coasting along in life without goals and who aren't living up to their potential. You take the best and worst of a situation or person and you learn from them both. When I see motivated people, I want to take a small piece of their excitement, passion, and knowledge and absorb it into myself. Because of the influential people in my life, and through the support of my family, my growth as a designer, artist, and human being has been pushed beyond what I would have been capable of on my own.

07 ATMOSPHERE

> " I BEGAN MY ART CAREER AS A CLASSIC PENCIL AND PAPER ARTIST, BUT SINCE I DISCOVERED FLASH, I HAVEN'T CARED TOO MUCH ABOUT DRAWING ON PAPER BECAUSE NOW I CAN DRAW MY IDEAS DIRECTLY INTO THE COMPUTER AND BRING MOTIONLESS CREATIONS TO LIFE. "

NATHALIE LAWHEAD
WWW.BLUESUBURBIA.COM

A Volaric Flower

I remember impatiently anticipating the day my grandfather, a well-known Slovenian sculptor, would teach me to pound the unyielding iron into submission and skillfully weld each piece of old metal into a masterpiece. Sneaking off to his basement, under the false impression that he wouldn't notice, I would admiringly finger the uneven surfaces of those timeworn rusted metal sculptures that cluttered every room. He had been sculpting for 30 years, turning his home into a crowded museum and his apple orchard into a towering sculpture garden.

Despite the overwhelming size and complexity of his pieces, the very first thing he taught me to weld was a simple flower. We eventually made several of them, which I used for the animated short, A Volaric Flower (included on the CD as `volaricFlower.swf`). The animation, made for his website (www.volaric.com), is a mixture of video and sequential photography.

I have a deep respect and awe for the process of welded metal sculpting. The fact that I'm bending, then melting together something as unsubmissive as iron at temperatures up to 6,000 degrees Celsius fascinates me. The threatening white sparks, the unbearably bright light, the hissing and crackling, and finally, that molten aftermath when rays of light pierce through the hot metal's twisting streaks of smoke all greatly influence my work.

This chaotic symphony of light, smoke, fire, and shadow, the violent combination of cold metal and blindingly hot fire colliding to shape something as delicate as a flower, bore a strange metaphorical similarity to life's constant struggles. It struck me powerfully that something so beautiful could be born out of such harsh and violent conditions.

BlueSuburbia

It was this metaphor of conflict and beauty that deeply shaped the mysterious atmosphere in BlueSuburbia (www.bluesuburbia.com). The entire site is a constant battle between darkness and light, cold and warmth, all squeezed into a perceptively warped world, a metaphor for the never-ending conflicts in life, of which each room is a different manifestation.

The only trace of human life in these winding halls and disintegrating rooms are poems, which pull the visitor into the world of BlueSuburbia. The site is my experimental creative outlet—a mirror for the world I observe and experience. This constantly growing labyrinth of rooms is painted with poetry and interactive images.

Flash gave me the ability to animate my art, and through the simplest code in ActionScript, my creations can dance independently of predefined beginning and ending keyframes. They can be as random as life itself.

I began my art career as a classic pencil and paper artist, but since I discovered Flash, I haven't cared too much about drawing on paper because now I can draw my ideas directly into the computer and bring motionless creations to life.

I jumped on the program because it opened up the possibility of incorporating all that I loved about environments, atmosphere, motion, and interaction into my art so that I could display this online. Flash, along with the Web enabled my work to become part of something bigger.

Living poetry

I wanted to create an environment for my site in which the visitor can experience my poems, not just read them.

The first image that sets the mood for this experience is a dark blue suburbia lost amidst silhouettes of branches cloaked in cold strands of fog, all of which are dimly lit by the vague sphere of a moon wrapped in twisting clouds. Within the cold grip of skeleton-like trees, the only sign of life is the occasional shimmer of light, and a human shadow suddenly appearing in a window. The journey begins with two choices: to follow the curious stranger in that far-away window, or to take the easier way out and pick up a red key lying in the darkness.

If the visitor chooses the key, he will be redirected to a page containing a weatherworn parchment, upon which a map is roughly scribbled. This map provides quick access to rooms in BlueSuburbia. However, if the visitor chooses to follow the figure in the window, they are lead on a journey of discovery, through strange rooms with flickering candles, and doors left ajar. . . .

The atmosphere in BlueSuburbia is primarily set by alpha gradients. Flash's gradients are very powerful tools for creating fog-like effects. They easily imitate haziness because, if placed in small clusters side by side, they seamlessly flow into one another. I find this especially convenient while animating, as I can quickly create a "mist moving in the wind" effect, or in other cases, fire. The gradients are also very simple to use as fills for drawing elements such as light rays, and they play an important role in emphasizing shadow, or silhouettes. This is best demonstrated in scenes like the beginning blue village, where I have placed clusters of gradients behind the trees. The trees are a solid black color standing in front of a solid black background. By placing gradients behind the trees, I push them to the foreground, creating the gloomy night environment.

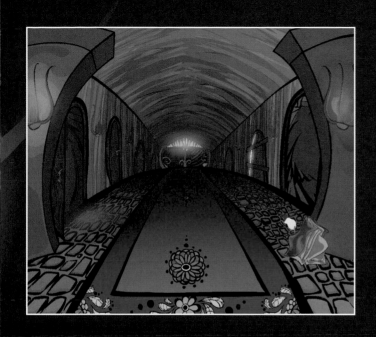

BlueSuburbia forces the viewers to interact with its environment. It surprises or scares them with small secrets scattered about. A moth softly flutters to the floor, a brittle page suddenly glides through a doorway, books tip over above a fireplace, or a little white rat scampers into the jaws of a hungry stairwell.

I was able to easily incorporate such surprise elements using ActionScript. The visitor becomes part of the environment to such an extent that they even become responsible for their choices. For example, inside the main hallway a wrinkled blue book leans against a column. If the visitor touches the book with her mouse, the book falls over, frightening a small rat that

Following the rat will eventually lead the visitor into a wooden room in the basement, where she finds the animal in a trap. Spurring this sequence of events causes small elements of the site, such as the map, to change.

If the visitor leaves the book alone or abstains from following the rat down the corridor, the rat survives her visit.

I believe in love,
though it is absent
I believe in the laughter of
happiness, though it is
silent
I believe in peace, though
life is violent

MY MONITOR IS MY CANVAS, AND THE WEB MY GALLERY

I strive to create my art with an anticipation of the future, aspiring to outlast trends and fads, or monitor resolutions and hardware improvements, because I believe art is immortal. I see my monitor as my canvas and the web as my gallery. As in the quote from Roman Polanski, "Cinema should make you forget you are sitting in a theater." I believe a good web page should make you forget that you are sitting in front of your computer. TV, movies, and games can all be very fascinating and immersive, and I believe Flash's forte is to bring all this to the Web.

During the Web's younger days, when tediously handcrafted HTML dominated pages, and frames or no frames was still a heated debate, I couldn't find much interest in the Web as an artistic medium. Printed media and canvas were still much more visually appealing. The Internet was only a small commodity in my life, nothing I really took seriously or considered as a possible creative outlet. However, with the arrival of Flash, the Web became immersive, taking on the ability to deliver powerful visual content.

AlienMelon

Old computer game classics like *Blade Runner*, *Space Quest*, *The Curse Of Monkey Island*, and *Day of the Tentacle*, where one finds oneself engrossed in a strangely beautiful, bizarre, or simply humorous environment full of foreboding mystery strongly influenced my work.

The sound of *Blade Runner*'s nighttime bustling market cluttered with fast food joints, continuously interrupted by the vague echo of police sirens emphatically howling in the distance, mixed with the far-away clamor of people always fascinated me.

All of a sudden, you find yourself lost in a claustrophobic back street alley behind one of the many busy pubs where the endless rhythm of music slowly thrums, luring you to further explore that mysterious urban world. Some of these elements found their way into the back alley of AlienMelon.

The Back Alley

I specialize in web design with Flash in our family business. We're an art collective that spans three generations: it begins with my grandparents, who are an odd mix of an engineer/ professor and a linguist both turned artist; my parents follow, both having developed an interest in the digital side of life,

computers; and it ends, of course, with me and my siblings. We love working together, and experimenting, so we needed a site to serve as our collective creative outlet, displaying anything from the impulsive to the nonsensical. The majority of the stuff we wanted to use was definitely not material for a corporate looking site. Thus AlienMelon (www.alienmelon.com) came about. A back alley was the perfect scene where we could graffiti our corner of the Internet with just about anything we wanted.

AlienMelon is a curious combination of pixel and vector art. I used the keyboard, and Flash's grid to create the pixelated menus and accompanying graphics in Flash. So I created pixel graphics with vectors—we jokingly call them vixels.

AlienMelon's navigation is part of the scene, which reinforces the environment's underlying story. The site opens to a late night in another graffiti ridden alley. You meet a girl who has roughly spray-painted a menu on the wall. The paint is still fresh, and dripping. After making your choice, she "talks" the selection to you. Through conversation, so to say, you explore the site. Her less talkative friend, idly leans against the wall playing the site's music which may be turned on or off by clicking on his weatherworn boom box.

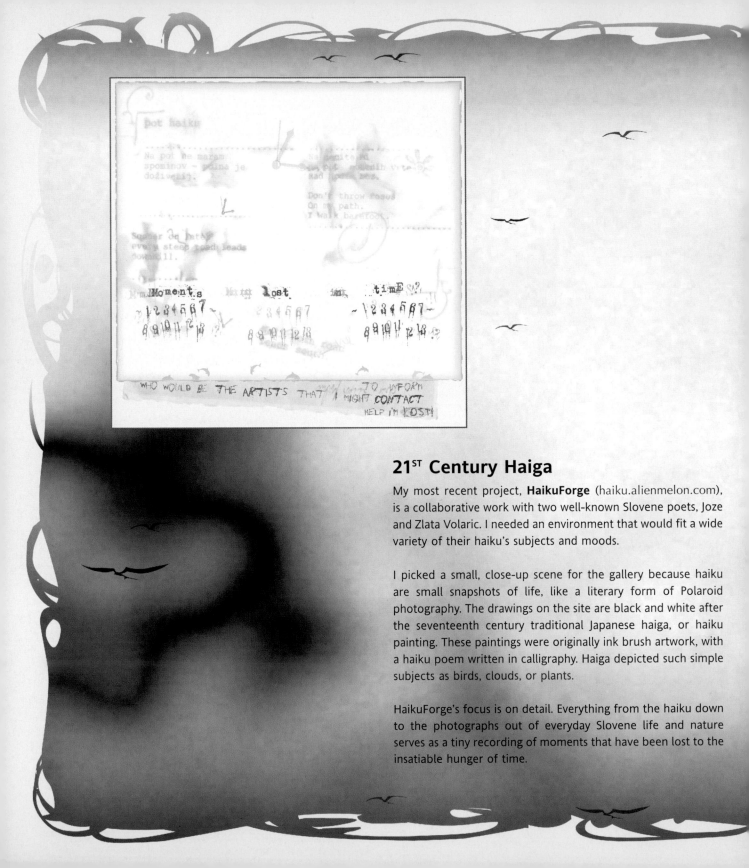

21ˢᵀ Century Haiga

My most recent project, **HaikuForge** (haiku.alienmelon.com), is a collaborative work with two well-known Slovene poets, Joze and Zlata Volaric. I needed an environment that would fit a wide variety of their haiku's subjects and moods.

I picked a small, close-up scene for the gallery because haiku are small snapshots of life, like a literary form of Polaroid photography. The drawings on the site are black and white after the seventeenth century traditional Japanese haiga, or haiku painting. These paintings were originally ink brush artwork, with a haiku poem written in calligraphy. Haiga depicted such simple subjects as birds, clouds, or plants.

HaikuForge's focus is on detail. Everything from the haiku down to the photographs out of everyday Slovene life and nature serves as a tiny recording of moments that have been lost to the insatiable hunger of time.

Moments in Time

The haiku are connected by an underlying theme of migrating birds, a metaphor for traveling through life. An old, travel-worn, lost letter serves as the interface, with a living stamp depicting a bird trapped in a spinning storm. The haiku and portions of the site are framed in with a calligraphic border, to echo haiga's quick, sketch-like lines.

Selecting the language triggers the intro animation, which shows the bird being swallowed up by a brooding mass of twisting gray clouds. This elicits the vague feeling that the bird was carrying this envelope, and thus lost it. Three words for the menu appear categorizing the haiku: moments, lost, and time. These depict the different feelings the author had in those particular situations.

These words, two of them nouns (moments and time) are linked by the verb, lost, because essentially moments are lost, and time is lost. The gallery's theme loosely hangs around the word lost—a lost envelope, a lost bird—thus the word "lost" is placed in the middle of the screen.

Choosing any of these three moods plays one of three random Haiga. Each of these haiku categories contains thirteen sets of haiku; every number is linked to three different poems that randomly load. No matter how often one visits the site, the experience is always different.

Old pond,
Frog jumping into
Water sound

Basho Matsuo (1644–1694)
Translation by Fumiko Saisho

Following the ancient traditions of the Japanese haiga masters, we will study a frog pond for our tutorial. You might eventually wonder why so much detail is involved in such an insignificant subject as a frog sitting on a lily pad. . . . But remember, it is the unanticipated beauty of seemingly insignificant details, and the occasional "special effects" in our world that surprise us and make life fascinating.

Lily, Fireflies, and a Hungry Frog: Tutorial Overview

The major part of this tutorial will focus on drawing in Flash. I like drawing in Flash because it's quick, simple, scalable, easy to animate, and it allows me to add detail. I can mix, match, and change colors to my liking. Flash lets me remove or add elements without having to redraw large portions of my image, and vectors keep the file size low. The viewer can zoom in and view yet another intricate piece of the art work. I can freely reuse the same graphic in different sizes and scenarios without having to worry about distortion.

The first portion of this tutorial will focus on creating such customizable graphics in Flash and using gradients to create atmosphere. To complete the drawing part of the tutorial, you will need a digitizer or drawing tablet. For those of you who don't have one, or who want to move directly into the Fireflies, or Animating sections, all the completed graphics are provided in oldPond_graphics.fla.

After all our elements are drawn, we'll create a single bug, which will serve as both the animated cursor and as a cluster of fireflies hovering above the lily. In this section, we'll also write the ActionScript to transform our user into one of these bugs and to generate our firefly herd.

The last section will focus on animating the frog, writing the ActionScript for his random movement, and incorporating the interactivity. If the visitor gets too close to the frog he'll be eaten. You can find all the completed animations, and code in oldPond.fla on the CD.

Drawing: The Frog

Open oldPond_drawingFrog.fla from the CD. To keep things simple, I have already completed the lily and lily pad.

There are two ways I draw in Flash: by using many quick lines as you can see from the lily and lily pad, or by using very smoothed-out blotches of colors, like the frog. The second method is a lot easier on the CPU; because Flash doesn't have to render so many corners and edges, the file size is significantly lower, and the animation is simpler.

Small static objects, such as the lily and lily pad, can be drawn with many sketchy lines. For the frog, we will focus on the second method—using clean smooth shapes. In order to easily create clean and smooth lines, I zoom in to my object as close as I can so that the lines turn out more exact. The closer I am to the stage while I draw, the fewer "edges" my lines will have. This significantly reduces the file size.

It's important to keep each color on a separate layer so that when you want to change the color or shape of your object, you only need to edit the contents of that specific layer. In the end, it makes making changes and fine-tuning a lot simpler.

Because the frog is the most important, he's going to be the most detailed part of the tutorial. You don't have to make the frog look exactly like mine; feel free to experiment and create your own character. The following methods are applicable to any type of graphic, or sprite.

1. Create a new layer between the LilyPad, and Lily layers, named Frog.

2. Zoom in to the lily pad and directly above the fold in the leaf, sketch out your frog's body using the brush tool. Use the default brush size (the third selection from the bottom) and shape (circular). In the Properties panel, make sure that you set Smoothing at a comfortable range. 60–70 works best for me.

3. Turn your frog sketch into a symbol named `frog`. Edit the new `frog` movie clip in place and rename the current layer inside it to outline.

Next we will separate and "smooth out" all the edges for each element of the frog outline. We'll essentially end up with a nose, eyes, face, mouth, left foot, left leg (the top part of the leg, above the elbow joint), right foot, right leg, chest, and back in this order, all on their own layers.

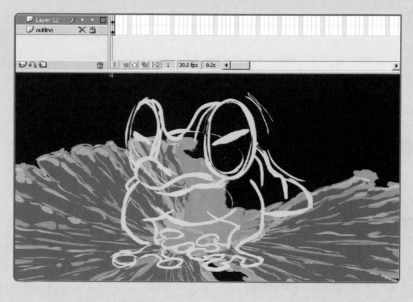

> *If you have trouble with this, I've included a finished version of the frog outline in this FLA's library, named `frogOutlineFinished`, with all the outlined body parts predistributed to their layers. Just drag this onto the Frog layer in the root timeline, edit it in place, and skip to step 5.*

4. Create ten layers with the aforementioned names. Cut out and distribute all the elements of the frog to those layers. Tint each element a different color so that lines are easier to keep apart. When everything is distributed, zoom in until you see the jagged edges of the lines and smooth them out using the Selection tool to grab any corners and pull them into your line's body. When you're doing this, make sure that Snap to Objects (the magnet icon) is selected.

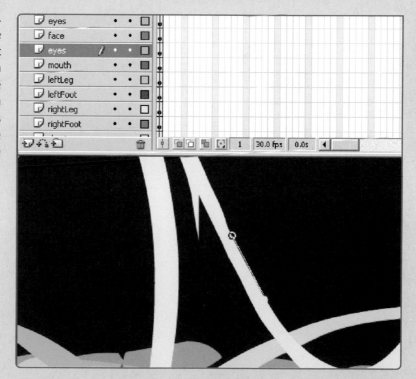

When done, your frog should look something like the screen-shot. A clean and clear outline for complex, animated graphics is crucial—the cleaner your lines are the lower the file size, and as a result, your image will be sharper. Having each element on its own layer makes it easiest to animate.

5. Each outlined body part will be a symbol. Go to the back layer and make all its contents a movie clip called `frogBack`. Edit `frogBack` in place.

6. Name the layer midCol. Use the paint bucket to fill the outline with the middle color #FFBE63.

7. Select the outline, tint it black, and cut and paste it in place on a new layer called outline. All outline layers, for each body part, should be the top layer.

8. Insert a new layer above midCol named darkCol. Paint in the shadows with #F78E00 and smooth out the lines using the Selection tool.

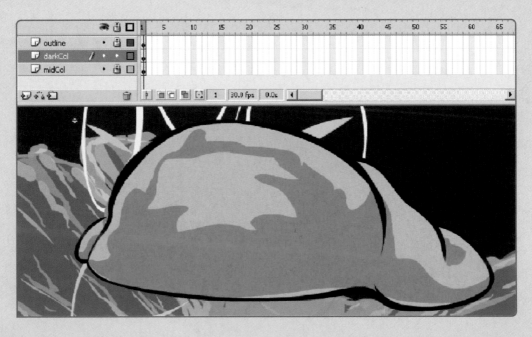

9. Insert a new layer named lightCol and paint in the light colors (#FFE7C6). Smooth out its lines.

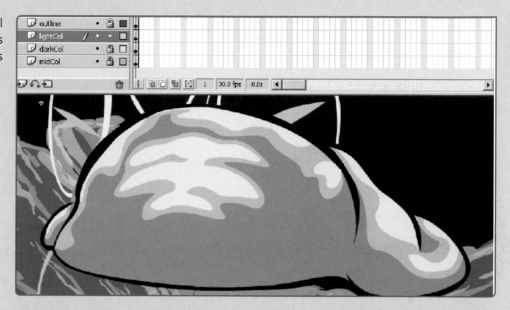

10. Paint the highlights (#FFFFEF) on their own highlights layer.

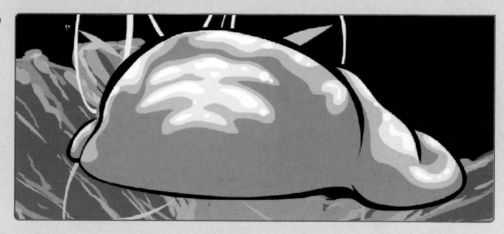

11. Follow the same process as above (steps 6–10) for the frog's chest (the chest layer), his nose (the nose layer), his feet (rightFoot, leftFoot), and his legs (rightLeg, leftLeg). Convert them into separate movie clips named according to each body part; create the following five layers for each of the colors shown here:

- outline: #000000
- highLights: #FFFFEF
- lightCol: #FFE7C6
- darkCol: #F78E00
- midCol: #FFBE63

12. Paint in the body parts using those colors and smooth out the lines with your Selection tool. Note that where the body part ends, you should let the colors slightly overflow over the outline. It's better to draw in a little extra; this will make animating easier.

Most of the frog's body should be painted and converted to movie clips by now.

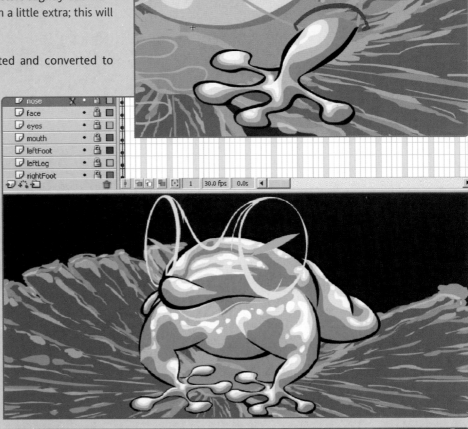

13. We still have the face, eyes, and mouth left. His mouth is somewhat complex. The frog will "snap" at the cursor, so we have to add the slimy red interior. Convert the contents of the mouth layer to a movie clip called mouth.

14. Name the layer outline and tint its contents black. Fill in the lip portion of his mouth with midCol #FFBE63. Paste it in its own layer behind outline called midCol.

15. Insert a layer folder named lip. Drag your layer midCol into the lip folder. Make sure that the outline layer is always on top.

16. Create the other three layers (lightCol, darkCol, highlights) and colors for his lip the same way you created his other body parts inside this lip folder.

17. Insert a folder just above the lip folder, and name it inside. We need the following five layers, and their respective colors, in the lip folder:

- highlights: #FFD7C6

- lightCol: #E7717B

- darkCol2: #213021

- darkCol: #6B1818

- mainCol: #A53031

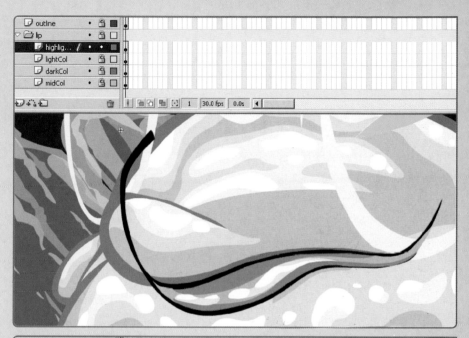

18. Using the same process that you used for the rest of his body, create the mouth.

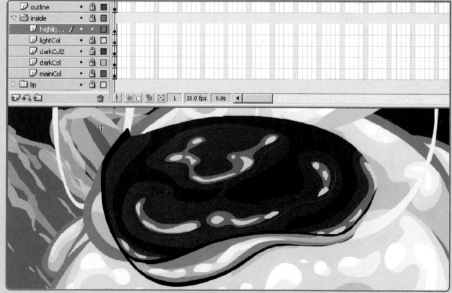

19. Return to the parent timeline. A rather eerie looking headless frog will greet you. Let's give him a head and eyes. On the eyes layer, turn both of his eyes into two symbols eyeRight, and eyeLeft.

20. Edit each in place and color them. The main color to use is #000800 50% alpha, with a small white outline of #FFFFEF 70% alpha.

21. On the parent timeline in the face layer, convert its contents to a symbol called face. Edit face in place.

22. Follow the same procedure as you did to create the other body parts. Create an extra layer below outline layer named eyeCols with two new colors in it: #223326 for the center of the eye, and #5B1D1A for the outer edges.

23. We need highlights for the eyes. Above the eyeCols layer, insert a new layer called eyeLight1 and use the color #9CDFDE with 70% alpha to paint the first set of highlights. Use the color #F4FEFF with 90% alpha applied to paint the second set in a new layer named eyeLight2, above the eyeLight1 layer.

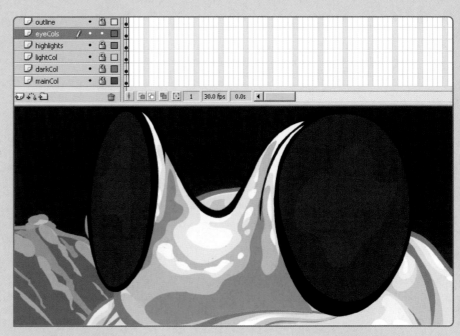

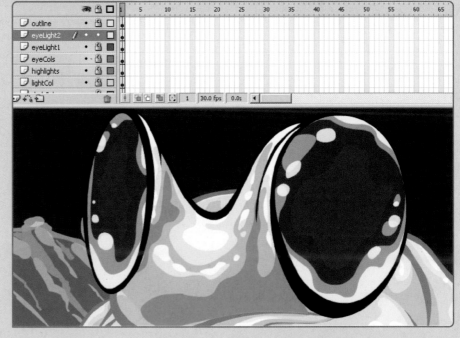

Drawing: Atmosphere and Gradients

Let's add a little touch of mist to strengthen our atmosphere. We'll do this with gradients. When I create hazy light effects, I don't let my gradient have too many solid colors. The alpha should be generously reduced, with colors similar to those of the background they're on. This set of gradients should consist of greenish blue colors like our movie's background.

1. On the root timeline, insert a new layer called fog1 above layer Lily. Insert a new symbol called fog.

2. In this symbol, draw a circle (no stroke) with a width and height of 130. Place it in the center. Fill the circle with a radial gradient with three swatches:

   ● #BCD0FE with an alpha of 20%

   ● #8282D5 with an alpha of 5%

   ● Background color #091617 with an alpha of 0%

   Play around a bit with the swatches' alpha levels if you are having trouble seeing your gradient. The visibility is strongly influenced by your monitor's brightness level. Make sure that they appear OK on the default monitor's brightness and contrast settings. This might take some experimenting to get right.

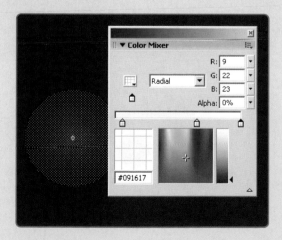

3. Use the Fill Transform Tool to slightly enlarge the gradient, as shown in this screenshot.

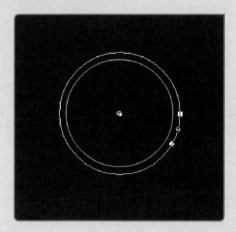

4. Return to the root timeline. Drag four of these new fog symbols onto the fog1 layer and skew/rotate them to form a semicircle around the left part of the lily pad. Refer to the image as a guide. Place them close together so single circular shapes aren't discernable. Keep turning up and down your monitor's brightness level to see if it looks good on lighter levels. These symbols always look better on darker settings.

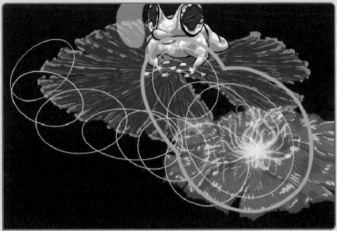

6. Insert another three gradients above the lily clustering near the frog. Tint them the same color at 100%.

7. Insert a new layer fog2 beneath LillyPad. In it insert eight fog symbols and place them around the right side of the picture, as shown below.

5. Add three gradients beside the lily. Tint these three a color of #FFFFEF, at 30%. See this image for placement.

Our environment is finished. We'll now create our fireflies.

Fireflies: Creating a Bug

Let's make some bugs. We'll use the same graphic for the cursor. If you've skipped the drawing section, all the completed graphics can be found in oldPond_Graphics.fla. Simply open the file and start working from there.

1. Above the fog1 layer, add a new layer, Bugs_Cursor.

2. Zoom in to the maximum (2000%) in any clear area of your movie.

3. Draw one long, pointed wing, with the color #EFEFD6 and alpha 70%, about two or three pixels wide and long. These are small bugs.

4. Turn your wing into a movie clip called bugWing. Duplicate it, and flip it horizontally. Move it to create a set of wings.

5. Select your set of wings and convert them both into one symbol named bug_mc. Edit the bug_mc symbol in place. Inside this new movie clip, we will create and animate our bug.

6. Make sure that the registration point of this new symbol is *exactly between* the two wings. This is important for the animation, and for the bug that will act as the cursor.

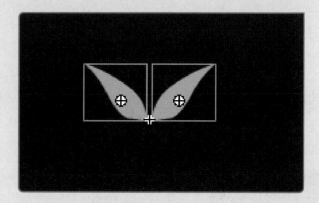

7. Name the current layer wings. Above wings, insert a new layer called body.

8. Draw a dot, the same color as wings, which represents the bug's body. Because the bug is so small, there's no point in making it detailed.

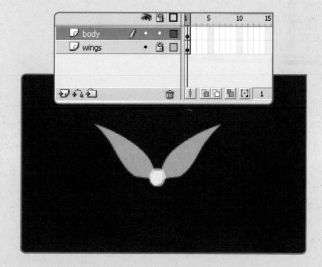

9. Insert a new top-level layer named gradient. Select the oval tool with no stroke. Draw a horizontal oval circle around the bug. Fill it with a radial gradient. The first color swatch is #C5E7FE with an alpha of 60%, the next is #FFBE63 with an alpha of 0%.

10. Extend your bug_mc timeline for three frames. On the wings layer, make sure that both graphics' transformation points are at the joint of the wings on the bug's body.

11. Insert three keyframes in the wing layer. Animate the three stages of flapping by skewing the wings frame to frame.

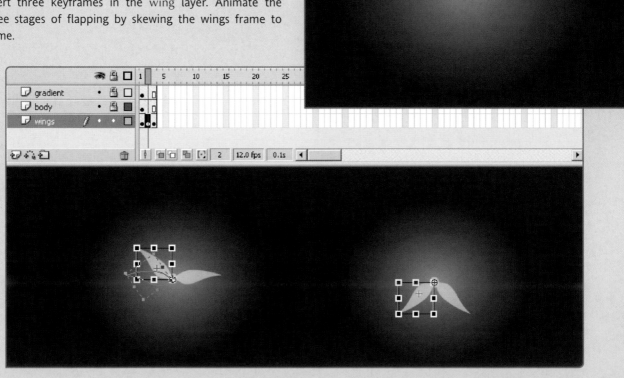

Fireflies: Scripting Simple Movement

Next we will use some ActionScript to control our fireflies.

1. Go back to your root timeline and select the new `bug_mc` movie clip. Using the transformation tool, skew it to a width and height of roughly 30 pixels. Place it at the bottom left, off the stage. Give it a target instance named `cursor_mc`.

2. Insert a new top-level layer named `actions` and open your Actions panel. In the actions for frame 1 of the `actions` layer, set the movie's general properties to hide the mouse and set the `scaleMode`:

```
Mouse.hide();
Stage.scaleMode = showAll;
```

3. We want the visitor to become the bug, so we'll swap the cursor for our insect. The bug will follow the mouse, rotating with the movement of the mouse. Create a function called `mouseRotFunc`, and in it declare an `onEnterFrame`. Type the following in your Actions panel:

```
mouseRotFunc = function() {
    this.onEnterFrame = function() {
```

4. Declare two variables that will contain the friction equation for the movie clip's x and y values.

```
var disX = (_xmouse-this._x)/6;
var disY = (_ymouse-this._y)/6;
```

This measures the distance between the movie clip's registration point and the x or y position of the mouse, calculating how far our movie clip is from the mouse. It divides that value by 6 because we want the movie clip to gradually reach its target location.

5. We'll do the same for the next line, but this time, our variables will calculate the rotation. The following code calculates the angle in radians (first line) and converts it to degrees plus 90 (second line) so that our clip rotates.

```
var myRads = Math.atan2(disY, disX);
var myDegs = Math.round
➡ (myRads*180/Math.PI)+90;
```

6. We now apply all the above values to the movie clip's x, y, and rotation. In the last line, apply `mouseRotFunc` to `cursor_mc`.

```
this._x += disX
    this._y += disY
    this._rotation = myDegs;
    };
};
mouseRotFunc.apply(cursor_mc);
```

7. Test your movie. You'll see the mouse transformed into a bug. Simple enough. Create an empty movie clip called `target` and place it on the stage, anywhere above the lily's center. Give this movie clip an instance name of `light_mc`. This will be the light source for our bugs, so I've placed it on the Bugs_Cursor layer.

8. Find the `bug_mc` symbol in the library, right-click (or CTRL-click) on it, and open up its Linkage properties. Give it an identifier of `bug_mc`, make sure that Export for ActionScript and Export in first frame are checked.

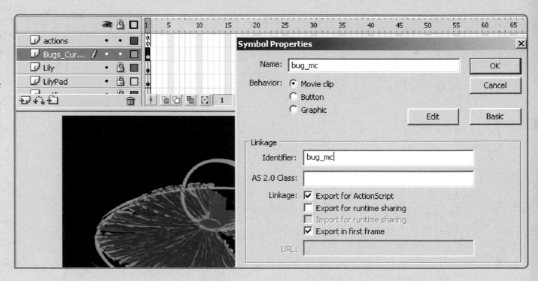

9. Open your Actions panel with frame 1 of the actions layer selected. We'll add the following ActionScript after our previous script. Basically, this will be a simple version of random movement. We'll generate a random x and y position for each separate instance of our upcoming cluster of bugs, have each bug movie clip move in that direction, check to see if it's arrived, and if it has, pick another location. First, you'll declare a function called `randMovFunc`, with a parameter called `targetClip`.

```
randMovFunc = function(targetClip) {
   var targetClip, i;
```

10. Then declare two variables that will pick a random target x and y position for our movie clip.

```
this.target_x =
➡ (Math.random()*100)+targetClip._x;
   this.target_y =
   ➡ (Math.random()*100)+targetClip._y;
```

11. Next, declare a variable `i` with the value of 0 and create an `onEnterFrame`, which will increment our variable `i`.

```
i=0;
this.onEnterFrame = function() {
   i++;
```

12. Within this `onEnterFrame`, we'll create an equation for measuring how far our movie clip is from its target. The concept here is the same as it was for the cursor.

```
this.xdiv = (this.target_x-this._x)/20;
this.ydiv = (this.target_y-this._y)/20;
```

13. Apply all the above values to our movie clip.

```
this._x += this.xdiv;
this._y += this.ydiv;
```

14. Check to see if our movie clip has arrived at its location. If it has, call the `randMovFunc` function again and begin the whole code cycle again.

```
if(i>20) {
  this.onEnterFrame = undefined;
  randMovFunc.apply(this, [targetClip]);
  }
 };
};
```

Done! Now let's create the bugs and apply `randMovFunc` to them. We're going to do this in a function called `makeBug`. This function is going to have a parameter of `bugAmount`, so we can change the number of bugs to our liking. It's going to duplicate the bugs through `attachMovie`, randomly size them so that they're not all the same, and apply the `randMovFunc` to them.

15. Initiate the function:

```
function makeBug(bugAmount) {
  var bugAmount, i;
```

16. Create a loop for cloning them:

```
for (i=0; i<bugAmount; i++) {
    this.attachMovie("bug_mc",
➡ "bug"+i+"_mc", i+100);
```

17. Now set their spawning x and y position to that of `light_mc`, otherwise they're going to spawn at the top right of the movie and then collectively fly towards `light_mc`, which isn't the intended effect.

```
var bugs = _root["bug"+i+"_mc"];
bugs._x = light_mc._x;
bugs._y = light_mc._y;
```

18. Randomly size them, apply the `randMovFunc`, and make five of them.

```
bugs._xscale = Math.ceil
➡ (Math.random()*100)+30;
bugs._yscale = bugs._xscale;
randMovFunc.apply(bugs, [light_mc]);
  }
}
makeBug(5);
```

Five bugs spawn and then move randomly, and the cursor is swapped for a naturally moving bug.

Animating: Frog and the Idle State

I animate my sprites so that they move a lot like marionettes. I use this method because it allows me to use movie clips instead of redrawing everything frame after frame, or shape tweening. This method reduces the file size and it's less demanding on the user's system. I first create all my movie clips and sort them on separate layers. I then place each movie clip's registration point on the body part's joint (that is, where the limb connects to the body or other limb). It's important to do this because the movie clip's transformation point is aligned with its registration point. So when I'm scaling the limbs, rotating them, tweening them, or simply controlling them through ActionScript, the sprite's body doesn't just float apart at its joints; instead, each limb is locked in place. The body parts are attached to the body, which allows for some nice organic movement.

We will create two types of animation for the frog. The first one will be **idle**; this occurs when the user isn't interacting with the frog and the frog is moving on his own. During this state, three sets of animations play. His legs are moving randomly, as are his eyes, and his eyelids are blinking. To incorporate a touch of random, we'll have ActionScript make these body parts either `gotoAndPlay` or `gotoAndStop` a random frame via `setInterval`.

The second state is **interactive**. In this state, the user is interacting with the frog. This is when he snaps at the cursor. All the animation for both of these states primarily consists of frame-by-frame animation. We'll begin with the idle state.

We'll need four moving body parts:

■ Eyes (eyeRight and eyeLeft movie clips)

■ Eyelids (blink1 to blink8 movie clips)

■ Left leg (leftFoot and leftLeg movie clips)

■ Right leg (rightFoot and rightLeg movie clips)

1. In the frog movie clip, insert a new layer above leftFoot called leftLegAni. Select both the leftFoot and leftLeg layers, right-click (CTRL-click on a Mac), and choose Cut Frames from the menu.

2. Create a new symbol (movie clip) called leftLegAni. Paste your frames into it. Make sure the leg is at an x and y of 0.

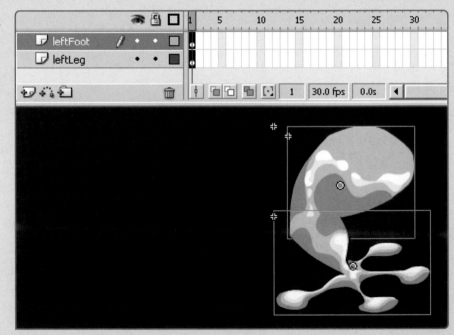

3. Return to the frog movie clip, and drag your leftLegAni movie clip from the library into the leftLegAni layer. After you placed the leg back in its original position, edit it in place.

4. Reposition the registration points of both leftFoot and leftLeg where the joints of these body parts would naturally be. Mark the position of the foot on the lily pad, using guides so that you don't forget where it should be placed.

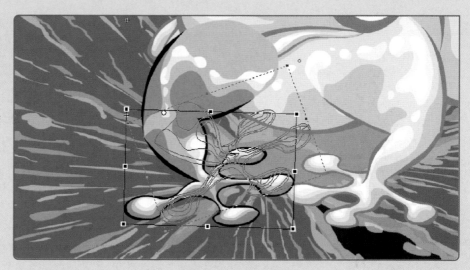

5. Use the Transform tool to move it to your liking, frame by frame, until you have a set of keyframes. Make sure that both body parts stay attached to each other; that is, keep your leftFoot symbol attached to leftLeg. Animate enough to allow for plenty of diversity in the frog's leg movements.

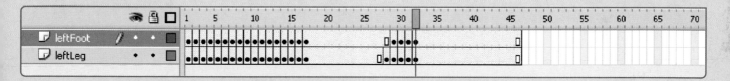

6. Choose a handful of areas in the animation, insert an equal amount of frames in both the leftFoot and leftLeg layers in those areas, and make them a tween.

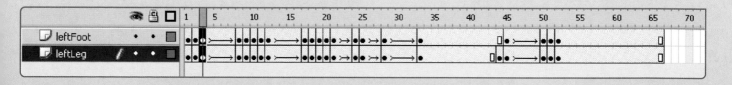

All your tweens should either have Easing In set at –100%, or Easing Out set at 100%. In real life, objects movements depend on friction, so I always use easing in my animations. They slowly accelerate and come to a crashing halt (In), or dart off in a speedy burst of energy and comfortably decelerate (Out). Easing In has the tendency to make you feel like you're witnessing a car crash—it starts out nice and slow but comes to an abrupt halt. I also normally use a little Easing Out to conclude an animation, so that it ends gently. For cases like this, the positive values are a lot more natural looking because the animated object glides to a halt, thus the end is less of a shock.

7. Insert a new layer called actions. Insert a keyframe as the last frame, and add a stop() action in this frame.

8. Now that the left leg is done, repeat all of the above with the right leg (rightLegAni), and both eyes (eyesAni) by

   ■ Inserting a new layer in the frog timeline (above the layer in which the to-be animated movie clip is currently nested) named with a structure like currentBodyPartAni.

   ■ Cutting the frames of your body part and pasting them into a new movie clip.

   ■ Making sure that both instances are selected and, when they are initially pasted into the movie clip, that they are placed at an x and y coordinate of 0.

   ■ Distributing the two parts onto separate layers.

   ■ Dragging that new symbol onto the frog timeline and reattaching the symbol in its proper location.

   ■ Editing the new symbol in place and placing your body part's movie clip registration points where they attach to the body (the eyes registration point can stay the way they are).

   ■ Animating your frog's body part to your liking—in my version, the right leg is fairly similar to the left leg, and the eyes move up and close before they open and return to their original position.

   ■ Inserting a stop() action in the end frame.

9. For the eyelids, return to the frog timeline. We will make the eyes blink with a frame-by-frame animation.

10. Insert a new layer above your eyesAni layer and name it blinkAni. Paint the first stage of an eyelid closing with #FFBE63, with an alpha of 85%, and a thin black outline. If you look carefully at the screenshot, you can just see that I've drawn the very start of an eyelid at the top and bottom of each eye.

11. Convert the drawing into a movie clip named blinkAni. Edit blinkAni in place and rename the layer to blink.

12. Use keyframes as before to gradually enlarge the eyelids, moving the black outline each time, to animate the eyelids to a fully closed position.

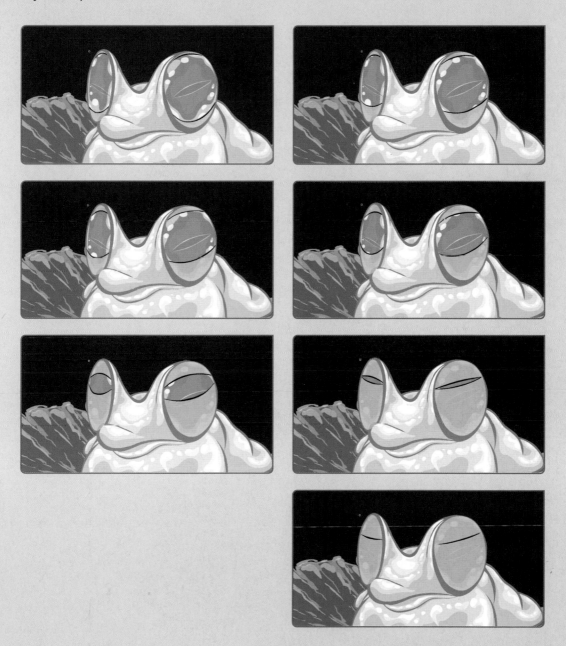

13. Go through all the frames and convert their contents to movie clips so that we can reuse them for the opening sequence. Name the movie clips `blink1`, `blink2`, `blink3` . . . in this order. Copy all the `blink` frames, and paste them further on in the timeline, starting at frame 20.

14. Select all the newly pasted frames. Right-click over them and chose Reverse Frames. Delete the **first two** frames of the newly pasted group.

15. Select all your frames, and drag them three frames ahead so there are three blank frames at the beginning. Insert a blank keyframe at the end. Insert a new layer called actions, and add a `stop()` action in that last frame.

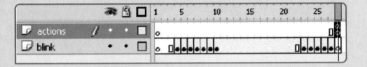

16. In the `frog` movie clip timeline, give the animated body part movie clips the following associated target instance names—we'll be using these in the ActionScript in the next step:

- lblinkAni: blinkAni_mc

- leyesAni: eyesAni_mc

- lleftLegAni: leftLegAni_mc

- lrightLegAni: rightLegAni_mc

17. In the root timeline, give the `frog` an instance name of `frog_mc`. Open up the Actions panel for the actions layer, and type the following after all the firefly code.

```
randFrameFunc = function (myMC) {
  var myMC;
  function chooseFrameFunc() {
      var randNum = Math.ceil
      ➡ (Math.random()*myMC._totalframes);
```

```
      if (randNum<myMC._totalframes/2) {
         myMC.gotoAndPlay(randNum);
      }
      if (randNum>myMC._totalframes/2) {
         myMC.gotoAndStop(randNum);
      }
  }
  setInterval(chooseFrameFunc, 1800,
  ➡ "myMC");
};
randFrameFunc(frog_mc.blinkAni_mc);
randFrameFunc(frog_mc.eyesAni_mc);
randFrameFunc(frog_mc.leftLegAni_mc);
randFrameFunc(frog_mc.rightLegAni_mc);
```

We're defining a function called `randFrameFunc` that has a parameter of `myMC`, which would be our movie clip. In `randFrameFunc`, we define another function called `chooseFrameFunc`. We declare a variable, `randNum`, that chooses a random frame according to the length of our movie clip's timeline. We then use an `if` statement to check if `randNum` is less than the movie clip's totalframes/2, or greater than the movie clip's totalframes/2, and act accordingly.

After our `chooseFrameFunc` we initiate a `setInterval` to call upon it every 1,800 milliseconds, using `myMC` as a parameter. You can play with the interval numbers and adjust them to the length of your body part's animations. The longer your animation the longer the interval between calls to `chooseFrameFunc` should be. The very last bit applies our `randFrameFunc` to the frog's body parts.

When you use `setInterval` on a movie clip and end up removing that specific movie clip, the interval will still continue to run code. We're going to add an interactive state of animation to our frog, and those specific movie clips with `setInterval` applied will be removed from the timeline for a short period of time. Normally I would recommend that you use `clearInterval` to stop the interval because leaving a bunch of `setIntervals` to idly run can sometimes be unnecessarily demanding on the user's system. In this case, our frog will always return to its idle state, thus returning the movie clips to the timeline for our `setInterval` to continue to apply code to. This conveniently serves the purpose.

Animating: Frog and the Interactive State

If you test your file now, then you should have a perfectly working random frog and firefly mouse pointer. If you look at the final file, you'll see that there's one more dimension that I've added: the ability of the frog to respond to user movements. I'm not going to go into as much depth in this section, as most of what is involved simply uses the animation techniques we've seen already. As always, take a look at the final FLA, `oldpond.fla`, if you get stuck.

The first thing to do is to open up the `frog` movie clip, and add a layer called actions at the top, with a label of idle and a `stop()` action on the first frame. Now add two layer folders called interactive and idle. The idle folder will contain all the random elements that we've just created, so move these layers into this folder and add a blank keyframe at the end of each layer.

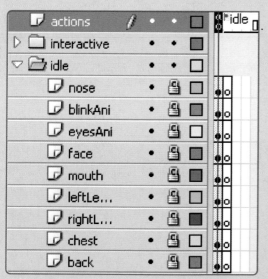

The next thing to do is to add some graphics to our interactive layer. We essentially want the same set of layers as we had earlier, before we created the animated movie clips of the legs, nose, face, and so on. So your layers should look something like this screenshot when you're done.

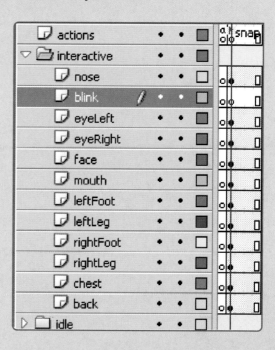

As you've probably guessed, frame 1 is going to include our idle animation, and frame 2 will hold our interactive animation. To do this, add a keyframe in frame 2 of the actions layer and label it snap. Insert an empty keyframe at the start of all the interactive layers.

Our interactive frog animation has seven stages:

1. Jump, where he jumps at the cursor

2. Snap, where he mauled the cursor and now has it in his mouth

3. Step back, where, with cursor in mouth, he contently steps back to his usual position

4. Gulp, where he gulps down the cursor

5. Wait, where he sits there and blinks unsure of what he just ate

6. Analyze, where he realizes what he just ate

7. Regurgitate, where he returns the cursor to the user. Here the animation ends, and timeline returns to the idle state. Make sure the animation ends the same way it started for a seamless loop.

The first thing to do is to take a look at the item that triggers this—the button. Create a new layer just under actions and call it buttons. We only want to trigger the sequence above when we're in the idle state, so add a blank keyframe to frame 2, and then add an invisible button to frame 1. The button needs to cover the area just in front of the frog's mouth (see the screenshot for details of mine).

Give the button a target instance name of snap_btn. Still in the frog movie clip, open the Actions panel for frame 1 of the actions layer, and insert the following code just before the stop() action you added earlier:

```
snap_btn.onRollOver = function() {
    gotoAndPlay("snap");
};
```

Now we can take a look at animating the different parts of the frog to give us our sequence. The frog should open his mouth wide enough so that when he snaps down, it looks believable that he ate the cursor. If your **hit area** is larger than his open mouth, the cursor disappears too early. The **snap area** is where he bites down.

At this point, I would strongly recommend opening up the completed chapter FLA (oldPond.fla) and refer to the animation in it for guidance. I've marked the seven stages of the snap animation with frame comments.

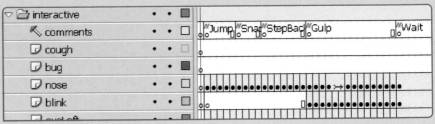

To animate the frog snapping sequence, use the same process that we employed in the previous section for the leftLegAni, rightLegAni, and eyesAni movie clips, this time referring to the above seven stages as a guide. Remember to use movie clip registration points properly. You can animate the head (nose, eyeLeft, eyeRight, face, and so on) as a whole; just skew them all at the same time. The only part of the frog that isn't animated is the back movie clip.

For the blinking, I took the existing blinking sequence, cut it up, and spread it around. For the blink at the Analyze stage I cut up two existing blink movie clips and rearranged them to give him his disgruntled expression.

Throughout the snapping process beginning at Gulp, there is a blinking sequence that runs like this:

- The frog's eyes stay closed until Wait.

- He opens them and begins blinking in a disturbed manner until Analyze where he jumps back with a new blink symbol, which is a combination of the left eyelid more closed than the right.

- Finally, in the Regurgitate stage, the frog opens and closes his eyes very slightly with each jerk forward.

In the `Regurgitate` stage are two new movie clips: `bug_mc` flying out of the frog's mouth stretched out, and an animated gradient cluster.

To create the bug, duplicate `bug_mc` and name the new symbol `bugHurl_mc`. In `bugHurl_mc`, delete all the frames except frame 1. In the body layer, stretch the body, then the wings, rotating them to an almost vertical position.

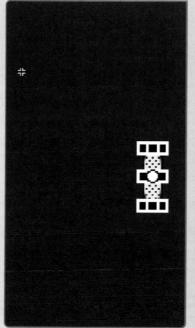
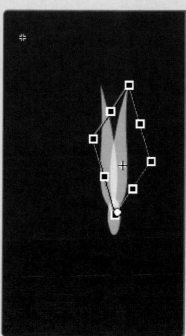

Stretch the gradient, and extend all layers to frame 2. Insert a new keyframe and rotate the wings to a completely vertical position—this is our "bug hurling through the air" animation.

Back in our interactive layer folder in the `frog` movie clip, insert a new layer named `bug`. In the `Regurgitate` stage in the `frog` timeline, create a tween that is eight frames long, with `bugHurl_mc` starting from the frog's mouth and ending off the stage when the frog is regurgitating.

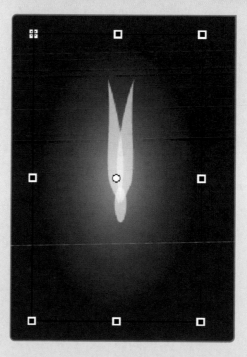

Here we want a cough effect to accompany the regurgitated bug; we'll use a series of frame-by-frame alpha clusters, which animate the frog's mouth. Create a new movie clip `coughGradient`. Edit it in place, and in the center, draw a circle (no stroke color) with a width of 32 and height of 32.

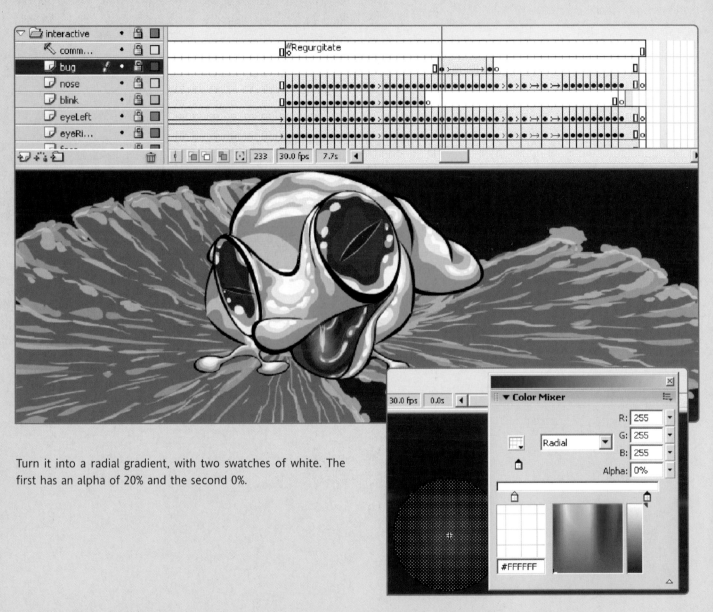

Turn it into a radial gradient, with two swatches of white. The first has an alpha of 20% and the second 0%.

In the frog's timeline, insert a new layer above the bug layer named cough. Insert a new keyframe in this layer at the same frame that your bug tween begins. Cluster the gradients around the frog's mouth.

Distribute them farther away with each frame. The animation should be six frames long, as you can see from the following series of images:

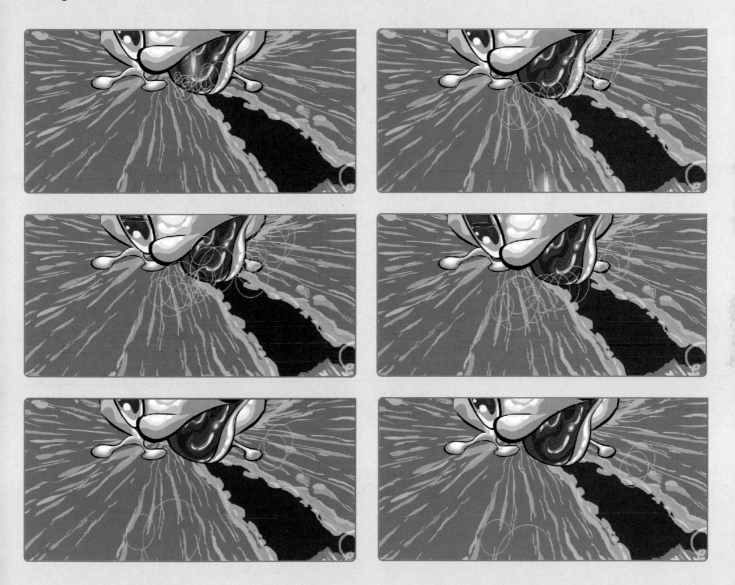

Finally, we need to hide our cursor while the animation is playing, and then reveal it again when it has finished. Insert a new keyframe on the actions layer a frame before the frog bites down—this is frame six in my file. Open the Actions panel for that new frame and type:

```
_root.cursor_mc._visible = false;
```

Now the frog snaps and the cursor disappears. We have to return the bug to the user. Anywhere after the frog has regurgitated, insert a new keyframe in the actions layer (in my file, I've used frame 250). Insert the following actions:

```
_root.cursor_mc._visible = true;
_root.cursor_mc._x = 0
_root.cursor_mc._y = 400.0
```

This sets the cursor to visible and back to its starting x and y position. It should be sent off the stage so that it appears to fly back to your mouse after being spat out. For the sake of tidiness, make sure your layers are all the same length, and finally, test your movie—you have a fully animated frog comfortably sitting on a lily pad ready to eat.

Summary

This tutorial was very detailed, but we've created graphics that give you a lot of elements for other projects because they're customizable. All the colors are on different layers, so you can change the colors and create variations of our lily pad to populate the whole pond. You can animate other parts of the frog's body without restructuring large parts of the graphic because each body part is already a separate element.

With gradient light or fog effects, you can quickly and easily add different atmospheric touches. You can even add more interactive stages. Have the frog periodically eye the cursor and have his gaze follow it around the screen. Try adding interactive sound. Set up more button hotspots that trigger a set of random animations instead of predefined ones. You could animate all the elements so that the lily and lily pad calmly and slowly float around in the water. To enhance the atmosphere, add the darkened silhouettes of fish swimming. Or, if you hate frogs, turn the frog into a dragon.

Flash is a powerful animation and art tool offering an infinite range of possibilities for creating reusable and fully customizable graphics. I took advantage of it to capture the viewer in the middle of a completely random and unexpected moment. Artists today don't have to be bound to physical media—technology has progressed to become an equally, or even more powerful, source of expression.

08

GRAPHICS DIRECTLY MANIPULATED BY CODE BRING
THE ETHEREAL TO LIFE. HEAVENLY APPARITIONS OF
COMPUTATIONAL STRUCTURES ADORN MY WALLS
AND INVADE MY DREAMS.

JARED TARBELL
WWW.COMPLEXIFICATION.NET

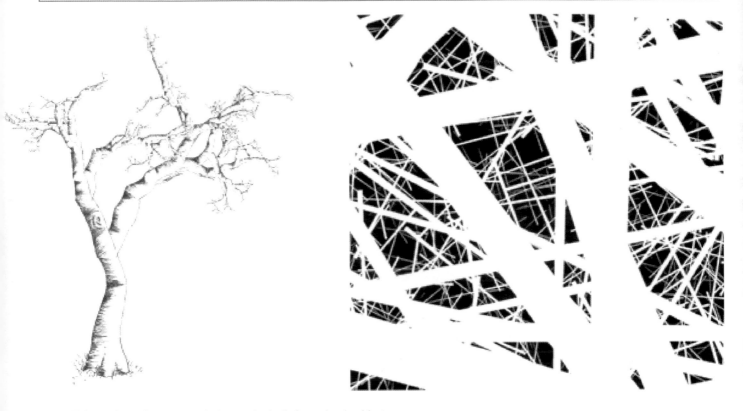

Beautiful creations of great complexity can be built from simple objects.

Inspirations, aesthetic influences, and artistic imperatives

Inspiration and discovery of the bizarre

Before you lies a computational world of never-ending possibilities. Within the pages of this chapter, I will take you on an adventure in a strange land of exponential proportions. The projects presented here have been crafted from a love of the beauty found in complexity. There is much yet to be discovered.

While I would like to say that programming the computer was love at first sight, the love, in fact, was developed over the course of many years. With enough afternoons spent staring into the depths of my Commodore 64, I found that I could manipulate large blocks of color on the screen by arranging commands within a simple text file.

I was amazed at this process, something I eventually came to relate as "creating something from nothing."

As the realm of what was possible increased with the sophistication of computer design, I found it more and more difficult to stay away. In all my experiences with the computer, graphic output intrigues me most. Whether the graphics are on the screen or outputted in some physical form, the visual representation of what is going on inside the machine is absolutely my favorite part of the process.

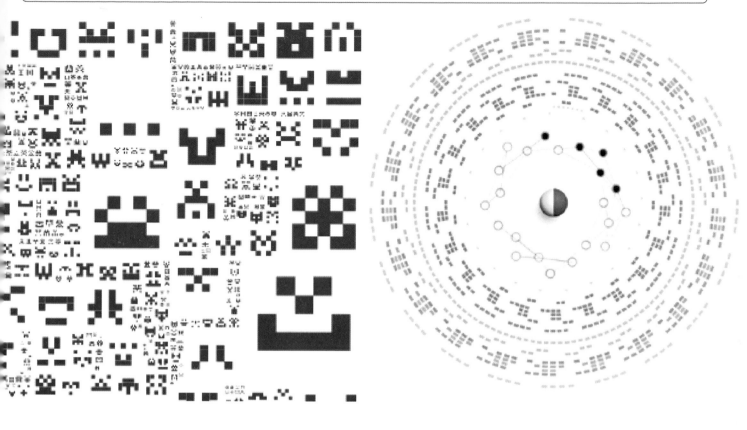

Driving philosophy

I am interested in the exploration of computational systems. The more bizarre and unexpected the output of a program, the higher it sits in my worldview. This attraction can be traced easily to my idiosyncratic social behavior. I love surprises. Complex systems are surprising.

Complexity theory is a central topic in computer science. It primarily deals with the measurable complexities of a computer program within its computational environment. It asks the question "How difficult is this problem to solve?" More interestingly, topics arise within this theory that describe beautiful systems, both real and imaginary. These topics include emergence, self-organization, and chaos theory.

I have often thought of the space this theory describes as an ancient oak tree. This tree is enormous, a giant in any landscape, with thick branches extending several hundred feet from the ground, weighed down by the weight of their fruit. It is impossible for any individual to see the whole tree, even over the course of a lifetime. Fortunately for us, we are focusing on a very small limb of this enormous tree, perhaps no bigger than your thumbnail. Let's zoom in close to get a better look.

Of course, the most fun way to explore the workings of a computer program is through the visualization of its processes. We do this by assigning graphic representations to objects and values. Graphics directly manipulated by code bring the ethereal to life. Heavenly apparitions of computational structures adorn my walls and invade my dreams.

Design and code/code and design

The application of graphic output inevitably involves principles of design. This at first confused me. I neglected to give much thought to design, as I considered it to be a tertiary concern behind computational accuracy and well-formed code. Many programmers share this perspective.

Edward Tufte is one person who altered my perspective forever. I point to him in particular because it was in forcing myself to do some exercises with his ideas that Levitated.net was born.

His three beautiful books, *The Visual Display of Quantitative Information*, *Envisioning Information*, and *Visual Explanations*, detail countless techniques for improving the rate of information transfer between a visual record and its human observer. What is amazingly great about these books is that they illuminate and map several kingdoms in the world of design. Confusion melts away with simple, effective rules of design.

While I still believe design is a close third behind computational accuracy and well-formed code (it is the accuracy bit that is losing ground), I have a new sense of peace and well-being. There are three examples in particular that I should mention because you will encounter them here, within the projects of this chapter.

One example is shown in the following figure. A man is levitated by his female counterpart against a cosmic background map of the solar system. The spacecraft carrying this message, *Pioneer*, is shown at the bottom of the image, passing between Jupiter and Saturn on its way to deepest space. This image is a redesign of the classic Pioneer 10 and 11 plaque originally created by Carl Sagan. It is both amusing and enlightening of what men and women are actually doing with themselves here on spaceship Earth.

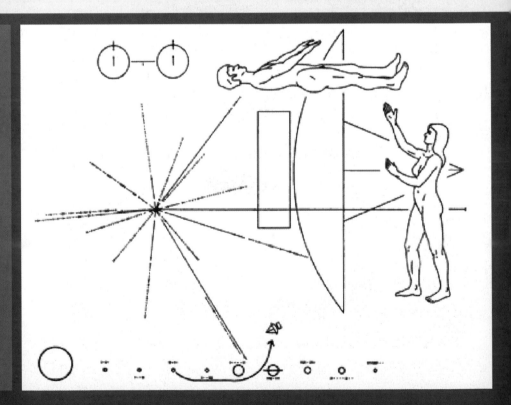

Reprinted by permission,
Edward R. Tufte, Visual Explanations,
Graphics Press 1997.

A technique especially well suited to displaying the output of computer programs (especially random ones) is something Tufte calls **small multiples**. When dealing with several instances of the same kind of object, it is sometimes best to arrange them within close visual proximity of each other. This allows the viewer to observe the objects themselves while also making comparisons. The small multiples technique has been applied to all four projects in this chapter.

Shown here are some hand-drawn renderings by Ernst Heinrich Haeckel (1834–1919). I strongly recommend a visit to Kurt Stüber's impressive online library at www.BioLib.de, which presents a fine collection of biology-related imagery by Haeckel and other important scientists and artists.

Another technique of Tufte's is **data-ink maximization**, the deliberate erasing of all unnecessary elements in a design. The goal is to represent the greatest amount of information with the smallest amount of ink. Of course, in our case, ink equals pixels. We all know that the more pixels we ask the computer to use, the harder it has to work. Therefore, using data-pixel maximization speeds up programs. Fast programs give us a greater amount of creative freedom. I will often reach a point in a program where I have assembled the essential minimum required to show the structure in memory.

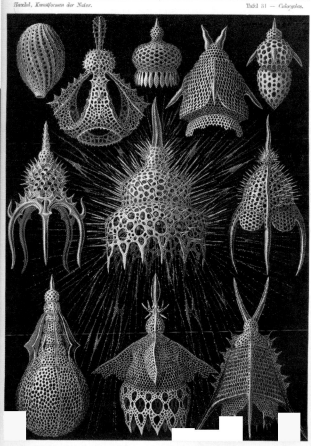

Cyrtoidea. — Flaschenstrahlinge.

Prosobranchia. — Vorderkiemen-Schnecken.

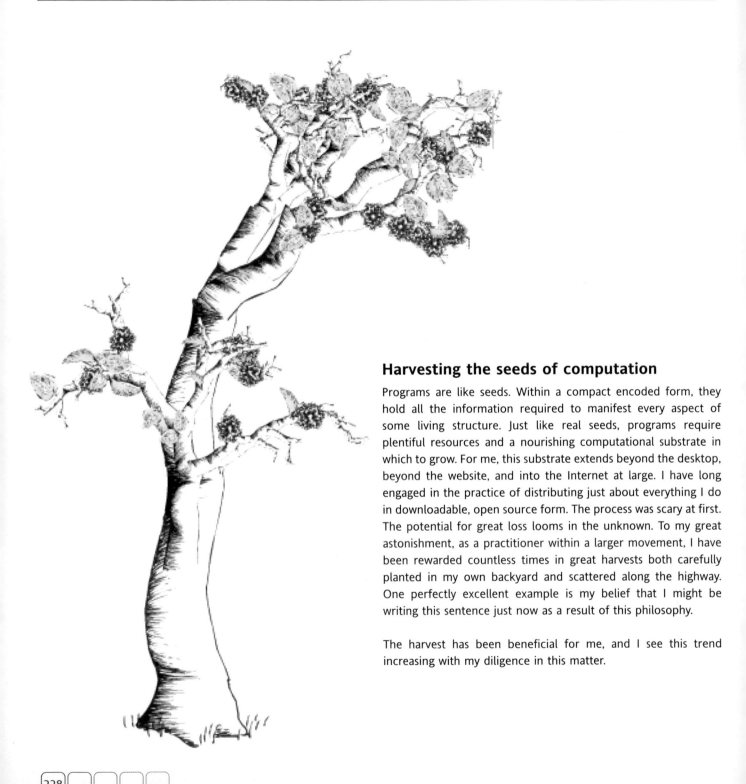

Harvesting the seeds of computation

Programs are like seeds. Within a compact encoded form, they hold all the information required to manifest every aspect of some living structure. Just like real seeds, programs require plentiful resources and a nourishing computational substrate in which to grow. For me, this substrate extends beyond the desktop, beyond the website, and into the Internet at large. I have long engaged in the practice of distributing just about everything I do in downloadable, open source form. The process was scary at first. The potential for great loss looms in the unknown. To my great astonishment, as a practitioner within a larger movement, I have been rewarded countless times in great harvests both carefully planted in my own backyard and scattered along the highway. One perfectly excellent example is my belief that I might be writing this sentence just now as a result of this philosophy.

The harvest has been beneficial for me, and I see this trend increasing with my diligence in this matter.

Why Flash?

I often am asked why I use Flash. The primary reason is the enormous audience capable of seeing the work. With Flash, I am not limited to showing my work to other geeks with computers just like mine. This new audience is simply huge in size and diversity. So for this funny reason, I get a warm nervous feeling inside when publishing something in Flash, like I am stepping out onto the stage of a theater.

There are many other reasons for using Flash, of course. You know of these yourself, or you would not be reading this book. One reason that applies especially to this chapter is the ease and speed with which rich, complex graphics projects can be built from scratch. It really is great being able to bring ideas into being with just a day's work.

So enough about me! Let's start building.

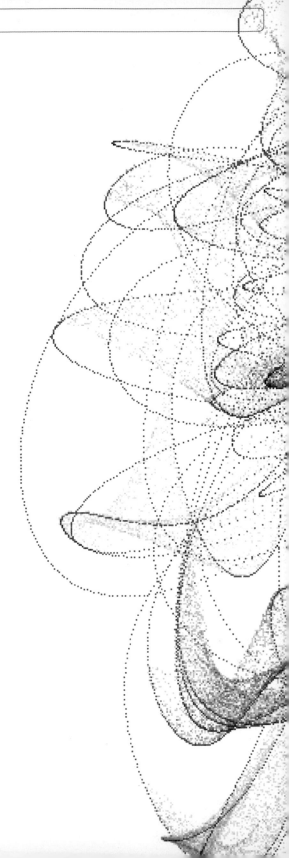

Tutorial deconstruction

In this chapter, I would like to introduce and deconstruct four different Flash projects, each a technique taken from topics in complexity. When I say "complexity," I am not talking about the code. I am talking about the results of the code's execution.

The four projects explored in this chapter rise within topics of recursion, chaos, combination, and emergence. Together we will examine each object of every project, how it works, how it fits into the whole, and what might be done differently to arrive at different results. This final topic is covered in much more detail at the conclusion of the chapter and in project files on the CD included with this book.

A note about the code

All the following projects use a style of ActionScript that relies heavily on the `prototype` property, with occasional frame action extensions where necessary. While not entirely pure, this technique of working allows you to take advantage of the unique properties of Flash while also providing a robust platform for more familiar object-oriented requirements.

If you are working within any version of Flash greater than 6 (Flash MX), you must set your publishing properties to **Flash Player 6** using **ActionScript 1.0**.

I like to present all the code for an object all at once. This is similar to the way the code exists within the movie clip: all in the first frame of the first layer. Code is reasonably commented, although more complete descriptions follow.

Presenting the code uninterrupted allows you to view it as a complete work, in the style and spirit of object-oriented programming (OOP). Another reason for following the complete code with a more verbose description is that the logical necessity for coded elements does not necessarily follow the order in which they appear in the program. If at any time you get lost or need confirmation, base FLAs are included on the CD that are identical to what is presented here.

An eternal root

A familiar problem encountered by Flash programmers is referencing the _root level of a movie in instances where the movie itself has been loaded into another movie. The fundamental problem is that there can only ever be one _root.

The solution to this problem is quite elegant. Taken from examples by Colin Moock, this code is the first line of the movie:

```
Object.environment = this;
```

This statement gives the _root of the movie a name that is recognized everywhere within the Flash player. Now, anywhere in your movie that you need to reference the _root, you use `Object.environment` instead. Of course, the object does not need to be named `environment`. It can be named just about anything. I use the word "environment" because it aptly describes what the _root is to my objects. You will notice it used in many Flash projects.

A quick guide to the prototyped Flash object

There are two good reasons to use the prototype method in Flash MX. First, it gives the programmer a consistent framework in which to lay down code. Second, prototypes are fast and extendable.

I should note that the prototype method has been deprecated in favor of ActionScript 2.0. Ideally, prototyped objects will convert nicely into ActionScript 2.0. Let's leave it as an exercise for the author. . . .

No doubt you are by now familiar with the many ways behavior can be programmed into Flash. Using the prototype to define functionality within a movie clip can speed execution considerably. It is especially advantageous when dealing with several hundred (or thousand) instances of the same movie clip, as is the case for most projects in this chapter.

You need not understand how the prototype works to use it. Believe me, I know. My basic approach to creating a new prototyped Flash MX object is described next.

Create a new movie clip that is also exported with a linkage identifier. Note that in the following screenshot I am using a linkage identifier of `linkID`. This is the bond between the movie clip asset in the Library and the code that will affect the movie clip.

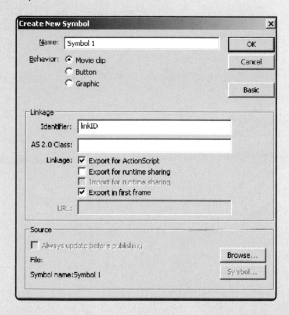

Paste in skeleton code of the prototype in the first frame of the first layer of the movie clip being prototyped (you might name this layer prototype or logic). It looks like this:

```
#initclip
// Constructor
function ClassName() {
}

// Allow component to inherit MovieClip
// properties
ClassName.prototype = new MovieClip();

// Instance methods
ClassName.prototype.doSomething = function() {
  // do something wicked

};
```

```
// Connect the class with the linkage ID for
// this movie clip
Object.registerClass("linkID",
ClassName);
#endinitclip
```

`#initclip` and `#endinitclip` are directives that instruct Flash to read these lines of code first. This is important so that the objects might be fully defined before being instantiated.

The first function, with the name of the class itself, is the constructor. The constructor function is important because it is executed immediately after the object is instantiated. Any code in the constructor function will be executed immediately after an instance of this object is created. It is here that variables are defined, events are set, and general setup of the object occurs.

The inheritance statement is crucial to giving the class life. If you allow your class to inherit all the properties and methods of a movie clip, you have almost unlimited control over it. This is required.

The instance methods are where the beef is. It is here that you define custom methods for the object. All logic interfacing with this object should be done through the methods contained here.

The format is simple. You begin the function with the class name, the keyword `prototype`, and then the name of the function (this is of your choosing). Finally, you insert an equal sign (=), followed by the keyword `function` with optional parameters listed between the parentheses.

For all references to the object itself, within the code, you use the keyword `this`, for example:

```
this.radius = 10; or this.grow(101);
```

As a final step for the prototype, you must link the movie clip instance in the Library with this class definition. You do this with the `registerClass` method, using the linkage identifier and the class name as parameters.

The quick and dirty method I have come to rely on is as follows:

1. Paste the prototype skeleton.

2. Change `Class` to `YourClassName`.

3. Change the linkage identifier and class name in the `registerClass` method.

4. Set any number of instance properties in the constructor.

5. Write any number of custom methods.

6. Rinse and repeat.

RECURSION: Tree Gardens

The first deconstruction of this chapter is a garden arrangement of classic recursive structures. The structures are similar to trees and have been enhanced to make this representation clearer. Each structure is as unique as a snowflake. They are arranged in a grid so you may observe each individual specimen, possibly for collection or comparison.

Mind the depth

There is great complexity in the instantiation of the indefinite —such complexity that you must stop the growth process of the tree with brute force or suffer certain doom. Many times I have enjoyed describing the dire consequences of recursive constructs that spiral into the depths. For this text I will simply say, mind the depth.

Preparation

Before you do any work in Flash, it might be nice to start working on paper. You need to create some assets that will give your trees some artistic life. In this case, let's draw or otherwise render a small set of limb graphics to add additional detail to the final rendering. The mechanics of how this will actually work are described later.

If at any time you would like to check your work, you can follow along in the file `treeGardenBase.fla` on the CD. This file is a representation of what you will build if you follow these instructions precisely.

The Sticks movie clip

Find a blank piece of white paper and measure out several rectangles of equal dimension. You will be drawing one stick illustration in each rectangle. You want to make sure the ends of each limb line up and that they are all of a similar size. This is also known as the formalization of the system's limits. You can assume that each limb will fit into a specific area.

With a little help from my colleague Dr. Lola Brine, I have drawn a set of seven different limb graphics. The trick now is to get these hand-drawn illustrations into Flash in such a way that I can easily use them as resources. To do this, I import the graphic images into Flash in the following manner:

1. Scan the hand-drawn illustrations into a bitmap image (JPG, TIFF, etc.).

2. Import the bitmap into Flash (File ➤ Import).

3. Vectorize the bitmap using the Trace Bitmap function in the menu. Pay close attention to the balance of polygon complexity and detail. Ideally, you want something that looks great and also has as few vector nodes as possible. To reduce the complexity of a vectorized bitmap, select the group of output vectors after the process and select Modify ➤ Shape ➤ Optimize from the menu. Generally, each stick should have no more than 200 shapes. Choose the amount you feel is necessary, and click OK. Flash will analyze the vector group and reduce as many nodes as possible while still preserving the overall appearance. A report at the end of this process tells you how successful the optimization was.

4. Once the vectors have been optimized, organize each limb by grouping its shapes into a single object.

5. Convert all objects into a single movie clip named Sticks.

6. Edit the Sticks movie clip and place one limb object on each frame.

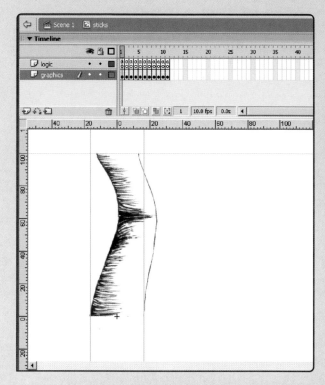

7. Align all limbs to a shared origin and scale. Orient the limb so that it points up, heavy end on the bottom. Scale the graphic so that it is approximately 100 pixels high (preserving the original aspect ratio). Position the limb so its bottom rests at the origin and is centered horizontally.

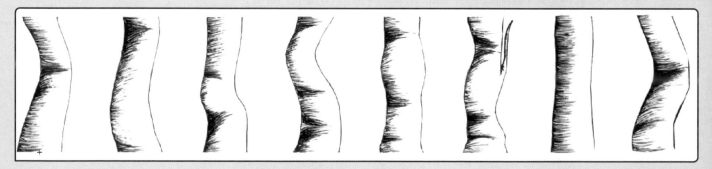

The Trunks movie clip

It might also be nice to have a set of trunks. Adding trunks to the trees will give the trees more of a grounded appearance.

If you would like to skip these steps and get right to the code, open the file lolaBrineTreeIllustrations.fla on the CD. Within this Flash movie are the two movie clips you are creating here, ready to be dragged and dropped within your project.

The trunks should be in the same style as the limbs, so you repeat the process for the trunk illustrations:

1. Repeat steps 1 through 4 from the previous (Sticks) section.

2. Convert all objects into a single movie clip named Trunks.

3. It's important that you export the Trunks movie clip with the linkage identifier of trunks. This is required so that you might dynamically attach the trunk to the limb when required.

4. Edit the movie clip and place one object on each frame.

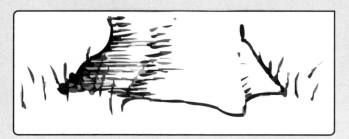

5. Align the objects to a shared origin and scale similarly to the sticks.

The Limb movie clip

Next, you will create the single most important element of the Tree Garden system: the Limb movie clip. The limb is the object that will be duplicated, scaled, and arranged hundreds of times to create the tree.

The limb is a recursive object. That is, the limb's special property is that it attaches copies of itself to itself. This is a strange thing to do, especially since the limb copies repeat the process, and on it goes.

What allows one simple object to create complex treelike forms is a continuous reduction of size and variation of rotation. Another important property is the ability to attach more than one new limb. Each time two or more limbs are attached, a fork is born, and the complexity of the tree increases dramatically.

1. Create a new movie clip. Name this movie clip Limb and export it for ActionScript with the linkage identifier limb. Be sure to export the movie clip or you will have no way to access it later when you are trying to build your trees.

2. Edit the Limb movie clip.

3. Rename the first layer as logic and create a second layer underneath it named stick. The logic layer is where all movie clip code will be placed. This is a coding convention I use throughout most of my work. While Flash allows you to place code just about anywhere, I have found this the more reliable and consistent place to keep it.

4. Drag an instance of the Sticks movie clip created earlier onto the stick layer. Place this instance on the stage at 0,0. Select the instance and give it an instance identifier of stick. This step is important; otherwise, you will not be able to reference the stick from within ActionScript. Not giving the instance a name is similar to saying "Hey, you!" to a roomful of people—no one will likely respond.

5. Type the following code into the first frame of the layer logic:

```
#initclip
// constructor
function LimbClass() {
  // place trunk graphic if required
  if (this.drawtrunk) {
   this.attachMovie("trunks","mytrunk",0);
   this.mytrunk.gotoAndStop(random(5)+1);
   this.mytrunk._xscale=this.core;
   this.mytrunk._yscale=this.core;
  }
  // scale the stick to the correct core
  // size
  this.stick._yscale = this.core;
  this.stick._xscale = this.core;
  // show some random stick graphic
  this.stick.gotoAndStop(random(9)+1);
  // on rare occasions, display these stick
  // graphics
  if (random(100)>96)
➡ this.stick.gotoAndStop(10);
  if (random(100)>98)
➡ this.stick.gotoAndStop(11);
  // continue if not too complex
  if (this.core>5) {
     this.onEnterFrame = this.addLimbs;
  }
}

// allow component to inherit MovieClip
// properties
LimbClass.prototype = new MovieClip();
// instance methods

LimbClass.prototype.addLimbs = function() {
  // do something wicked
  var mydepth = 0;
  var maxr = 100;
```

```
// continue limb
var nombre = "lmb"+String(mydepth++);
var r = (Math.random()-Math.random())*
➡ (40+maxr-this.core);
var c = this.core*(random(20)+64)/100;
var lx = 0;
var ly = this.core*0.96;
// ready to attach
var init = {_x:lx, _y:-ly,
➡ _rotation:r, core:c, d:this.d+1};
this.attachMovie("limb", nombre,
➡ mydepth, init);

// add at least one child limb
var newlimbs = 1;
// add more limbs if core is thick

newlimbs+=random(Math.floor(this.core/20));

  for (var n=0; n<newlimbs; n++) {
   var nombre = "lb"+String(mydepth++);
   var r = (Math.random()-Math.random())
➡ *(maxr-this.core);
    var c = this.core*(Math.random()
➡ *40+38)/100;
    var init = {_x:lx, _y:-ly,
➡ _rotation:r, core:c, d:this.d+1};
    this.attachMovie("limb", nombre,
➡ mydepth, init);
  }
  delete this.onEnterFrame;
};
// Connect the class with the linkage ID for
this movie clip
Object.registerClass("limb", LimbClass);
#endinitclip
```

6. The first few lines of this code are a requirement of the prototyped object in Flash. If you are not familiar with the prototype style of ActionScript, please refer to the quick guide earlier in this chapter.

7. The constructor function of the limb does a number of things. First, it checks whether or not it needs to draw the trunk. Only the first limb of a tree needs to draw the trunk. This condition is stored in a Boolean variable named `drawtrunk`. If the trunk needs to be drawn, its movie clip asset, the `trunk`, is attached, set to a random illustration, and scaled to the limb's `core` size.

The `Sticks` movie clip is also scaled to the limb's `core` size. The `core` value comes from the movie clip that created the limb. You'll see where this happens within the `Limb` object itself and again at the level of the garden environment.

Using three consecutive statements, you randomly set the illustration graphic for the limb. You do this quite simply by placing a unique graphic on each frame and then randomly stopping on one of those frames. Note that some negative bias is given to frames 10 and 11. These frames contain unusual variations of the limb that should be seen less frequently.

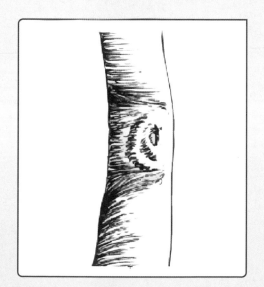

As a final step of the constructor, an important decision is made about whether or not to continue. This decision relies on the current size of the limb (stored as `core`). If it is too small (below 5), stop. Otherwise, call the one and only method, `addLimbs()`, and let the growth begin.

8. The method `addLimbs()` is used to do all the important work of the structure growth. In a nutshell, it continues the growth by attaching at least one limb, and then it randomly selects a number of additional limbs to attach. Each attached limb is given slightly different properties to produce the irregular appearance.

For the first new attachment, a name stored in variable `nombre` is constructed using the string `lmb` and then a number as determined by `mydepth`. The variable can be used as a safe determination of level in which to place attachments because it is incremented each time a new instance is being named. In this fashion, your limb names will be `lmb`, `lmb1`, `lmb2`, `lmb3`, and so on.

Variable `r` is the new rotation. The rotation can swing in either direction, positive or negative, with a magnitude inversely relational to the `core`. That is, the thicker the limb, the smaller its rotation will be. (This is a wildly fun relation to play with. Changing the magnitude, variability, or relationship to the `core` can produce some astonishingly different forms.)

Variable `c` is the new core. The `core` of new limbs is always smaller than the `core` of the limb they are attached to. Otherwise, you would have very strange-looking trees indeed. In this implementation, the new `core` will be somewhere between 64% and 84% of the original `core`.

Variables `lx` and `ly` store coordinates where the new limb will be attached. You want this first limb to be at the end of the current one, so you use the `core` to determine where this actually is. Note that you place your new limbs at 96% of the `core` value. Making the new limb just a little bit shorter like this eliminates gaps (that will still sometimes occur).

Now that you have calculated all the variables required to create a new limb, you prepare an initialization object with all the variables plugged into the right place. This initialization object is called `init`, and it is passed to the `attachMovie` method as a parameter. The advantage of the initialization object is that the values are available for the object's use immediately (within the constructor function).

Attaching the new limb is now a one-step operation. You attach the `limb` movie clip asset, with the name stored in `nombre`, at the level of `mydepth`, with the attributes contained in `init`.

Next, you calculate some number of additional limbs to attach. You want at least one, so you immediately set `numlimbs` to 1. Then perhaps you would like more. More specifically, the thicker the limb is (the larger the `core` value), the higher the chance for additional limbs. This desire is enumerated using a random function with some fraction of the `core` as the range. It is important not to get too carried away here. Every time you add a new limb to the system, the complexity increases significantly.

With `numlimbs` calculated, you begin a loop to attach new limbs. This method of attaching new limbs in the loop is similar to that of the first limb, with a few differences.

The final step of the `addLimbs()` method is unusual, but required. Deleting `this.onEnterFrame` stops the movie clip from executing the `addLimbs` function again on the next tick of the frame clock. If this statement were not here, it would be disastrous. Why is it here, then? Why don't you just call the `addLimbs` function from within the constructor? Quite simply, the one-frame delay allows Flash to keep up with the recursion while also providing a nice animation for the human observer to watch.

The code of the `Limb` movie clip concludes with the required steps for a prototyped object in Flash. It is always a good idea to check the parameter supplied to the `registerClass` method with the linkage identifier assigned to the exported movie clip. If they don't match up, none of this code will work and no error will be given to you.

The environment

You are now ready to start growing trees. To do this, you only have to instantiate a couple limbs in locations of your choosing and watch them work their magic.

A nice way to do this is with a simple grid. You will use two loops to iterate through positions in a grid, placing a limb in each one. You stop when all positions of the grid have been filled. Arranging your tree specimens this way is ideal for studying the similarities and differences of the system.

1. In the main timeline, rename the first layer as logic.

2. In the first frame of layer logic, type the following code:

```
Object.environment = this;
var dim = 1000;
var num = 3;
var g = dim/num;
var depth=0;

for (var py=0;py<num;py++) {
  for (var px=0;px<num;px++) {
    var nombre="limb"+String(depth++);
    var lx = g*px+g/2;
    var ly = g*py+9*g/10;
    var s = 150;
    var init = {_x:lx,_y:ly,core:
    ➥ 42+px+py*2,_xscale:s,_yscale:
    ➥ s,drawtrunk:true,d:0};
    this.attachMovie("limb",nombre,depth,
    ➥ init);
  }
}
stop();
```

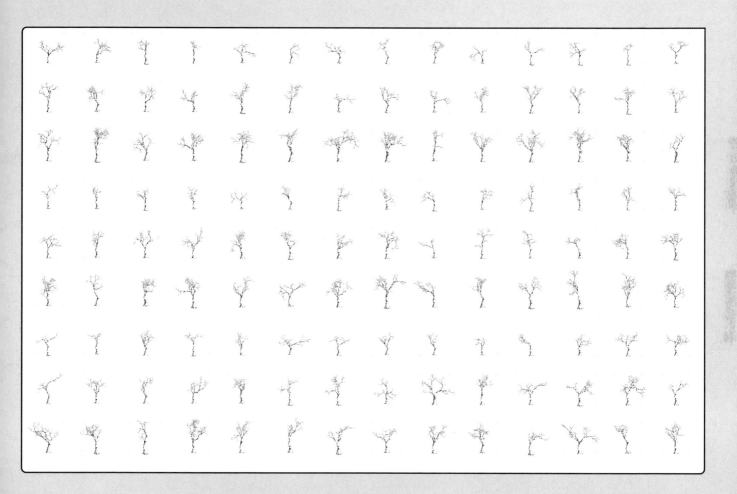

3. The first statement gives the `_root` of your movie the name `Object.environment`. This simple trick allows you to refer to the `_root` of your movie from any location in any object by using the keywords. The single greatest advantage of this technique is portability. Suppose, for example, that later you decide to bring the Tree Garden into a larger Flash project. The new project works well with the garden because it is completely self-contained, making no references to the `_root`, which is now at a higher level than the garden.

4. The next few statements set up properties of the garden as a whole. The variable `dim` sets the dimensions of the stage (considered a square) in pixels. The variable `num` describes the number of rows and columns (thus the total number of trees is num^2). The variable `g` is a calculation of the spacing between trees (each tree gets an equal amount of space within the dimensions). The variable `depth` is an integer that keeps track of the current level at which movie clips are placed.

5. Two nested loops are used to create the grid of starting limbs. Both loops run a number of times, as specified by `num`.

6. Each time through, the loop does the following things. First, the new limb is given a name. The name is constructed with the keyword `motherlmb` and the integer `depth`. So the names of the limbs are `motherlimb`, `motherlimb1`, `motherlimb2`, and so on. Next, the position, scale, and other important attributes are assigned within an initialization object. Note that the x- and y-coordinates of the new limb are directly determined by the count through the loops and the amount of space available. These relational functions are nice in that you can quickly change the number or dimensions of the scene and still have perfectly arranged trees. Note also that the `drawtrunk` variable is set to `true`. This is because you want the first limb place to be the trunk of the tree. The final `attachMovie` statement combines all your variable preparation and creates the new limb. From this point on, the limb is free to begin growing, which, if all is well, it most readily does.

Manifestation

You are now ready to test your new system. This is always an exciting time for me. The reason is simple: this kind of computer work is dangerous. The entire development environment can explode. The trees can come out all funny, like some kind of genetic experiment gone wrong. Sometimes catastrophic events can occur that will send the whole operating system into peril. For these reasons, you should save now and save often.

Ancient one

You may want to generate a single, massively complex tree instead of a group of less detailed ones.

You need change only three values to do this properly. First, in the first frame of the main timeline, change the value of `num` to 1. You want one row and one column, which gives you precisely one tree. Next, you want to increase the scale of the screen so that it more fully fills the screen. Both horizontal and vertical scale values are edited within the initialization object. Where `var s = 150`, change the number 150 to something larger, perhaps 420. You can also increase the detail of the tree limbs by lowering the minimum size of new limbs.

In the first frame of the `Limb` movie clip:

```
// continue if not too complex
if (this.core>5) {
   this.onEnterFrame = this.addLimbs;
}
```

change the number 5 to 4, 3, or 2. Setting this number lower than 2 may cause your recursion to run on forever.

You may need to run the program a few times before you get a tree that you like. The beauty here, of course, is that your system is sufficiently complex to guarantee a unique tree every time you run the program.

Limb staggering

You can also add to the variation and complexity of the structure by allowing the limbs to attach to the sides of other limbs, instead of just at the ends. I have done this and saved the results in the file `treeGardenStag.fla`.

Blossoms

A natural extension of this system might include the addition of leaves, flowers, or even fruit. I completed the first two of these ideas. The work is saved as `treeGardenBlossom.fla` on the CD.

Tweaks

Changing just a few of the constants in this project can reveal some wildly different results.

CHAOS: Trema Field

The Trema Field is the most straightforward of this chapter's projects. It is a complex graphic construction built from the exhaustive repetition of a simple random step. More elaborate variations of this particular technique have been used in the scientific community to study the distribution of galaxies in the universe and the surface of planets cratered by meteor impacts. Revealed in the output is something greater than the sum of its parts.

You will use the technique just described to create a beautiful portrait of randomness.

The Trema movie clip

"Trema" is a word invented by Benoit Mandelbrot to describe removed elements. I am using the word to describe the primary graphic object of this system (although you will actually be adding, the graphic appearance allows you to consider it a removal).

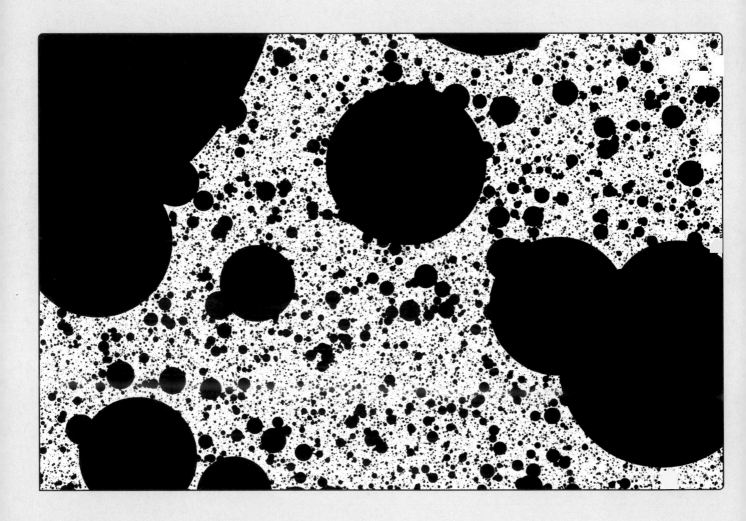

1. Create a new movie clip and call it `Trema`.

2. Export the `Trema` movie clip with a linkage identifier of `trema`.

3. Edit the movie clip and name the first layer graphic.

4. Draw a circle with a diameter of 100 pixels on the first frame of the graphic layer. Fill the shape with black. Delete the outline. Center the circle on the stage.

For this example, I have used a black circle with no outline. Some other shapes to consider are a square, a triangle, a line, or even something irregular like a string. You may eventually create thousands of instances of the shape, so it is important that the shape is not too complex.

Let's create a field as a simple placeholder for all your `Trema` object instances to be attached to. The field is totally empty and contains no code. You want to create it for two reasons. First, it would be nice to have a container to move, resize, rotate, or remove all the `Tremas`, all at once. Second, you can mask it. So go ahead and create a new movie clip (CTRL+F8) and name it `field`.

The environment

Now that you have created the `Trema` and `field` objects, you are ready to write some code that will generate your Trema Field. Here you go:

1. In the main timeline, rename the first layer as logic.

2. Create a new layer below logic and name it frame.

3. Create another layer below frame and name it box mask.

4. On the layer box mask, draw a simple rectangle about 300 pixels wide and 200 pixels high. Delete the outline and center the box within the stage of the movie.

5. Now set the layer box mask to be a mask by double-clicking the layer icon and selecting Mask. The mask is now in place, so it is OK to hide this particular layer.

6. Create yet one more layer below box mask and name it field.

7. Drag the field layer underneath the box mask layer so that it will indeed be masked by the box.

8. Drag an instance of the `field` movie clip onto the field layer. Center it within the stage. Give it an instance name of `field`. This is kind of an old-fashioned way of doing things in Flash, but it is nevertheless very effective.

9. In the first frame of the layer logic, type the following code:

```
this.dim = 10000;
this.dimlg = Math.log(this.dim);

this.onEnterFrame = function() {
    // random tier scale
    var s = 1+5*(this.dimlg -
    ➥ Math.log(1+random(dim)));

    for (var k=0;k<6;k++) {
    // name and attach new trema
    var nombre = "trm"+String(depth++);
    var neo = field.attachMovie("trema",
    ➥ nombre, depth);
    neo._x = random(400)-200;
    neo._y = random(300)-150;
    // neo._rotation = random(360);
    neo._xscale = s;
    neo._yscale = s;

    // show complexity count
    txtCount.text = "tremas: "+depth;
    }
};
stop();
```

Next, you define the `onEnterFrame` event (a method that is called repeatedly) to name, attach, and randomly position the new `Trema` object. In the previous project (the Tree Garden), you used an initialization object to define the properties of newly attached movie clips. Here, I present an alternate method, which is just as effective as, and in some cases superior to, the previous method. Instead of setting up all the properties before the attach event, you grab a handle to the new movie clip (stored as `neo`) and with it make direct changes to the new instance's attributes. In this case, position, and later on, scale.

The scale of your new trema is determined in an interesting way. Very large tremas will have the unfortunate effect of covering up smaller tremas. Worse, if too many large tremas are attached, your field will turn solid black and the observer might be left wondering what the point is. To disproportionately ensure you have more small tremas than large, you use an inverse logarithmic scale.

Logarithmic scales are especially well suited for this type of work because the levels of detail imposed by `Math.log` closely resemble the way the human eye perceives light, pattern, and complexity.

It should be noted that the observer might still be left wondering what the point is.

At this point, you could test this movie and get good results. But something is missing! There is no stop condition. If you were to run this movie (and some of you might have already done this), it would continue indefinitely, or at least until all available memory was consumed and the computer ground to a halt. What you need here is some kind of condition or event that will stop the generation of new `Trema` movie clips. Since each one of us has a different view on how this thing is supposed to look, let's make the stop condition user-determined using the mouse.

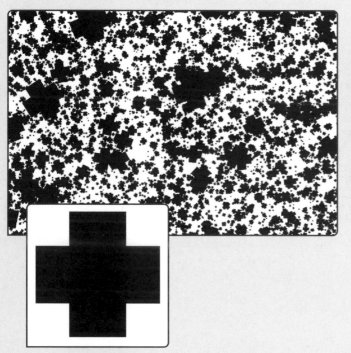

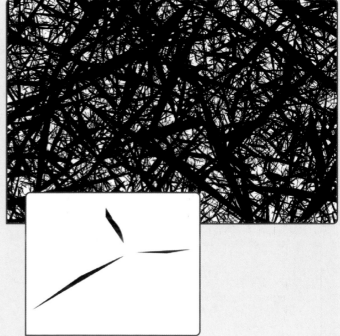

10. Add the following code to the first frame of the main timeline:

```
this.onMouseDown = function() {
  delete this.onEnterFrame;
};
```

This is a quick and clean way to stop the show. There is no consideration for those who would like to start up the system again. I will leave that as an exercise for the reader.

Manifestation

You are now ready to set your Trema Field in motion. You will make one final change to the movie. Set the frame rate of the movie to something high, like 60 fps. While you are not exactly sure what the eventual outcome will look like, you do know that it is going to take some time to get there, so you might as well do this as fast as Flash allows you.

Quick variations on this project involve drawing unique shapes for the `Trema` movie clip. The following are examples with approximately 10,000 tremas in each image:

Let the program run long enough (on a well-equipped machine), and the results are outstanding. At some point in the execution, the background object will transform into the foreground object. This technique is not much different from splattering paint on a canvas or dropping pennies into a wishing well. All these activities require only simple steps, repeated indefinitely, with random variations introduced into each. Everyone has a fantastic attraction to complete irregularity. The beauty is unquestionable.

COMBINATION: Invader Fractal

One of my very favorite disciplines of computer science is **combinatorics**, or the complete manifestation of all possible combinations in a discrete system. Here, we have small 15-bit combinatoric constructions affectionately called invaders.

There are only three objects in the system, the **invader** (a combinatoric self-assembler), the **spaceship** (a recursive space-filling container), and the **environment** (an oversight system that tracks and manages recursive calls). Let's first concentrate on the invader.

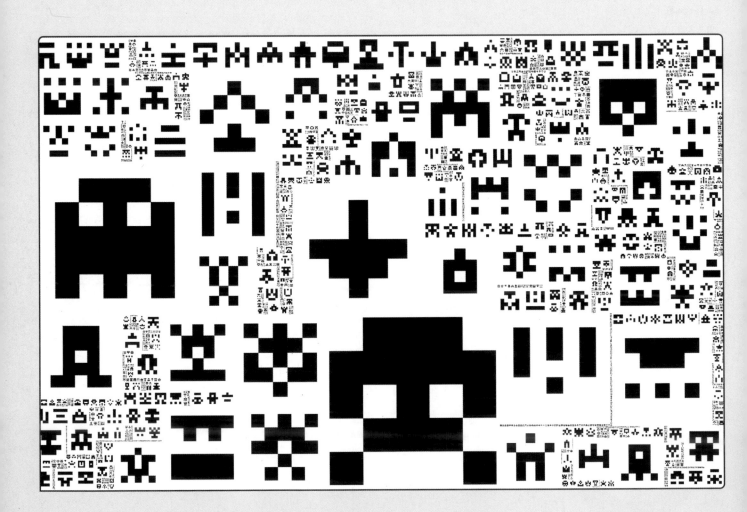

The Invader movie clip

Suppose you have two objects, a white square and a black square. The invader then is a collection of 25 of these squares, arranged in a 5x5 grid. Some squares are black; others are white.

Internally, the invader is represented with only a 3x5 grid of blocks. The full 5x5 grid of blocks is rendered using a mirroring technique. The left two columns are a mirror image of the right two columns. The center column is unique. This technique imposes a nice vertical symmetry in the invader. It also conserves memory and provides an easy method of rendering the invader as a whole.

As humans, we are compelled to examine vertical symmetry.

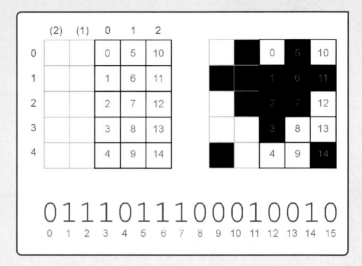

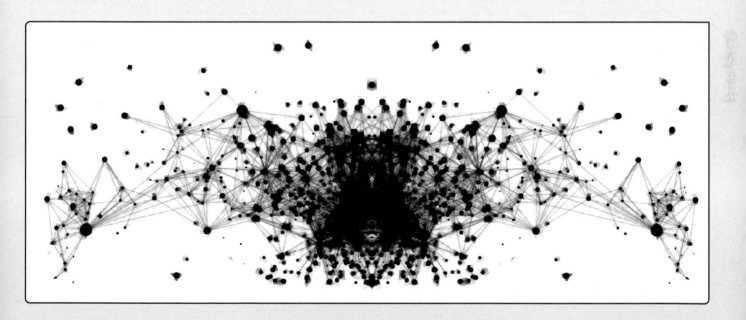

You can prove it to yourself by casually glancing into the preceding image. Your eyes will immediately move to the center. Quickly, they will then start finding and losing meaningful patterns. The process is almost involuntary. The image is a randomly generated network. The little invaders will have a similar effect on observers, multiplied by several thousand.

To begin, you need to create a new, 500x500-pixel Flash MX movie. Set the frame rate at a comfortable 22 fps. Also set the publishing version to Flash 6 and ActionScript 1.0 (if you are using MX 2004 or greater). You can follow these steps to build your own project, or follow along with invaderFractal.fla on the CD.

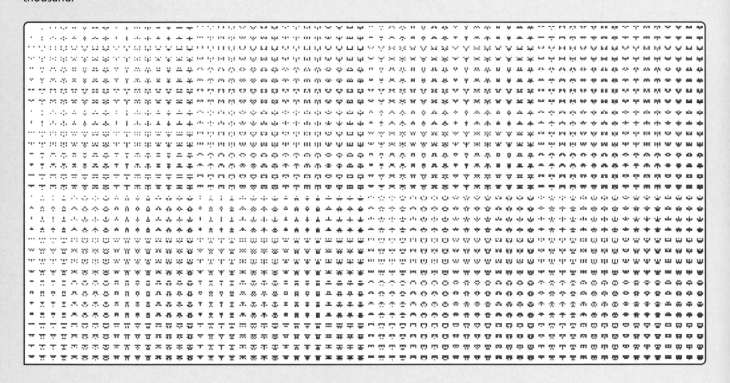

This image shows the iterative generation of the first 2,048 invaders (just 16% of the total number possible!). They are also sequentially listed, such that the top-right invader has a bit representation of 000000000000000 and the bottom-right invader has a bit representation of 000100000000000. Here, in their unshuffled arrangement, you see clearly the exhaustive process of lighting each possible combination of squares.

Let's build the Invader movie clip:

1. Create a new movie clip and name it Invader.

2. Export Invader with a linkage identifier of invader.

3. Name the first layer of the new movie clip logic.

4. Type the following code into the first frame of the logic layer:

```
#initclip 1
// constructor
function InvaderClass() {
  // wait to be built by spaceship container
this.build(random(32768));
}
// allow invader class to inherit MovieClip properties
InvaderClass.prototype = new MovieClip();
// instance methods
InvaderClass.prototype.build = function(s) {
  // build the graphical appearance of invader using squares
  this.seed = s;
  var seedbits = Math.dec2bin(s);
  for (var x = 0; x<3; x++) {
    for (var y = 0; y<5; y++) {
      var i = y*3+x;
      if (this.lit(seedbits, i)) {
        this.drawSquare(x*100, y*100);
       // mirror last two columns
       if (x>0) {
         this.drawSquare(-x*100, y*100);
       }
      }
    }
  }
};
InvaderClass.prototype.drawSquare = function(x, y) {
  // draw a 100x100 pixel square at x,y
  this.moveTo(x, y);
  this.lineStyle(0, 0x000000, 0);
  this.beginFill(0x000000, 100);
  this.lineTo(x+100, y);
  this.lineTo(x+100, y+100);
  this.lineTo(x, y+100);
  this.lineTo(x, y);
  this.endFill();
};
InvaderClass.prototype.lit = function(bits, i) {
  if (bits.substr(i, 1) == "1") {
    return true;
  } else {
    return false;
  }
};
// Connect the class with the linkage ID for this movie clip
Object.registerClass("invader", InvaderClass);
#endinitclip
```

The constructor function of the invader self-organizes its appearance with a call to the build method. The parameter passed to the build method is an integer between 0 and 32,768. This number will determine the unique graphical appearance of the invader.

There are only three methods for the Invader movie clip: one method to actually build the invader (build), another to draw a square (drawSquare), and another to determine if the square is white or black (lit).

The drawSquare method is the simplest of the three methods. When called, two values (x and y) are passed that instruct the function where to place the top-left corner of the square. Assumed to be black and with a 100x100-pixel dimension, the square is drawn using Flash's drawing API. Basically, you move to the starting point, draw left, draw down, draw right, and then draw back to the starting point. The whole thing is filled with black and given a transparent outline. You need not worry about size because this is taken care of by the space-folding, fractalicious Spaceship movie clip.

The lit function is a simple Boolean calculation that returns true or false. It is passed a string of bits (1010010111001) and an index number (a value between 0 and 15). The function then checks the bit character at the index, and returns true if the bit is a 1 and false if the bit is a 0.

The build function is passed a seed value (which can also be considered the invader's ID number). The seed is an integer between 0 and 32,767. The range that seed can be expected to be is determined by the number of bits you use to represent the invader, which in this case is 15, as you can see here:

```
3 x 5 = 15
215 =   32,768
```

For the easiest possible assembly of the invader, it would be nice to have the binary representation of the seed value stored as an easily searched string. The conversion of decimal numbers to binary strings is outside the scope of this chapter, but I have included a quick method to perform this conversion using an extension of the Math object at the root level (discussed in more detail in the section "The Environment movie clip").

After converting the number seed into the binary string seedbits, you use two loops to place squares where appropriate. The inside loop runs through rows (y), and the outside loop runs through columns (x). For each grid position, you draw a square if the bit is lit (using the lit method discussed earlier). When x is 1 or 2, you are working with a column of the invader that is mirrored, so you need to place squares on both sides to maintain vertical symmetry.

The registerClass method makes the connection between movie clip asset and class definition. The prototype is then closed using the #initclip directive. These are standard elements of working with the prototype object and must be included for the object to function properly.

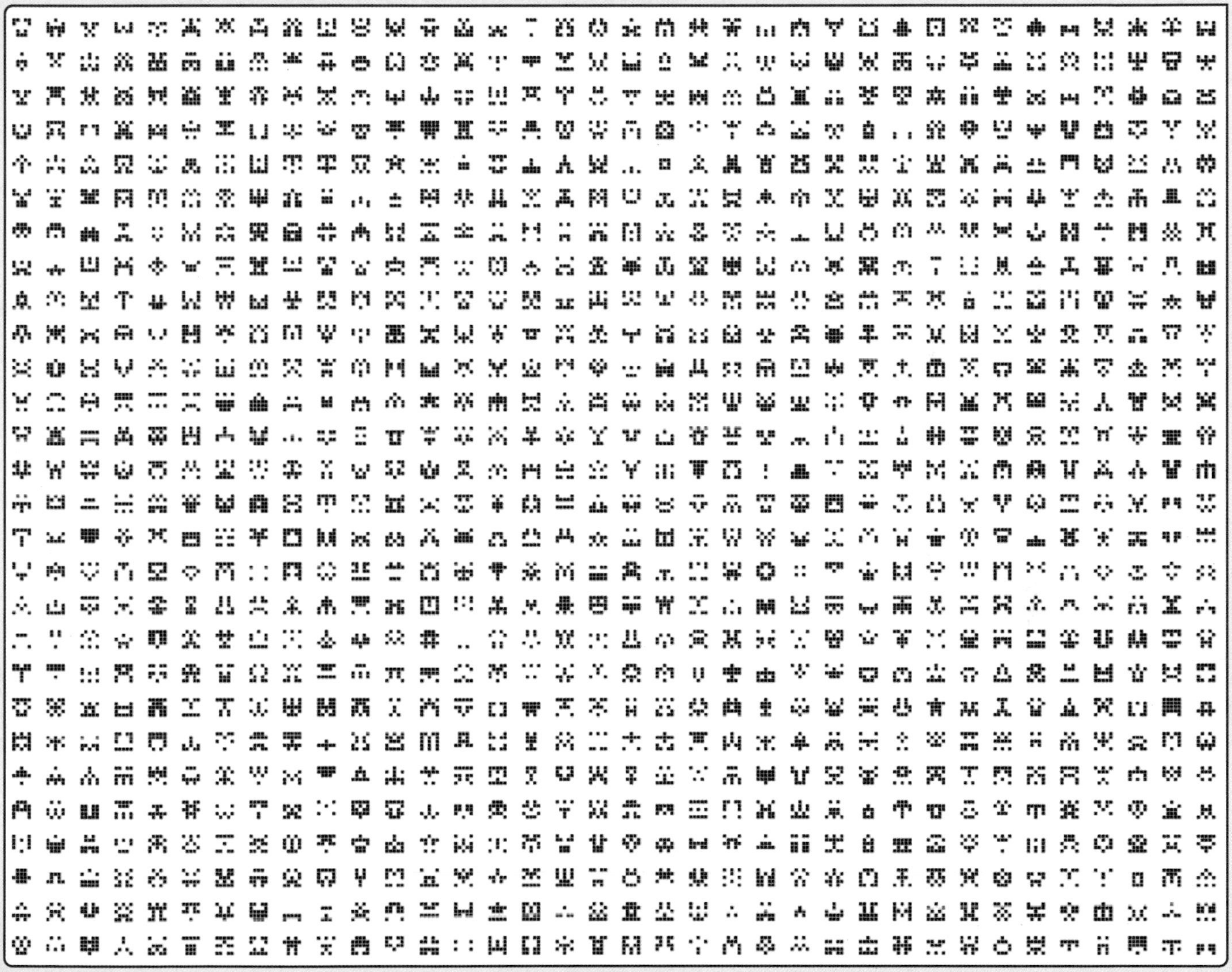

The Spaceship movie clip

The spaceship is a recursive, space-filling time machine the invader rides within. The spaceship itself is not required to see the invader. The spaceship simply gives you the unique fractal arrangement techniques that make the invaders seem so menacing.

Each spaceship contains exactly one invader. The movie clip works recursively, so that only a single instance needs to be created to get the "invasion" started. The spaceship is also dependent on the environment. For now, assume that certain functions in the environment exist, such as the ability to call down more spaceships once a proper landing spot has been found. These functions are described in detail in the next section, "The Environment movie clip."

Let's create the Spaceship movie clip:

1. Create a new movie clip and call it Spaceship.

2. Export the Spaceship movie clip with the linkage identifier of spaceship.

3. Rename the first layer as logic.

4. Create a new layer underneath logic and name it my invader.

5. Drag an instance of the Invader movie clip into the first frame of the my invader layer. Give this clip the new instance name myInv. Center it within the stage.

> A brief reminder here that the instance name is critical to the success of this movie clip. If the invader instance contained within has no name, it is not directly accessible. You can make no changes to it.

6. Type the following code in the first frame of the layer logic:

```
#initclip 2
// constructor
function SpaceshipClass() {
  // begin to fade in
  this._alpha=0;
  this.onEnterFrame = this.fadeIn;
}
// allow ParticleClass to inherit MovieClip properties
SpaceshipClass.prototype = new MovieClip();
// instance methods
SpaceshipClass.prototype.fadeIn = function() {
  if (this._alpha<100) {
    this._alpha+=10;
  } else {
    delete this.onEnterFrame;
  }
}
SpaceshipClass.prototype.getWidth = function() {
  // return actual width (width padding)
  var dynopad = 700 - 180 * (this.regionpad/850);
  return Number(dynopad*this._xscale/100);
};
```

```
SpaceshipClass.prototype.getHeight = function() {
  // return actual height (with padding)
  var dynopad = 700 - 180 * (this.regionpad/850);
  return Number(dynopad*this._yscale/100);
};
SpaceshipClass.prototype.fitInto = function(x0, y0, x1, y1, d) {
  // region width and height
  var rWidth = x1-x0;
  var rHeight = y1-y0;
  var rAspect = rHeight/rWidth;

  // dynamic padding (smaller objects get more padding)
  this.regionpad = rWidth;
  this.myInv._x=300 - 90 * (this.regionpad/850);
  this.myInv._y=100 - 90 * (this.regionpad/850);

  // spaceship width and height
  var wWidth = this.getWidth();
  var wHeight = this.getHeight();
  var wAspect = wHeight/wWidth;

  // determine what percentage of space to fill
  if ((rWidth<Object.environment.thresholdRegion) ||
    ➤ (rHeight<Object.environment.thresholdRegion)) {
    var percent = 100;
  } else {
    var percent = random(80)+20;
    // if this is the first spaceship
    if (d==0) {
      // force to occupy 61% of space
      var percent = 61;
    }  }

  // make sure we are not  exceeding the space provided
  var dWidth = rWidth * percent/100;
  var scale = dWidth/wWidth;
  this._xscale *= scale;
  this._yscale *= scale;

  if (this.getHeight()>rHeight) {
    // recalculate width to fit height
    scale=rHeight/this.getHeight();
    this._xscale*=scale;
    this._yscale*=scale;
  }
```

> **"THIS IS A BEHEMOTH OF RECURSIVE LOGIC!"**

Code continues overleaf

```
  var placeH=random(2);
  if (placeH==0) {
    // left side
    rx0 = x0+this.getWidth();
    rx1 = x1;
    this._x = x0;
    if (random(2)) {
      // place invader top left
      this._y = y0;
      // fill region to right
      Object.environment.fillRegionRequest(rx0, y0, rx1, y0+this.getHeight(), d);
      // fill region on bottom
      Object.environment.fillRegionRequest(x0, y0+this.getHeight(), x1, y1, d);
    } else {
      // place invader bottom left
      this._y = y1-this.getHeight();
      // fill region to right
      Object.environment.fillRegionRequest(rx0, y1-this.getHeight(), rx1, y1, d);
      // fill region on top
      Object.environment.fillRegionRequest(x0, y0, x1, y1-this.getHeight(), d);
    }
  } else {
    // right side
    rx0 = x0;
    rx1 = x1-this.getWidth();
    this._x = x1-this.getWidth();
    if (random(2)) {
      // place invader top right
      this._y = y0;
      // fill region to left
      Object.environment.fillRegionRequest(x0, y0, rx1, y0+this.getHeight(), d);
      // fill region on bottom
      Object.environment.fillRegionRequest(x0, y0+this.getHeight(), x1, y1, d);
    } else {
      // place invader bottom right
      this._y = y1-this.getHeight();
      // fill region to left
      Object.environment.fillRegionRequest(x0, y1-this.getHeight(), rx1, y1, d);
      // fill region on top
      Object.environment.fillRegionRequest(x0, y0, x1, y1-this.getHeight(), d);
    }
  }
};
// Connect the class with the linkage ID for this movie clip
Object.registerClass("spaceship", SpaceshipClass);
#endinitclip
```

Wow, this may seem pretty complicated. That is because for many reasons, it is. I will break down each method as much as I can, although many aspects of this code cannot be fully conveyed through discussion. Certain insights can be gained only by playing around with the code and closely examining it.

The constructor function sets the _alpha of the spaceship (including its invader contents) to 0. You want to the ship to make a dramatic appearance, not just pop in from nowhere. You do this with a simple function named fadeIn, which executes with the onEnterFrame method.

The fadeIn method checks the _alpha level of the movie clip. If the _alpha level is less than 100, this method increases it by 10. If the _alpha level is 100 (or greater), the movie clip has become completely opaque and you no longer need to fade in. To stop fading in, delete the onEnterFrame method.

The getWidth and getHeight methods are used to return more precise values of actual width and height. They also give you room to pad the invader by some dynamic amount (smaller invaders actually get more padding).

Next up, consider the fitInto method. This is a behemoth of recursive logic! Essentially what is happening here is that the spaceship is being instructed to "fit into" a rectangular space as defined by the top-left coordinates x0,y0 and the bottom-right coordinates x1,y1.

Except to make things interesting, the invader does not fit into the space entirely. It randomly chooses some percentage of the space and fits into that. This creates unused portions of the "fit into" region. To continue the invasion (fill process), the spaceship sends the coordinates of the unused spaces back to the environment.

The four orientations of an invader within its spaceship are as follows:

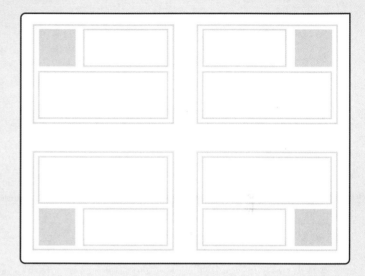

Special cases of how to behave when the spaces become smaller are checked before the invader is positioned and the remaining space is filled. Quite simply, if the space is small enough, go ahead and fill the whole thing. This produces a more intelligible arrangement overall and wastes less space. You should set this limit to hover around your own abilities of perception (why render something smaller than can be observed?).

7. The spaceship's code is concluded with a prototype class registration and #endinitclip directive.

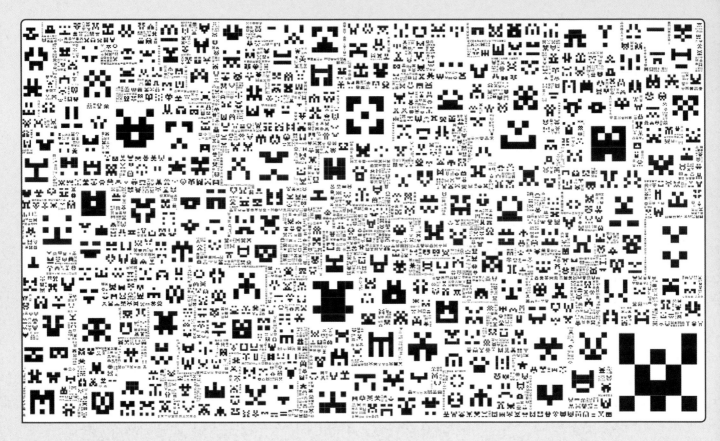

The Environment movie clip

Now you need to set up an environment in which to land and otherwise direct all your spaceships. (Is this metaphor getting old?)

1. Rename the first layer in the main timeline as functions.

2. Create a new layer below functions and name it logic.

3. Place a small text field somewhere on the stage, but out of the way, and give this text field an instance name of `txtInv`. You will use this text field to output the current status of your program—essentially, the totally number of invaders landed.

4. On the first frame of the layer functions, type the following:

```
// register root as environment
Object.environment = this;
function fillRegion(x0, y0, x1, y1, d) {
  // place the word object
  var nombre = "ship"+String(depth++);
  var neo = this.attachMovie("spaceship", nombre, depth);
  neo.fitInto(x0, y0, x1, y1, d);
}
function fillRegionRequest(x0, y0, x1, y1, d) {
  // request has been made to recursively fill a region
  var rW = x1-x0;
  var rH = y1-y0;
  // allow only if reasonable
  if ((rW>Object.environment.minRegion) && (rH>Object.environment.minRegion)) {
    addFillRequest(x0, y0, x1, y1, d+1);
  }
  txtInv.text = "total invaders: "+String(cnt++);
}
function addFillRequest(x0, y0, x1, y1, d) {
  // queue up a request to fill a region
  var freq = {x0:x0, y0:y0, x1:x1, y1:y1, d:d};
  fillRequests.push(freq);
}
// convert decimal number to binary string
Math.dec2bin = function(iNumber) {
  var bin = "";
  var oNumber = iNumber;
  while (iNumber>0) {
    if (iNumber%2) {
      bin = "1"+bin;
    } else {
      bin = "0"+bin;
    }
    iNumber = Math.floor(iNumber/2);
  }
  // left pad with zeros
  while (bin.length<15) {
    bin = "0"+bin;
  }
  return bin;
};
```

There are a number of interesting methods here. The style of this code's ActionScript is a departure from the prototype method. This is perhaps confusing, but the intention is to keep it simple. The prototype is not needed because there will only ever be one instance of the environment. Let's look at each function in the context of the spaceship.

First, of course, you register the root timeline as the environment. You may have noticed the `Object.environment` references in the spaceship created just a moment ago. Now you know that the references refer to `this`, the `_root` of the movie.

The `fillRegion` function is the engine of this system. Based on the coordinates of a rectangle (x0, y0, x1, y1) and a depth (d), it names, attaches, and commands a new spaceship instance. This function is called repeatedly for the duration that the movie runs or until all available space has been filled.

The `fillRegionRequest` function is a clever way to control the amount of recursion occurring in the system and display it in a constant, orderly fashion. The spaceship uses this function to request that regions of space be filled with additional spaceships. For a region to be filled, it must be big enough, and it must wait for its turn in the order it was received. If the region is too small (here the total pixel area is compared to a constant defined as `minRegion`), the request will be ignored. Otherwise, it is added to the end of the queue of requests (an array named `fillRequests`).

`addFillRequest` is a convenience function designed to add a coordinate object to the array of regions to be filled. It works by combining the function parameters into an object, which is pushed into the queue array.

At the end of the function list I have added a small extension of the `Math` object that converts a decimal number into a string binary. The necessity of this function was discussed in the section "The Invader movie clip."

5. On the first frame of the layer logic, type the following:

```
Object.environment.minRegion=25.0;
Object.environment.thresholdRegion=15.0
;

// array to hold all fill requests
fillRequests = new Array();

// fill the page with words!
fillRegion(0,0,500,500);

this.onEnterFrame = function() {
  // pull fill requests from queue and
  // execute
  if (fillRequests.length>0) {
    freq = fillRequests.pop();
    fillRegion(freq.x0, freq.y0,
    ➡ freq.x1, freq.y1, freq.d);
  }
}

// required because of extra-long comment
// layers
stop();
```

This is the gear that really makes the fractal machinery work. The first two lines are constants that define the detail and complexity of the system. `minRegion` is the smallest area in pixels that will be filled by an invader. `thesholdRegion` defines the amount of space an invader needs before deciding to occupy the entire thing. You can force invaders of a certain size to dominate the filled space by adjusting this value.

The single line of code that actually begins the process is the first call to the `fillRegion` method. Here, you are asking it to fill the extents of the movie with the upper-left coordinate of 0,0 and the bottom-right coordinate of 500,500. This one line begins the recursive fractal domino effect.

To nicely animate the fill process, you use the `onEnterFrame` event of the main timeline (`this`, `Object.environment`). Each time through, you check to see if fill requests exist in the queue, and if so, you send the request to the `fillRegion` method. Pretty simple, and amazingly fun!

So let's sum things up and discuss how these movie clips you just created fit together. You have the invader that uses black squares to represent itself in a symmetric fashion.

It is riding inside a spaceship, which uses an advanced, fractalicious space-drive technology to fit into any given space with room left over for yet more spaceships. All these spaceships are landing in the same environment. The environment enforces a kind of regularity in the invasion process, like time itself, ensuring that everything doesn't happen at once.

Manifestation

With patience and multiple renderings, it is possible to generate every single possible combination of bits. The overwhelming variety of individuality is unexpected. It is as if you have generated a gold mine of iconic forms.

Here are all 32,768 possible invaders.

EMERGENCE: Binary Network

I cannot describe the pure wonder found in the self-organizing orders of the binary network. The fundamental laws governing such systems can be understood in seconds, while the consequences of these laws may evade a lifetime.

What I am most concerned with describing within the scope of this project is the method through which I have visualized such a system. I will describe only briefly the principles of the binary network. You can find more information on the topic as applied to Flash in the book *Fresh Flash: New Design Ideas with Flash MX* (friends of ED, 2002).

Simple theory

A **binary network** is a collection of switches tied together in an ad-hoc network. Each switch can be in one of two states: off or on, charged or uncharged, 0 or 1. A giant systemwide clock determines when the nodes change state, and all nodes change state at precisely the same time.

The next state of the switch is determined by the states of the switches it is connected to. The simplest determining rule (and the one applied in this project) works like this:

> *If an **odd** number of connected switches is on, then the switch turns **on**. If an **even** number of connected switches is on, then the switch turns **off**.*

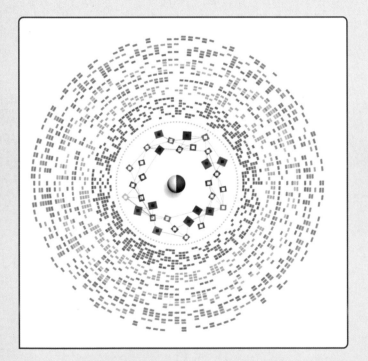

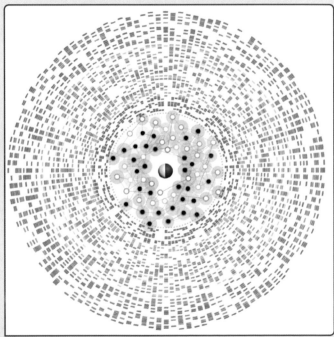

You might expect that a network created with these simple rules would behave in a predictable fashion, either chaotically or with boring, obvious patterns. But what in fact happens is something quite amazing.

The duality of computation

This project contains two major elements: a network (represented by the `Bnetwork` movie clip) and a network history visualization (represented by the `Bhistory` movie clip). Both movie clips use instances of other movie clip objects to realize their full function.

The Colorchip movie clip

By now you've probably realized that I like to build things from the inside out, starting with the simplest objects. The simplest object in the binary network is a small block of color—several small blocks of color, actually. I like introducing naturally selected color into my projects, as it helps a project escape the instant label of "computer art" because only mathematically simple color values have been used. To do this, I often use an external application to generate squares of nice color for import into Flash. For this project, you will need a dozen or so color squares for representation of unique binary switches.

To begin this project, create a new Flash movie or follow along with `binaryNetworkBase.fla` on the CD. Set the stage size to something sufficiently large, and set the frame rate to 30 fps.

Again, as with all the projects in this chapter, set the publish settings to Flash 6 and ActionScript 1.0.

1. Create a new movie clip named `Colorchip`. Give it a linkage identifier of `colorchip`.

2. Edit the `Colorchip` movie clip.

3. Import a selection of colored squares. Create a sufficient number of frames so that one square can be placed in each. All the squares should be the same size. In this example, the squares are 10x10 pixels, but your squares really can be any size (or any shape, for that matter). You will be sizing them with ActionScript. Just make sure they are not so big that overlapping becomes a problem.

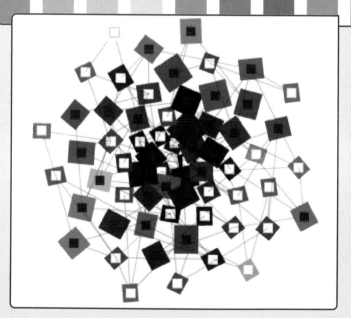

The `Colorchip` is going to be used as a unique identifier of different nodes. **Nodes**, which I will describe in detail later, are simple switching objects that connect to each other. Additionally, each node can hold a **charge**. The charge of a node is a value of "on" or "off" and is determined by the charges of the nodes it is connected to. Nodes are the substance of this network.

The Bfreq movie clip

You are going to use the `Bfreq` movie clip as an indication of the frequency with which each node has been charged. The `Bfreq` movie clip will be one part of the `Bnode` object you will build later on. Essentially, each time the node changes state, you want to show this visually with an increase in the size of the `Bfreq` instance. At the end of a network simulation, those nodes that were most active will have the largest `Bfreq` instances.

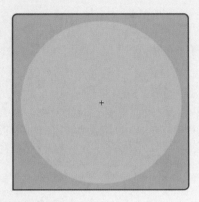

Visually, I thought it would be nice if `Bfreq` were round like the `Bnode` body, but also the same color as what will be recorded in the network history (which I discuss later). You can have both features if you do the following:

1. Create a new movie clip named `Bfreq`.

2. Edit `Bfreq`, and rename the first layer as `chips`.

3. Drag an instance of the `Colorchip` movie clip into the first frame of the `chips` layer.

4. Select the instance and give it an instance name of `chips`.

5. Create a new layer above the `chips` layer and name it `mask`.

6. Within the layer `mask`, draw a circle with a diameter just slightly smaller than the `Colorchip` instance. Convert this layer into a mask.

7. Drag the `chips` layer under the `mask` layer so that it is masked by the circle.

The Body movie clip

The `Body` movie clip is a simple on/off graphic that shows the charge state of the node. Its creation is simple:

1. Create a new movie clip named `Body`.

2. Edit the `Body` movie clip, and rename the first layer as `states`.

3. Draw a white circle on frame 1.

4. Add a `stop();` command to frame 1.

5. Draw a black circle on frame 2. Make sure both circles are the same size. You don't necessarily want your nodes to change sizes when they charge. I have drawn my node bodies about 15 pixels in diameter, centered about the origin.

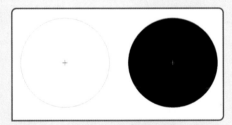

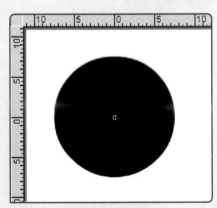

You may choose to create something more elaborate here. One of the variations of this project included on the CD contains a three-dimensional rendered cube that is capable of changing to both black and white.

The Bnode movie clip

The Bnode is the composite binary switch that keeps state and makes connections with other Bnodes. It is composed of the two elements you just created, Body and Bfreq, plus some pretty serious ActionScript to provide the behavior you would like to see.

1. Create a new movie clip named Bnode.

2. Export the Bnode movie clip with a linkage identifier of bnode.

3. Name the first layer logic.

4. Create a new layer underneath logic and name it Body.

5. Drag an instance of the Body movie clip to the layer Body. Center it on the stage. Give the new Body instance an instance name of body. You can do this by selecting the instance and typing the name into the Properties panel.

6. Create a new layer underneath Body and name it Bfreq.

7. Drag an instance of the Bfreq movie clip to the layer Bfreq. Center it on the stage. Give the new Bfreq instance an instance name of bfreq.

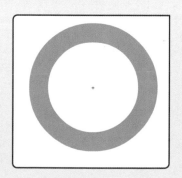

8. Type the following code into the first frame of the logic layer:

```
#initclip
// constructor
function  BNodeClass() {
    // registry to hold all connections
    this.connectList = new Array();
    // set random initial charge
    if (random(100)>50) {
        this.charge = 1;
    } else {
        this.charge = 0;
    }
    // set color chip
    this.bfreq.chips.gotoAndStop
    ➥ (this.colorID+1);
    this.bfreq._alpha=25;
}

// allow component to inherit MovieClip
// properties
BNodeClass.prototype = new MovieClip();

// instance methods
BNodeClass.prototype.connectTo =
➥ function(esta) {
    // enter new connection in connection list
    this.connectList.push(esta);
    // draw connection
    this._parent.lineStyle(0,0x000000,22);
    this._parent.moveTo(this._x,this._y);
    this._parent.lineTo(esta._x,esta._y);
};
BNodeClass.prototype.calcNext =
➥ function() {
    // calculate the new charge state
    var potential=0;
    // add a potential charge for each
    // connected node that is charged
```

```
    for (var n=0;n<this.connectList.length;n++) {
      potential+=this.connectList[n].charge;
    }
    if ((potential%2)==1) {
      // potential charge is odd, set local charge
      this.nextCharge=1;
    } else {
      // potential charge is even, remove local charge
      this.nextCharge=0;
    }
    return this.nextCharge;
};
BNodeClass.prototype.setNext = function() {
  if (this.nextCharge==1) {
    // add historic marker
    Object.environment.bhistory.addChip(this.colorID);

    // increase frequency marker
    this.bfreq._xscale+=2;
    this.bfreq._yscale+=2;
  }
  // make charge change
  this.charge = this.nextCharge;
  // show change of charge
  this.body.gotoAndStop(this.charge+1);
};
// connect the class with the linkage ID for this movie clip
Object.registerClass("bnode", BNodeClass);
#endinitclip
```

The constructing function of the Bnode does a couple of important tasks. First, it declares an array to keep track of connections. This connectList will store references to the other Bnode objects it is connected to. Next, the Bnode sets a random initial charge. The charge is either 0 or 1. Visually, the Bnode is represented by an on/off body light (body) and a colored disc (bfreq).

The connectTo method is a nice way to make meaningful connections between nodes. With a reference to some target node, the parameter esta is pushed into the connectionList array. In this way, every node is aware of all of its connections.

To visualize this connection, draw a line on the _parent movie clip between the two nodes (which will eventually be the location to which these nodes have been attached, Bnetwork).

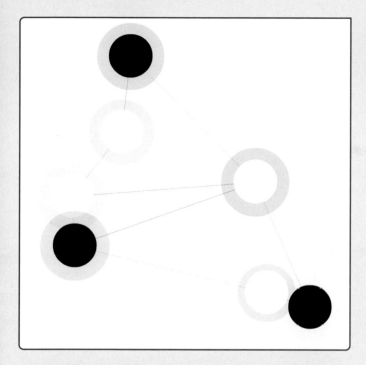

Note that the current state of the node (lit or unlit) is stored in the variable charge. The charge of the node is handled by two separate functions, calcNext and setNext. Executed in this order, the two-step process is necessary since state changes between the nodes are dependent on each other. If Bnodes are changing states while other Bnodes are trying to calculate their state, you get a latency effect that, while interesting, blurs the pure logic of the network. Later, in the Bnetwork, you will see that two basic loops, repeated one after the other, drive the mechanics of the network. The first loop instructs all the nodes to calculate their next state, and the second loop instructs all the nodes to go ahead and switch into that state.

Method calcNext loops through all connections in the connectionList. Each time a connection is found to have a charge, the local potential charge is incremented. After all connections have been examined, the nextCharge is set according to the modulus of the potential. Odd potentials result in a nextCharge of 1, while even potentials result in a nextCharge of 0.

Method setNext simply takes the nextCharge and assigns it to the charge. Before this actually happens, though, the Bnode does all the things necessary to record and visualize this charge event. If the Bnode is receiving a charge (that is, it has a nextCharge value of 1), you increment the size of the Bfreq movie clip (to show that this node has been busy) and add a color chip to the Bhistory movie clip (which I will discuss later). Also, of course, the body is set to display either a white circle (for charges of 0) or a black circle (for charges of 1). Note that the frame of the body movie clip is actually set to the charge plus 1. This is because the charge value starts at 0, while the frame numbers start at 1. A charge of 0 goes to frame 1 and a charge of 1 goes to frame 2.

The Bnetwork movie clip

The Bnetwork is the collection of all Bnodes and their connections. The Bnetwork contains the clock that works as an engine, driving the Bnodes to calculate and set their next states at a rate of about four times per second. The Bnetwork is almost entirely code. In my example, I have included a single graphic element as homage to the binary node. This is a shaded sphere with unified white and black sides. You may skip this graphic, draw your own, or retrieve the "duality" graphic stored in the file binaryNetworkBase.fla.

The construction of the Bnetwork is as follows:

1. Create a new movie clip and name it Bnetwork.

2. Export the Bnetwork movie clip with a linkage identifier of bnetwork.

3. Rename the first layer as logic.

4. Create a new layer underneath logic and name it icon.

5. Place any decorative graphics on the layer icon. My example uses the duality graphic mentioned earlier.

6. Type the following code on the logic layer:

```
#initclip
// constructor
function BNetworkClass() {
  // make the network of binary nodes
  this.makeNetwork();
  // make random connections between nodes
  this.connectNetwork();
  // set network rocking interval (250 ms = ~4 ticks per second)
  this.rInt = setInterval(this,"rock",250);
}

// allow component to inherit MovieClip properties
BNetworkClass.prototype = new MovieClip();
// instance methods

BNetworkClass.prototype.makeNetwork = function() {
  // registry to keep track of nodes
  this.nodeList = new Array();

  // seed placement variables
  var theta = 0.0;
  var radius = 64.0;

  // attach binary nodes in radial seed pattern
  for (var n=0;n<16;n++) {
    // choose name and increase depth
    var nombre = "node"+String(this.depth++);
    // calculate next seed position
    var x = radius*Math.cos(Math.PI/180*theta);
    var y = radius*Math.sin(Math.PI/180*theta);
    // define initialization object
    var init = {_x:x, _y:y, colorID:n, charge:random(2), nextCharge:0};
    // attach the bnode
    var neo = this.attachMovie("bnode",nombre,this.depth,init);

    // register this binary node for future reference
    this.nodeList.push(neo);
```

```
      // natural seed transformation
      theta += 137.5;
      radius += 2.0;
   }
};
BNetworkClass.prototype.connectNetwork = function() {
   // clear any previously drawn lines
   this.clear();
   // connect network
   for (var n=0;n<this.nodeList.length;n++) {
      // attempt to make at least 2 connections for each node
      for (var t=0;t<2;) {
        var neo = this.nodeList[n];
        var o = n;
        while (o==n) {
           // pick some random other node that is not self
           o=random(this.nodeList.length);
        }
        // calculate distance to other node
        var dx=neo._x-this.nodeList[o]._x;
        var dy=neo._y-this.nodeList[o]._y;
        var d=Math.sqrt(dx*dx+dy*dy);

        // only connect to nearby nodes
        if (d<120) {
          // connect to the node
          neo.connectTo(this.nodeList[o]);
          t++;
        }
        // crude method to prevent infinite loops
        if (random(10000>9990)) t++;
      }
   }
};
BNetworkClass.prototype.rock = function() {
   // calculate next states
   for (var n=0;n<this.nodeList.length;n++) {
      this.nodeList[n].calcNext();
   }

   // set states
   for (var n=0;n<this.nodeList.length;n++) {
      this.nodeList[n].setNext();
   }

   // advance age of history
   Object.environment.bhistory.age();
};

// Connect the class with the linkage ID for this movie clip
Object.registerClass("bnetwork", BNetworkClass);
#endinitclip
```

The `Bnetwork` constructor function does some pretty hard work right away in the creation of the network. It can be broken up into three distinct events.

First, the nodes of the network are created using the method `makeNetwork`. Second, the nodes are randomly connected using the `connectNetwork` method. Finally, the entire network is put into motion with an interval that executes every 250 ms, or about 4 times a second. Each time the interval executes a method named `rock`. This method calculates and then sets new charges for all the nodes in the network.

The `makeNetwork` method iterates through a finite loop, instantiating `Bnodes` in a radial seed pattern. If you are unfamiliar with the natural order of seed arrangement, its construction is quite simple. First, initialize a variable (`theta`) to keep track of a placement angle and another variable (`radius`) to keep track of some distance from the center. Now iterate within a loop to create a specific number of nodes. In this case, you hard-code the number of nodes in the network to be 16. Each time through the loop, you calculate the position of the node using `theta` and `radius`, attach a new `Bnode` movie clip instance, register the new node with the `nodeList`, and finally increase `theta` by the golden rotation of 137.5 degrees and increase `radius` just slightly.

The `connectNetwork` method loops through all nodes within the network and connects each to precisely two other nodes. To make things interesting (or challenging, depending on your point of view), you let nodes attach only to nodes that are nearby. Specifically, the distance between the two nodes must be less than 120 pixels. I like this limitation because it creates networks more likely to be connected in loops, which ultimately are the constructs that give you such weird behaviors.

If the `makeNetwork` and `connectNetwork` methods are the brain of the network, the `rock` method is the heart. Keeping a steady beat, it analyzes and mandates the state switching of all the nodes of the network.

The `rock` method does three things. First, it loops through all nodes in the `nodeList` and instructs them to calculate their next state. The nodes store this next state internally. Second, it loops through all the nodes again, this time instructing them to change state (to what they had previously calculated). From your perspective, the whole process happens instantaneously. Third, it advances the age of the history recorder, which is very important if you want to make any progress.

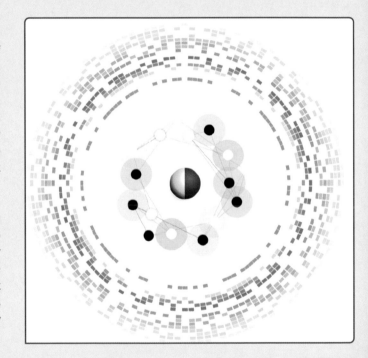

The Bhistory movie clip

For many years I have stared at these binary networks, quite foolishly trying to spot order within the chaos. With so many nodes flickering on and off, pattern matching is tough. Especially when the patterns are long, repeating after 100 or more unique state changes. I created the Bhistory movie clip to try and visualize each state of the network as it is happening.

Note that within the Bnode setCharge method that you created earlier, there is a call made to the Bhistory addChip method. The addChip method is a nice little function that places a corresponding color chip in a radial pattern as indication of a Bnode charge event. Now, you need not remember the unique network states, as this information is rendered in concentric rings around the network itself. Patterns, if they exist, are immediately evident. As humans, we are good at this kind of visual pattern recognition.

Here are the steps to create the Bhistory object:

1. Create a new movie clip and name it Bhistory.

2. Export this movie clip with a linkage identifier of bhistory.

3. Edit the Bhistory movie clip.

4. Rename the first layer as logic.

5. Type the following code in the first frame of layer logic.

```
#initclip
// constructor
function BHistoryClass() {
  // marker of historic action
  this.theta = 0;
}

// allow component to inherit MovieClip
// properties
BHistoryClass.prototype = new MovieClip();
```

```
// instance methods
BHistoryClass.prototype.age = function() {
  // increment by one section
  // circle is divided into 128 sections
  this.theta+=(360/128);
};
BHistoryClass.prototype.addChip =
➥ function(id) {
  // pick name and increase depth
  var nombre = "chip"+String(this.depth++);
  // calculate radius using id (the higher
  // the id, the further out chip is)
  var r = 150+id*5.2;
  // calculate position
  var x = r*Math.cos(Math.PI / 180 *
➥ this.theta);
  var y = r*Math.sin(Math.PI / 180 *
➥ this.theta);
  // define initialization object
  var init = {_x:x,_y:y,_xscale:45,
➥ _yscale:30+r*Math.PI/12,
➥ _rotation:this.theta, _alpha:100};
  // attach the new colorchip
  var neo = this.attachMovie
➥ ("colorchip",nombre,this.depth,init);
  // instruct colorchip to show id
  // corresponding color
  neo.gotoAndStop(id+1);
};
// Connect the class with the linkage ID for
// this movie clip
Object.registerClass("bhistory",
BHistoryClass);
#endinitclip
```

Note that the only thing the Bhistory movie clip does when starting up is set theta to a value of 0. theta is the variable used to track the current location in which new color chips can be attached. You might also start at −90 to compensate for the rotational coordinate system of Flash. This would place the first chips at high noon.

The age method adds precisely one tick to `theta`. The size of the tick is determined by the value derived from dividing 360 degrees into a number of equal segments. In my example, there are 128 sections. Incrementing `theta` in this manner allows you to quickly change the number of historic ticks before a complete revolution is made. To change the number, simply change the value of 128 to some positive, nonzero integer. Recall that the age method is called by `Bnetwork` each time the `rock` interval executes.

You will remember from earlier that the `Bnode` movie clip made a call to `Bhistory`'s `addChip` method each time a positive charge was set. As a parameter, the `addChip` method requires only the `colorID` of the `Bnode` that called it. This, combined with `theta`, gives the method enough information to correctly size and place a new instance of the `Colorchip` movie clip. The radius (`r`) is directly proportional to the `colorID`. The higher the `colorID`, the further away from the origin the `Colorchip` is placed. All chips start at 150 pixels from the center. The `x` and `y` position of the chip is a straightforward trigonometry operation. Note the one unusual calculation is the `_yscale` of the new movie clip. My original approach was to create continuous rings of charge where applicable. Instead, I settled for this compromise that simply increases the width of the chips at further distances.

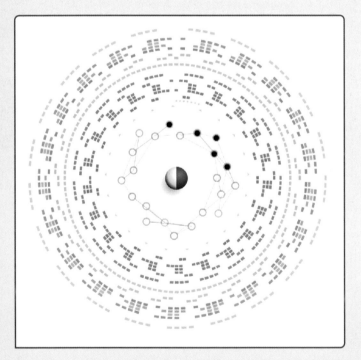

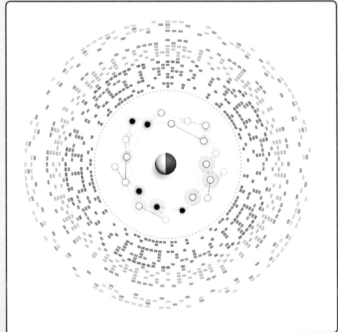

The environment

The environment of the binary network project is very simple.

1. In the main timeline, name the first layer logic.

2. On the first frame of layer logic in the main timeline, add the following code:

```
Object.environment = this;
stop();
```

3. Create two new layers and name them network and history. Make sure that network is above history. The original layer logic can be anywhere, but I like to keep it on the top.

4. Drag an instance of the Bhistory movie clip into the first frame of the layer history. Center the instance on the stage.

5. Drag an instance of the Bnetwork movie clip into the first frame of the layer network. Center this instance on the stage as well.

That's it!

Manifestation

Run the binary network. If all is well, you should now be watching an emergent system unfold as ripples of complexity move through the nodes of the network. Pay close attention to the story being told in the rings of history. Write to me if you discover something interesting.

Of all the projects in this chapter, this one especially is wide open for further experimentation and tweaking. There are several additional files on the CD that contain both interesting and bizarre variations on this theme. I will quickly describe them here.

Increased network complexity

Right away, you might want to crank up the complexity of your network. The simplest way to do this is increase the number of nodes in the network. Take a look at binaryNetworkLarge.fla on the CD. Here's what has been changed:

- The number of nodes was increased to 42. This change is made in layer logic of the Bnetwork movie clip within the makeNetwork method. At about line 25, there is a for loop. The number 16 in the loop was changed to 42.

- The starting radius of the seed arrangement was decreased. Since you have many more nodes, you might start attaching them closer to the center so you do not run out of screen space too soon. Also within the makeNetwork method, the value of radius was set at 50 instead of 64.

- The maximum connection distance was decreased to 70 from 120. This is simply because you have so many nodes now that we do not need to necessarily search very far for a good connection. The connection distance is set in the connectNetwork method.

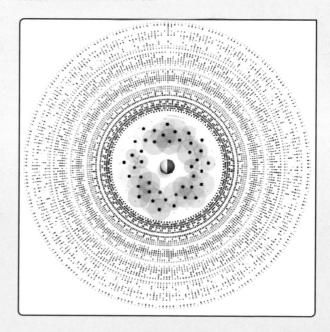

Another interesting modification might be to increase the number of connections. However, it is unclear what effect this would have on the complexity, if any. This would be a worthwhile experiment for more motivated readers.

Automatic pattern detection

Wouldn't it be nice to have the network search out and discover patterns on its own? With a little bit of work, you can make this possible. Take a look at `binaryNetworkPatterns.fla` on the CD. Notice that in addition to color chips being added to the history, pattern markers and unique state markers are added. These appear as a triangle and a dot, respectively.

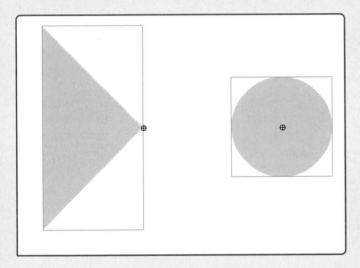

There are too many code changes to address in detail here, but a basic description of the process follows:

1. Within the `Bnetwork`, the `rock` method captures the state of the network each time just before it changes. The states are stored as long strings of 1s and 0s, with each digit corresponding to a particular node in the network (that is, 00010101011010100).

2. The state strings are stored in an array. Before a state string is added to the array, however, the array is searched for previous instances of that string. If none exists, the state is considered unique and a marker is added.

3. In the special case where the first nonunique state is found, this state is flagged as the **pattern head**. Once a pattern head has been flagged, you know that the network has fallen into a loop pattern. Consequently, each time the pattern head is again detected, that state is marked in the history as the beginning of the pattern.

Fancy nodes

A lot of readers probably groaned when they saw how simple the node objects were going to appear. A black and white circle that occasionally blinks on and off? Admittedly, this is not very exciting. The file `binaryNetworkCubeNodes.fla` on the CD contains an enhanced version of the node that not only looks cooler, but also displays more information. The nodes in this file are white cubes. The cubes turn black when charged, and they also spin.

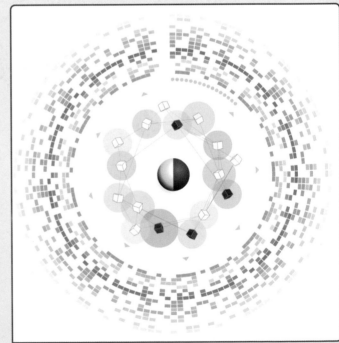

The spin of the cubes is determined by the speed with which the node changes charge. Each time the state of a node is different from the previous state, the cube is given a little rotational acceleration. This creates a network in which the most active nodes are spinning crazily, while less active nodes turn slowly or sit completely still. Together with the frequency indicator (remember, this records only positive charge events), you have a complete story of the node's behavior.

Binary sound machine

So far I have neglected the use of sound in these projects entirely. It is a natural conclusion that a binary network of this type could be used in the automatic generation of beats. By assigning each node a unique sound and then playing that sound every time the node is charged, you can compose some interesting rhythms.

Open the file binaryNetworkSoundMachine.fla on the CD. Run it a few times. Notice now how the activity of the network and history are reinforced dramatically with the inclusion of sound. There are only two changes required to make this possible. First, a new movie clip called Bsound has been added to the Library. Bsound is basically a long timeline with sound events every five frames. An instance of the Bsound movie clip is included within the Bnode. Each time the Bnode charges, it instructs the Bsound to gotoAndPlay a particular frame containing the unique sound for that node. Simple, right?

Since the network is moving very fast, the sounds should be short and sweet. I should note that the micro sounds used in my example were generated by www.seraph.nl.

Summary: The infinite reaches of Complexification

It almost makes me sad to come to a conclusion. There are so many topics to explore in this field that I feel compelled to keep going. While we have no room for new projects, we do have a great collection of systems that open themselves for endless variation.

The source code for all of these projects and a great many enhanced variations have been included on the CD. I encourage you to explore the disc.

Complexification is a theme that runs through much of my work. If I am lucky, the path before me will remain unobstructed, so that we might continue these constructions together. I thank my friends and especially you, the reader, for taking this journey with me.

09 MASQUERADE

These sources of inspiration have meant a lot to me in my creative development. There are others as well, but these two are the most important. So the world I'm exploring now probably has influences from both John Bauer and Astrid Lindgren.

I believe my love for storytelling is the main reason I've come this far as an artist. To listen to or read tales written and created by others is indeed something special, though to write a tale yourself and touch others might be an even greater experience. To explore the world created in my mind, to find out who's living there and what they look like, is very exciting.

Sometimes when I'm scribbling away in my sketchbook, some figure pops up, just like that. I ask myself, "Where did you come from?"

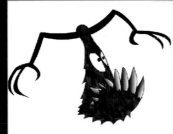

Sometimes when I'm scribbling
away in my sketchbook,
some figure pops up, just like that.
I ask myself, "Where did you come from?"

Everyone has his or her own worlds to explore. I probably have thousands more hidden away somewhere. It's all about taking the time to search for them.

I've always thought animation would be the best way to tell my tales. As a youth watching old Disney movies, I was swept away into the world of the animators' minds—it was exciting. But as a young lad without animation skills or any industry contacts, working in this medium seemed like a distant dream. On top of that, Sweden didn't have any real animation schools at the time.

After many years of adventure, I stumbled upon a computing course that later on led me to Flash 3.0. Love didn't strike at once—it was quite a while before I saw how this Flash could help me out. The first film I made was about a man who sat under a palm tree, and a coconut fell on his head. Unfortunately, he broke his neck and couldn't tell anyone about the laws of gravity. That was long before Newton got acquainted with a more suitable fruit. Five grieves and eleven sorrows later I ended up with a 7-second film and I still felt skeptical. But then again, it did at least move.

In December 1999 I decided to give animating in Flash a serious try. I had bought a marvelous piece of music by The Chieftains called *Don Oiche Ud I mBeithil*, and I thought I should do something with it and create a kind of Christmas card. The song opens with Burgess Meredith reading an English translation of the song's lyrics, which are about the birth of Jesus, and I decided to make an animation based on those lyrics.

I found the result revolutionary. I managed to make this candlelight, using shape tweens, and I was so proud. The rest of this Christmas tale was made like a shadow play, but the results convinced me to continue.

I had at last found the tool to visualize the journeys I take in my mind. The following December I visited the pixie world for the first time. I decided to make a more advanced film about a pixie that on Christmas Eve wakes up the forest playing his flute and then dances off through the woods.

> *Many people believe I used 3D to create the bumblebee, but that wasn't the case. I was just thinking in 3D.*

This was a tougher task, as the background became complex and there were many moving figures. I created the background images for this film in Flash and converted them into bitmaps later on. After this point, I would make most backgrounds in Photoshop.

In this film I was especially satisfied with the intro, which pans down through the dense and hilly woods while snow gently falls. It was during this scene that I started to realize what Flash was actually capable of.

I decided that I would put Flash through a serious test, *The Gooberstory* (www.humbugz.com/hela.htm). When I began this project, I was a Flash novice; when I finished, I knew most of Flash's secrets. Many people have had opinions, both positive and negative, about this film. For me it was a great experiment and a serious journey into Flash. The film itself gives viewers an idea of what Flash can achieve and at the same time tells a weird fable about the creation of the peanut.

The creation of *The Gooberstory* was a long and tedious process. I thought I would never finish it. Weeks would pass without me opening the source file, but in the end I made it. Some people think the story is strange, the film is long-winded, or some of the artwork doesn't match. Others love its easygoing, peaceful mood. For my part, I'm not satisfied. If I could do it all over again, I would change quite a few things. Maybe that will be a future project.

Most animations in the film are made with motion tweening, but there's one character in the film that I put a lot of work into: the bumblebee. Many people believe I used 3D to create the bumblebee, but that isn't the case. I was just **thinking** in 3D. This little fellow was mostly done with shape tweening—many layers and lots of hard work.

I made a full 3D-like rotation, which I reused in some of the scenes.

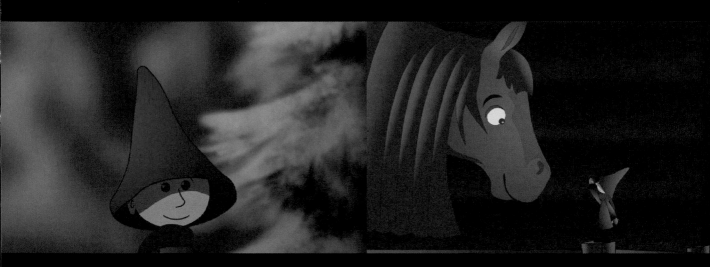

At that time, the possibility of masking animated symbols didn't exist. So I had to animate each shape on its own to get that effect. I had already used this technique on the firefly in my website intro. But this time I had to animate the stripes of the bumblebee. Even though it might look simple, it was actually very tricky. This is where I started to understand and appreciate shape hints. I realized that with shape tweening I could accomplish far more than with regular motion tweening, but it was much more time-consuming.

In the following film, *Nim's Winter Tale*, I went back to the pixie theme once again.

By now, this new world was forming in my head and I wanted to try out a couple of ideas. I used a lot of shape tweening, because I wanted to see how well it would work and if I could find a way to make a Flash film not look like a Flash film. I tried working with some 3D-like effects here and there: when Nim is turning around, when the lantern is moving, when the horse is turning his head, and so on. It worked out quite well. I made all

the backgrounds as well as a couple of effects in Photoshop. One of those effects is the sunrise at the end of the film. I didn't want a silly gradient popping up behind a mask; I wanted a soft, beautiful sunrise. Because I couldn't make this effect in Flash, I had to find another way.

I achieved the effect by fading nine different bitmap images into each other in Flash, putting them on top of the bigger background image. Each bitmap was put in its own symbol and animated from 0%–100% alpha on top of each other in even intervals. Quite a simple trick, but I hadn't thought of using it before.

Now I've continued the journey started in *Nim's Winter Tale* with a film that takes place in the very world where Nim was born. For this task I needed more advanced Flash animation methods. I had to look at the tools Flash provides and use them in a new way. What could I do to make complex characters easier to animate? How could I use texture so that it didn't look so flat? Could I achieve something with Flash that hadn't been done before? In the following exercise I reveal one of my secrets.

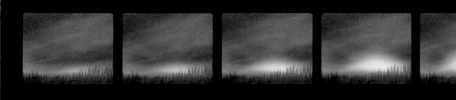

Animating the masks: A Grodd is created

There are many creatures in this new world, and one of them is the Grodd, a tiny fishlike being that lives in the deep lakes of the forests. At one point in my new tale, Nim sits fishing by a lake. I wanted a little water creature to play tricks on him, so I started sketching. I thought of a tadpole, with its big head and delicate tail. I just mutated it a bit.

The evolution of the Grodd

After a while I came up with a result that I liked, and since then the Grodd has been in constant development. Most Grodds are different from each other—some have two eyes, while others have one. Most of them have different patterns and colors. One thing all Grodds have in common is that they communicate through blowing bubbles that form images.

This Grodd is speaking about pixies.

The project that I'm now working on is huge. I've always wanted to make some kind of feature film, and now I've begun to do it. I started with some storyboarding and thinking about which parts of the world I'll have to explore in detail. I've realized that I'm researching a world that no one knows anything about, and that's quite strange in its own way. I've promised myself that I'll finish the storyboarding before I start animating, which isn't that easy to do (I'm a very eager person!). The Grodds are a small part of this story.

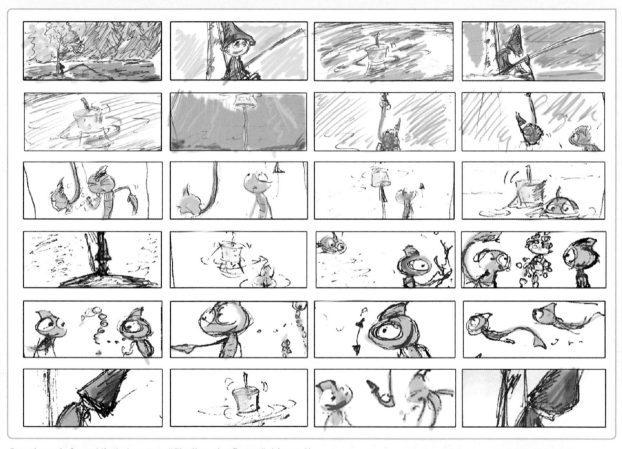

Storyboards from Nim's Journey: "Finding the flower" (shoot 1)

I want to give the figures more detail while still being able to animate them without too many shape tweens. The way to do this is through **animated masking**. Using a symbol as a mask isn't new to Flash, even if there's an animation nested within the symbol. It's how you use it that makes the difference.

In this exercise you'll learn how to use animated masks to give the Grodd detail and color without too much hassle. The great thing about it is that it's easy to experiment with the result as soon as the hard work is done. You can apply and use what you'll learn here in many different situations, so it's up to you to use it in your own way.

I made a complete swimming Grodd animation for you to use. I set the frame rate on this document to 25 fps. This is because I'll export my animations to video (PAL) later on. If you're going to export to NTSC format, you can change the frame rate to 30 fps. You can find the animation on the accompanying CD with the filename `GroddOriginal.fla`.

The figure is in black and gray so that you easily can see all its different parts.

The Grodd consists of 13 parts spread out on 13 named layers. All these parts are animated with shape tweens. The animation is 68 frames long and resembles a Grodd's swim cycle. The animation is nested within a graphic symbol (GroddOriginal) that's placed on the stage.

Let's get started! Once you've opened `GroddOriginal.fla`, double-click the graphic symbol representing the swimming Grodd. Once inside the symbol, you can check for yourself how the layers are organized. Be careful not to move the shapes, as some of them have shape hints attached and can easily start to live their own lives.

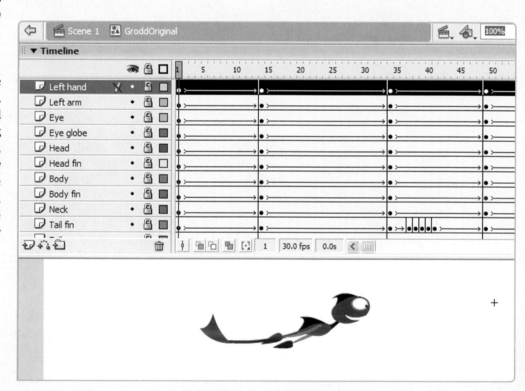

Shape hints

Before we begin, let's take a closer look at **shape hints** in general. Shape tweens are by far my favorite way of animating, but there's one problem with them: Flash has a hard time translating the shape tweens into the precise motions I prefer. To help Flash understand better, I use shape hints. Though shape hints are a great tool, they aren't that easy to handle.

The reasons for using shape hints instead of key-by-key animations are many. The main benefits are less work and a smaller file size, but shape hints also provide great control of the tweens.

I try to use as few keyframes as possible, and I try to put them on the same frame numbers. Then I can easily make the animation shorter or longer by removing or adding frames to all layers at once. This might make the animation less precise at certain times, as you might notice in the swimming Grodd animation. There's only one place in the animation where I've used key-by-key animation because the shape hints just couldn't help me: a certain area of the tail-fin animation.

The secret to success in using shape hints lies in simple shapes. The more complex the shape, the more nodes it has, and the more difficult it is to control. Let's take a closer look at that tail fin. I wanted the tail fin to follow the motion of the tail and at the same time change its shape depending on the motion.

This is the motion of the tail fin from frame 1 to frame 14 without hints. It doesn't look like a very smooth animation.

I had to use shape hints (four of them, to be exact) placed at strategic points on the shape. There's no way to tell where you should place the hints—you just have to keep trying until you get the result you want. Sometimes you'll need only one hint; sometimes you'll need four. I've never used more than five shape hints, because I've noticed then that using shape hints doesn't have the desired effect anyway. In those cases, I use key-by-key animation.

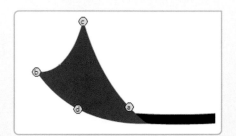
Frame 1 with the hints correctly attached

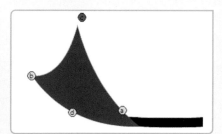
Frame 1 with hint C unattached

Each of the inserted shape hints is assigned a letter. The hints on frame 1 have counterparts on frame 14. All the hints have to be attached to the shape in order for them to work. If they aren't attached to the shape, the hints are colored red. If they're properly attached to the shape, the hints on frame 1 are colored yellow, and those on frame 14 are green.

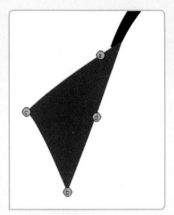
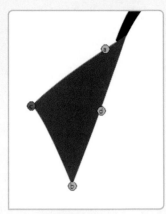

Frame 14 with the hints correctly attached

Frame 14 with hint C unattached

This is the motion of the tail fin from frame 1 to 14 with working shape hints. This looks much better.

Sometimes when you're adding shape hints, the shape might disappear when the animation is played. At that point, you'll have to either start adding the hints all over again or figure out which hint caused the problem. Also, I noticed that Flash MX 2004 sometimes doesn't manage to convert shape-hinted animations from Flash MX. In cases where I wanted to use in Flash MX 2004 an animation created in Flash MX, I had to add the shape hints all over again or continue to work in Flash MX.

There are quite a few unwritten rules when you're working with shape hints. I could dedicate a whole chapter to them. My best advice to you is to just dive right in and start using shape hints. After many tough hours and much less hair, you might in the end start liking them. I wish you the best of luck!

Now back to the tutorial. Each Grodd has a head, fins, arms, and a tail. In this exercise I'll go through each of these in turn so you can see exactly how they all work. All these parts are made with shape tweens, and you're going to put a texture on each one, except for the neck. First you'll put a pattern on the head, then you'll repeat the same steps on the body, and finally you'll put a pattern on the tail.

The head

Remember that you're starting with `GroddOriginal.fla`.

1. I think the head is a good starting point. First you need to create a new layer just below the Head layer. Name the layer Head texture. This is where you're going to make all the textures for the head.

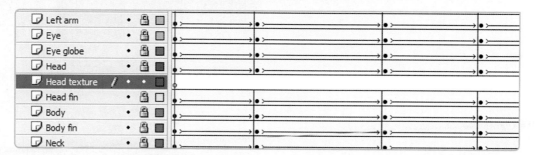

While you're working with the head, you don't need to see all the other moving parts—this only makes matters confusing. I recommend that you hide all layers except for the Head and Head texture layers by clicking the eye icons next to the layer names. Also, make sure that all layers except for the Head texture layer are locked.

2. Because you're going to make the texture drawing on the layer beneath the head, it's a good idea to put the Head layer into **outline mode**. This way, you can see what you're doing, and you can use the outline of the head as a reference.

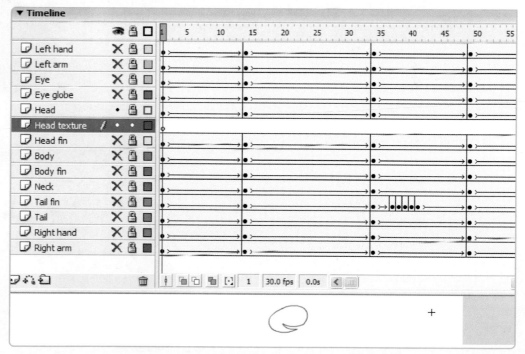

Now you can concentrate on the head without any further distraction.

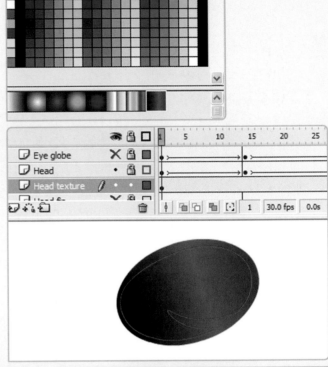

3. Next, you have to decide what color the head should be. I've chosen an olive green/black color gradient. If you want to use the same gradient, you can find it in the Color Swatches panel.

4. On the Head texture layer, use the **Oval tool** to draw a circle that's slightly bigger than the head. Make sure to get rid of the stroke around the circle. Place the circle at the same position as the head. You might have to rotate it a little to make it fit. Zoom in on the head if you need more control.

5. Now select the circle and convert it into a graphic symbol. I usually do this by clicking the appropriate keyframe to make sure everything is selected and then pressing F8. Name this symbol Head texture.

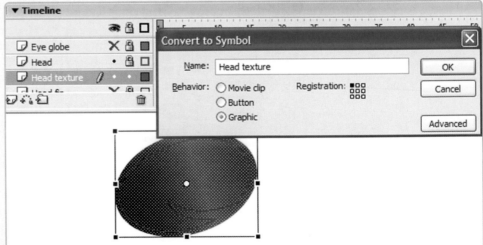

6. Because you're going to make the texture or pattern on the head, it would be great to use the eye as a reference. So make the Eye globe layer visible and put it into outline mode by clicking the appropriate icons.

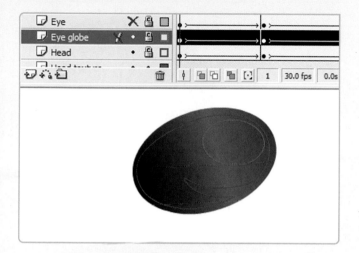

7. To continue working on the texture, you have to navigate into the graphic symbol Head texture. Do this by double-clicking the symbol.

Remember that you can always check where in the symbol hierarchy you are by looking above the timeline.

8. It's a good idea to always name the layers. Try to make this a habit. In the graphic symbol Head texture, name the first layer Head colour.

9. It's time to make some nice patterns. Put the layer Head colour into outline mode and create a new layer named Head pattern.

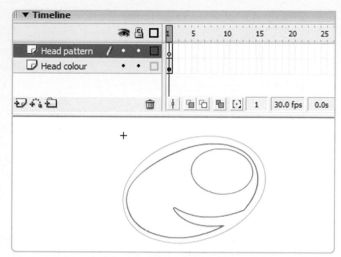

10. You can now see where the head and the eye are. On the Head pattern layer you can now draw your pattern. I chose to create a speckled pattern. I used circles with a color of black and a 60% transparency setting. Try to create a simple pattern, because the more detail you have, the tougher it will be for the computer to keep up the frame rate. It all depends on the computer that you watch the animation on and how fast its processor is. If you're going to export to video later on, you obviously don't have to bother with such frame optimizations. Try to keep the pattern within your circle, and avoid drawing within the eyes.

11. Turn off outline mode on the Head colour layer.

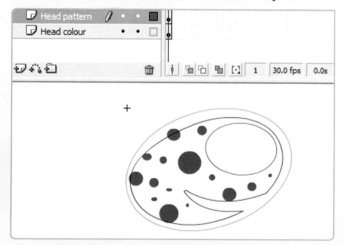

12. This looks fine to me. Navigate back to the GroddOriginal symbol. Now you're going to make this thing move. The head texture has to follow the same path as the head. To do this, you'll use **motion tweening**. Apply a motion tween to the Head texture layer.

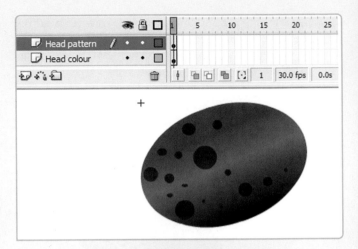

To get the smooth motion in the animation, I've used **easing**. Easing makes the whole animation smoother and more lifelike. It accelerates and decelerates depending on the motion. Natural motions follow the rules of gravity. For example, if you jump up and down on the floor, you'll go from standing still to launching up in the air. But gravity won't let you jump that high, so it constantly slows you down until you reach that unavoidable truth: you have to fall back down again. But for a millisecond of time, you actually hang in the air until you start accelerating back down again, hitting the floor with a thump.

> *In Flash, 100 gives the biggest easing effect, while 0 gives the least. So if a tween goes from 100 to 0, it's very fast in the beginning of the animation and then it slows down to a halt.*

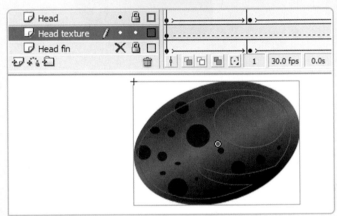

The texture and the head have to move in the same way, therefore you have to use some easing on the Head texture layer.

13. Set the keyframes on the Head texture layer to the same intervals as those on the Head layer.

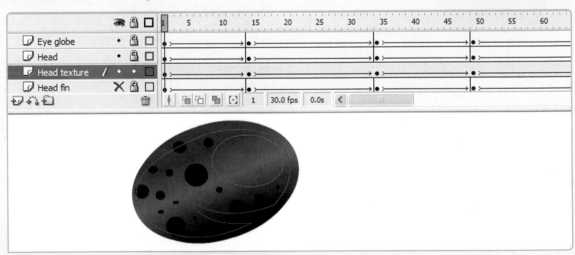

Now you can apply the easing. The motions of the two layers have to be the same, so it's important that the Head texture layer has the same easing as the Head layer.

14. Select the appropriate keyframe in the Head texture layer and take a look in the Properties panel.

15. Use the Ease option in the Properties panel and fill in the correct values. Also, make sure that the Scale box is checked and that Rotate is set to Auto.

This is how the easing should look on the different keyframes in the Head texture layer (note that there's no need for easing on frame 68 as this is the last frame in the animation):

Frame 1: easing =   100
Frame 14: easing = –100
Frame 34: easing =   100
Frame 49: easing = –100
Frame 68: easing =   0

16. The last step is to place the actual head texture in the same position as the head graphic. So, select each keyframe in the layer, and move/rotate the head texture so that it covers the head at each point. Try to be as precise as possible when positioning the head texture. Use the pattern (the speckles) as a reference to the edge of the head.

The last keyframe is a little special. The secret to creating a good looping animation is to make it seamless. There's an easy way to do this. The trick is to avoid the first and last keyframes being in exactly the same position. To accomplish this, you have to find the position of the frame that is prior to frame 1.

What you'll do is copy the first frame and use it to get a similar position on the last frame. It's crucial that the loop becomes as unnoticeable as possible, because the human eye is so sensitive that it will register any glitch in the motion.

17. Right-click (CTRL-click for Mac users) frame 1 in the Head texture layer and choose Copy Frames.

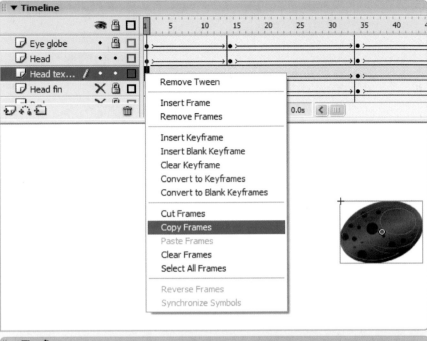

18. Paste frame 1 on frame 69 in the same layer.

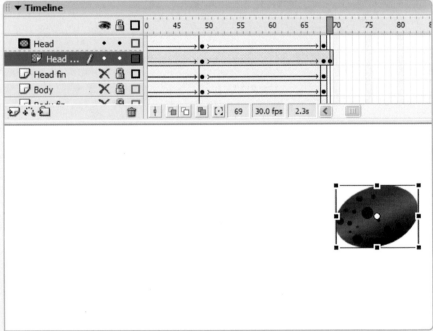

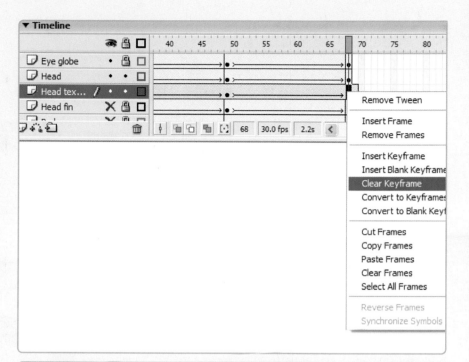

19. Clear keyframe 68 by right-clicking (CTRL-clicking) and selecting Clear Keyframe.

Now the position of the head texture on frame 1 and frame 69 is exactly the same. If you play the animation now, those two frames show as a tiny pause in the otherwise smooth flow.

20. To get a fluid motion, insert a keyframe on frame 68, and then delete keyframe 69.

21. The Head texture layer is now complete. There is one final step: creating the mask. This is the easy part. Just right-click (CTRL-click) the Head layer and choose Mask.

22. The Head layer now masks the Head texture layer.

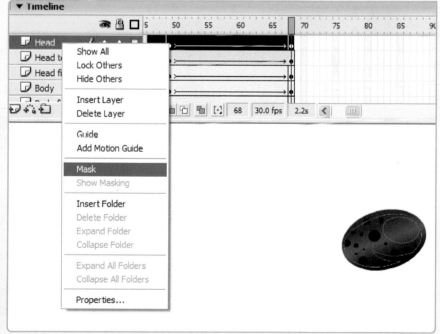

For the mask to work properly, the two layers have to be locked.

Now test the movie to see the result. If Head texture isn't following Head properly, you can always correct it later on. If you want to change the texture of the head, just navigate into the graphic symbol Head texture and change the color and pattern.

You've already done the hard work of making the animated mask, so now you can play around. You can see some texture examples on this page.

You've now finished the first part of this exercise. If you get stuck with any part of it and want to compare files, or if you want to skip straight to the next part of the exercise, open GroddHead.fla from the accompanying CD.

So, the advantage of using the body parts as masks is that you can quickly customize the basic Grodd by adding new textures, much like you can skin a component.

As we will see in the following pages, there are also other advantages: you can reuse your textures, and you also gain more control of how the texture moves with the body part.

The body

The next step is to make a Body texture layer. You can do this by yourself—I've used the same gradient on the body as on the head, and I've also used the same pattern, black dots. The process for the body is the same as that for the head, so use the previous exercise as a guide. Check out `GroddBody.fla` from the CD if you need any more help.

The tail

Now you'll work with the tail, the delicate area between the body and the tail fin. You'll look at the tail fin later on, so don't worry about that for now. Making a pattern on the tail is trickier than it is on the head and body, because the motion is more vivid. The tail is bent, therefore it will be hard to use dots in a symbol. On this tail, you'll use stripes.

1. Unlock the Tail layer so you can work with it, and lock all other layers.

2. First you need to change the tail's color. I'll use the same color gradient I used previously for the head and body textures.

To make the tail look like a part of the body, it's essential that the colors at the transition between the tail and the body are similar.

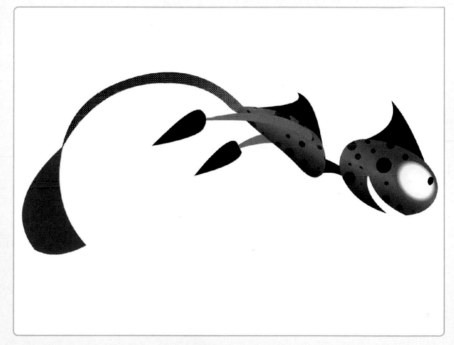

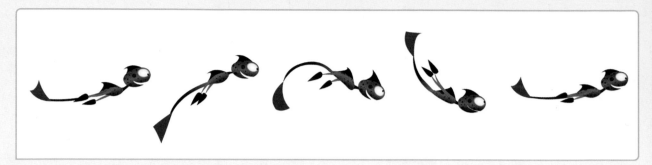

3. You can use the Fill Transform tool to perfect the gradient. Change the color of the tail in **all the keyframes** in the Tail layer. I've made the end of the tail fade to black in this version.

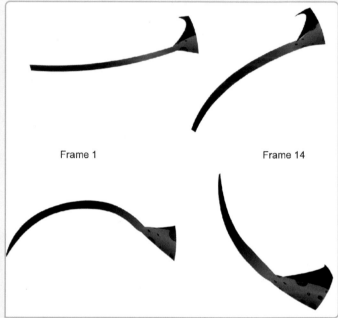

Frame 1   Frame 14

4. Create two new layers above the Tail layer. Name the layers Tail texture and Tail mask.

You're going to leave the Tail layer as it is. It will function as the main color of the tail. This way, you have full control over the motion of its color gradient.

On the Tail texture layer, you'll create the stripes, and on the Tail mask layer, you'll transfer a copy of the keyframes from the Tail layer. Those frames will be used to mask the Tail texture layer. Let's start out with copying the keyframes.

5. Select all frames in the Tail layer, right-click (CTRL-click) somewhere on the selected frames, and choose Copy Frames.

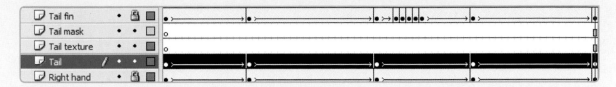

6. Select all the frames in the Tail mask layer and choose Paste Frames.

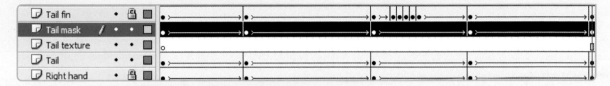

You now have an exact copy of the tail and its motion to use as a mask later on.

Now it's time to stretch your brain a little. The texture of the tail has to be able to follow the motion of the tail, so you have to make a texture that can accomplish this without it looking weird.

7. Create a stripe pattern on the Tail texture layer. I've used broad stripes because I think it looks better. You can either make a narrow oval with no stroke and cut it in half, or make two lines and bend one of them a little to create the fin shape. Copy and paste to create five "fins," and then select them all and fill them with the gradient from earlier (delete any outlines left). Because the tail will move a lot, make sure that the stripes will be able to cover the whole tail at all times. You'll see what I mean in the following screenshot.

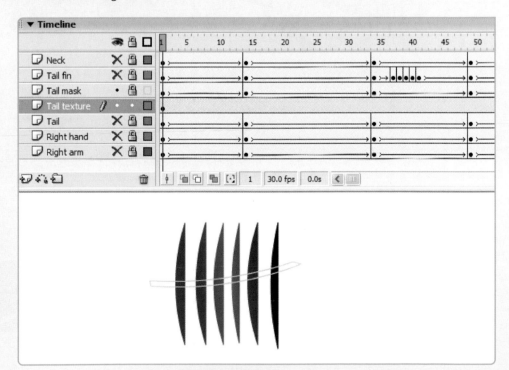

8. Select all stripes and turn them into a graphic symbol. Name the symbol Tail texture.

9. As with the Head texture and the Body texture symbols, the Tail texture symbol needs motion and easing applied to it. Before adding any keyframes, you can add a motion tween. This makes the process a lot simpler.

Frame   1: easing =   100
Frame 14: easing = −100
Frame 34: easing =   100
Frame 49: easing = −100
Frame 68: easing =   0

10. The stripes must follow the tail as closely as possible. To achieve this, you can use the Free Transform tool to stretch, scale, and rotate the Tail texture symbol to your liking. It may take a few attempts to get it right, so you need to be patient.

11. The final step is to activate the mask.

Voila! The Grodd has stripes that move with the tail. Once again, if you have any problems, take a look at GroddTail.fla on the CD.

The arms

1. Let's not waste any time. Try to color the arms with a gradient, just like you did with the tail.

When you've done this, you'll need some contrast on the left arm so that it doesn't blend in too much with the body of the Grodd (if you've used the same types of colors).

2. The left arm is positioned farthest to the left from your point of view, so you'll create a shadow. To do this, you need to have two copies of the left arm's motion on two new layers. Create two new layers above the Left arm layer and name them Left arm shadow and Left arm mask.

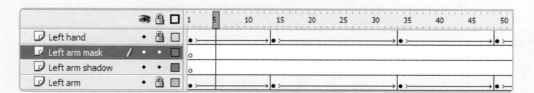

3. Select all the keyframes in the Left arm layer, right-click (CTRL-click), and choose Copy Frames.

4. Now select all the empty frames on the Left arm mask layer, right-click (CTRL-click), and choose Paste Frames. Make sure that no extra frames have popped up after frame 68. If you do find any extra frames, delete them.

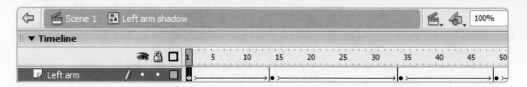

To make the shadow of the arm, you're going to use the same animation, but you'll have to reposition it a little. The easiest way to do this is to place it into a new symbol.

5. Create a new graphic symbol (Insert > New Symbol or CTRL+F8), and name it Left arm shadow. Choose Paste Frames on the first keyframe in the layer.

6. Navigate back to the graphic symbol GroddOriginal. Open up the Library (Window > Library or CTRL+L).

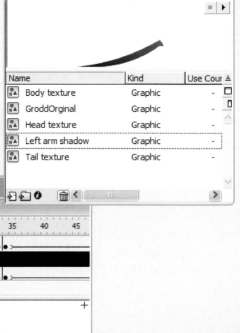

7. Select frame 1 in the Left arm shadow layer. Drag the graphic symbol Left arm shadow from the Library to the stage.

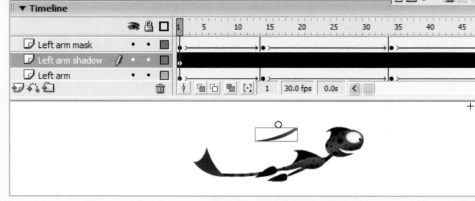

8. This symbol will be the shadow of the arm, so you have to make it a little darker. Select the symbol and look in the Properties panel. Select Brightness from the Color drop-down menu. Set the value to –60%.

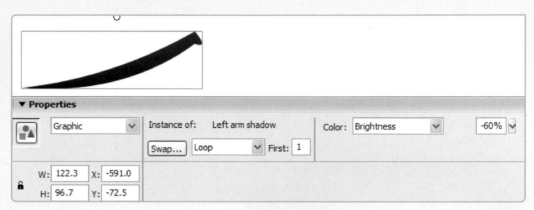

9. Position the symbol a little to the left below the left arm. I've put the Left arm shadow layer into outline mode here so you can see it clearly.

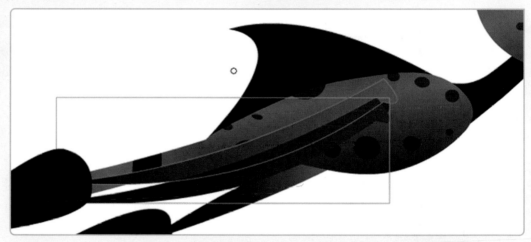

10. Now turn the Left arm mask layer into a mask.

There you have it: a thin shadow on the arm. A small detail like this makes a big difference. If you need something to compare your work against, the completed file up to this stage is saved as `GroddArmShadow.fla` on the CD.

The fins

To make the Grodd look more fishlike, I want the fins to be transparent. I also want to use lines as texture. Because the tail fin bends differently throughout the motion, the lines have to follow and bend as well.

1. Create a new layer below the Tail fin layer and name it Tail fin texture.

As before, concentrate on the layer that you're working with. All other layers should be locked and hidden or outlined apart from the Tail fin layer, which should be locked but shown.

2. On the Tail fin texture layer, draw a circle that encircles the tail, and use a transparent color of your choice. I've used a greenish hue so that the tail fin matches the rest of the Grodd. Make sure to get rid of the stroke around the circle.

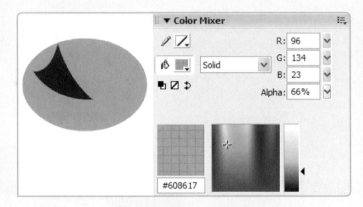

3. Select the circle shape and convert it into a graphic symbol. Name the symbol Tail fin texture.

4. To continue with the texture, navigate into the graphic symbol Tail fin texture by double-clicking it.

5. Here you'll find one layer with the circle. Now create one more layer on which to make the lines. Name the two layers Lines and Circle.

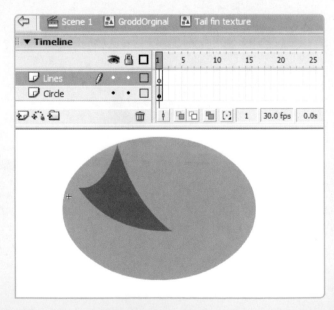

"How can I create the illusion that the lines seem to bend, without too much work?" was the question I asked myself at this point in the process. The answer is quite easy, but it took me some time to figure it out. If I used S-shaped lines, I could move them back and forth within the tail. In this way, it would seem as if the lines were bending when the tail did. This is what it looks like:

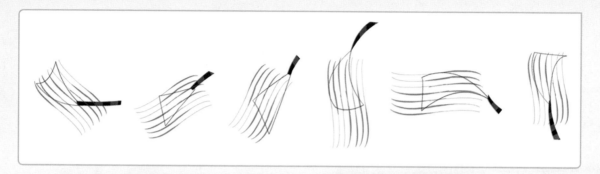

How curved the lines should be depends on the motion of the tail. Make sure that the lines look OK and work well within the context of the moving tail; the rest will be masked later on. You have to find the right *look* through rigorous trial and error.

You can either use the brush or draw curved lines using the Pen tool and turn them into shapes, which you can then alter. Do this by grabbing hold of the edge of the shape and pulling it.

Let's continue.

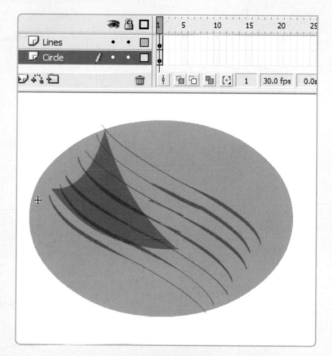

6. In the Line layer, draw the lines.

7. Navigate to Grodd original and start duplicating the keyframes and easing in the Tail fin layer.

    Because the tail fin was so difficult to animate, I was forced to use key-by-key animation in a certain area: frames 37 through 41. You have to do this with the Tail fin texture layer as well. Make sure that the easing on the keyframes of both layers matches.

8. When you're satisfied with the motion, you can turn the Tail fin layer into a mask, so that it masks the Tail fin texture layer. The results should look something like the following image:

I leave it up to you to finish this animation. The rest of the fins need to have the same transparent texture. The file up to this point is saved on the CD as GroddTailFin.fla, and the finished file is GroddFinished.fla.

In the end, this is what you accomplish with the mask technique.

If you want to change the colors and the textures, it's very easy. Just navigate into the appropriate symbol and change it. You've already finished all the motion and masking, so don't bother changing those. You can see a couple of examples in GroddFinished2.fla and GroddFinished3.fla on the CD.

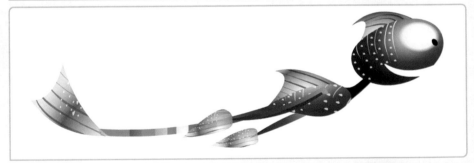

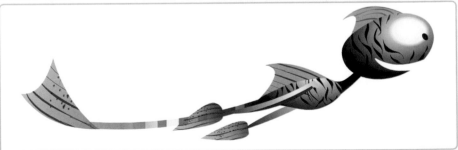

Using animated masking to create 3D-type animations

You've looked at just one way to use this technique, but there are many more. Mostly I developed this technique because I wanted to make some 3D-like animations involving textures. A texture means not only using vector graphics, but also using pixel graphics. In Flash you can fill a shape with a bitmap image. Unlike ordinary gradients that you can move within the shape, however, bitmaps can only fill the shape.

I've seen bitmap textures used before in Flash, but usually the result looks flat and boring. If you can combine the motion of a shape and the form of the texture, though, you can achieve amazing results. In this section, I'll give you a little taste of this.

My idea was to put some texture on a pixie hat, and at the same time make it rotate.

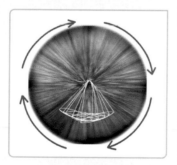

I made a circular texture in Photoshop that I put into a symbol (included on the CD as `PixieHatTexture.png`). Then I made that symbol rotate. The hat is just a shape moving back and forth a little. This shape is used to mask the rotating texture.

I used the same mask to make a couple of shadows on the hat. The result is a rotating pixie head. No 3D is involved—only good old shape tweens. (You can see this for yourself by opening `RotatingPixieHead.fla` from the CD.)

Now on to the nice part: this spinning animation's size is about 30KB, and most of this is the result of the bitmap texture. The more you compress the animation, the smaller the size will become.

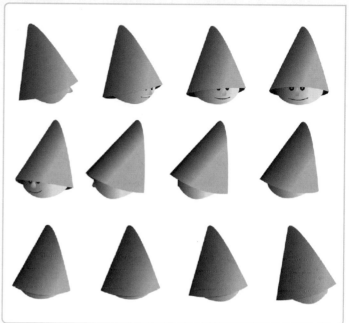

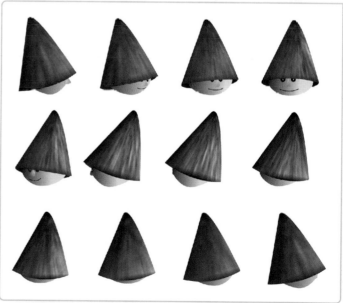

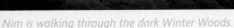

Nim is walking through the dark Winter Woods.

The windmill in the borderlands.

Summary

So there you have it, a short introduction to the world of masking. I'm waiting for the day when we can distort symbols in Flash, animate bitmap fills, and scale them without those jerky movements. Then we'll be able to achieve really great things. Until that day comes, we have to stick with the tools Flash provides and use them to the best of our ability.

Flash is a rare program that's expanding in many directions: games, web development, applications, education, commercials, cartoons, television, cinema—the list goes on and on. It attracts programmers, designers, developers, and artists alike. All in all, Flash is an amazing program for animators all around the globe, and I'm sure that the more we discover what we can do with this program, the more accepted it will become. In response to the question "Do you think Flash will continue to be the animator's tool of choice?" my answer is that I believe it will attract even more traditional animators as our knowledge of how we can use this program deepens. It's giving people a wonderful opportunity to make animations in a fast and inexpensive way. Flash has already proven itself capable of making good animations, and soon I hope we'll be able to make really high-class animations. Much depends on us as artists pushing the limits and also on Macromedia helping us get there.

I'll continue working on my *Nim's Journey* film and its website, which I hope will be up and running by the release of this book. The website, www.nimsjourney.com, will cover the progress of making the film from scratch—a kind of diary for the interested.

It's still a long way until any animation will be published, but I hope to at least publish some screenshots and illustrations, among other goodies. Because I'm doing this in my spare time, and because I work alone, I can't guarantee when the first episode will be released. This is a long-term project that will most likely span years. I'll leave you with some concept images from *Nim's Journey*.

Nim fishing at Shadowmere

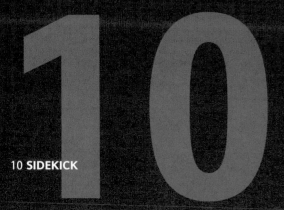

"WHILE I SEE BEAUTY IN EVERYTHING
AROUND ME, IT IS THE LOGIC BEHIND
IT THAT INTRIGUES ME THE MOST."

TODD MARKS
WWW.MINDGRUB.NET

Inspirations and influences

I believe everything is defined by the most beautiful mathematics in the world. Each of us has free will, yet there are forces within and around us that push and pull us in a preordained direction. While I see beauty in everything around me, it's the logic behind it that intrigues me the most.

> "I BELIEVE EVERYTHING IS DEFINED BY THE MOST BEAUTIFUL MATHEMATICS IN THE WORLD."

Tree branches, for instance, grow in relation to other branches because they following the mathematical Fibonacci sequence. In itself, a tree branch has much beauty, but the equation that dictates its growth is pure genius.

That type of information keeps me jazzed about the world. I've always had a strong desire to know everything worth knowing, and I've never run out of things to learn. This in turn has led me to specialize in information display systems as well as working with Flash, so that I can develop better ways of sending and receiving information.

My primary influences have been events in my life and a strong desire to disseminate information. Design is a skill I picked up along the way to help me present information more successfully. Lucky for me, I've had the chance to work with some outstanding designers—from my early dot com days to my current work with mediaEdge, The Unity Project, and Mindgrub Technologies. Although I haven't had any formal design training, I've been exposed to some of the best design in the world, and I learn by osmosis.

I suspect that I've also always followed a path of least resistance, or some sort of destined track in my life. I've never had to consciously choose what to do next—things have just crossed my path or developed from what seemed like the most fun at the time. If you know me, you'd think that this way of living might have lead me to fill my time with entirely outdoor activities. Instead, I feel drawn toward web-based information display, and specifically, to training development.

The Dining Hall, wood block print by Todd Marks

Ki-Yi Ki-Yi Ki Flippity Bim!
Come out of the woods, sandpaper your chin.
We're wild we're wooly we're rough like a saw,
Pathfinder Pathfinder raw, raw, raw!

Mom and Dude

My parents were the first major influences in my life—and not simply for their genetic contribution. My mother gave me her time and nurturing and my father shared his wealth of knowledge and his passion for sharing that knowledge with others. I believe my father's affinity for distributing knowledge has been the single most influential thing in my life. His influence caused me to go to school and concentrate on education, and all the while, he has been the guiding force that explains why I am currently looking for new ways to distribute knowledge.

Pathfinder

Between the ages of 12 and 22, I spent the better part of my summers at a wilderness camp and outdoor leadership school located in Canada's Algonquin Park. In fact, I still travel there most summers. It is at Pathfinder that I realized that I wanted to educate. Pathfinder is a Mecca for freethinking, or at least non-commercialized thought processes; there is no electricity to run a TV and everyone lives in tents. As a result, we entertained ourselves with conversations about philosophy, sociology, and the sciences. These experiences didn't necessarily play into my design aesthetic, but they did contribute to why I'm so enthralled with the sharing of information.

Because it is the place that I had my first formal teaching experience, Pathfinder additionally influenced me. I was a canoe and rock-climbing instructor and had the opportunity to learn climbing from a great instructor, Jon Benjamin; I then passed on what he taught me to others. From this experience on, I've enjoyed sharing information, which has led me to teach at the high-school level, to lecture at colleges and universities, to hold online classes, and to author for a number of years now. In addition, I've recently shifted my focus to concentrate on creating training software and learning management systems.

Pathfinder was also the first place where I worked in a very open environment with a dedicated team. The other people involved in the climbing program were particularly passionate about the cause. Working with such a small group of individuals who are really into what they are doing has become a theme to all the things that draw me in life.

The final aspect of spending my summers at Pathfinder that has heavily influenced me is that it is where I adopted my favorite color pallet: the colors of nature.

I enjoy colors found naturally in the environment and therefore, it is probably not surprising that I am most drawn toward fall. I think that this too is a path of least resistance since I've clashed with too many other colors my entire life—I have red hair and freckles. I always find that natural colors suit me best, and therefore, I'm paying homage when I select such colors for my work.

Self-reproduction, mono-print by Todd Marks

Tom Thomson

One painter who used the nature-based color scheme that I admire the most is Tom Thomson (1877-1917). Tom Thomson was a Canadian painter who lived and spent much of his time painting in Algonquin Park. Thomson also happened to have been a member of a group of friends called the Group of Seven and was a very driven person. Unfortunately for him, he died mysteriously while out in a canoe on one of his many outings. His work, however, is full of bold color and plays off the vibrant colors found naturally in Algonquin Park.

Of course, other well-known artists have inspired me, such as Leonardo da Vinci and M. C. Escher, though in this case, I think my admiration stems from the fact that I consider myself a kindred spirit to the two: part inventor, part mathematician, part artist. Escher and da Vinci also demonstrated a strong drive that I admire, and indeed that has been recognized historically.

Atholton

The next group to whom I can definitively point as being a major influence on me after my years at Pathfinder are the students I worked with at Atholton High School. The second year I taught at Atholton, the Instructional Leader from the Computer Science department, Reg Hahne, pulled me aside and asked me to pick up a few classes in the Computer Science department.

This experience was similar to my Pathfinder experience in that I ended up working with a small group of extremely dedicated students who very readily shared information. This was at the height of the dot com boom, however, so I soon left education to get a start-up company rolling with friends. However, had I not gained significant confidence working with these students and with Reg Hahne, I might not have ended up where I am today.

*om Thomson, The Jack Pine, 1917, Oil on canvas
National Gallery of Canada, Ottawa)*

digitalorganism

When I got the bug in me that caused me to leave public education and start an Information Technology company, I teamed up with one of my friends who had a similar idea. He and his brother pulled me in to a multimedia company called digitalorganism (www.digitalorganism.com). The company grew from one that inhabited a less then glamorous apartment to a chic pad in Baltimore's Fells Point district.

It was here that I had my very first experience with Flash. Someone showed me Rand Interactive's site, where Branden Hall, Asako Nagata, and others had created a 3D navigation that used a beta version of Flash 4. At the time, I can say I was bewildered and totally amazed! I also remember that my computer could barely handle the animation.

It was soon after digitalorganism was founded that I came on board, and we then developed digitalorganism's Genesis site, which put us on the map. That site, which we created entirely using Flash, had a 3D rotating and interactive helix. This was originally coded, once again, by Branden, but I reworked it before we incorporated it into the site. That navigation, and the Genesis site as the whole, earned us three Flash Film Festival nominations, two ADDY awards, you name it. It truly was a genesis, and it is what sparked the majority of the client work we received.

During my two years at digitalorganism, I headed up research and development and worked on several sites and presentation media for companies such as Verve Music, Motown Records, Universal Studios, and KurzweilAI. By this point, we had pulled in Asako Nagata, and hired the likes of Chrissy Rey and Brian Espinola. The sites that we produced were cutting-edge and the individuals we hired were some of the best in the industry. digitalorganism is also the place where I first picked up multimedia tools such as Flash, Dreamweaver, Director, PHP, and Photoshop.

Mindgrub Technologies

After I left digitalorganism, I started working for myself and founded Mindgrub Technologies, LLC (www.mindgrub.net). When I originally left teaching, it was to create an information display system that could be used to present data and advertising. As soon as I got Mindgrub Technologies off the ground, I fell into a contract with ARINC Information Technology doing just that. I began working on a Flight Information Display System (FIDS), which features a presentation client design with Macromedia Flash.

The amazing folks at ARINC are another group of passionate developers who have really helped shape my developmental outlook, and specifically, have helped me hone my skills developing information display systems. Developing the FIDS display at ARINC was the first enterprise-scale application that I helped build and bring to fruition. I've since developed and released a simplified version of the same system called *easyIDS*, which was recently showcased in the book *Macromedia Flash MX 2004 Magic* (New Riders, 2004). Building from these experiences, I've now helped bring over a dozen products to market and have assumed the roll of a Product Manager.

While I'm talking about Mindgrub Technologies, I should take a moment to give a plug for and a shout out to Bill Spencer, AKA Pope de Flash. Bill gave me a cool color scheme and the logo for Mindgrub Technologies. In addition, Bill and I have recently joined forces to create the Unity Project. Right now, The Unity Project, www.theunityproject.com, is still under construction. When it is finished, we intend for it to function as a portal where designers and developers can come together and share ideas. Ultimately, we feel that the best work is achieved through collaboration, and we want The Unity Project to facilitate this level of collaboration. Bill has been a good friend and design confidant when I need one. And likewise, I have helped him out with some programming projects when he has needed it.

Mind

search _____ GO

NEWS

House and Studio Nearing Completion
1/1/2004
New House and Studios are nearing completion. We should be moved in within the month.

Plumtree Showcases Gavel
12/10/2003
Plumtree showcases MediaEdge's electronic courtroom management software, Gavel

Plumtree Odyssey
10/12/2003
mediaEdge attends Plumtree users conference

EDIA

Sidekick Intro
Sidekick, made with Macromedia Flash, allows developers to build training modules on the fly. Incorporate custom animation, video, and Macromedia RoboDemo simulations to make captivating and interactive training.

For more information
10.694.0240

Exceptional Branding
Exceptional animation for

CODE

Sidekick
mediaEdge's software simulation training

Video Transcriber
mediaEdge's searchable courtroom video software

Rich Media Server
mediaEdge's portal video asset management software

REVIEWS

Flash MX Components
MindGrub and PopeDeFlash created a sliding panel component which is showcased in this book published by Friends of Ed

Flash MX Video
This book demonstrates how to use Flash MX's new video features. Chapters written by MindGrub Technologies

Advanced Php for Flash

SHOWCASE

mediaEdge

www.media-edge.com
mediaEdge is a division of Exceptional Software specializing in content management, information display, and video services and solutions. mediaEdge brings you Building Block Technology which was used in the creation of this site

MM Certified Developer, Designer | MM SME | t. 410.446.3901 | info@mindgrub.com

ARRIVALS

3 : 54 am
Dec 19, 2002

Aerolinea	Vuelo	Destino	Hora	Sala	Comentario
NORTHWEST AIRLINES	NWA 0524	Port of Spain	03:25 AM	G2	Aterizado
SOUTHWEST AIRLINES	SWA 34	Port of Spain	03:25 AM	A32	Aterizado
SOUTHWEST AIRLINES	SWA 2151	Dakar	05:00 AM	A32	
UNITED	UNI 8864	Sao Paulo	07:30 AM	D03	
UNITED	UNI 4150	Sao Paulo	07:30 AM	B16	
Lufthansa	LUF 1300	Buenos Aires	08:20 AM	A4	
LANCHILE	LAN 0530	Santiago	08:30 AM	B13	
NORTHWEST AIRLINES	NWA 530	Santiago	08:30 AM	B15	
KLM	KLM 6641	Amsterdam	12:15 PM	G9	
NORTHWEST AIRLINES	NWA 0061	Amsterdam	12:15 PM	G36	
UZBEKISTAN airways	UZB 0130	Accra	01:30 PM	E12	

Any unattended baggage will be subject to search and may be destroyed.

Screenshot of Flight Information Display System created with Flash

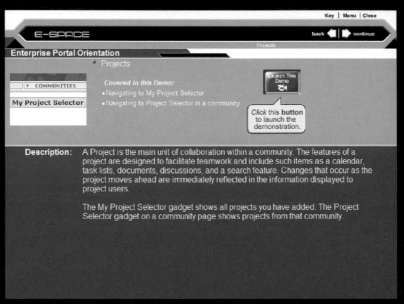

Sample screenshot of Sidekick training application

mediaEdge

By now it's clear that several passionate groups have helped shape me into the designer and developer that I am today. The most recent of these is mediaEdge, a division of Exceptional Software Strategies Inc. (www.media-edge.com), where my desires to create information display systems and disseminate knowledge has culminated.

I initially started Mindgrub Technologies to focus on visual information systems, and I've had tremendous success with this venture, with clients such as ARINC, Zurich Insurance Company, and Oracle. This path brought me to work with mediaEdge—I've really enjoyed working with these guys. In the course of a year, we were able to bring five new products to market, double in size, and require new office space.

It's pretty exciting right now at Exceptional Software Strategies—like many new media companies, mediaEdge is at the point where it could really make it huge over the next couple of years. mediaEdge is really the location where a lot of things have come together for me, specifically my development of web- and computer-based training. When I first started at mediaEdge, the initial contract that I worked on was to create a computer-based training CD-ROM. From my past experiences creating information display systems, I'd learned that I wanted to develop the architecture for the training so that it could be used to deliver any web or computer-based training in a similar fashion as an information display system. So we made a system that reads an XML file that contains all of the information about each training lesson, and auto generates a tailored navigation to linearly progress through the training lessons. We later added a content administration tool, called the backroom, and have since dubbed the entire application *Sidekick*.

Web-based training

Currently my main goal is to create hardware and software solutions that allow information to travel an infinite distance in zero time, thereby allowing an individual to know anything and everything instantly. I believe Flash offers the best tools for creating a solid presentation tier for an information display system. This, in turn, makes it good for educational purposes. I also like Flash because it has a solid balance of design and development tools, meaning you can have everything from animation to the digestion of web services within a single medium.

Currently, as humans, we must distribute information to the minds of others by passing data via our senses.

Until we override these senses, and most likely even after we do, the human mind will continue to import data and re-create a mental picture of that data. The design of that picture is a key ingredient to how well that information is learned, stored, and retained by the user.

So, by creating a web-based training system, I am looking to develop a way to best pass information. Since we are so governed by visual experiences and want to be entertained, I have not only created a interactive Flash-based training application, but I have created an avatar, the Sidekick trainer, to add some visual excitement in this chapter's tutorial.

Creating an XML-driven animated trainer

In this part of the chapter we are going to create an animated lip-sync training utility. This will allow you to create a web-based figure, such as the Sidekick trainer, and give it the ability to mouth the words of an MP3 file. In this fashion, you can add voice-overs to an instructional piece and have, in addition, an entertaining figure to deliver that knowledge.

To see an example of the application in action, check out the file `lipSyncInstructions.mov` on this book's CD.

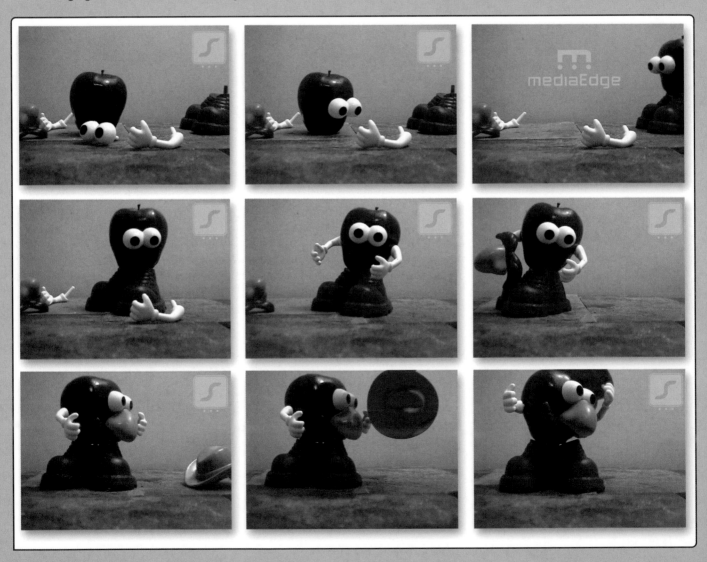

Overview

This utility allows you to synchronize phonemes with an MP3 file. A *phoneme* is essentially the smallest aspect of speech used for pronunciation—typically a single or double character that you move your lips and tongue in a certain manner to produce.

The utility outputs XML that will control the attributes of a character's animations. The XML is parsed and the timelines for the lips and actions of the Sidekick trainer are animated. This forms an animated trainer who can deliver specific training soundtracks.

This greatly enhances the entertainment value of your educational content, which directly correlates to the amount of information retained by the learner.

With all of my current projects I like to create a system written with entirely reusable code. In the case of this lip-sync utility, all of the code can easily be ported over to an ActionScript 2.0 object. For now, however, I have left it as a series of functions on the first frame of the main timeline so that it is easy to see how it works.

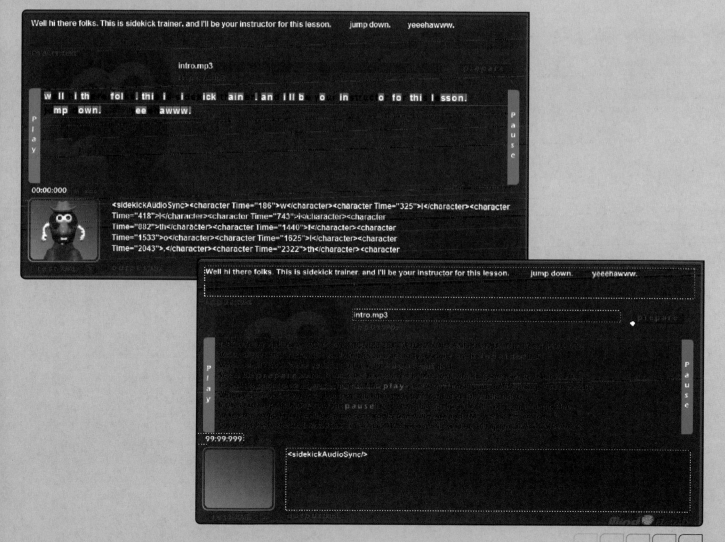

Project development

In the following sections, I'll highlight the main stages in the development of our animated trainer that enable us to synchronize phonemes with an MP3 file and output those timings as XML. We'll cover the following stages:

- Creating graphics and setting up our project file

- Incorporating buttons and text fields

- Adding the actual Sidekick trainer movie clip

- Adding ActionScript and constructing the functionality of the utility

Graphics and set up

On any project, I typically like to look for ways to reduce the amount of time it takes me to do things—this explains my love of reusable and modular code. In this case, instead of drawing an animation from scratch, I took a series of pictures of my Sidekick model using a small stage and a digital camera mounted on a tripod. I then batch processed the images using Photoshop to crop and scale them. Next, I opened the series of images in Flash and vectorized them, so that the end result looks like an animation that I slaved away in a 3D modeling program to create. This isn't cheating, this is efficiency!

In this tutorial we are going to start with all of the images (animations) in the timeline, organized within the various movie clips for lip and body movement. We will place each of the movie clips within the file and add the relevant code to make it work.

1. To start, open the file `synchronizer_start.fla`. You will notice that the file is already set to have dimensions of 800~TMS420, a background color of #300000, and a frame rate of 31 frames per second (31 fps is a reliable rate; its playback is the same speed on both Macs and PCs). If you look in the Library (CTRL+L), you will see that all of the assets have been organized into five main folders: backgrounds, buttons, character, loadAudio, and sidekickTrainer.

We are going to look at each folder individually and build the utility in the order in which the folders are organized.

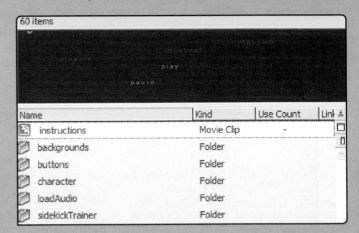

2. Now add seven new layers, in addition to the default layer, to the main timeline. Name the layers: actions, sidekickTrainer, textFields, instructions, loadingAudio, graphics, grey, and background.

As a rule of thumb, I always like to have my layers organized with actions *as the first layer and* labels *as the second layer. With this main timeline, we are only going to use the first frame, so in this case, we don't need a* labels *layer. When we look at some of the other movie clip timelines, however, you will notice that this layer is included.*

3. We are going to start developing by adding the background to the stage. The background is a combination of a picture of the Sidekick trainer as well as borders for each of the text fields and the utility as a whole. All of these graphics sit within the border movie clip where I gave them a 70% tint of our background color #300000.

Open the backgrounds folder in the library and drag a copy of border to the background layer in the main timeline.

4. Next up, open up the Properties panel and give the border movie clip an X value of 1.0 and a Y value of 1.0 with the registration point set in the top-left corner.

5. Drag a copy of the movie clip grey from the backgrounds folder in the Library to the background layer.

6. Open the Properties panel and give the grey movie clip an X position of 13.2 and a Y position of 293.4. This graphic will become the background behind the animated trainer.

7. We are now going to add the static text fields and buttons to the stage. These assets will all be added to the graphics layer of the timeline. Open the buttons folder in the Library and select the graphics layer of the main timeline.

8. Drag the pause button out of the Library and give it an X position of 767 and a Y position of 121.

You will notice that a couple of these buttons are blue-green in appearance. If you add a graphic to the last frame of a button's timeline, and no other frames, you get what is referred to as an **invisible button**. When working within the Flash authoring tool, these invisible buttons show up as this blue-green color. But don't be fooled by my buttons—in fact, they're not actually invisible buttons, they just happen to be the same color; they will indeed show up in the final movie. In this case, I have added graphics to the first frame of each of these buttons but have colored them the blue-green color, #188080.

9. Drag the `pauseTest` button out of the Library and give it an X position of 104 and a Y position of 398. As you'll see later when you come to use the utility, the pause button is used to pause the audio, thus enabling you to make changes to the XML or to synchronize just a portion of the audio.

10. Drag the `play` button out of the Library and give it an X position of 14 and a Y position of 121. The `play` button is used to start the audio before synchronization.

11. Drag the `prepare` button out from the Library and give it an X position of 688 and a Y position of 77. This button initiates string detection of the different phonemes and outputs those characters as buttons with a visible hit state.

12. Drag the `stop` button out from the Library and give it an X position of 82 and a Y position of 275. The `stop` button stops the audio during synchronization or testing.

13. Finally, drag the `testXML` button out from the Library and give it an X position of 20 and a Y position of 396. The `testXML` button plays the audio and initiates parsing of the corresponding XML.

Buttons and text fields

Now that we have added all of the buttons to the stage, we now need to add the function calls that are triggered when each of the buttons is selected. For each of the buttons, you will need to open the Actions panel and add the prescribed actions. Note that, in keeping with my love of all things modular, I'm relying on the traditional attached scripting technique here.

To begin, there are two pause buttons. The first pause button on the right of the stage pauses the audio while synchronization takes place. The second pause button, pauseTest, appears on the bottom of the stage, beneath where the animated trainer resides; it is used to pause the audio while testing the XML output.

1. Starting back from the top, select the pause button and add the following:

```
on (rollOver) {
   PauseTranslation();
}
```

2. Next select the pauseTest button and add the following code.

```
on (release) {
   PauseTest();
}
```

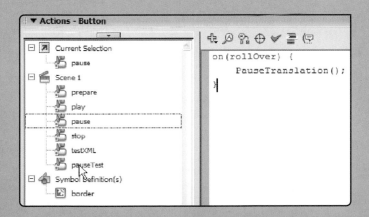

With Flash MX 2004, we now have the ability to navigate the different elements on stage directly within the Actions panel, without having to select the object on the stage first. You can now click each successive object in the menu to the left of the ActionScript pane.

3. Next, select the play button and add the following code. In the case of this button, we only want the function `StartTranslation()` triggered if we have yet to prepare the text (_global.bTranslationInProgress) or we have prepared the text but have already started the synchronization process. Essentially, the first time we hit the "process" button, we set _global.bSynchronizeInProgress equal to true. This way if we roll over the start button and _global.bSyncronizeInProgress is true, we know to start synchronizing from where we left off, as opposed to at the beginning.

```
on (rollOver) {
   if (_global.bTranslationInProgress &&
   ➥ !_global.bSyncronizeInProgress) {
      this.StartTranslation();
   }
}
```

4. Next, we need to add the following code to the stop button.

```
on (release) {
   StopTranslation(true);
}
```

5. Add this final bit of code to the testXML button.

```
on (release) {
   this.TestXML(oAudio.text, oXML,
   ➥ oLoadingAudio);
}
```

6. The next things that we want to add are all of the text fields. These come in the flavors of static, input, and dynamic. Let's start by adding the static text fields. Keeping to the graphics layer, add four static text fields with the following text: input:text, input:mp3, output:xml, and stop. The font that I used was Eras Demi ITC, but you can use anything similar. The following screenshot shows the placement and relative sizes of these text fields:

7. Now, we need to move to the textFields layer where we are going to add three input text fields and one dynamic text field.

8. Start by selecting the Text tool option in the toolbar and move the text type to Input in the Properties panel. Add a first text field with a width of 771, a height of 47, an X position of 15, and a Y position of 10. Give this text field an instance name of oText.

9. Now add a second input text field with a width of 423, a height of 19, an X position of 247, and a Y position of 76. Give this text field an instance name of oAudio.

10. Now add a final input text field with a width of 647, a height of 99, an X position of 143, and a Y position of 295. Give this text field an instance name of oXML.

11. Finally, switch to dynamic text in the Properties panel and add a fourth text field to the stage. Give this last text field a width of 74, a height of 18, an X position of 3, and a Y position of 272. Give this text field an instance name of `oTime`.

Note that the file `synchronizer_final.fla` *has some default text and a path to a corresponding MP3 file so that a user can test the file and have immediate results. These values, however, are not a necessity for building the utility.*

The next two items that we will add are helpful, but trivial to the utility as a whole. The first item includes the instructions to the user, which are just static text, and the second item is an animated loading movie clip that plays while an MP3 file is loading.

12. Select the instructions layer of the timeline and drag a copy of the `instructions` movie clip out from the Library. Give it an X position of 36, and a Y position of 124. Give this movie clip a name of `oInstructions`.

13. Select the loadingAudio layer of the main timeline and drag a copy of the `loadingAudioMC` from the loadAudio folder in the Library. Give this movie clip an X position of 688 and a Y position of 96. Give this movie clip an instance name of `oLoadingAudio`.

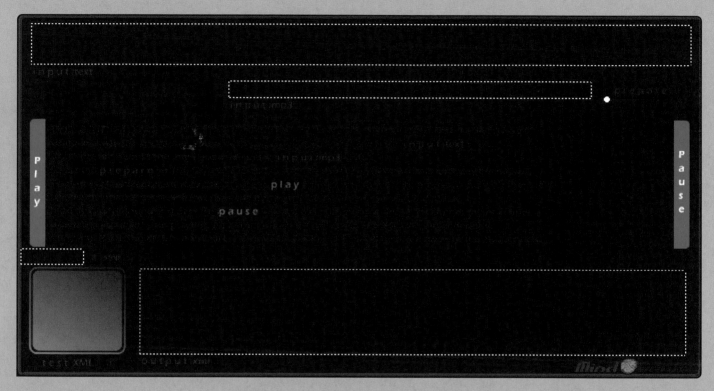

Sidekick trainer

The Sidekick trainer movie clip is no more than a bunch of imported PNG files with `stop()` actions and frame labels. We will explore these timelines so that you really understand how everything fits together. I've used PNG files here so that I can have an invisible background with the imported graphic. It's not possible to do this with an imported JPG, GIF, or BMP because you will end up seeing the rectangular border with these formats.

1. Start by selecting the sidekickTrainer layer of the main timeline. Drag a copy of `sidekickMC` from the sidekickTrainer folder in the Library. Give this movie clip an X position of 23 and a Y position of 286. You should be placing the trainer over that grey circle we added to that corner earlier. Give this movie clip an instance name of `oSidekickTrainer`.

2. Double-click the `sidekickMC` clip and let's start examining the timelines. The first timeline that you see is little more then a tween to bring the trainer to the foreground of the stage.

3. If you double-click the `sidekick` movie clip, you'll see that this is where things start to get more exciting. Embedded in this movie clip you will see all of the different animations to make the trainer's body move to walk, talk, point right, and stop.

The selection of animations included in the file is very limited—though of course several hundred could be added to this timeline. Then, after you added such animations, and depending on the `Action` attribute of the XML synchronization data, the Sidekick trainer could demonstrate all of the different movements and actions.

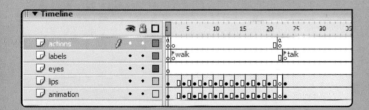

Now look at the ActionScript based on this timeline—aside from a bunch of `stop()` actions throughout the timeline, frame 1 has some relevant code. The first function here, `PlayNext()` simply has a `gotoAndPlay()` action that tells the timeline to go play the next animation. The value of `action` is set in the main body of code and is parsed from the attributes of the XML.

```
function PlayNext() {
  this.gotoAndPlay(action);
}
```

The next functions, `Blink()` and `setInterval()`, simply makes the animation for the eyes blink every ten seconds when the trainer is playing the `stop` animation. `oEyes` is the name of the movie clip that contains the animation for eye movement.

```
function Blink() {
  oEyes.gotoAndPlay(2);
}
setInterval(Blink, 10000);
```

4. Finally, if you drill down one more movie clip into the `mouth` movie clip found on the `lips` layer, you'll find each of the different images for the different phonemes. In this case, not all of the different phonemes are included, though you could certainly add a graphic for each, as well as corresponding facial and jaw moments.

For a handy phoneme reference, take a look at this page: www.auburn.edu/~murraba/spellings.html.

Creating these lip images was pretty fun—I started by trying to determine what I thought were the significant phonemes by simply looking at myself talking and miming in a mirror. After taking a base picture of my Mr. Potato Head lips, I then morphed the image of the lips to look like my lip movements.

Before I explain the crucial code, let's talk about the final piece of the puzzle that makes this entire thing work, the `characterMC` movie clip. The `characterMC`, which gets attached to the main timeline for every character or multiple characters processed from the text, contains a button and a text field for displaying the associated character or characters.

The button's visibility is set to true or false when it is attached, depending on whether that particular character has a corresponding animation or not. Lucky for you, I have also already included everything that we'll need for this movie clip in the Library.

If you look at the linkage column, you will notice that this movie clip is exported as character. The code I add next dynamically grabs this movie clip out of the Library, so you don't need to do anything with this movie clip.

Code outline

The core of this utility is the code behind it. A heavy description would put most folks to sleep, so I'll summarize the functionality of each section of code. Once again, I encourage you to view the file lipSyncInstructions.mov and play around with the FLAs to see everything work together.

I started by adding the following code to the prepare button:

```
on (release) {
  var iXPos = 36;
  var iYPos = 124;
  // order array based on significance,
  // comparison will continue up until first
  // match.
  var arrPronunciation = new Array(".",
  ➥ "a", "b", "ch", "ck", "ee", "f",
  ➥ "i", "l", "m", "n", "oo", "o", "p",
  ➥ "ss", "th", "v", "w");
  this.PrepareTranslation(oText.text,
  ➥ oAudio.text, oTime, oXML, oLoadingAudio,
  ➥ iXPos, iYPos, arrPronunciation);
}
```

To keep to an object-oriented practice, I had to pass in all of the elements that reside outside of the main code functionality as parameters. In this case, all of the phonemes that have corresponding animations within the Sidekick trainer are passed in to the PrepareTranslation function as the array arrPronunciation. (As mentioned before, the code included with this utility could be broken out into a separate AS file and converted to an ActionScript 2.0 object.)

Note: If you want to add additional phonemes and animations, you can easily do so by adding their characters to the arrPronunciation array, and to the corresponding graphic to the lips movie clip that we added earlier in this chapter.

You will also notice that the object names for the different text fields are passed into the PrepareTranslation function, which I will cover shortly. This is once again to keep the code object oriented, and because the code itself doesn't create these graphical elements.

In this last step in creating the synchronization utility, I added the following code to the actions layer of the main timeline.

This code is going to prepare the text for synchronization as well as text XML and animate the Sidekick trainer—I'll skim through the finer details here.

This first function, CompareXML() walks through the phoneme array, which I added first (discussed above), compares the time when each phoneme was encountered during synchronization, and tells the lips movie clip to play each phoneme when that time is reached during playback. It does this by looking at the Time attribute in the XML and comparing that to the current time in the sound file during playback. When the times are the same, it tells the oLips movie clip to stop on the frame with a corresponding label as the phoneme.

```
// **** THIS SECTION FOR TESTING XML DATA ****
// sample XML Data
function CompareXML() {
  this.iArrPosition = 0;
  var action = null;
  this.onEnterFrame = function() {
    DisplayPosition(this.oTime, this.oTempSound);
    if (this.iArrPosition == this.arrTempResults.length) {
      this.oSidekickTrainer.oSidekick.oLips.gotoAndStop(1);
      this.bTestPaused = false;
      this.onEnterFrame = null;
    } else if (this.arrTempResultsTime[this.iArrPosition]<=this.oTempSound.position) {
      if (this.arrTempResultsTime[this.iArrPosition]>=(this.oTempSound.position-200)) {
        this.oSidekickTrainer.oSidekick.oLips.gotoAndStop
        ➥ (this.arrTempResults[this.iArrPosition]);
        if (this.arrTempResultsAction[this.iArrPosition] == undefined) {
          action = "stop";
        } else {
          action = this.arrTempResultsAction[this.iArrPosition];
        }
        this.oSidekickTrainer.oSidekick.action = action;
      }
      this.iArrPosition++;
    }
  };
}
```

The parse function is a recursive function that walks through all of the nodes in the XML file and stores times and phonemes in arrays as they are encountered:

```
function Parse(_firstchild) {
    //Recursive function that parses XML
    if (_firstchild != null) {
        var sNode = _firstchild.nodeName;
        var oAttributesArray = _firstchild.attributes;
        switch (sNode) {
        case ("sidekickAudioSync") :
            break;
        case ("character") :
            this.arrTempResultsTime.push(oAttributesArray["Time"]);
            this.arrTempResultsAction.push(oAttributesArray["Action"]);
            this.arrTempResults.push(_firstchild.firstChild);
            break;
        default :
            //unexpected tag encountered
            error = true;
            break;
        }
        var oNextChildXml = _firstchild.firstChild;
        while (oNextChildXml != null) {
            this.Parse(oNextChildXml);
            oNextChildXml = oNextChildXml.nextSibling;
        }
    }
}
```

The PauseTest function pauses the audio when the button is pressed:

```
function PauseTest() {
    this.oTempSound.stop();
    this.iPause = this.oTempSound.position/1000;
}
```

The `TestXML` function is triggered by the test XML button and kicks off the parsing of the XML, the storing of the times and phonemes, and the creation of the sound object to play.

```
function TestXML(sAudio, objXML, objLoadAudio) {
  // create storage arrays
  this.arrTempResults = new Array();
  this.arrTempResultsTime = new Array();
  this.arrTempResultsAction = new Array();
  // create XML object
  this.xmlTemp = new XML(objXML.text);
  Parse(this.xmlTemp.firstChild);
  // grab current position
  var iPos = this.oTempSound.position;
  if ((iPos != undefined) && (iPos != 0) && (iPos != this.oTempSound.duration)) {
    this.oTempSound.stop();
    this.oTempSound.start(this.iPause, 1);
    CompareXML();
  } else {
    // create sound obj and load sound
    this.oTempSound = new Sound();
    var iNewFrame = 0;
    this.onEnterFrame = function() {
      if (iNewFrame) {
        this.oTempSound.loadSound(sAudio, false);
        objLoadAudio.gotoAndPlay("loading");
        this.oTempSound.onLoad = function() {
          objLoadAudio.gotoAndStop(1);
          CompareXML();
          this.start();
        };
        this.oTempSound.onSoundComplete = function() {
          iPause = 0;
        };
      }
      iNewFrame++;
    };
  }
}
```

This next function keeps track of when the text field with the audio link is changed. When is it changed, the oTempSound object is set to false so that a new sound object is created with the new MP3 file:

```
oAudio.onChanged = function() {
  this.oTempSound = null;
};
```

The next section of code processes the text and finds all of the phonemes. It then attaches the characterMC movie clip (via its linkage name character) and affects the visibility of the attached button depending on whether or not it encounters a marked phoneme.

Firstly, the OutputXML function outputs the XML after synchronization has taken place.

```
// ***THIS SECTION FOR GENERATING XML DATA ****
function OutputXML() {
  this.oXML.text = "<sidekickAudioSync>";
  for (var iPos = 0; iPos<this.arrResults.length; iPos++) {
    this.oXML.text += "<character Time=\""+this.arrResultsTime[iPos]+"\">"
    ➥ +arrResults[iPos]+"</character>";
  }
  this.oXML.text += "</sidekickAudioSync>";
}
function LogChar(sChar) {
  // record the timings for the special characters
  this.arrResultsTime.push(this.oSound.position);
  // and what characters are recorded
  this.arrResults.push(sChar);
}
function RemovePreviousCharacters() {
  if (this.iChar != null) {
    for (var iChar = 0; iChar<=this.iChar; iChar++) {
      removeMovieClip(this["char"+iChar]);
    }
  }
}
```

The AddCharacter function attaches the different instances of the characterMC movie clip. It keeps track of the position of the last written character and wraps to the next line if the end of a line is achieved.

```
function AddCharacter(iHotSpotLength, sCharsToWrite, iXMax, iYMax) {
  // write out text with hotspots to grab timing.
  this.iChar++;
  this.attachMovie("character", "char"+(this.iChar), this.iChar);
  // determine if a hotspot needs to be visible
  if (iHotSpotLength == 0) {
    this["char"+this.iChar].oTextField.textColor = "0xC23000";
    this["char"+this.iChar].oHotSpot._visible = false;
  }
  // add the character and size the hotspot
  this["char"+this.iChar].oTextField.text = sCharsToWrite;
  this["char"+this.iChar].oHotSpot._width = this["char"+this.iChar].oTextField.textWidth;
  // determine next place to write text.
  this["char"+this.iChar]._x = this.iCumXPos;
  this["char"+this.iChar]._y = this.iCumYPos;
  // determine next x and y position
  this.iCumXPos += this["char"+this.iChar].oTextField.textWidth+1;
  if (this.iCumXPos>=(iXMax-17)) {
    this.iCumXPos = this.iStartXPos;
    this.iCumYPos += this["char"+this.iChar].oTextField.textHeight+4;
  }
}

function Div(iDividend, iDivisor) {
  return iNumDivides=Math.floor(iDividend/iDivisor);
}

function Mod(iDividend, iDivisor) {
  return iDividend-(Div(iDividend, iDivisor)*iDivisor);
}
```

The variables iXmax and iYMax are used to denote where the maximum x and y positions occur to dictate whether the next character in succession must wrap or not.

The `DisplayPosition()` function displays the current time location within the MP3 in a *minute:second:millisecond* format.

```
function DisplayPosition(oTextField, objSound) {
    // returns time in 00:00:000 time format
    var sAudioPosition = objSound.position;
    var iMinutes = Div(sAudioPosition, 60000);
    (iMinutes<=9) ? (sMinutes="0"+String(iMinutes)) : (sMinutes=String(iMinutes));
    var iSeconds = Div(sAudioPosition-(iMinutes*360), 1000);
    (iSeconds<=9) ? sSeconds=("0"+String(iSeconds)) : (sSeconds=String(iSeconds));
    var iMilliSeconds = sAudioPosition-(iMinutes*60000)-(iSeconds*1000);
    if (iMilliSeconds<=9) {
        sMilliSeconds = ("00"+String(iMilliSeconds));
    } else if (iMilliSeconds<=99) {
        sMilliSeconds = ("0"+String(iMilliSeconds));
    } else {
        sMilliSeconds = String(iMilliSeconds);
    }
    oTextField.text = sMinutes+":"+sSeconds+":"+sMilliSeconds;
}
```

Next, the `InitializeClock` function initializes the time display.

```
function InitializeClock(objTime, objLoadAudio, objSound) {
    // keeps track of the timings as well as
    // displaying the time duration
    objLoadAudio.gotoAndStop(1);
    // boolean to disable StartTranslation()
    // if preperation is not complete
    _global.bTranslationInProgress = true;
    DisplayPosition(objTime, objSound);
}
```

The function `CreateSoundObject` does just that—it creates a sound object and initializes the clock when a sound is loaded:

```
function CreateSoundObject(sAudio, objTime, objLoadAudio) {
    // create sound obj and load sound
    this.oSound = new Sound();
    this.oSound.loadSound(sAudio, false);
    // initialize clock after sound loads
    objLoadAudio.gotoAndPlay("loading");
    this.oSound.onLoad = InitializeClock(objTime, objLoadAudio, this.oSound);
```

```
    // create event call now to initiate XML output
    this.oSound.onSoundComplete = StopTranslation;
}
```

The function prepareTranslation does the bulk of the work in setting up the text for synchronization. As mentioned previously, it attaches the characterMC movie clip from the Library for each character in the text, making the button visible or not, depending on whether or not the character is a phoneme with a corresponding animation.

```
function PrepareTranslation(sText, sAudio, objTime, objXML, objLoadAudio, iXPos, iYPos,
➥ iXMax, iYMax, arrPronunciation) {
  RemovePreviousCharacters();
  StopTranslation(false);
  // turn visibility of instructions off,
  // output text with hotspots.
  oInstructions._visible = false;
  var sTextLowerCase = sText.toLowerCase();
  this.arrResults = new Array();
  this.arrResultsTime = new Array();
  // keep track of the cumulative X and Y positions.
  this.iCumXPos = iXPos;
  this.iCumYPos = iYPos;
  this.iStartXPos = iXPos;
  // create an object to point to the time text field.
  this.oTime = objTime;
  // create a string to hold the path of the sound file
  this.sSoundPath = sAudio;
  // create an object to point to the XML text field.
  this.oXML = objXML;
  // start a character counter
  this.iChar = 0;
  // make the character comparisons.
  for (var iTextPos = 0; iTextPos<=sTextLowerCase.length; iTextPos++) {
    var sStringMatch = false;
    var sChar = sTextLowerCase.substring(iTextPos, iTextPos+1);
    var sChars = sTextLowerCase.substring(iTextPos, iTextPos+2);
    for (var iPronunPos = 0; iPronunPos<=arrPronunciation.length; iPronunPos++) {
      // we assume that we are only looking for
      // 1 char or max 2 char matches
      if (sChars == arrPronunciation[iPronunPos]) {
        iTextPos++;
        sStringMatch = true;
```

Code continues overleaf

```
            AddCharacter(2, sChars, iXMax, iYMax);
            break;
        } else if (sChar == arrPronunciation[iPronunPos]) {
            sStringMatch = true;
            AddCharacter(1, sChar, iXMax, iYMax);
            break;
        }
    }
    if (!sStringMatch) {
        AddCharacter(0, sChar, iXMax, iYMax);
    }
  }
  CreateSoundObject(sAudio, objTime, objLoadAudio);
}
```

The next three functions are fairly self-explanatory: they start, pause, and stop the translation accordingly:

```
function StartTranslation() {
  if (this.oSound.position == 0) {
    // start from the beginning
    this.oSound.start();
    sDisplayInterval = setInterval(DisplayPosition, 100, this.oTime, this.oSound);
  } else {
    // start from last position
    this.oSound.start(this.iCurrentLocation, 1);
  }
  _global.bSyncronizeInProgress = true;
}

function PauseTranslation() {
  _global.bSyncronizeInProgress = false;
  // grab the current location within the sound object
  this.iCurrentLocation = this.oSound.position/1000;
  this.oSound.stop();
}

function StopTranslation(bOutput) {
  if (_global.bTranslationInProgress) {
    this.oSound.stop();
    clearInterval(sDisplayInterval);
    _global.bSyncronizeInProgress = false;
```

```
      _global.bTranslationInProgress = false;
      if (bOutput != false) {
        OutputXML();
      }
    } else {
      // maybe they wish to stop the testing of XML
      this.oTempSound.stop();
      this.oTempSound = null;
      this.onEnterFrame = null;
    }
  }
}
```

The variable and XML code at the end of this root timeline ActionScript is an example of the type of output and actions that can be called by the Sidekick trainer. When I initially tested the file synchronizer_final.fla, the trainer mouthed this XML as well as performed the walk animation. You will notice that the name of an audio file as well as the corresponding text is also included in the synchronizer_final.fla file. I've included this information so that you have something to test initially. For reference, a snippet of this XML is shown below—refer to the FLA for the full listing.

```
oSidekickTrainer.oSidekick.action = "walk";
oXML.text = "<sidekickAudioSync>
<character Time=\"1300\" Action=\"talk\">w</character>
<character Time=\"1440\">l</character>
<character Time=\"1486\">l</character>
.
.
.
<character Time=\"5062\">o</character>
<character Time=\"5387\" Action=\"point right\">th</character>
<character Time=\"5526\">i</character>
.
.
.
<character Time=\"7848\">w</character>
<character Time=\"7941\" Action=\"stop\">.</character>
</sidekickAudioSync>";
this.TestXML(oAudio.text, oXML, oLoadingAudio);
```

Now that I've finished with the overview of the coding behind this utility, let's test it out. Try grabbing your favorite song and synchronizing the trainer to its lyrics.

Using the Utility

To use the lip-sync utility to generate and test XML, open `syncronizer_final.swf` and follow these steps (for reference, these steps are also included in the opening screen of the SWF, along with the default introductory demo text):

1. Type or paste in the text of the audio track you want to synchronize in the input: text field.

   Remember that any time you want the trainer to pause or stop moving its lips you should include a period. When a period is received in the XML, it tells the trainer to go to a closed lip appearance. Also, if there are breaks between some of the spoken text, it is helpful to include spaces in the text to remind you to pause as you synchronize with the MP3 file.

2. Write the file path to the MP3 audio file in the input: mp3 field. If your MP3 is in the same directory as the SWF, you'll just need to add in the name of the file here.

3. Select the prepare button to have the text written to this area with hotspots over key characters.

   When you mouse over each of these hotspots, after first rolling over the play button, the time within the MP3 file will be recorded and both the phoneme and the corresponding time will be written as XML in the output: xml field.

4. To start synchronization, start to the left of the play hit area and move your mouse along with the audio.

5. Note that if the text wraps to a new line, by rolling over the pause hit area you can pause the audio till you begin the next line.

   It is sometimes helpful to add spaces to the original text before selecting the prepare button to force the text to wrap in helpful locations.

6. When the audio finishes playing, the synchronization will cease and XML will be generated. Note that you can also hit the stop button at any point while you synchronize. When you do hit the stop button, it will output the XML up to that point. This is key if you want to synchronize phrase by phrase and then piece the XML back together in an external editor.

7. You can add an `Action` attribute to the generated XML to animate the trainer along with the lip-syncing of the text. If you look at the sample XML or the included `lipSyncInstructions.mov`, you will see the additional `Action` attribute that makes the trainer walk and talk.

8. Select the test XML button to see the animated trainer lip-sync with the MP3 file you have synchronized with and generated the XML for.

Summary

I believe that I have come full circle; I was first a teacher, and now I create applications to aid teaching. If I can only get the "infinite distance in zero time" thing programmed, I will have reached my goals and can die happy—but I think that will take a little more planning. . . .

Right now, I am working on incorporating the Sidekick trainer with a light information display system that I've developed (*easyIDS 1.0*), to allow the character to enhance any Flash-based lesson. Another step I might try next, would be to take the XML generated from the lip-sync utility and have it reside within the schema for *easyIDS*, so that all the data can be pushed into a lesson or a presentation piece at the same time, using the same architecture. Be sure to check back with www.mindgrub.com for future updates.

Now that you have made the utility and worked with the current lip and body animations, it is time to create your own figure and corresponding animations.

Inspirations

Coming of age in San Francisco in the late 1980s had a profound impact on me and my life's work. The music scene was fantastic—from the street musicians to the stadium stars. Art supplies were cheap. Used book-stores carried books I could afford on everything that interested me . . . which was just about everything.

Back then, I spent a lot of time looking at the city through the lens of an old Canon AE1. I'd go on long walks to discover interesting patterns and architectural details. Black and white film was not only a wonderful medium, but a number of darkrooms could be rented by the hour and I could develop and print photos myself.

Combine this with my love of graphic artists like M. C. Escher, whose impossible geometrical structures and fantastical worlds have always fascinated me, and you're starting to get to know me.

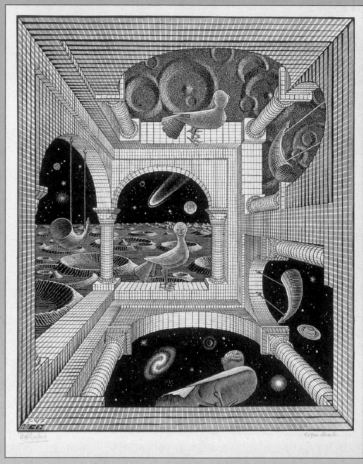

M.C. Escher's "Other World" © 2004
The M.C. Escher Company - Baarn - Holland.
All rights reserved.

I was having a great time, but my neighbors were dying of AIDS. I couldn't help but get at least a little depressed about that. I've always taken the path less traveled, and my response was to pursue studies in Biological Anthropology and Biology in hopes that I could help find a cure. I later found that my talents lie instead in communicating science, and gave up the path to research and founded GalaxyGoo.

GalaxyGoo is a non-profit organization that I founded in the late '90s. Basically, it's a web-based think-tank where volunteers develop educational software (www.galaxygoo.org). We focus on math and science topics, and our contributing members range from science enthusiasts with high school diplomas to research scientists with PhDs. While I have to spend a lot of time on paperwork and the business of running a small non-profit organization, I spend as much of my time as possible working on projects and encouraging others with their own.

The inspiration for many of my projects comes from subjects that I found interesting or challenging as a student. When I started GalaxyGoo, I thought it would be great to build games that helped with all the rote memory a science degree requires.

Electron micrograph of spleen tissue

Lots of ideas are still on my to-do list, like a Tetris-based game that uses organic chemistry molecular diagrams instead of blocks. I also thought it would be great to have an online community where developers and educators could come and get ideas for educational projects and share techniques.

As a biology student, I took a course in electron microscopy. It turned out to be one of my favorite classes ever, and it was the beginning of my explorations in visualizing science and data. It also introduced me to the concept of "preparation artifacts," which are traces left by the process of preparing an image—traces that can be confused with what is really there. Without training, these additions to the information could be misunderstood. This can also happen in the design process of graphics, so I try to make my visualizations as free of design artifacts as possible.

I spent many hours with the microscope and in the dark room, amazed at the images that developed. I was taking pictures of microscopic patterns! They may not have been as clear as the photos I could take with a regular camera, but they sure were intriguing. It wasn't just a diagram from a textbook of a T-helper cell, it was an actual T-helper cell!

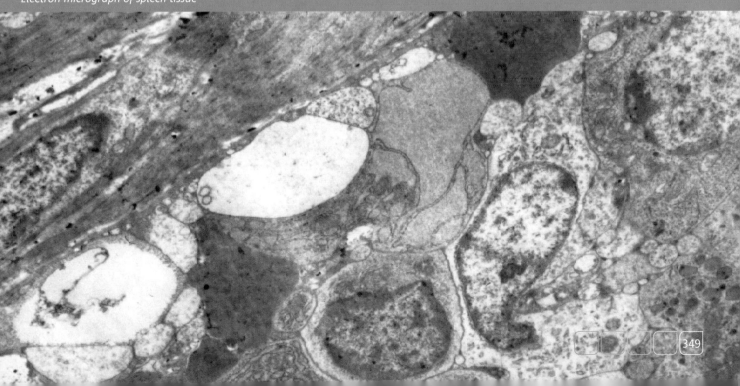

I'm still a shutterbug, but I don't have time to develop and print anymore. My photographic and artistic interests usually involve space filling and patterns, whether it's the natural view of sky through a tree or a designed bridge of stones in the Japanese Tea Gardens of San Francisco. Some of the most interesting views are only noticeable when you change your perspective. Try looking up, or down. Very interesting patterns can be found when we let our eyes stray from the view directly ahead, both literally and figuratively.

To me, negative space is what makes a composition interesting —whether it's an expressive piece or an educational illustration. I try to keep my compositions uncluttered. In fact, to some, my work may seem sparse. However, with science animations and learning tools, there is a delicate balance between too much and not enough information. Visual organization can help the user take in a lot of information at once, and it can maintain context for that information.

"Some of the most interesting views are only noticeable when you change your perspective."

LOOKING UP
LOOKING DOWN

I love science museums. One of my favorites is the Monterey Bay Aquarium. A while ago, they had an exhibit with giant tanks of all kinds of jellyfish. Entire walls of jellyfish slowly moved through backlit water. I spent hours just watching them and their different forms of movement. What colors and patterns; stunning!

One of my early experiences with the Internet was as a volunteer for the Mad Scientist Network, an organization founded by a medical student. The way it works (it's still online at www.madsci.org) is for people to submit questions; the moderators then assign them to scientists and science students to answer. Responses are restricted to text. At the same time I volunteered for this organization, I was starting to play around with Flash. Since I learn best when I can draw the subject, I wanted to help others learn the same way. Flash seemed to be one of the most promising tools for this. But at this point, I was still mostly exploring authoring illustrations in HTML documents.

My first big Flash project was a straightforward animation of the molecular biology of HIV. In my spare time, I'd been working on an illustrated booklet about the molecular biology of HIV with the hope that I'd eventually find a real illustrator who could turn my crude sketches into something more visually appealing.

When I discovered Flash, I decided to try animating the project myself. While it's never going to win an award for Flash animation, it is scientifically accurate and is still one of the most popular features on galaxygoo.org.

During my studies, drawing helped me prepare for exams. Many of my professors would accept a drawing, with labels, instead of an essay answer. In fact, this practice was encouraged and many of my fellow biology students did the same. This worked out great for me, and I learned the subjects better than if I had stuck with rote memorization of technical terms.

If drawing helped me learn biology, animating helped me understand it even more. I was surprised to find that as I worked on the HIV animation, I discovered questions that had never occurred to me before. This taught me the importance of the context and continuity that could be achieved with animation. I realized that science illustration captures a dynamic process in a static image, and that using these images as the storyboard for an animation wasn't enough. The transitions needed more work, and sometimes I needed to do more research.

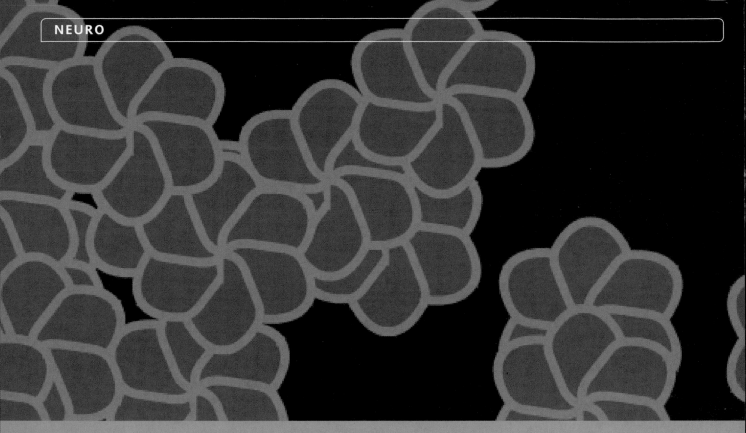

Big projects break down into small pieces, and like most folks, I work out how to approach these smaller pieces on their own. When possible, I take time to explore small experiments. On one project, I was looking for a way to get an overlapping circular effect, with every element overlapping on one side and underlapping on the other, and with the last element tucked under the first.

After tinkering around with a dynamically generated flower experiment, I cut the petal clip in half and saved each half as a separate movie clip. Then, on the last petal of the flower, I set the visibility of one petal-half to invisible. Flash is wonderful for this kind of solution to a visualization problem.

Adding a little color and lowering the transparency of the petals produced an x-ray effect. The outlines look almost like skeletal parts to me. I posted these experiments as part of the GalaxyGoo project during the 2003 Blogathon, and we won the best visual project award. Take a look at the source files on the CD, `zinnias_color.swf`, for example, and play around with them.

Although I'm not a designer in the traditional sense of the word, I like to think that I have something to offer the Flash community, whether it's the e-learning angle or the way I approach a project. I start with the subject, which usually has to do with science or math. Initially, I'll need to thoroughly research and truly understand a topic and then identify ways in which Flash can be used to overcome the challenges of communicating its concepts. I want the end-user to gain deep understanding of the subject, not just a superficial impression. Ideally, they'll have a satisfying "ah-ha!" moment.

On a really good day, I spend most of the workday researching and developing projects for GalaxyGoo. Most days, I spend about a third of my time on paperwork, community monitoring, and website maintenance.

When I'm studying an area for a potential Flash project, I look for the points where a student might get lost. The next step usually involves making a storyboard; after producing this, I'll put the project aside for a while. Sometimes an idea percolates in my brain for a long time before I attempt anything in Flash. Coming back to the project after a pause works very well for me.

I'm not a very flashy Flash developer. It's the inner logic of a project that I most enjoy working on. The more intricate the logic is, the more fun I have. It can be challenging to keep track of all the details of some projects, and pushing a pen around on paper helps me organize my thoughts, especially when I'm working with pseudo-code or straight out algorithm design. The act of writing things down by hand has a way of making things clear that just doesn't happen for me on a monitor.

When it comes to programming paradigms, I tend to go back and forth between object-oriented programming (OOP) and procedural programming in my Flash applications. To be honest, I often fall back into the comfort zone of procedural programming since that's how I started. I guess the point is there isn't necessarily a right way or a wrong way—in my opinion, you should use whichever technique you're comfortable with behind the scenes. With that in mind, let's take a look at the construction of one of my science communication pieces.

Neuromuscular Junction Simulation

One of the many challenging topics that anatomy students face is the Neuromuscular Junction (NMJ). It's not that it's mind-bending; it's just often presented in a confusing way. Since it's a system that extends throughout the body, and since textbooks usually break it up into various chapters, it can be difficult to understand how the system works as a whole and where the different parts of it fit together. When I took Anatomy and Physiology, muscle fibers and the synaptic cleft were in one chapter, and the nervous system wasn't discussed until a few chapters later. Not only was it split up, but there was a lot of material—very detailed material—in between. So, when I was asked to work on a simulation of a NMJ, I knew that context was a priority if I wanted to meet the end-user's needs.

Project background

Let's start with a quick and painless explanation of what the NMJ is so that the rest of the tutorial makes more sense. In the simplest terms, the NMJ is the point at which a nerve ending connects to a muscle fiber and sends a chemical signal to that muscle fiber. This is how your brain tells the muscles in your arm and hand to pick up that coffee cup.

The two main cells involved in the NMJ are the muscle cell and the motor nerve cell. Our muscles are made of bundles of muscle cells (fibers). The muscle shortens (contracts) when individual fibers within it contract. The signal for this action comes from the motor nerve cell.

The part of the nerve cell that we will focus on is called the axon. It's a long cable-like extension from the nerve cell body that reaches out to the muscle fiber. An axon can be as long as several meters.

An electric signal (action potential) is sent down the axon toward its target cell, the muscle fiber, where it releases a chemical into the synaptic cleft (the space between the end of the nerve cell and the muscle fiber).

In this project, I used a little texture and gradient along with the line drawings. I didn't use a lot—just a touch of texture on the background and some gradients on the axon and muscle fiber. The texture of the background is very simple, but it helps give a sense of depth. I've kept the graphics simple, like most medical illustrations. I also based the colors on those I've seen in medical illustrations, but made them a little more vibrant.

For this simulation we have three zones of action:

1. The axon of the nerve cell, down which an electric signal passes

2. The synaptic cleft, in which the chemical neurotransmitter (ACh) is released

3. The muscle fiber that contracts

These three stages are illustrated in the following diagrams, which form the foundation of the Flash simulation.

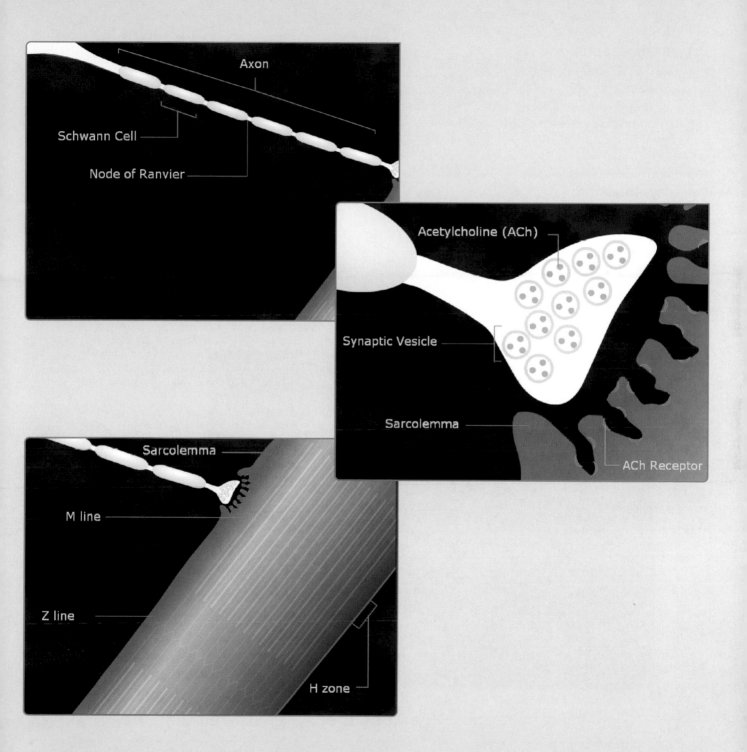

Axon

Schwann Cell

Node of Ranvier

Acetylcholine (ACh)

Synaptic Vesicle

Sarcolemma

ACh Receptor

Sarcolemma

M line

Z line

H zone

Project development

Before we start to look at the construction of this Flash project, it's worth running the finished Flash simulation, `NMJ_fin.swf`, to see the bigger picture of how all these technical diagrams fit together so that you can see what we're going to create.

We're going to place all code for this project on the first frame of the main timeline, unless otherwise noted. Commenting your code is always important.

Meaningful comments are sometimes a real challenge to write, but they are essential for code maintenance, not to mention being very helpful during initial development. In this project, I've used a lot of vocabulary from the content of the project. This helps me keep track of what the code is doing in the context of the simulation.

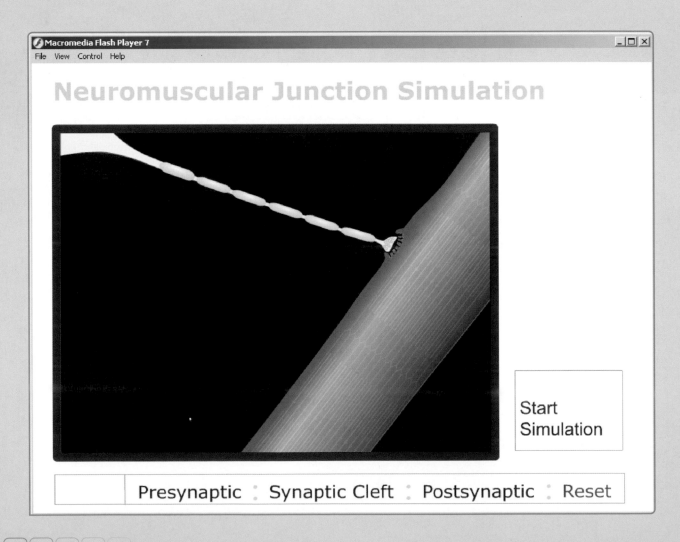

The visual design of this project is crucial to its function, which is to teach a complex subject to students. I want it to draw the student in, to make them aesthetically comfortable, so that they can absorb the information. The simulation should strengthen the student's understanding of the illustrations they've already seen in their textbook. But not only does the design have to communicate; it also has to avoid confusing or distracting the user from the content. It has to be simple.

The design of the user interface is also very simple. To start with, I put a mask in front of the movie clip for the simulation, creating a simple view of the content. The screenshot shows how the main graphic content spills outside of the window without the mask. Once the mask is added, the navigational elements can be placed around it. I wanted the user to be able to zoom in on the different areas, and see labels for all the relevant parts of the simulation—a snapshot illustration with labels. The goal is to keep the user focused on the animations without getting distracted by the navigation.

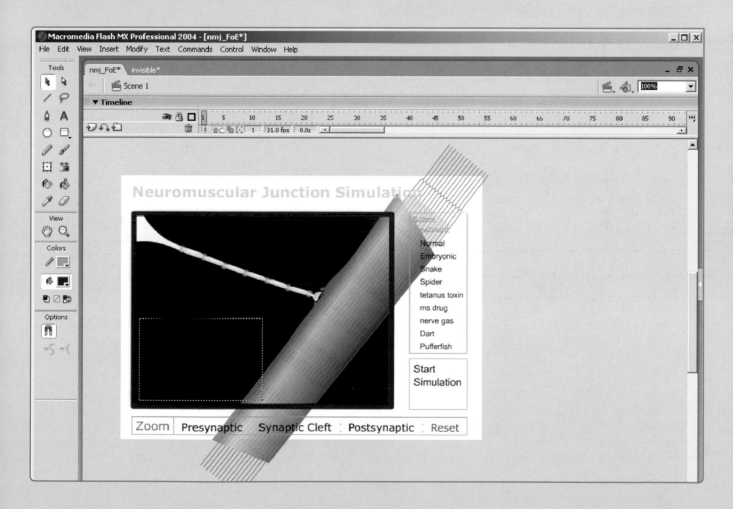

Adding the illustrations

We'll start out with the illustration that serves as the base of this simulation.

1. Open the source file NMJ_1.fla in the neuro directory for this chapter on the CD and save it as a local file (you'll see that there are two further interim files, NMJ_2.fla and NMJ_3.fla, as well as the final file, NMJ_fin.fla, for you to open and take a look at if you need any help at any stage in this exercise).

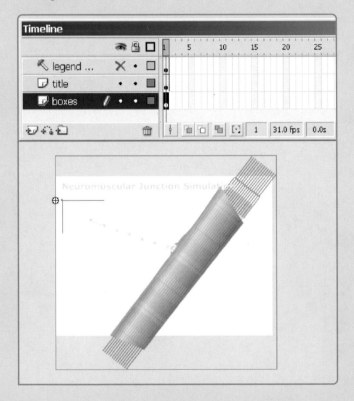

2. You will find a movie clip named boxes on the stage—it's in the boxes layer. Add two new layers to the timeline below the boxes layer, naming the first one background and the second one blue panel.

3. Find the graphic symbol blue_panel in the library, and drag it onto the blue panel layer. Align the upper-left corner of the symbol with the red guidelines. Repeat this with the nav-mask1 movie clip symbol on the background layer of the timeline.

4. Add a layer above the boxes layer, and name it mask. Drag the movie clip symbol frame_mask to the stage, in the mask layer of the timeline, and align it with the red guidelines.

5. Convert the mask layer into a mask, and make sure that it's locked and that the three layers below it (boxes, background, and blue_panel) are grouped under the mask. You should only see a masked area of the main illustration on the stage now.

6. Add one more layer above the mask layer and name it frame. Drag the outline_frame movie clip from the library and align it with the red guidelines. The following screenshot shows the timeline layers as they should be now.

   To check your progress, take a look at the NMJ_2.fla file from the CD.

7. Now it's time to add our legend movie clips, which label the different parts of the illustration with the appropriate vocabulary. Add a new layer, below the legend guide layer and name it legend pre. Drag the legend_pre movie clip from the library and align it with the green guidelines in the legend guide layer (you may need to make the legend guide layer visible and a few other layers invisible to do this).

8. Name the instance of the movie clip legend_pre. Repeat these steps for the movie clips legend_cleft and legend_post, creating a new layer for each for them and aligning the legend_cleft clip with blue guidelines and the legend_post clip with the yellow guidelines. Don't forget to give them instance names!

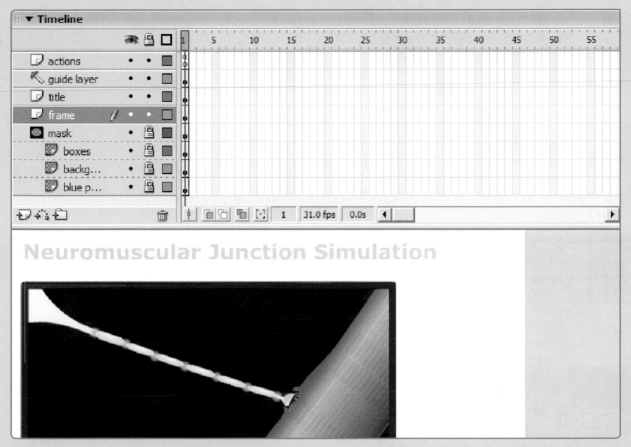

9. Since these legend clips should only be visible at specific times, they need to be hidden in default mode. Open the ActionScript editor for the layer named action and add the following code to hide the legend clips. Remember that unless specifically directed otherwise, you should place all code in the first frame of the timeline for this project.

```
hideLegends();

// hide legends
function hideLegends(){
  currentLegend = 0;
  // hide legend for presynapse
  this.legend_pre._visible = false;
  // for cleft
  this.legend_cleft._visible = false;
  // and for postsynaptic
  this.legend_post._visible = false;
  // clear info box
  this.info = "";
}
```

10. Add a new layer just under the actions layer, and call it explanation. Add a text field to this layer, and use the Properties panel to make it a dynamic text field. Set its dimension values to W = 186.0 and H = 124.0, and set its position values to X= 28.0 and Y=216.0. Give it an instance name of infoBox, and set its var to info. Make sure that the multiline option is selected.

Adding the zoom functionality

The scales of the different zones of action differ greatly. The boxes clip needs to be repositioned as the scale changes so that the child clips are centered properly in the viewing panel.

The zoom function is fairly simple and doesn't include any easing equations. I thought the likelihood of this running on a slow machine, say in a school, was pretty high, and I wanted to keep the computational demands on Flash as low as possible.

The variable myRate in the movement calculations controls how many frames the zooming takes place in. A counter is set, outside the onEnterFrame function, which increments each frame. The onEnterFrame is deleted to stop the zooming when the counter reaches the number of frames we've set with myRate. One advantage to using "rate" this way is that we could add a feature for the user where they can speed up and slow down the animation.

When the zoom is complete, I check to see if it was called from the simulation or from the zoom buttons (by the user). If it was called by the user, labels on the diagram should be displayed. This function (testLegend) tests for both the flag that indicates if a legend should be displayed and another flag, which indicates which legend should be displayed and then displays it.

1. First, we set up the variables for controlling the zoom function for each zone of action at the top of the code. Keeping the global variables at the top of the code means that they are easy to find if you want to change their values later.

```
// starting position
_global.initx = 20;
_global.inity = 40;
_global.initScale = 100;

// number of frames to take for movement
_global.myRate = 10;
```

```
// set simulation movie clip to initial
// position and scale
this.boxes._x = initx;
this.boxes._y = inity;
this.boxes._xscale = initScale;
this.boxes._yscale = initScale;

// dynamic values
_global.moveThis = 0;
_global.dx = 0;
_global.dy = 0;
_global.ds = 0;
```

2. Now we add the coordinates and scale for each of the three zones of action so that we can use them in the zoom functions.

```
// presynaptic position and scale
_global.x1 =-10;
_global.y1 = 20;
_global.scale1 = 140;

// synaptic position and scale
_global.x2 = -3600;
_global.y2 = -1400;
_global.scale2 = 1300;

// postsynaptic position and scale
_global.x3 = -300;
_global.y3 = -100;
_global.scale3 = 180;
```

3. Below the global variables, add a function that will move the boxes movie clip to the scale and position passed to the function when called.

A note about comments: I sometimes put equations that the code executes in a format that I'm more familiar with in code comments. This makes the code much easier to read. For example, I've commented this line:
```
var Vx = Math.floor(( newx this.boxes._x)/rate)
```
with Vx = x2-x1/s.

```
//-------------------------------
// move the simulation movie clip
//-------------------------------
function moveBoxes(newscale, newx, newy){
  var n=0;

    // Calculate velocities: Vx = x2-x1/s
    var Vx = Math.floor(( newx -
    ➥ this.boxes._x)/myRate);
    // Vy = y2-y1/s
    var Vy = Math.floor(( newy -
    ➥ this.boxes._y)/myRate);
    // Vxsc = xs2-xs1/s
    var Vsc = Math.floor(( newscale -
    ➥ this.boxes._xscale)/myRate);

    // zoom onEnterFrame
    this.onEnterFrame = function(){
      if(moveThis != 0){
        // move clip on X axis
        this.boxes._x += Vx;
        // move clip on Y axis
        this.boxes._y += Vy;
        // zoom in and out
        this.boxes._xscale += Vsc;
        this.boxes._yscale += Vsc;
      }
      if (++n == myRate) {
        moveThis = 0;
        // stop zooming
        delete this.onEnterFrame;
        // show legend? if yes, which one
        testLegend();
        if(zoomOnly != 1){
          return simStatus = 0;
        }
      }
    };
}
```

4. Add a function that tests if a legend should be shown and makes the right one visible:

```
function testLegend(){
  // test if show legend,
  // and which one to show
  if (showLegend == 1 && currentLegend
  ➥ != 0){
    if(currentLegend == 1){
      // show legend for presynapse
      this.legend_pre._visible = true;
    } else if(currentLegend == 2){
      // show legend for cleft
      this.legend_cleft._visible = true;
    } else if(currentLegend == 3){
      // show legend for postsynapse
      this.legend_post._visible = true;
    }
  }
}
```

5. Add a layer beneath the explanation, and call it zoom menu. From the library, drag the four zoom control buttons (control_pre, control_cleft, control_post, and reset) onto the stage, and align them along the bottom of the stage. Give them each the same instance name as their symbol name. For example, name the instance of the control_pre movie clip control_pre, and so on.

6. In our version of the application, the zoom functions are called from within the simulation. There is one function for each of the zones and another that resets the position and scale to the default settings.

```
// pre zoom-function
function zoomPre(){
  // set control flag to "go"
  moveThis = 1;
  moveBoxes(scale1, x1, y1);
  // ok to go to next step in sim
  nextStep=2;
}


// cleft zoom function
function zoomCleft(){
  moveThis = 1;
  moveBoxes(scale2, x2, y2);
  // ok to go to next step in sim
  nextStep = 4;
}


// post zoom function
function zoomPost(){
  moveThis = 1;
  moveBoxes(scale3, x3, y3);
  // ok to go to next step in sim
  nextStep=6;
}


// reset zoom function
function zoomReset(){
  hideLegends();
  // stop action after zoom
  zoomOnly = 1;
  // ok to show legend
  showLegend = 0;
  // which legend to show, default is none
  currentLegend  = 0;
  // set control of zoom to "go"
  moveThis = 1;
  // reset zoom
  moveBoxes(100, initx, inity);
}
```

7. To call the zoom functions and show the legend for the zone selected by the user, add the following functions to the code.

```
control_pre.onRelease = function(){
  // clear any visible legends
  hideLegends();
  // stop action after zoom
  zoomOnly = 1;
  // ok to show legend
  showLegend = 1;
  // show presynaptic legend
  currentLegend = 1;
  // zoom in on neuron axon
  zoomPre();
}


control_cleft.onRelease = function(){
  hideLegends();
  // stop action after zoom
  zoomOnly = 1;
  // ok to show legend
  showLegend = 1;
  // show cleft legend only
  currentLegend = 2;
  // assign function to button
  zoomCleft();
}


control_post.onRelease = function(){
  hideLegends();
  // stop action after zoom
  zoomOnly = 1;
  // ok to show legend
  showLegend = 1;
  // show postsynaptic legend
  currentLegend = 3;
  // zoom on muscle
  zoomPost();
}


// assign zoom to reset button
control_reset.onRelease = zoomReset;
```

8. The zoom control buttons will now allow the user to select a zone of action to zoom in on. Once the view reaches a new position, the appropriate legend should be displayed.

To check your progress, open source file `NMJ_3.fla` from the CD.

Controlling the action potential animation

The action potential animation is controlled programmatically. Along the axon there are nodes that are illustrated as exposed (or narrow) spots on the axon. When an action potential fires, an electrical charge jumps down the axon from node to node. There is a movie clip at each node. By default in this project, all of the jumping neuron movie clips have their _visible property set to false. When the `actionPotential` function is called, the clips are made visible, and then not visible, in sequence down the axon.

1. Add the action potential globals near the top of the code, with the other global variable declarations.

```
// set jump status to ready state
_global.jumpStatus = 0;
// set time between action potential jumps
in ms
_global.jumpDelay = 400;
// which axon is visible on this jump
_global.theAxon = 7;
// counter for number of jumps
_global.jumpCount;
```

2. Below the globals, add a short loop to hide the neuron movie clips.

```
// set all axon-jumps to invisible
for(var i=1; i<=7; i++){
  boxes.neuron["axon_j" + i]._visible =
  ➡ false;
}
```

3. Add the three functions needed to animate the action potential to the code.

```
function moveJump(jumpNumber) {
  // This function makes the next axon jump
  // (visible) and the previous axon falls
  // back (invisible)

  // get current time
  var lT = getTimer();
  // update current time
  sT = lT;

  // Since we know which axon is visible
  // (theAxon) we can make this current axon
  // invisible
  boxes.neuron["axon_j"+theAxon]._visible
  ➡ = false;
  // Update jumpCount & check if we can
  // make next Axon visible
  if (jumpCount++==jumpNumber) {
    // ok to go to next step in sim
    simStatus = 0;
    // signal for zoom in on cleft
    nextStep = 3;
    // we're done so finish the setInterval
    clearInterval(jumpID);

  } else {
    // we need to find the next axon so we
    //update theAxon, and stop if we went
    //too far
    if (++theAxon==8) theAxon = 1;
    // theAxon now holds correct value
    // so make appropriate axon visible
    boxes.neuron["axon_j"+theAxon].
    ➡ _visible = true;
  }
}
```

Code continues overleaf

```
function sIMethod(jumpNumber) {
  // jumps occur at constant intervals, so
  // setInterval is very useful. This
  // function creates the setInterval
  // so that moveJump gets called every
  // 'jumpDelay' milliseconds

  // create variable for 'current time'
  sT = getTimer();
  // reset number of jumps
  jumpCount = 0;
  // clear interval, just in case
  clearInterval(jumpID);
  //check to see if jump has been triggered
  //and if so run moveJump
  if (jumpStatus==1){
    _global.jumpID =
    setInterval(moveJump,
    ➥ jumpDelay,jumpNumber);
  }
}


// actionPotential function
function actionPotential(ap_fire_times){
  if(jumpStatus == 0){
    // set jump tigger to "go"
    jumpStatus = 1;
    // number of times jumps are supposed
    // to happen (multiple of 7)
    var jumpNumber = 7*ap_fire_times;
    // call setInterval method
    sIMethod(jumpNumber);
  } else  if (jumpStatus != 0){
    // reset jumpStatus to ready state
    jumpStatus = 0;
  }
}
```

Run Simulation

I like to keep as much in code, and as much code in one frame, as possible. For this project, I wanted to get a frame-by-frame-like action and zooming effect—where the movie would zoom in and play the action for that "scene" and then zoom out for the next. If I were doing this in the timeline, it would be very easy to put a little code at the last frame of a section with instructions on where to go next. But that approach can be a big pain to maintain and update.

To accomplish this in code, I started with a series of functions: one for each stage in the simulation, including the zoom sections. We zoom in for the first segment, and then run it. When that finishes running, we zoom in on the next segment and run it and then move on to the third.

In the functions for each step, we call either a zoom function or define what animation segment to run. I've also set the explanation text, which displays during the simulation, in the zoom functions.

One advantage to giving each step its own function is that it makes modifying any step easy. A prototype version can be mostly tweened animations, and a revised version can be called in an updated version.

1. Near the top of the code, add these global variables to set various flags that will be used in the simulation code.

   ```
   // which step are we currently in?
   _global.currentStep;

   // keep track of which step in sim to run
   // next, default is zero
   _global.nextStep = 0;

   // flag for play-status, default is off
   _global.simStatus = 0;
   ```

```
// flag for if action follows zoom
_global.zoomOnly = 0;

// ok to show legend
  _global.showLegend = 0;

  // which legend to show, default is none
  _global.currentLegend  = 0;

// Define text for the explanation text
// field for each of the three zones
_global.exp1Normal="Motor Neuron Action:
➥ propagation of action potential along
➥ the axon";
_global.exp2Normal="ACh released into
➥ synaptic cleft";
_global.exp3Normal="Myofibril contracts
➥ and then relaxes when bound ACh
➥ degrades";
```

2. Add the function for stepOne to the previous code in the actions layer. This function sets up the text explanation for the presynaptic animation and calls the function for zooming in on the axon of the nerve cell (presynaptic region).

```
function stepOne(){
  // zoom on presynaptic
  this.info = exp1Normal;
  zoomPre();
}
```

3. Add the function for stepTwo to the action frame. This calls the actionPotential function and triggers a single action potential animation.

```
function stepTwo(){
  // run presynaptic action & display
  // explanation
  actionPotential(1);
}
```

4. Add the function for stepThree to the action frame. This sets up the text for the explanation text field for the synaptic cleft animation and calls the function for zooming in on the synaptic cleft.

```
function stepThree(){
  // zoom on synaptic cleft
  this.info = exp2Normal;
  zoomCleft();
}
```

5. Add the function for stepFour to the action frame. This animation is tweened on a timeline, so use a gotoAndPlay for the movie clip we want to target (boxes.vesicles).

```
function stepFour(){
  // run synaptic cleft action & display
explination
  boxes.vesicles.gotoAndPlay("move10");
}
```

6. Add the function for stepFive to the action frame, setting up the text for the explanation text field for the muscle fiber animation, and calling the function for zooming in on the muscle fiber.

```
function stepFive(){
  // zoom on postsynaptic cleft
  this.info = exp3Normal;
  zoomPost();
}
```

7. Add the function for stepSix to the action frame. This animation is also tweened on the timeline of its movie clip, so a gotoAndPlay is used to target the movie clip with the muscle contraction animation.

```
function stepSix(){
  // run postsynaptic cleft action & display
  // explination
  boxes.muscle.myofibril.gotoAndPlay
  ➥ ("contract");
}
```

8. Add the logic function for the simulation. This uses the simStatus global variable as a flag. This function tests if simStatus indicates that we can go ahead to the next step and which step to go ahead to. It then sets the simStatus to pause and calls the function for the next step.

```
function getSimStep(){
  if(simStatus == 0 && nextStep == 1){
    // stop any other sim steps
    simStatus = 1;
    // start sim sequence
    stepOne();
  } else if(simStatus == 0 && nextStep
  ➥ == 2){
    // stop any other sim steps
    simStatus = 1;
    // action potiential
    stepTwo();
  } else if  (simStatus == 0 && nextStep
  ➥ == 3){
    // stop any other sim steps
    simStatus = 1;
    // zoom to cleft
    stepThree();
  } else if  (simStatus == 0 && nextStep
  ➥ == 4){
    // stop any other sim steps
    simStatus = 1;
    // ACh release
    stepFour();
  } else if  (simStatus == 0 && nextStep
  ➥ == 5){
    // stop any other sim steps
    simStatus = 1;
    // zoom to post
    stepFive();
  } else if  (simStatus == 0 && nextStep
    ➥ == 6){
    // stop any other sim steps
    simStatus = 1;
    // muscle contraction
    stepSix();
  }
}
```

9. Add the final function for running the simulation, which uses setInterval to call the getSimStep function.

```
function runSim(){
  clearAll();
  // select first step in sim to run
  nextStep = 1;
  // start sim
  simStatus = 0;
  // check for next step in simulation
  var simIntervalID =
  ➥ setInterval(getSimStep, 200);
}
```

10. From the library, drag the button symbol begin_sim onto the stage (I've placed mine on the zoom menu layer). Put it somewhere to the right side of the main simulation movie clip and above the Reset button. With the Properties panel, name the instance begin_sim.

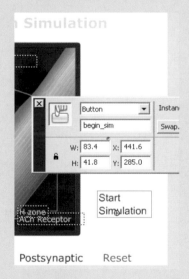

11. Below the runSim function, add this code to attach runSim to the begin_sim button.

```
// assign function to button
begin_sim.onRelease = runSim;
```

12. Below the `hideLegends` function, add this function to the code. This resets the simulation to run again.

```
function clearAll(){
    hideLegends();
    // which axon is visible on this jump
    theAxon = 7;
    // start at beginning of simulation
    nextStep = 1;
    moveThis = 0;
    // stop action after zoom
    zoomOnly = 0;

    // restart vesicle tweens
    boxes.vesicles.gotoAndStop(1);
    boxes.vesicles.myVesicle10.
    ➥ gotoAndStop(1);
}
```

Congratulations, you've built a neuromuscular junction simulation! To compare your finished project with mine, open the `NMJ_fin.fla` file from the CD.

Summary

From time to time, I've heard people questioning what an appropriate use of Flash is. In my opinion, the answer is anything that it's capable of doing! Your imagination is your only limitation. So I hope this project has shown you how Flash can serve as a medium for learning as well as entertainment, and how it is flexible enough to serve a variety of purposes.

This application is probably not the first way that you might think of using Flash, but that just goes to prove my point—Flash is a tool that allows you to look at the world around you in your own personal and unique way, and to gain inspiration from many different sources. What I love about Flash is that it is simultaneously an outlet for artistic expression and scientific communication. I'm sure that there are many thousands of areas in which Flash has yet to be used—and it's up to you to push it to the limits and produce even more unique creations.

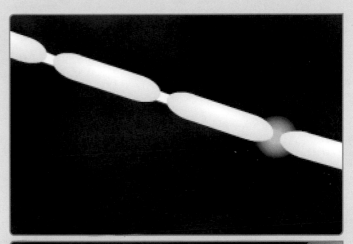

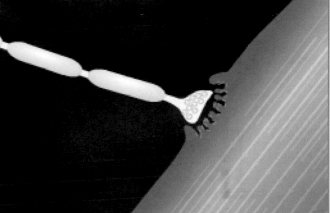

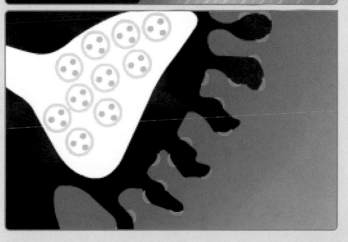

12

"FOR POSSIBLY THE FIRST TIME IN MY LIFE, I HAD ALL OF ME GOING IN THE SAME DIRECTION. I COULD FOCUS. I WAS UNSTOPPABLE!"

KEITH PETERS
WWW.BIT-101.COM

Who am I?

My name is Keith Peters. If you've received e-mail from me, I probably signed it "kp". Online, I'm often known as "bit-101" and some even call me "bit" for short.

Bit-101 (www.bit-101.com) is my personal website, which I started in August 2001. It's where I file away my Flash ideas after I'm done playing with them, or when it gets too late at night to continue working on them. People often look at them and say "Ooh" and "Ahh," and then complain about the design of the site.

MENU

- Content
- Calendar
- Comments
- Other Pages
- Color
- News
- Favorites
- Source
- Links

SOURCE

Click here to check source availablity.

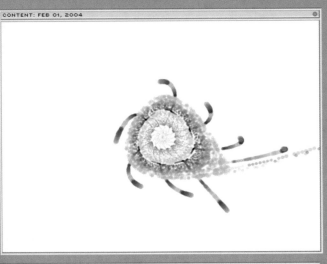

CONTENT: FEB 01, 2004

COMMENTS

Inspired by...ok, copied from Complexification. (I owed him one for BIT-10001!)
Click!

CALENDAR

Feb 08, 2004
Feb 04, 2004
Feb 02, 2004
Feb 01, 2004
Jan 31, 2004
Jan 29, 2004
Jan 27, 2004
Jan 26, 2004
Jan 25, 2004
Jan 24, 2004
Jan 23, 2004
Jan 22, 2004
Jan 18, 2004
Dec 30, 2003
Dec 29, 2003
Dec 28, 2003
Dec 27, 2003
Dec 25, 2003
Dec 24, 2003
Dec 23, 2003
Dec 22, 2003
Dec 21, 2003
Dec 19, 2003
Dec 17, 2003
Dec 11, 2003
Dec 10, 2003
Dec 05, 2003
Dec 04, 2003
Dec 03, 2003
Dec 02, 2003
Dec 01, 2003
Nov 29, 2003
Nov 28, 2003
Nov 23, 2003

OTHER BIT-101 PAGES

- Forum
- Blog
- Java
- Processing
- Resume
- The CD
- Tutorials
- Strange Attractors

LINKS

- Levitated
- Complexification
- Praystation
- Yugop
- 27Bobs
- Flash Extensibility
- FlashGuru
- RewindLife
- Friends of ED
- MM News Aggregator
- Person13
- Exit33 (my job!)
- Were-here
- Ultrashock
- Flashkit
- FontsForFlash
- GalaxyGoo

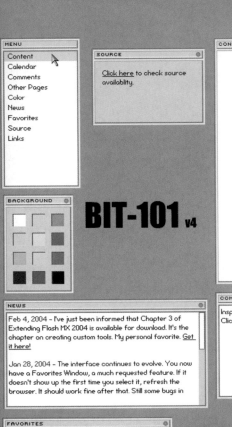

BACKGROUND

BIT-101 v4

NEWS

Feb 4, 2004 - I've just been informed that Chapter 3 of Extending Flash MX 2004 is available for download. It's the chapter on creating custom tools. My personal favorite. Get it here!

Jan 28, 2004 - The interface continues to evolve. You now have a Favorites Window, a much requested feature. If it doesn't show up the first time you select it, refresh the browser. It should work fine after that. Still some bugs in

FAVORITES

Sep 24, 2002: Node Walker
Sep 20, 2002: Original Node Garden
Sep 25, 2002: Node Dancers
Nov 22, 2001: 3D Message Board
Feb 16, 2003: 3D Grids
Mar 26, 2003: Gears

Description...

Add   Delete

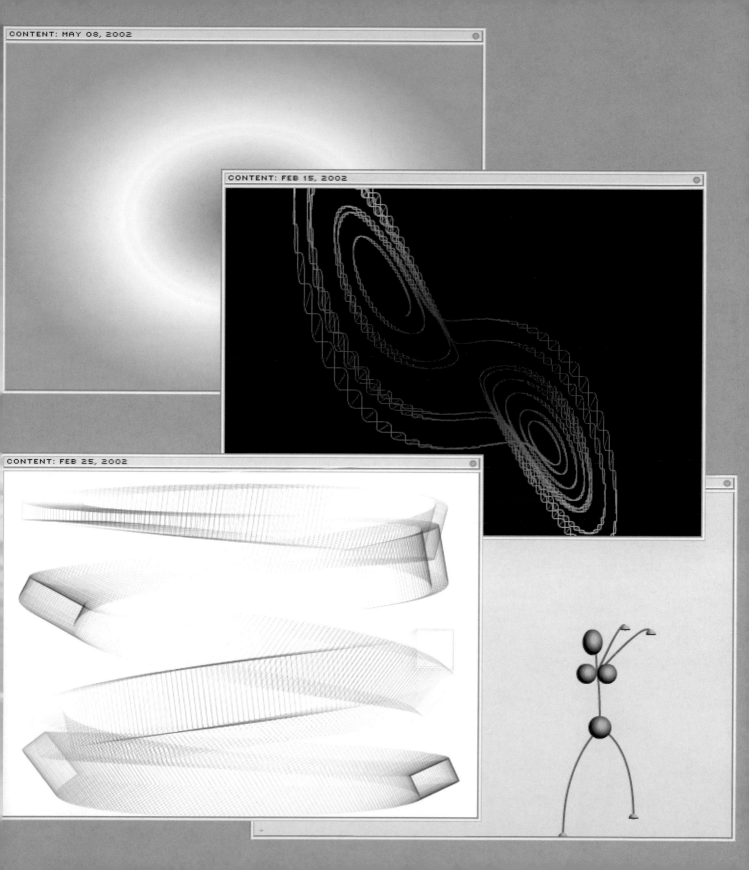

CONTENT: MAY 08, 2002

CONTENT: FEB 15, 2002

CONTENT: FEB 25, 2002

I've done a few interviews, and the interviewer always asks where I get ideas or inspiration for my experiments. It feels kind of lame to constantly say "Everywhere" and "From anything," but it's true. I once read a list entitled something like *"You know you're addicted to Flash when . . ."* One of the items was when you see some special effects in a movie and you think, "I could do that in Flash." Well, I think I must be addicted to Flash. For example, when I get stuck in a traffic jam, I start looking at the dynamics of the flow of vehicles and say, "I could do that in Flash!"

I don't know if there's any particular traditional artistic influence in the Flash work I do. If anything, I've been inspired by other Flash experimental sites. I started working with Flash back in what some are now calling the "Golden Age of Flash." You know, the good old days when Flash was 99% bad and there were contests for the best Flash intro. Back when nobody had ever heard of a Rich Internet Application and people just wanted to make stuff that looked cool and made people say "Wow!"

I'd scour the Internet looking for cool Flash sites. Of course there was www.gabocorp.com, www.balthaser.com, and www.rayoflight.net. But as cool as some of those intros were, how many times could you watch an intro before it got old?

What really got me were sites that had random or interactive elements, making each visit a unique experience. These were generally the experimental sites. Three in particular caught my attention: Joshua Davis's Praystation (www.praystation.com), Yugo Nakamura's Yugop (www.yugop.com), and Jared Tarbell's Levitated (www.levitated.net). In addition to being experimental sites with interactive—sometimes random—elements, they all had one other thing in common: they were based on a calendar theme with new experiments on a regular basis.

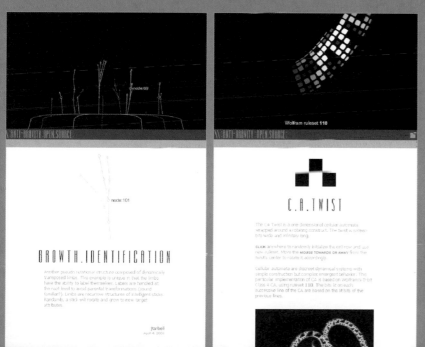

Jared Tarbell's Levitated (www.levitated.net)

Joshua Davis's Praystation (www.praystation.com)

One night after spending hours going through Praystation from start to finish, I decided to blatantly copy it. Well, I decided to copy at least the concept of keeping an experimental Flash diary. I already had a couple of dozen experiments going on my previous site, www.kpwebdesign.com (long since dead; if there's anything there now, it's not mine!). I started building a new site and just needed a new domain. Now here's a question that I'm surprised doesn't get asked more often: What does "bit-101" mean? Honestly, it doesn't mean anything. It simply rose to the top of a long list of potential cool-sounding domain names. It had a certain ring to it, so I registered it.

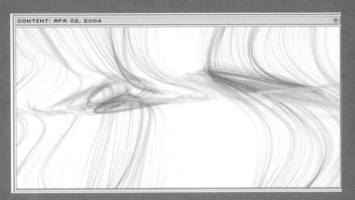

CONTENT: APR 02, 2004

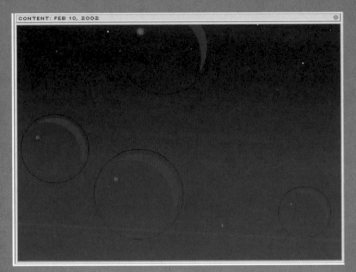

CONTENT: FEB 10, 2002

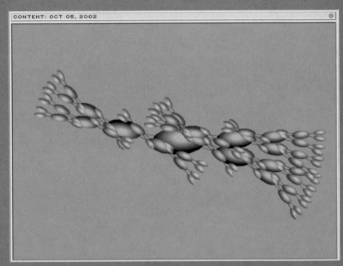

CONTENT: OCT 05, 2002

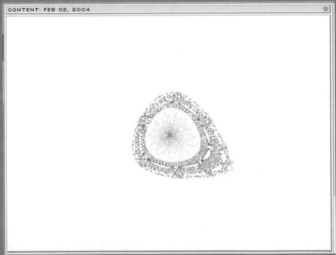

CONTENT: FEB 02, 2004

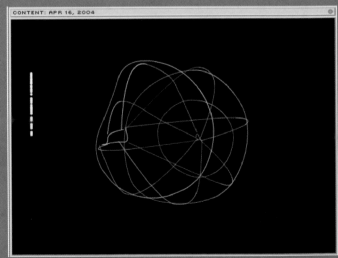

CONTENT: APR 16, 2004

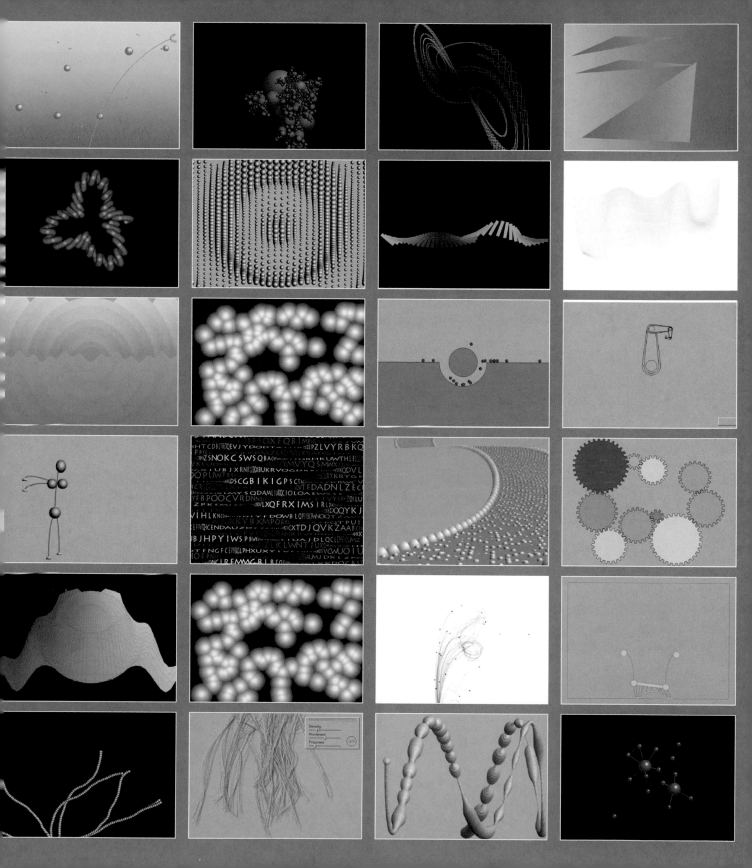

Now I hate to start sounding religious about a software package, but I'd be lying if I said that my life hasn't been transformed since I started using Flash. To explain why that might be, I'll have to go back a few years.

As long as I can remember, I've had an artistic side that has usually been expressed through drawing. As a kid, I copied cartoons out of *MAD* magazine. Later, I started doing portraits of my favorite rock stars. (Don't laugh at my use of the term "rock stars"—this was back in the 1970s, and that's what we called them.) Although I never went totally professional with it, I got good enough with pen and ink in the early 1990s to get a good amount of work published and make some decent money.

Way over on the other side of my brain, I've also always had a fascination with technology. My first experience with computers was in the Sears store at the local mall. There was a Texas Instruments TI-99 on display.

My first program was something along the lines of this:

```
10 LET X = 1
20 PRINT X
30 LET X = X + 1
40 GO TO 20
```

If you're not familiar with BASIC, that's about the equivalent of the following ActionScript:

```
x = 0;
onEnterFrame = function(){
   trace(x);
   x++;
}
```

In BASIC, if you let it run long enough, it would eventually overflow and crash. I soon found I could accelerate the process by replacing line 30 with the following:

```
30 LET X = X * 2
```

I may have become the first spammer when I let the following loose on the Sears computer-showroom floor:

```
10 PRINT "KEITH IS GREAT"
20 GOTO 10
```

Many years later, I tamed a wild Commodore 128 at work, when nobody else would touch it. This led to the purchase of my own Commodore Amiga for home use. I still admire that computer. An entire graphical operating system on two low-density floppies, half a megabyte of RAM, no hard drive, and a 7.16 MHz processor!

When that reached the limits of its usefulness after a few years, I graduated to my first PC, a 486 SX with 4MB of RAM and a 20MB hard drive. I had perfected the art of spaghetti coding in AmigaBASIC and thought I was ready to move on to C++ Windows programming. It was far too painful an experience to recount here. Let's just say that after C++, it was close to 5 years before I dared to program anything more complex than a VCR.

My career as an artist was moving along in fits and starts, and I thought there might be some way to combine creativity and technology, but nothing I tried seemed to click with me. The closest I got was using my computer to write cover letters to art directors.

Around the turn of the millennium, a friend asked if I'd ever used a program called Flash. I had downloaded a demo version of Flash 4 and played with it. I wasn't very impressed with the vector drawing tools and had uninstalled it. He said he needed some help on a project he had weaseled his way into and would pay me well. "Of course," I said. "I know all about Flash." After many all-nighters fueled by lots of greasy pizza and even greasier Chinese food, I actually did know a thing or two about Flash. I could make the cheesiest tweens you ever saw, and I even got brave enough to write some tellTarget code on some buttons.

I'd be embarrassed to show you any of the sites we created back then. Mercifully, they've all been put out of their misery and replaced by real websites. Or perhaps some of the companies just mysteriously went out of business shortly after their websites went live. Eventually, my friend's company went under as well. When he had no money to pay me, I accepted his Flash 5 CD and manuals as payment.

I was armed and dangerous and loose on the Internet, ready to start my own company making horridly amateurish Flash websites (hence www.kpwebdesign.com). Luckily, some higher power (the god of good taste, perhaps) intervened and sent me in another direction.

Don't tell anyone you saw this!

My revelation came in the form of a small interactive Flash movie I saw on someone else's portfolio site while looking for inspiration. It was a little metallic spinning flying saucer–type object in nicely rendered 3D. But the thing that took my breath away was that you could pick it up with the mouse and *throw it*! It would bounce off the "walls" and "ceiling" of the movie, and eventually come to rest on the "floor." I had never seen anything like it in Flash. I had done some similar stuff years before in AmigaBASIC, so I actually had a pretty good idea of the concepts and coding behind it, but it never occurred to me that you could do something like that in Flash. I had been shying away from using too much ActionScript, but now I knew I had to learn it. I picked up a friends of ED book, the original edition of *Foundation ActionScript* by Sham Bhangal, and read it cover to cover in about a week.

Again, I don't want to sound evangelical here, but it was really like I saw the light. It was as if two parts of me, which had both been searching for *something*, had found what they were looking for in, of all things, a programming language. Call it left brain/right brain, yin/yang, Mars/Venus, elf/dwarf—whatever you want. All I know is that for possibly the first time in my life, I had all of me going in the same direction. I could focus. I was unstoppable!

It's been a rocket ride since then, and it doesn't seem to be slowing down. Just about every aspect of my life is a hundred times better than it was. It's not that Flash is a magical software program that will change your life. It's just that for me personally, Flash was a tool that opened some doors and allowed me to get to a very good place. The very fact that you're reading this book most likely means that you know where I'm coming from.

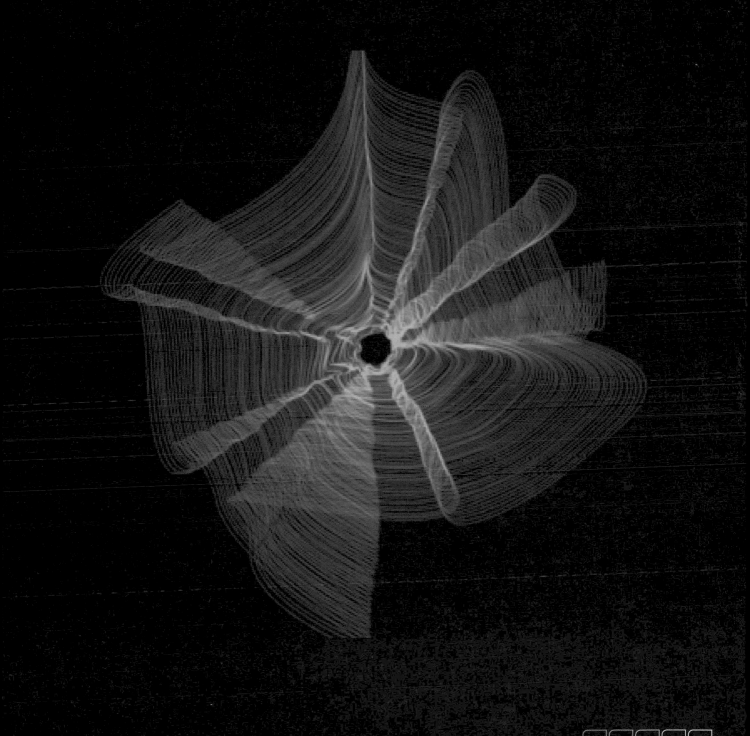

Experimental Flash

Before we move on to the hands-on section of this chapter, I want to take a little time and try to describe the kinds of things that really get me going in Flash, or any other computer animation/experimentation.

The first thing that intrigues me is the idea that you can write a program—whether it be long and complicated or short and simple—and just let it run, and it will go on as long as you let it. For me, "static" often means boring and dead. For instance, you could write a program that will run once and generate a static image that, although it may well be quite beautiful, will essentially just sit there. Whenever I make a Flash movie that does such a thing, I almost always add in some kind of loop that will display the image for a while and then randomly change some parameters and draw another one. One of the big paybacks of programming an experiment is sitting back and watching it do its thing, which is often something you might never have imagined on your own.

Building on that, the next thing that cranks up my interest is allowing the parameters of a program to change over time. While animation is certainly more interesting than a static image, even a very complicated scripted animation can get old quickly if it just sits there doing the same exact thing over and over. You might as well skip the scripting and make a tween of it. As an example of the program changing over time, imagine an object that starts out moving in a circle. Maybe after a while, the circle flattens out until it is just moving back and forth in a line. As it continues, its path goes back to a circle or perhaps some other shape.

Possibly the most used (or overused!) function in my files is `Math.random()`. It's a simple way to add variety to a Flash movie, and it can be used in infinite ways. Run a movie for a while with certain random parameters, then change the parameters, again randomly, and run it again. Or, as a movie is running and basing its actions and graphical elements on certain parameters, change those parameters slightly by random amounts. After a while, you'll notice that the movie isn't doing quite the same thing it started out doing. Alternatively, make a movie with several identical elements, with each having some randomly generated properties that make it behave just a bit differently than its peers. (Remember that one—you'll be coming back to it soon.)

An example of this is what has been dubbed the "Peters Wave" by Jared Tarbell (www.levitated.com). A series of wavy lines filled with gradient colors is drawn from the bottom to the top of the screen. It looks pretty cool, but each generation is only one of the billions of possible combinations of waves and colors. So I made it so that all the factors controlling the colors, wavelengths, and wave heights (amplitudes)—and even how these factors change within one screen—are *randomly* determined. As soon as one screen is drawn, new random factors are chosen and another one draws. I can sit and watch the endless variety for quite a while.

A far more powerful method of changing a program is basing the parameters of the program on variables that the program itself changes. This can become a sort of **iterative feedback cycle**. This usually occurs on a frame-by-frame basis. A function runs, checking various properties in the movie.

Based on what the function finds, it takes certain actions, which wind up changing some of those properties. The next time around, it reevaluates the situation and acts accordingly, again changing the situation.

I remember an experiment I did trying to imitate or simulate a flock of birds. The concept was that each "bird" could randomly wander around but wouldn't wander too far from the "flock." On each frame, I would average the positions of all the birds and get a point that represented the center of the group.

Each bird could then wander randomly unless it got too far from the center. If it did go astray, its direction would be adjusted to move it back toward the crowd. The further away a bird got, the more heavily weighted the adjustment would be. The center was determined by the bird's positions, and the bird's positions were affected by their relationship to the center.

A vital aspect in grabbing my attention is **interaction**. While a particular experiment might be engaging enough to sit and watch, if you can change it as it's running, that just kicks it up to a whole new level. I try to include some kind of interactive elements in most of my experiments. For me, this usually takes the form of checking the mouse position and incorporating the values into the program, but it can also involve listening for mouse clicks or keyboard events, or perhaps text fields, buttons, or any other user interface controls.

Finally, wrapping up my favorite points about computer animation experimentation is the concept of algorithms that are based on real-world physics, or that mimic the behavior of real or imagined life-forms (artificial life or artificial intelligence). The bouncing ball animation I described earlier mimicked gravity and reproduced a bouncing effect. Pretty simple formulas, but at the time that I was playing around with these experiments, I was completely awestruck. I've since learned about Hooke's Law for springs, conservation of momentum for collisions, and gravity between two large masses (as well as many other concepts). These few principles alone are enough to make endlessly fascinating Flash experiments.

As far as artificial life or artificial intelligence is concerned, I don't really know much about it at all. I just make it up as I go along, creating various states and rules. If the creature is hungry, it looks for food. If it finds food, it eats. If it is full, it watches TV. And so on. You'd be amazed at how such simple rule systems can start to make movie clips appear alive.

In the preceding shot, you can see such a system that I made for the book *Flash Math Creativity* (friends of ED, 2003). Take a look at hungry ai at www.friendsofed.com/fmc/keithpeters/index.html. The big sphere is the food, and the little creatures seek out this food and consume it. As they eat, they expand (much like myself over the last few years). When they get full, they wander off to a random location and sleep it off until they get hungry again. A pretty simple system, but when you see it in action, you could almost swear you're looking through a microscope at some new species.

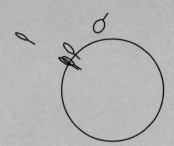
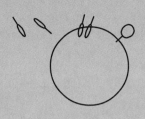
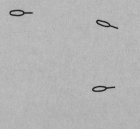

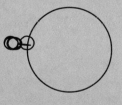

Particles

My roundabout discussion of experimental interactive Flash design brings me conveniently to the topics of particles and particle systems. Again, since I tend to make most of the rules up as I go along, I had better define what I mean by these terms, in case they differ from the *real* definitions.

A **particle** is simply a single element that has some physical form, some properties, and some behavior. A **particle system** is a whole bunch of related particles. Generally speaking, they have similar behaviors in common and differ mainly in their properties. Maybe they have slightly different speeds or sizes, or masses or friction.

Why do I find particles so fascinating? Mainly, I guess, because they can easily cover all of the points I just mentioned.

You can assign a bit of code to a particle telling it to move at a particular speed in a particular direction, and it will go on doing that as long as you let it.

You can randomly change the speed and direction at any point or have it change based on other factors in the environment (movie). You can use feedback by having each particle react to the other particles individually or as a whole. The flock of birds I described earlier was in reality a sort of particle system.

You can have each particle in the system start off with slightly different properties, such as position, speed, and direction. Their behaviors might all differ slightly, though generally they would be pretty similar. And the way in which each particle changes over time can differ.

The fun part comes when you start programming real-world physics or artificial life/intelligence algorithms into the particles. You start giving them gravity, attraction, repulsion, momentum, friction, elasticity, collision detection, and so on, or giving the particles "goals," barriers, predators, and prey. Then the whole system seems to come alive.

On top of it all, you add some interaction by way of the keyboard —or better yet, the mouse—and you can create something quite addictive.

There's something really cool about having dozens, scores, or even a hundred particles flying about in Flash. Although each one may follow a different path, you can plainly see the overall "intention" of the group. Watching a single ant traveling along might be somewhat interesting, but watching the entire colony build a nest or destroy an attacker is pretty amazing.

There are limitations in Flash as to how many particles you can realistically have on the stage at any one time and still maintain a decent frame rate. But the Flash 7 player is several times faster than earlier versions. Combined with increasingly faster CPUs, it isn't unrealistic to have up to 100 particles active at once, a number I wouldn't have believed just a year ago.

Of course, this doesn't compare to other, more efficient languages, such as Java, in which you can manipulate upward of 10,000 particles more smoothly than you can 100 particles in Flash, but since Flash is much easier to play with, I'm sure I won't be abandoning it anytime soon. That said, in addition to Flash, there's some great experimentation happening in Java with a system called Processing. You can check it out at http://processing.org.

The Particle class

In case you haven't done anything with object-oriented programming before, let's take a look at the concept of what a **class** is. In the simplest terms, a class is a package of variables and functions that can be used over and over. Take the `MovieClip` class, which I'm sure you're familiar with. It has variables, such as `_x`, `_xscale`, and `_alpha`, and functions, called **methods**, such as `attachMovie` and `gotoAndPlay`. In this section, you'll be creating a class for particles, which will give you some ready-made properties and methods you can use over and over, rather than having to redefine them each time you want to make a particle.

All right, let's get down to it. One of the coolest things about Flash MX 2004, and specifically ActionScript 2.0, is how easily you can create a class. In Flash MX, you created a function, not a class, and started messing around with its prototype. When you registered the class (function) to a symbol (movie clip), you had to stick everything between #initclip and #endinitclip. Personally speaking, it was usually more trouble than it was worth for anything but creating components.

With the new Flash MX 2004 class system, however, I find myself making classes for almost everything. Let's get started and see how easy it is.

Unfortunately, I don't have the space to go into detail on every aspect of the class (unless friends of ED wants to rename this book *New Masters of Crazy Particle Madness*). But I will go through the basic properties and methods, and enough of the principles to understand the rest of it. The full class file, along with several examples of its use, is available on the book's CD and at www.bit-101.com/particle.

Classes are created and saved as external ActionScript (AS) files. If you have Flash MX 2004 Professional, you can create them with the script editor. Otherwise, you can use any text or code editor out there. Actually, as of this writing, there are at least three third-party ActionScript editors out there that beat the pants off the one included in Flash MX 2004 Professional. If you're serious about coding, I highly recommend you spend the money on the PrimalScript 3.1 editor (www.sapien.com). It has many, many advanced features such as a class browser, code completion and hinting (even for your own classes), automation features, project management functions, and more. These features will save you many hours. Also available for free are SE|PY (www.sephiroth.it/python/sepy.php) and SciTE|Flash (www.bomberstudios.com/sciteflash).

As of this writing, SciTE|Flash was still in the process of being upgraded to handle ActionScript 2.0. SE|PY already supports ActionScript 2.0, and there are projects underway to port it to the Mac. Both of these editors have features similar to PrimalScript's.

Starting the class

Open whichever script/text editor you'll be using and start a new file. Start the class with the keyword class, followed by the name of the class and the class it extends (MovieClip in this case), followed by a pair of curly braces:

```
class Particle extends MovieClip {

}
```

Although there's no requirement that class names be capitalized, this has become the standard convention. Here, you're **extending** the MovieClip class. This means that you **inherit** all of the properties and methods that any movie clip has, plus you can add on your own or change the way the existing ones work.

The first thing you want to add to the class is its **constructor**. This is an internal function with the same name as the class. It will be called as soon as an instance of the class is created. Again, by convention, not requirement, the constructor usually doesn't contain much—usually just a call to another function, init(), which initializes the class object.

```
class Particle extends MovieClip {

  public function Particle() {
    init();
  }
  private function init(){
    trace("Particle initialized!");
  }

}
```

First note the keyword, `public`. With ActionScript 2.0, class members and methods can either be `public`, which means that any code outside the instance can access them, or `private`, which means that only other functions within the class can use them. The constructor needs to be public, since Flash will have to call it whenever it creates an instance of the `Particle` class. You don't want anyone arbitrarily recalling the `init` function again, so you make it private. This allows the constructor to call `init`, but prevents any code outside the class from having access to it. For now, just give `init` a trace statement to show that you were successful up to that point.

Save the file in a new empty directory and name it `Particle.as`. It's vital that the name of the file be the exact name of the class and that the constructor has the same name as both. Remember also that ActionScript 2.0 is case sensitive.

Creating an instance

Now let's apply this class to an object. Create a new Flash movie and save it in the same directory in which you saved the class. The name of the movie isn't important.

In this movie, draw a small shape—a circle will do. Select the shape and press F8 to convert it to a symbol. Choose Movie Clip as the type of symbol and name the clip whatever you want—for example, dot. You probably want to make the registration at the center of the shape. Check Export for ActionScript (you may need to click the Advanced button to see the additional options). Flash will assign a linkage name that's the same as the symbol name, which is fine. In the field labeled AS 2.0 Class, enter the name of your class, Particle. Click OK to save the settings.

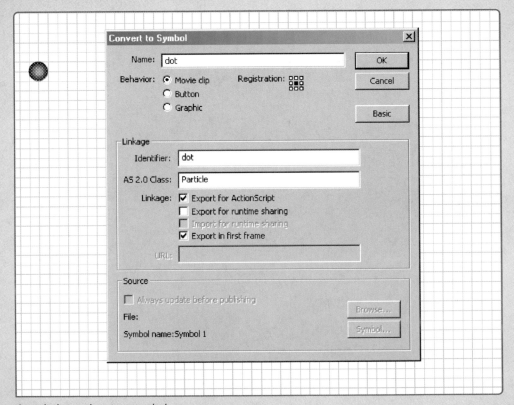

Associating a class to a symbol

As a heads up, I'll be calling my particles dot *throughout the chapter. You can name the movie clip symbol and any instances whatever you want, as long as the class name matches the class you've created, which in this case is* Particle.

You may now think you see a movie clip sitting on the stage. Actually, you now have a particle sitting on stage. Test your movie in the Flash IDE and you'll see that it traces the message Particle initialized! (see also stage 1 in the source files on the CD). Cool—you've just created and implemented your first class! OK, so it doesn't really do much yet, but you'll soon see how easy it is to add functionality.

It's worth reiterating here that, unlike ActionScript 1.0, Action-Script 2.0 is case sensitive. Something called MyVar isn't the same as myVar. If you run into any problems compiling and running the program, that's one place to start checking.

Making the particle move

Now let's extend the framework by giving it some properties and behaviors that ordinary movie clips just don't have.

```
class Particle extends MovieClip {
  private var __vx:Number;
  private var __vy:Number;

  public function Particle() {
    init();
  }
  private function init(){
    __vx = Math.random() * 4 - 2;
    __vy = Math.random() * 4 - 2;
  }
  public function onEnterFrame(){
    _x += __vx;
    _y += __vy;
  }
}
```

First of all, you'll declare a couple of private variables for velocity on the x-axis and y-axis. Variables inside classes are declared with the keyword var. Note that I start my private variables with two underscores: __vx, __vy. Again, this isn't required, but it's one of several conventions used. Some use a prefix like m_vx to show that the variable is a *member* of the class. It's just a way to remind yourself, and anyone else using the class, that this variable isn't to be used outside the class, and it makes it less likely that someone will accidentally attempt to do so.

Next, notice the colon and Number. In ActionScript 2.0, when declaring variables, you can specify what type of data they should hold by following the name of the variable with a colon and the type of data—Number, String, MovieClip, Object, and so on—that it should contain. Here you're telling Flash that these variables should contain only numerical values.

Now you use init to assign the initial values to __vx and __vy, making them random values from −2 to +2. (Math.random() returns a fraction from 0 to 1. Multiplying that by 4 gives you 0 to 4. Subtract 2 to get −2 to +2.) Note that you can assign a value to the variable when you declare it, but only a constant value such as

```
private var __vx:Number = 0;
```

If you tried to write

```
private var __vx:Number = Math.random() * 4
➡ − 2;
```

you would get an error at compile time. Thus you wait until init to assign values to your variables.

Finally, you create an `onEnterFrame` function that will be applied to every instance of the class. In it, you simply add the velocity on each axis to the position of the particle. You might be wondering about the absence of `this` in the code. You'd normally expect something like the following:

```
this._x += this.__vx;
```

In fact, if you're more comfortable with writing it that way, it's perfectly valid. But any properties or functions within a class are assumed to be scoped to that class. In other words, the `this` reference is added automatically. However, there are some cases where you need to use `this` for clarification purposes, such as the `startDrag()` function. If you used the `startDrag()` function without `this`, Flash assumes you're using the global `startDrag()` function, which expects a reference to the movie clip you want to drag as a parameter. You need to explicitly add `this` to `startDrag()` to tell Flash you're referring to the movie clip `startDrag()` method.

Go ahead and save the `Particle.as` file now and test your movie again. Your particle should wander off the stage in a random direction.

At this point, you're ready to start making your first particle *system*, which is to say a whole bunch of particles! Simply delete the existing particle from the stage and add this code to frame 1:

```
for (i=0; i<50; i++) {
    dot = attachMovie("dot", "dot"+i, i);
    dot._x = Stage.width/2;
    dot._y = Stage.height/2;
}
```

You can find this code in `particles.fla` in the stage 2 folder of the CD source files. Line 1 causes the code to loop 50 times. Line 2 attaches an instance of the particle to the stage, assuming you named the shape `dot` when you converted it to a symbol, and stores it in a variable called `dot`. The next two lines place the particle center stage.

Each particle will get its own `__vx` and `__vy` properties. The constructor and `init` function will run for each one, giving each a random velocity, and the `onEnterFrame` function will be assigned. The result is that each particle goes flying off in a different, random direction. Most likely, you've already played with Flash enough to get an idea of what frame rate you're comfortable with. In any case, the default 12 fps is probably way too slow for this experiment. I'd suggest going with 24–30 fps.

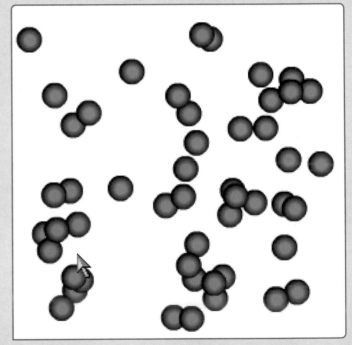

Particles are born!

Getters and setters

While random velocities are fine for demonstration purposes, let's build something that allows more control. Let's initialize the velocity to 0 and allow the user to set it. As it is, the velocity variables are private, which means that you don't want anything outside the class to access them directly. So you need to add a pair of **getter/setter** functions to allow for that. If you're unfamiliar with the concept of getters and setters, read on and all will be revealed. As the class is going to start growing in size, I won't always show all of it from here on out.

First, let's go back to the `Particle.as` class file and set the top lines to initialize the velocity values to 0:

```
private var __vx:Number = 0;
private var __vy:Number = 0;
```

Then go into the `init` function and delete the lines that set the random velocities—these ones here:

```
__vx = Math.random() * 4 - 2;
vy = Math.random() * 4 - 2;
```

Just leave the `init` function empty for now. Next, add the following code before the final closing brace of the class (as you can see in `\stage 3\Particle.as` on the CD):

```
public function set vx(x:Number):Void {
  __vx = x;
}
public function get vx():Number {
  return __vx;
}
public function set vy(y:Number):Void {
  __vy = y;
}
public function get vy():Number {
  return __vy;
}
```

OK, what do you have here? Taken from the top, you have a public function, so anyone can use it. Then you have the keyword `set`, followed by the name of the function, `vx`. This function takes a single parameter, `x`. Here you can see that in ActionScript 2.0 you can also specify the type of data a function parameter should be. So `x` should be a number. You can also specify the return value of the function by putting the colon and data type after the function parentheses. This first function doesn't return anything, so its return type is `Void`. Inside the function, you simply set `__vx` to `x`, the parameter passed to the function.

Next, you have a similar function with the keyword `get`, no parameters, and a return type of `Number`. And as you can see, it does return a number: the value of `__vx`. Finally, these two functions are repeated for `__vy`.

It's all pretty clear except for those `get` and `set` keywords. What these do is essentially make the function look like a variable. Instead of writing something like

```
dot.vx(5);
```

to set the value of `__vx`, you can write

```
dot.vx = 5;
```

To read the value of `__vx`, you can simply write

```
trace(dot.vx);
```

This is a little more natural and hides the fact that there's another private variable underneath. From a user perspective, `vx` and `vy` are simply properties, and the user never has to know about `__vx` and `__vy`.

So why do all this? It seems like this is adding an extra layer of complexity. Well, first of all, a principle of object-oriented programming is that you don't want any internal variables exposed to the outside world. In theory, you should be able to change your entire implementation of the class, and as long as the public functions and getters and setters took and returned the same values, everything should still work the same. If you had users hooking directly into __vx and __vy, you could never change the names of those variables or change how they worked without breaking the end users' code. However, as long as you have vx and vy, which always accept and return a number, you can mess with the class innards as much as you want and the users will never know.

Furthermore—and more immediately useful from my perspective—is that you can inspect, validate, process, or change, if need be, the incoming data before assigning it, or you can use it in more than one way. For instance, you could convert a number to a string or vice versa, and store it that way, or put it in an array or object rather than just storing it as a simple variable. You could check to make sure the value assigned wasn't too high or too low, or was one of a few acceptable values.

All right, save your class file and change the code on frame 1 of the FLA as follows:

```
for (i=0; i<50; i++) {
    dot = attachMovie("dot", "dot"+i, i);
    dot._x = Stage.width/2;
    dot._y = Stage.height/2;
    dot.vx = Math.random() * 4 - 2;
    dot.vy = Math.random() * 4 - 2;
}
```

You can now use vx and vy as if they were simple properties of dot. You can even retrieve their values just as easily by writing this:

```
trace(dot.vx);
```

The edge of the world

Now let's add some physics. You'll start by creating some boundaries. At present, if the particles go off the stage, they'll just continue to fly off forever. Let's make them bounce off the edges of the stage. Here's the strategy.

You'll create a bounds object that will hold the top, bottom, left, and right boundaries. These boundaries will be set to the stage size initially. You can find the files relating to this example on the CD under the \source\stage 4 directory.

In the onEnterFrame function, you'll check to see if a particle has gone past any one of these boundaries. You'll have to take into account the size of the particle here. If it has gone past a boundary, you'll replace it so it sits right on the edge of the boundary and then reverse its direction. You can even cause it to lose some energy in the bounce. How much energy it will lose will be stored in a bounce variable.

Finally, you'll make some getter/setters to allow the user to access these variables.

To start, you'll create and initialize the variables. Add the following lines near the top of the class, after the other variable declarations:

```
private var __vx:Number = 0;
private var __vy:Number = 0;
private var __bounds:Object = {top:0,
bottom:Stage.height, left:0,
right:Stage.width};
private var __bounce:Number = -.9;
```

Here you have an object containing the size of the stage. The bounce variable will cause the particle to bounce away with 90% of the speed it hit with.

Next, change the onEnterFrame code to check for and handle any boundary condition, as follows:

```
public function onEnterFrame(){
    _x += __vx;
    _y += __vy;
    if(_x > __bounds.right - _width/2){
        _x = __bounds.right - _width/2;
        __vx *= __bounce;
    } else if(_x < __bounds.left + _width/2){
        _x = __bounds.left + _width/2;
        __vx *= __bounce;
    }
    if(_y > __bounds.bottom - _height/2){
        _y = __bounds.bottom - _height/2;
        __vy *= __bounce;
    } else if(_y < __bounds.top + _height/2){
        _y = __bounds.top + _height/2;
        __vy *= __bounce;
    }
}
```

That's a lot, but it's really the same three lines repeated four times for the four different boundaries. Let's consider the first set:

```
if(_x > __bounds.right - _width/2){
    _x = __bounds.right - _width/2;
    __vx *= __bounce;
}
```

You're comparing the x-coordinate of the particle with the right boundary, minus half of its width. If the x-coordinate is greater, you move it back so it's just sitting on the edge. Then you multiply the x velocity by the bounce value, causing it to go off in the other direction. The rest of the code just repeats that for right, top, and bottom.

Test the file again. If you watch it long enough, the particles will eventually slow down and come to a stop as they lose a little speed on each bounce. If you set bounce to a smaller value, such as −0.5, this will happen a lot quicker.

Now since __bounce is private, you'll need to supply a getter and setter to allow outside access. While you're at it, you'll also create a getter/setter for __bounds. This will allow the user to limit the particles to a different area than the stage if required. Here's the code, which can go right after the vx and vy getters and setters:

```
public function set vy(y:Number):Void {
    __vy = y;
}
public function get vy():Number {
    return __vy;
}
public function set bounce(b:Number){
    __bounce = b;
}
public function get bounce():Number {
    return __bounce;
}
public function set bounds(b:Object){
    __bounds.top = b.yMin;
    __bounds.bottom = b.yMax;
    __bounds.left = b.xMin;
    __bounds.right = b.xMax;
}
public function get bounds():Object {
    return {yMin:__bounds.top,
➥ yMax:__bounds.bottom, xMin:__bounds.left,
➥ xMax:__bounds.right};
}
```

The getter/setter pair for bounce is pretty straightforward, but bounds might require more information. The setter takes an object, rather than four individual parameters. It's assumed that this object has four properties: yMin, yMax, xMin, and xMax. These properties were chosen because this is the same object that's returned from the preexisting function MovieClip.getBounds(). Since they're performing similar functions, I thought it would be good to give them the same format. This allows you to confine your particles to the shape of a rectangular movie clip by simply writing this:

```
var myBounds = my_mc.getBounds(_root);
myParticle.bounds = myBounds;
```

The getter returns an object in the same format. I can't think immediately where I might use that, but it seemed best to keep it the same. At any rate, it's a good example of how you can transform data within getters and setters, rather than just passing values to private variables.

You can implement the bounce factor by changing the frame code to the following:

```
for (i=0; i<50; i++) {
    dot = attachMovie("dot", "dot"+i, i);
    dot._x = Stage.width/2;
    dot._y = Stage.height/2;
    dot.vx = Math.random() * 4 - 2;
    dot.vy = Math.random() * 4 - 2;
    dot.bounce = -.2;
}
```

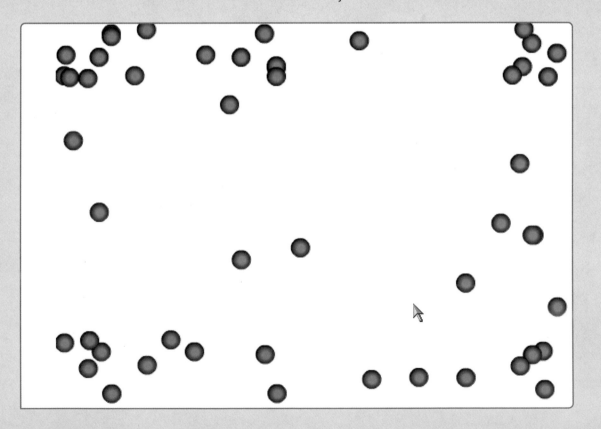

Friction and gravity

Moving along, let's add some more physics: pseudo-friction and gravity. Let's call the friction factor `damp`, and gravity will be `grav`. Again, you'll create private variables and getter/setters. `damp` will slow down the velocity a little bit on each frame, rather than just when a particle bounces, and `grav` will increase the y velocity on each frame, effectively pulling the particle down. And again, you'll declare the private variables at the top of the class, implement them in the `onEnterFrame` function, and then supply the getter/setters. Refer to the `stage` 5 folder on the CD for the relevant source files for this example.

First, here are the declarations:

```
private var __damp:Number = .95;
private var __grav:Number = 0;
```

Then you have the `onEnterFrame` function (I'll show just the first few lines here—the rest doesn't change):

```
public function onEnterFrame(){
    __vy += __grav;
    __vx *= __damp;
    __vy *= __damp;
    _x += __vx;
    _y += __vy;
...
```

And finally, here are the getters/setters:

```
public function set damp(d:Number):Void {
    __damp = d;
}
public function get damp():Number {
    return __damp;
}
public function set grav(g:Number):Void {
    __grav = g;
}
public function get grav():Number {
    return __grav;
}
```

Next, you'll add some gravity in the timeline code
(\stage 5\particles.fla):

```
for (i=0; i<50; i++) {
    dot = attachMovie("dot", "dot"+i, i);
    dot._x = Stage.width/2;
    dot._y = Stage.height/2;
    dot.vx = Math.random()*4-2;
    dot.vy = Math.random()*6-3;
    dot.bounce = -.8;
    dot.grav = .1;
    dot.damp = .99;
}
```

Be sure to play around with the `damp` variable to see what effect that has.

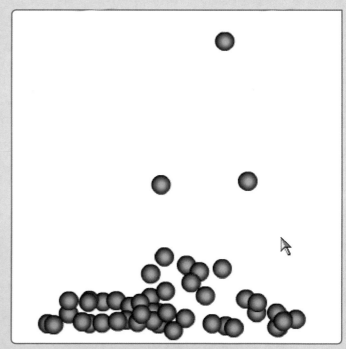

Beware of falling particles!

Wandering

You can add a little random motion to make the particles wander around. I called this one wander. It basically adds a random velocity to the particles on each frame. The same process as before applies: declare the variable, implement it, and provide getter/setter pairs.

Here's the declaration:

```
private var __wander:Number = 0;
```

Here's the implementation:

```
public function onEnterFrame(){
    __vx += (Math.random() * __wander - __wander/2);
    __vy += (Math.random() * __wander - __wander/2);
    __vy += __grav;
    __vx *= __damp;
    __vy *= __damp;
...
```

And here is the pair of getter/setter functions:

```
public function set wander(w:Number):Void {
    __wander = w;
}
public function get wander():Number {
    return __wander;
}
```

This should be quite familiar to you by now. You'll change the frame code to eliminate gravity and plug in wander:

```
for (i=0; i<50; i++) {
    dot = attachMovie("dot", "dot"+i, i);
    dot._x = Stage.width/2;
    dot._y = Stage.height/2;
    dot.vx = Math.random()*4-2;
    dot.vy = Math.random()*6-3;
    dot.bounce = -.8;
    dot.wander = 1;
    dot.damp = .99;
}
```

You can see this wandering effect in action if you open \source\stage 6\particles.swf.

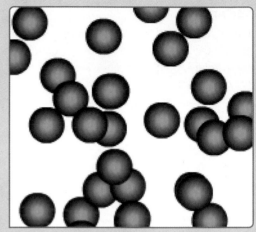
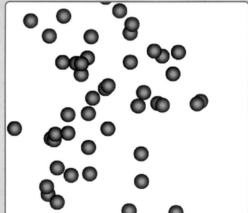
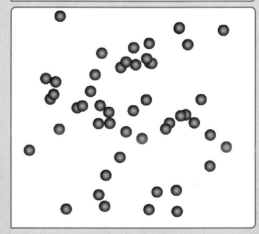

Wandering particles

Adding interactivity

You're doing great so far. Let's now add some interactivity with the mouse. In particular, you'll make a function called `repelMouse`, which will cause the mouse to repel the particles if it gets within a certain distance. This function will take three parameters:

- `bRepel`, which can be `true` or `false`. This allows you to turn off or on the repelling at any point.

- `force`, which relates to how much the mouse will repel the particles. Generally, it's a small fraction such as 0.1.

- `minDist`, which is how close the mouse must be to a particle to affect it.

Here's the function. It can go anywhere inside the class, but I like to group all my getters and setters together, so I put this right after `onEnterFrame` (see \stage 7\Particle.as for the code in full):

```
public function
repelMouse(bRepel:Boolean, force:Number,
minDist:Number):Void {
  if(bRepel){
    if(!force){
      var force = .1;
    }
    if(!minDist){
      var minDist = 100;
    }
    __repelMouseK = force;
    __repelMouseMinDist = minDist;
    __repelMouse = true;
  } else {
    __repelMouse = false;
  }
}
```

Here you have the three parameters just described. First you check if `bRepel` is true. If so, you check if values for `force` and `minDist` have been passed to the function. If not, you supply the default values 0.1 and 100. This allows you to just call the function with `true` or `false` and accept the default values. You then store these in three private variables, `__repelMouseK`, `__repelMouseMinDist`, and `__repelMouse`. If `bRepel` isn't `true`, you don't need to worry about `force` and `minDist`; you just set `__repelMouse` to false.

Next, of course, you need to make sure that these three private variables are declared, or you're going to get compilation errors. You declare them at the start of your AS file:

```
private var __repelMouseK:Number = .1;
private var __repelMouseMinDist:Number =
➥ 100;
private var __repelMouse:Boolean = false;
```

You should be extra careful and supply default values too. This makes certain that you'll never wind up with undefined values here.

Finally comes the implementation. You wrap the whole thing in an `if` statement, as you won't need to do anything if `__repelMouse` is false:

```
public function onEnterFrame(){
   if(__repelMouse){
      var dx = _parent._xmouse - _x;
      var dy = _parent._ymouse - _y;
      var dist = Math.sqrt(dx * dx + dy *
      ➥ dy);
      if(dist < __repelMouseMinDist){
         var tx = _parent._xmouse -
         ➥ __repelMouseMinDist * dx / dist;
         var ty = _parent._ymouse -
         ➥ __repelMouseMinDist * dy / dist;
         __vx += (tx - _x) * __repelMouseK;
         __vy += (ty - _y) * __repelMouseK;
      }
   }
   __vx += (Math.random() * __wander -
   ➥ __wander/2);
   __vy += (Math.random() * __wander -
   ➥ __wander/2);
   ...
```

I guess this deserves some explanation. First, you get the distance between the mouse and a particle. If it's less than the minimum, you need to act:

```
var dx = _parent._xmouse - _x;
var dy = _parent._ymouse - _y;
var dist = Math.sqrt(dx * dx + dy * dy);
if(dist < __repelMouseMinDist){
```

The next two lines create a target x and y point for the particle to move to. This is calculated by taking the angle between the mouse and the particle, and finding a point along that line that's the minimum distance away from the mouse.

```
   var tx = _parent._xmouse -
__repelMouseMinDist * dx / dist;
   var ty = _parent._ymouse -
__repelMouseMinDist * dy / dist;
```

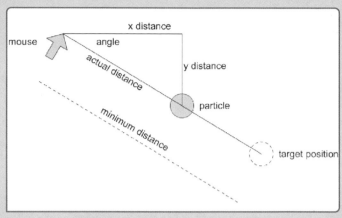

Calculating the target point to repel to

Finally, you accelerate the particle toward that point with the next two lines:

```
   __vx += (tx - _x) * __repelMouseK;
   __vy += (ty - _y) * __repelMouseK;
```

You can find more information on a lot of these physics and motion principles in the tutorials on my personal site at www.bit-101.com/tutorials.

Now you can throw some code on the timeline to make all your particles repel:

```
for (i=0; i<50; i++) {
   dot = attachMovie("dot", "dot"+i, i);
   dot._x = Stage.width/2;
   dot._y = Stage.height/2;
   dot.bounce = -.6;
   dot.wander = .1;
   dot.repelMouse(true, .01, 50);
}
```

That gives you a pretty gentle repelling. Something like this would be a lot harsher:

```
dot.repelMouse(true, .1, 150);
```

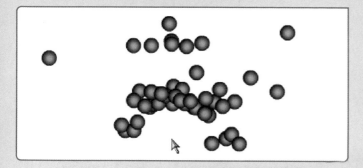

Spring points

I want to demonstrate one final set of class methods. These classes allow you to specify any number of points or movie clips that will have an effect on the particles. You can add points that will repel the particle or attract it with a spring formula or with a gravity formula. These functions are addRepelPoint, addSpringPoint, and addGravPoint. Or you can specify movie clips that will repel or attract the particle in the same way with addRepelClip, addSpringClip, and addGravClip. Each of these will also have a method to remove a specific point or clip, or clear out all of them.

Here I'll just cover the spring point functions addSpringPoint, removeSpringPoint, and clearSpringPoints, but it's worth investigating the other functions when you have a chance. You can copy the other methods from the finished class file or just use that file. Again, the rest work in exactly the same way, except the formulas for the motion are changed.

First you need a way to store all these points. You'll use an array called __springPoints. Obviously this will be private. You can declare it at the top of the class:

```
private var __springPoints:Array;
```

One mistake I make often is declaring an array in a class and then trying to add items to it. But unlike a simple variable type, such as a number or string, you need to perform one more step for an array or object before you actually use it: you have to create it! This would happen in the init function with the following line:

```
private function init(){
    __springPoints = new Array();
}
```

Next you have the function addSpringPoint. This is pretty simple, actually:

```
public function addSpringPoint(x:Number,
➥ y:Number, force:Number) {
  if (!force) {
    var force = .1;
  }
  __springPoints.push({x:x, y:y,
  ➥ k:force});
  return __springPoints.length - 1;
}
```

Just put this at the end of the class definition. You can see it takes three arguments. The first two are the x,y coordinates of the point to spring to. The final argument is how much force it will spring with. This is similar to the force value used in repelMouse.

The first lines of the function check if force exists, and if not, they set it to a default value of 0.1.

Then you push an object onto the array. This object merely contains the three values passed to the function. You call them x, y, and k. (k is the letter used to refer to the force of a spring by scientists and people who know about such things. I use it too, so I can look smart.)

Finally, you return a value of one less than the length of the __springPoints array. Remember that array indexes start with 0, so *length* — *1* will be the index of the last item in the array—the object we just added. Why return that? This allows the user of the class to store this number in a variable by writing this, for example:

```
var p = myParticle.addSpringPoint(100,
➡ 100, .1);
```

If, for some reason, the user wanted to remove that point, he or she could use this value in the removeSpringPoint function like so:

```
myParticle.removeSpringPoint(p);
```

Let's take a look at that function now:

```
public function
removeSpringPoint(index:Number) {
    __springPoints.splice(index, 1);
}
```

Even simpler than adding a point. It uses the splice method of the array to remove one element starting at a particular index.

Finally, even simpler is the clearSpringPoints method:

```
public function clearSpringPoints() {
    __springPoints = new Array();
}
```

It merely creates a new array, storing it in __springPoints. This overwrites the reference to the existing array, which is then automatically destroyed.

Now, what do you do with these points now that you've added them to the array? Let's take a look at the new onEnterFrame function.

```
public function onEnterFrame(){
    if(__repelMouse){
        var dx = _parent._xmouse - _x;
        var dy = _parent._ymouse - _y;
```

```
        var dist = Math.sqrt(dx * dx + dy * dy);
        if(dist < __repelMouseMinDist){
            var tx = _parent._xmouse -
            ➡ __repelMouseMinDist * dx / dist;
            var ty = _parent._ymouse -
            ➡ __repelMouseMinDist * dy / dist;
            __vx += (tx - _x) * __repelMouseK;
            __vy += (ty - _y) * __repelMouseK;
        }
    }
    for (var sp = 0; sp <
    ➡ __springPoints.length; sp++) {
        var point = __springPoints[sp];
        __vx += (point.x - _x) * point.k;
        __vy += (point.y - _y) * point.k;
    }
    __vx += (Math.random() * __wander -
    ➡ __wander/2);
    __vy += (Math.random() * __wander -
    ➡ __wander/2);
...
```

Here you add a for loop that loops through each element in the __springPoints array. Obviously, if no spring points have been added, the length of the array will be 0 and Flash will jump to the next chunk of code.

For each element Flash does find, though, it will store a reference to that object in the variable point. It then finds the distance between the point and the particle's current position, and adds some velocity based on the distance. Remember that the farther the distance, the more force it will spring with.

To demonstrate this, I've altered the frame script a bit as follows:

```
for (i=0; i<50; i++) {
    dot = attachMovie("dot", "dot"+i, i);
    dot._x = Stage.width/2;
    dot._y = Stage.height/2;
    dot.bounce = -.6;
    dot.wander = 1;
    dot.damp = .8;
    dot.repelMouse(true, .1, 100);
}
```

```
onMouseDown = function () {
  for (i=0; i<50; i++) {
    dot = _root["dot"+i];
    dot.addSpringPoint(_xmouse, _ymouse,
Math.random()*.1);
  }
};
Key.addListener(_root);
onKeyDown = function () {
  for (i=0; i<50; i++) {
    dot = _root["dot"+i];
    dot.clearSpringPoints();
  }
};
```

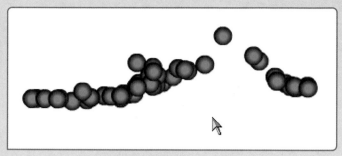

Attracted to two points, but repelled by the mouse

I changed a few of the original parameters to each dot. Then I added some handlers for onMouseDown and onKeyDown. (Note that you have to make _root a listener for Key events before you can respond to them with a handler.) The onMouseDown handler loops through each particle and adds a spring point at the current mouse position, and with a random velocity. The onKeyDown handler loops through and clears all the spring points on each particle.

Summary

At this point, I think the class, and therefore any associated particle instance, has enough interesting properties and behaviors that you can really start having some fun with it. I'm sure that if you followed through to the last example, you've already started experimenting with it on your own, changing values and switching in and out other properties I've already covered. I urge you to check out the full version of the class from the CD or from www.bit-101.com/Particles, which has the other methods mentioned here, as well as a few other goodies I didn't even have time to mention. I guarantee that if you're half as much into this stuff as I am, this will keep you occupied for hours.

You can use this class not only to create what you would normally think of as particles, but also to simulate smoke, fire, water, explosions—the sky's the limit! I'm looking forward to seeing what you can come up with.

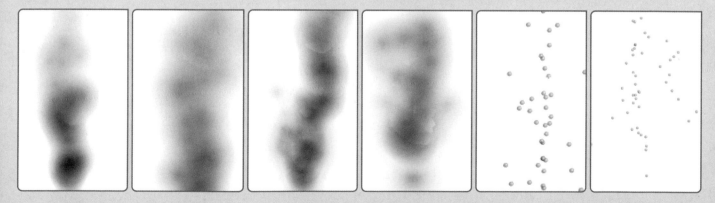

13

13 DESIGNERGOKKO

I AM TOTALLY AMAZED BY EVERYTHING THAT
COMES FROM JAPAN, FROM THE SHEER BEAUTY
OF JAPANESE ANCIENT TRADITIONS TO THE
SUPER-POP-FLASHY ASPECTS OF ULTRAMODERN
CITIES LIKE TOKYO.

SIMONE LEGNO
WWW.DESIGNERGOKKO.IT

Inspirations

The first time I created any animation was when I sketched little frames on the corner of a thick notebook. I would carefully draw some little characters in every miniframe with the aim of bringing them to life by fanning the book in my hands. I loved to take this magic paper notebook out of my pocket and watch it over and over, again and again. I always loved drawing and didn't have that many toys, so by making this book, I was inventing the best way to spend time, by creating fun by myself.

Now I'm a designer and produce animation for a living.

I love animation. Like many Italians, before I went to kindergarten and elementary school, I spent my early childhood drinking lots of caffe latte and watching Japanese animation from the late '70s and early '80s. I was in love with the robots and with their pilots, who risked their lives to save humanity and to protect the world (well, generally, these shows involved just Japan being attacked by aliens and androids). I always believed in these heroes and their good judgment.

Designergokko

Growing up, I loved drawing and had boxes full of chewed, broken, unsharpened pencils. On my new personal site, www.designergokko.it, I plan on including some of the things that I drew as a kid so that people can see how my style developed over the years. "But what does Designergokko mean?" you're probably asking yourself. Well, *gokko* is a fun little Japanese word used to explain the game that children play when they imitate what adults do. For example, *Oishagokko* means playing doctor, *Cowboygokko* means playing cowboy, and so on. Gokko can refer to any kind of imitation kids make when they imagine themselves in the adult world.

Memories of my childhood, and a child's world in general—the games, the toys, the fun, the behavior—are one of the major inspirations for my designs.

In addition to being inspired by the fun of kids' games and toys, in most of my designs, a strong female character forms the central graphical element. I use a female figure, generally with oriental features, with their soft gentle lines, to capture her sweet behavior and beauty. I love the sensual, often shy, nature of the Japanese women I've met, and their funny and fun attitude toward life. I adore the fact that a strong personality always lies behind such a fragile and delicate composure.

Tokidoki

I first created www.tokidoki.it as a way of collecting
and presenting all of my illustrations that were just
sitting around on my computer, hidden from everyone. I used this site as a gallery for my drawings,
largely of pale young girls. For me, publishing a
personal website is not just self-promotion, not just
the need to send a part of myself into space in a
capsule, but it's fun! I love doing design; it fulfills my
need to be happy, but it's also the reason I have so
many sleepless nights.

I wanted to use vectors in the same way that traditional Japanese art represents the beautiful female
figures: by creating a flat image, with dark soft lines
and pale skin. Around this time, I was spending long
hours in the Japan Foundation's library, reading and
leafing through anything about Japan, mostly the art
of masters like Utamaro, Hiroshige, Hokusai, and
also traditional and contemporary graphic, texture,
and environment design books.

When tokidoki.it first went online, it was pretty
different from any other site around. I think this was
because, rather than looking within the Internet
community or at the design trends of the time, I was
mostly looking into my past, my memories and my
dreams, to get inspiration. This is also partly due to
the fact that, at the time, my knowledge of online
design and the Flash community as a whole was
almost nonexistent when compared to the present.
Nowadays, inspiration from the digital art community
is just as valuable to me as motivation from other
sources.

tokidoki.it
トキドキ
SimoneLegno

Japanism

It's hard to explain my love for Japan and all things Japanese. I use the art concept *Japanism* to describe the craze and love of things from this wonderful country. It's something I feel inside—I am totally amazed by everything that comes from Japan, from the sheer beauty of Japanese ancient traditions to the super-pop-flashy aspects of ultramodern cities like Tokyo. I love Japanese people: I love their kindness, politeness, seriousness, and how, at the same time, they can be quite funny, playful, and extremely creative.

Not only my art but even my everyday world is colored and decorated by Japanese objects, souvenirs, packaging, textiles, toys, books, prints, t-shirts, and food.

Illustration, animation, and gaming

After many years of sketching and doodling and trying to imitate the Japanese icons, objects, and people that I'd grown so fond of, I started to learn some computer graphic programs. At the beginning, I had fun using Adobe Photoshop. I did some collage posters for punk gigs and for my own band. Then I fell in love with the clear lines and shapes of Adobe Illustrator. I think my adolescence spent in punk venues, with tattooed and pierced friends, colored hair, and alternative clothing, influenced my design and a good portion of the characters I invent. Right now I design *everything* in Illustrator, mostly working initially from a sketch on paper. I still always travel with a sketchbook in my hand because my mind is constantly active when I'm watching people in various environments.

When I design a female character, I typically start from a simple sketch: pencil on white paper. After making an initial draft, I'll scan it into digital form and then add all the intricate little details, like facial characteristics, makeup, tattoos, nail polish, and so on, using vectors in Illustrator. After the image is traced, I also add some shading to give the body more volume.

Finally, directly in Illustrator, I draw in the environment in which the character lives.

DESIGNERGOKKO

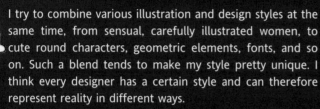

I try to combine various illustration and design styles at the same time, from sensual, carefully illustrated women, to cute round characters, geometric elements, fonts, and so on. Such a blend tends to make my style pretty unique. I think every designer has a certain style and can therefore represent reality in different ways.

If I'm drawing a cute little character, sometimes I'll start out with the Adobe Illustrator Pen tool because I don't really need the soft lines that hand drawing produces.

Illustrator is a perfect application for making an image seem shiny, soft, and glittering. With Illustrator, I can produce high-quality vector designs that will export perfectly in SWF format and keep the file size pretty small, even with fairly complex illustrations. One of the things I do once I've exported an image from Illustrator to SWF is optimize it further by taking any repetitive graphical elements and converting them into symbols so that I can clone them and save as many KB as possible.

414

As I've mentioned earlier, as time passed and as my personal style evolved, I felt I could mix my female Japanese characters with the cute little cartoon figures that I had developed to complete their overall appeal. The cute, or *kawaii*, elements are something Japanese life is soaked with. Kawaii is a word used constantly in Japanese everyday life, simply meaning cute, little, and adorable.

Kawaii images are stuck or printed on any kind of object: they give color to the modern city, or they give a friendly sense to the cold image of a huge industrial or financial corporation. I think in Tokidoki I create a strong sense of proportion and respect for the rules of design, but really I just want to hide behind this and create a virtual town inhabited by the little made-up friends of my world in various styles.

yukochan ti amo ♥

princess
bianca

So I was becoming pretty clever with vectors, but I needed to move my characters and bring them to life; they needed to be free to play around in my screen on their own! I started by exporting JPGs from Photoshop and building them in Premiere, frame by frame. But when started using Flash, I discovered a whole new world. No more JPG-by-JPG sticky motion. I spent many days and nights trying to understand Flash and use it intuitively. Little by little, everything started to become normal and natural, and now I'm completely at home working in Flash. When I see some object moving in the real world, I already start imagining the animation technique I will need to make this behavior happen in Flash. In the WWW galaxy, a single website is just a baby star amongst millions of stars. But thanks to Flash, you can make it shine brighter than all the others. I was so happy when people started to discover and explore my Tokidoki site.

IN THE WWW GALAXY, A SINGLE WEBSITE IS JUST A BABY STAR AMONGST MILLIONS OF STARS.
BUT THANKS TO FLASH YOU CAN MAKE IT SHINE BRIGHTER THAN ALL THE OTHERS.

Animation helps me describe things—it enhances the static image and allows me to tell a story, to express a feeling, and to maintain the attention of the audience. Adding interactivity to my animations led naturally to developing games. I've always loved video games: Atari, Nintendo, even the old-school Commodore 64 arcade games. So as soon as I could, I wanted to convert my graphics into games.

A couple of friends, Ubi and Emanuele, first started programming simple Flash games, so we decided to experiment with something tougher—my creative view and animations combined with their ActionScript power.

So for this chapter, we've prepared a tutorial based on the character movements from a popular platform game we developed: you can play this game at http://yuko.benq.it. As well as being the name of my girlfriend, Yuko is a character I designed for our client BenQ. She's a beautiful secret agent, who turns into a cute little kawaii form once she is immersed in the arcade world. Vianet created an online competition based on her adventures in a set of three games. To explain the way she moves, kind of like a digital puppet, I'll introduce you to her sister, Chiharuchan.

Creating a digital puppet

Let's now start the tutorial that will show us the basics of how to move our Chiharuchan character—the way she would move in a platform game scenario. The goal of the following explanation is to demonstrate how, thanks to Flash and ActionScript, we can make our little kawaii character interactive, and control her movement using the keyboard.

In my opinion, Flash is the best environment for making interactive animated vector graphics for web distribution. However, when we design and program a game for the Flash plug-in, it's always worth considering the fact that it has to work on very different kinds of computers, with different CPUs. So we have to try to make the scripts as optimized as possible to make the game enjoyable on any processor.

Chiharuchan   **Yukochan**

BenQ
Enjoyment Matters

Character

First of all we have to design our game character in a profile position. After sketching out ideas, I always design my characters using Illustrator, keeping the vectors as clean as possible and avoiding too many finer details that would make the animation difficult to render for slower processors. Sometimes I complete the little details of the illustration by adding some color with the Flash design tools.

We have to divide the character into parts that will be posed in different layers: the two legs, the two arms, the head, and the body. Open up `chiharu_tutorial_char.fla` and look in the library to see how I've structured my Chiharuchan character.

It's important to put the center of the motion, the registration point, in the right place so that it is the character's pivot point. Just select it and move it using the black arrow.

Then we make the character move within its own movie clip by using a new keyframe for each movement, and between every keyframe, we add a motion tween to make the movement fluid. At this point, my Chiharuchan is finally walking and moving, and can even throw her magic flower.

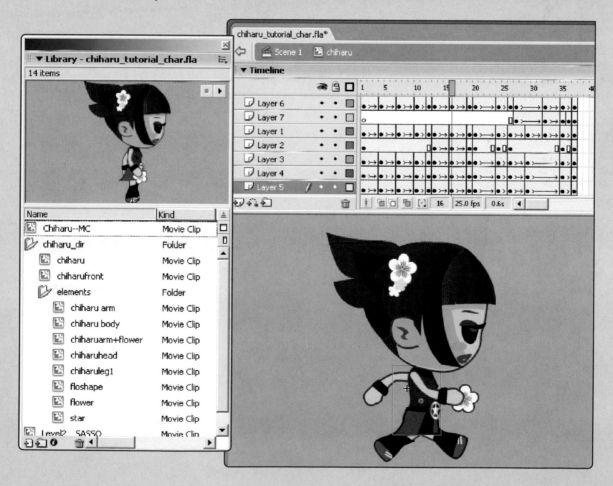

In the accompanying FLA file, `chiharu_tutorial_char.fla`, you'll find Chiharu with two kinds of animations: one that uses motion tweening, as mentioned earlier, and one that doesn't.

Note that we now have two positions of the character: a profile and a front view. We have to integrate them to give to our puppet the ability to walk, jump, and be interactive.

The secret to this is found in the Chiharu–MC movie clip, which in turn contains instances of the chiharu and chiharufront movie clips. Here you'll find all the movement you need to make her change position on the screen—from left to right, and the waiting position she takes when you decide to stop and don't use the keyboard for a short while.

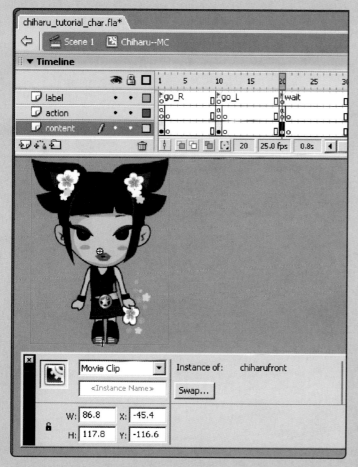

Chiharu–MC contains the frontal and lateral positions of the character. I've organized the timeline in such a way that, when we need to, we can start to control and call the functions and animations using the ActionScript.

One of the characteristics of Flash I really appreciate is that we can incorporate a mix of programming and motion tweening that will make our work easier and faster, and that will save a lot of time and effort, resulting in effortless controls and a clean timeline.

You can see that in this movie clip I've used three layers:

1. The label layer contains some textual markers for the three main actions of our little Chiharu: go_R, meaning go right; go_L, go left; and wait, which is the default stance when no command or input arrives from the keyboard.

2. action contains the three actions required for each movement stage.

3. content contains the prepared movies of Chiharu's movements (walking, jumping, throwing the magic flower). Note that I've flipped the chiharu movie clip on both sides so that she can turn, and I've also included the frontal view chiharufront movie clip for the waiting view.

To see the next developmental stage, open the second tutorial file: chiharu_tutorial_char2.fla. Here you can see that I've given each of the movie clips the same instance name, body. Also, even the chiharu movie clip has been organized and divided into different markers with labels that identify actions of the characters like stop, walk, jump, and shot.

With this kind of organization and structure in the movie clip, it will be very easy to control our character with ActionScript.

Environment

Next we have to build up the environment where our character is going to perform. Take a look at chiharu_tutorial_env.fla; the first thing we have to do is create a building block movie clip to form the bricks of our boundaries. In this case, my floors and walls will be made up of a graphic part (the gray bricks in the bg movie clip) and an invisible part (with alpha quantity set to 0), which is useful for making the movements more homogeneous (refer to the invisible_fill and vertical_fill movie clips).

We use the bg clip to build up the horizontal floors (base_mc) and vertical walls (vertical) so that our character has a surface to jump against and obstacles to impede her path.

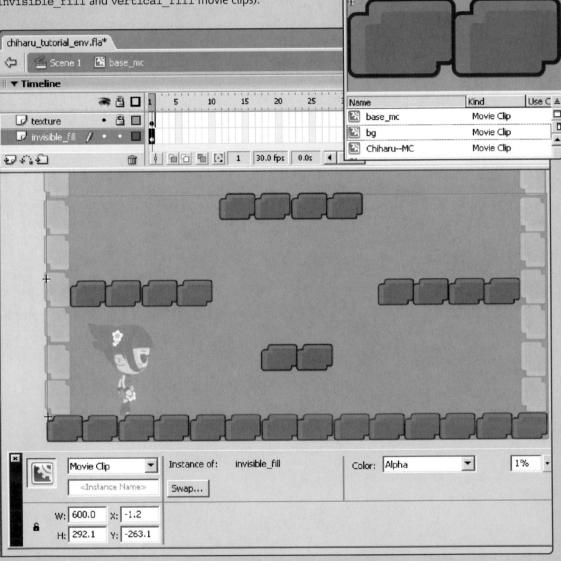

Interactivity

Once we have prepared all of our character movie clips and a background environment for Chiharu to move around in, we need to prepare the code that is necessary to make our game character truly interactive. At this point, it's worth jumping ahead to the finished piece o see at what we're trying to achieve here—so go ahead and open up `chiharu_tutorial_fin.swf` and play around to see how the cursor keys and space bar allow you to control the little Chiharu. (This is obviously a fairly limited game environment for the purpose of demonstration and learning.)

Now we're ready to dive into the FLA and study the relevant control code, so open up `chiharu_tutorial_fin.fla`. The first thing you might noticed here is that I've set the frame rate to 30 fps, a nice quick rate suitable for this kind of game development in which we use both timeline and ActionScript effects.

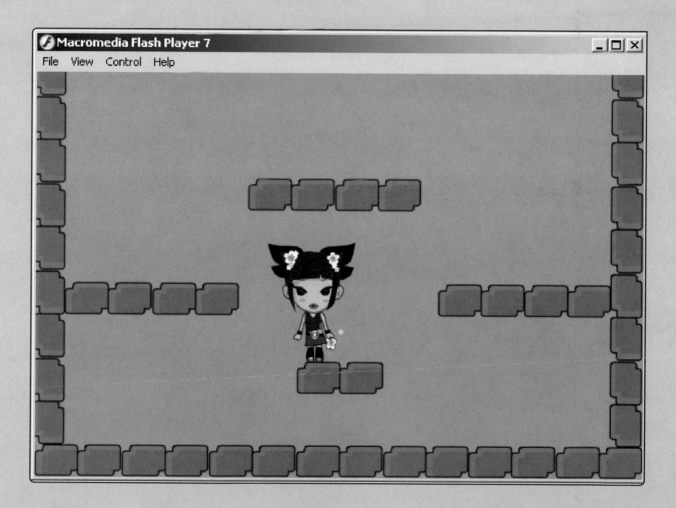

Open the action layer in this Flash document, and refer to your Actions panel (F9). First up, we have to set some variables that will provide us with the way to make the character move—their meaning will become clear as we progress through the code:

```
// variables
incrSpeed = .8;
maxSpeed = 6;
gravity = 1;
defaultDeceleration = .3;
jumpHeight = 14;
jumping = 0;
speedHoriz = 0;
speedVert = 0;
shot_on = 0;
//========================
```

Next, we construct some simple sound objects and associate them with jumping and shooting actions:

```
// sounds
jumpS = new Sound();
jumpS.attachSound("j");
shotS = new Sound();
shotS.attachSound("s");
//========================
```

If you move on to the movement control functions, the first one you'll come across is the moveRight() function:

```
// moveRight
function moveRight() {
  chiharu.gotoAndStop("go_R");
  myDirection = 1;
  resetInterval_wait();
  if (speedHoriz<maxSpeed) {
    speedHoriz += incrSpeed;
  }
  if (!jumping) {
    chiharu.body.gotoAndStop("walk");
  }
}
//========================
```

From this ActionScript, it's clear that increasing the value of the variable speedHoriz results in rightward movement. Moreover, if the character is not jumping, then we move the player movie clip chiharu.body to the walk position on its timeline. Note that the myDirection variable allows us to keep track of the direction of the character; this is used later in the Shot_the_flower() function.

The moveLeft() function is very similar to moveRight() and looks like this:

```
// moveLeft
function moveLeft() {
  chiharu.gotoAndStop("go_L");
  myDirection = -1;
  resetInterval_wait();
  if (speedHoriz>(-1*maxSpeed)) {
    speedHoriz -= incrSpeed;
  }
  if (!jumping) {
    chiharu.body.gotoAndStop("walk");
  }
}
//========================
```

In the jump() function, the jumping variable is immediately set to 1 (true), and then the value of the speedVert variable is decreased to counteract the simulated gravity effect:

```
// jump
function jump() {
  jumping = 1;
  speedVert -= jumpHeight;
  chiharu.body.gotoAndStop("jump");
  jumpS.start(0);
  resetInterval_wait();
}
//========================
```

The myStop() function is called when no key has been hit for a short while—this calls setInterval_wait() (discussed in the following code) and makes Chiharu turn to face front as if she is waiting for your next command.

```
//stop
function myStop() {
  speedHoriz *= deceleration;
  chiharu.body.gotoAndStop("stop");
  setInterval_wait();
}
//========================
```

The waiting functions are as follows:

```
// waiting
function Wait() {
  isWaiting = 0;
  chiharu.gotoAndStop("wait");
  clearInterval(intervalW);
}
function resetInterval_wait() {
  clearInterval(intervalW);
  isWaiting = 0;
}
function setInterval_wait() {
  if (!isWaiting) {
    intervalW = setInterval(Wait, 3500);
    isWaiting = 1;
  }
}
//========================
```

In setInterval_wait() we set a time interval of 3,500 milliseconds. This means that after 3.5 seconds, Wait() is called and Chiharu turns into her waiting state. Whenever a movement function is called, the resetInterval_wait() function resets the interval with clearInterval().

Next up, let's now see the functions that will allow Chiharuchan to shoot the magic flowers—the shot() and Shot_the_flower() functions:

```
// shooting
function shot() {
  if (!jumping) {
    speedHoriz = 0;
  } else {
    if (speedHoriz>1) {
      speedHoriz -= incrSpeed;
    }
  }
  chiharu.body.gotoAndStop("shot");
  resetInterval_wait();
}

function Shot_the_flower() {
  numF += 1;
  shotS.start();
  flower.duplicateMovieClip
  ➡ ("flower"+numF, 10+numF);
  var tg = eval("flower"+numF);
  tg.xInit =
  ➡ tg._x=chiharu._x+20*myDirection;
  tg._y = chiharu._y-50;
  tg.dir = myDirection;
  tg.onEnterFrame = function() {
    if (this.dir == undefined) {
      this.dir = 1;
    }
    tg._x += 5*this.dir;
    if (this.dir == 1) {
      if (this._x>(this.xInit+220)) {
        this.play();
        delete this.onEnterFrame;
      }
    } else {
      if (this._x<(this.xInit-220)) {
        this.play();
        delete this.onEnterFrame;
      }
    }
  };
}
//========================
```

When `shot()` is called, the variable `speedHoriz` is at first set to 0, meaning that the movement on the x-axis is stopped. Then the player movie clip `chiharu.body` is moved to its `shot` frame. As we can see in the following screenshot, the animation of the movie clip `Chiharu—MC.chiharu.Chiharu_shot` will call the function `Shot_the_flower()`that will duplicate the flowers. To each duplicated magic flower we assign an `onEnterFrame` function that allows the flower to move 220 pixels left or right, depending on the direction the character is turned. At the end of the movement, we cancel the function `onEnterFrame` from the memory and play the duplicated flower (`flower_explosion` movie clip). This is a good example of how the game is effectively built up from tweened animation interacting with ActionScript.

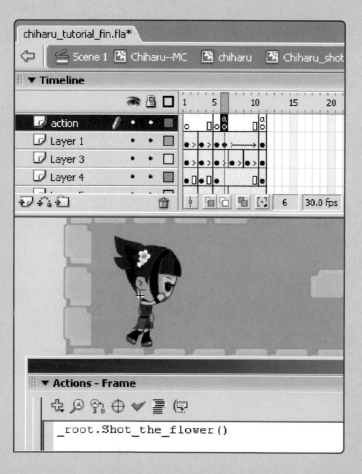

Now we need to set the function that will give the interactivity to Chiharu—that is, the code that traces the pressed keys, `MyKeyPress()`:

```
// keyboard interactivity
function MyKeyPress() {
  if (Key.isDown(Key.UP) && jumping ==
➥ false) {
    jump();
  }
  if (Key.isDown(Key.LEFT)) {
    moveLeft();
  } else if (Key.isDown(Key.RIGHT)) {
    moveRight();
  }
  if (Key.isDown(Key.SPACE)) {
    shot();
  }
  if (!Key.isDown(Key.LEFT) &&
➥ !Key.isDown(Key.RIGHT) &&
➥ !Key.isDown(Key.UP) &&
➥ !Key.isDown(Key.SPACE) && !jumping) {
    myStop();
  }
}
//========================
```

This function will be inserted into our final `onEnterFrame`, to allow the character to instantly react to the typing on the keyboard. Once we press the up, left, and right keys, the corresponding movement functions, `jump()`, `moveLeft()`, and `moveRight()` will be called on every `EnterFrame` cycle. If no key is typed, then the `myStop()` function is invoked. In addition, we use the `Key.SPACE` property to associate the pressing of the SPACE bar with the `shot()` function.

The penultimate block of code is the collision detection function:

```
// collision detection
function Collision() {
  // Y collision
  if (base.hitTest(chiharu._x, newY,
➡ true) && speedVert>-1) {
    speedVert = 0;
    jumping = false;
  } else {
    chiharu._y = newY;
  }
  // X collision
  if (vertical.hitTest(newX, chiharu._y,
➡ true)) {
    speedHoriz = 0;
  } else {
    chiharu._x = newX;
  }
}
//=========================
```

Here, `Collision()` detects the collisions on both the x- and y-axes, modifies the values of the variables `speedHoriz` and `speedVert` respectively, and also modifies the position of the character on the screen. The actual detection work is achieved through the classic `hitTest()` function, using vertical and horizontal elements and Chiharu's position.

And finally, the `onEnterFrame` event handler runs all the time event programming and references the two important functions: `MyKeyPress()`, for the keyboard control, and `Collision()`, for collision detection.

```
this.onEnterFrame = function() {
  MyKeyPress();
  // gravity
  if (speedVert<maxSpeed) {
    speedVert += gravity;
  }
  // x and y movement
  newX = chiharu._x+speedHoriz;
  newY = chiharu._y+speedVert;
  Collision();
};
//=========================
```

Summary: Italy to California, via Japan

Japan has obviously been a major influence in my life. In addition, I believe that I inherited my love of art, cuisine, and design—especially vintage and retro design—from my own country, Italy. Now that I live in California, I have a whole new world of influences to explore. Right now, I'm working on many exciting projects; I'm involved with product development and managing the Tokidoki brand, including printing t-shirts, making gadgets with the heart and crossbones Tokidoki logo, and so on. But my multimedia development will always continue with the help of my best friends from my studio in Rome (www.vianet.it). Flash gaming is one of the things we really love to do and base our business on—we have an incredible team, and I thank them for the friendship that binds us together. In particular, Emanuele Petrungaro (www.aoirobot.it) assisted me greatly with the technical aspects of this chapter's tutorial.

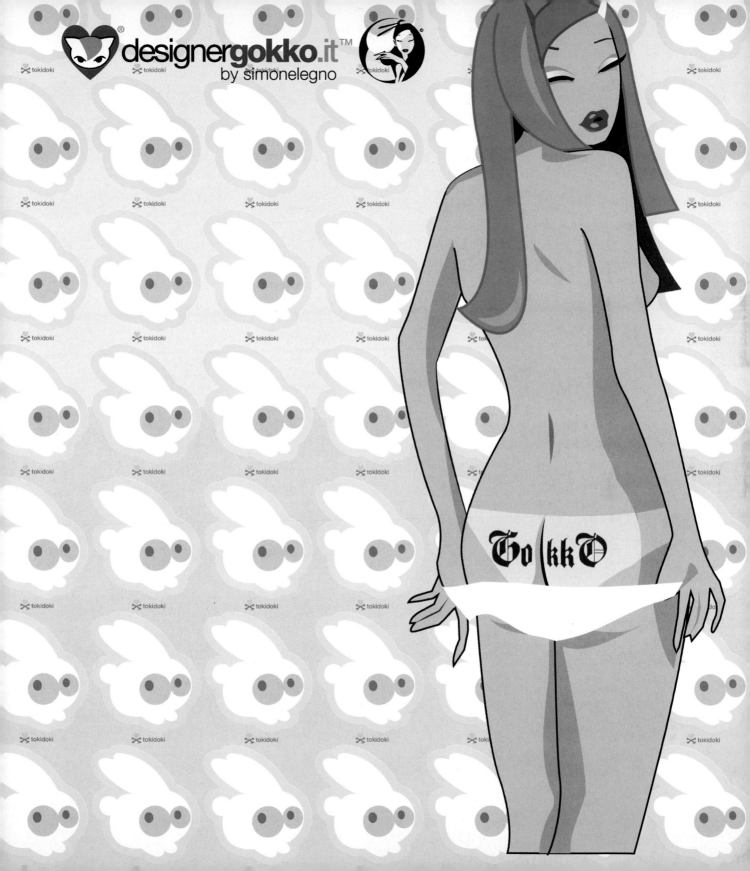

14 PROCESS

"I LIKE THE THOUGHT THAT NEARLY EVERYTHING IS IN A PERPETUAL STATE OF CHANGE: IDEAS DEVELOP, GOALPOSTS ARE CONSTANTLY SHIFTED, AND YOUR PERSPECTIVE IS INFLUENCED BY THOUSANDS OF DIFFERENT INTERACTING OBJECTS ON A DAILY BASIS."

DANNY FRANZREB
WWW.TAOBOT.COM

Inspirations

I like the thought that nearly everything is in a perpetual state of change: ideas develop, goalposts are constantly shifted, and your perspective is influenced by thousands of different interacting objects on a daily basis.

Quite a few people tend to think that they can clearly identify major goals for their life and work. Some individuals believe they're able to define all the problems and needs of a project in its initial stages. Furthermore, a person or a group of people might think that they know all alternatives and consequences of a project decision, that their preferences are consistent, and that the rules on which their decisions are based are well defined. In this way, people feel their decisions and goals for a project are based on a rational decision-making process.

(mt) Media Temple NRG Bar Graphic © Taobot

All Our Deal cover © Taobot

I guess that holds true for some simple decisions, but I believe a lot of us have a very different experience. Typically, problems are murky, they can be hard to define in detail, and they change over time. Likewise, goals are inconsistent, ambiguous, and sometimes difficult to achieve in exactly the way they conceived in the beginning. Getting hold of all the alternatives isn't that straightforward—normally, information is incomplete and thus consequences are also unclear, preferences are inconsistent, and rules are vague. If you now consider that all of this strongly depends on the composition of participants who dynamically join and leave a project or group, decision-making during or defining goals for a project is often a highly fluid process influenced by various fluctuating factors.

This idea might seem chaotic at first, but its implications are important to the way I tackle tasks and interact with my surroundings. I believe being aware that projects and goals constantly undergo changes is important to how we work and live. Don't get me wrong—I'm not saying that I don't have any goals or that I can't focus. Sure, I work on projects according to clearly defined goals, and I'm focused on trying to put as much effort as I can into everything I do, but I feel the need to also have an understanding and appreciation of different opinions, methods, interests, and styles along the way. Having a static approach might ultimately lead to more chaos and confusion than adapting and redefining, because you'll try to prevent something that isn't appropriate anymore, which will blur or compromise what you could have achieved.

One small example of this is a decision I made while developing a website for SMIRNOFF ICE. At the time, Flash MX and Flash Communication Server MX were just around the corner, and I didn't have much experience with the new features—I'm sure you'll know that when you have a tight deadline, it doesn't normally help to experiment. I decided to use the new tools for various reasons. One reason was the video support of Flash MX, which meant I could display SMIRNOFF ICE's TV commercials directly in the Flash interface in a unique isometric design, which was very important to the client. Another reason was the multiuser capabilities of Flash Communication Server MX, which helped me create a popular chat application. By incorporating these new features, I enhanced the site and made it more successful. I also sped up my development process once I learned the new language constructs introduced with Flash MX. By the way, I believe we're at a similar point with the ActionScript 2.0 classes introduced with Flash MX 2004. There will always be new features, and normally they'll help you in your work once you've mastered them. Personally, I hope to continue learning new skills and techniques with each new project by being open-minded and interested, and by incorporating different perspectives from various disciplines.

Texelseboys poster © Taobot

Paperkut magazine © Taobot

I would now like to share with you my personal background and events that influenced me over the years, so that you're better able to understand why I approach things the way I do. When I was very young, I loved to draw, play with LEGOs, and do all the things other kids my age did. I remember one thing, however, that wasn't normal for a 4-year-old boy in the mid-1980s: I had a personal computer. I didn't really do much with my computer at that time, other than madly play some of the computer games my father brought home from work. He worked at IBM for more than 30 years, which is the reason we had stuff like computers to experiment with at home.

Like I said, I didn't really care much about those sorts of things, and I used the computer only for playing games or figuring out how to install the latest programs. I was far away from being a coding whiz kid—things like the command line bored rather than exited me. I guess that's because I've always been very much attracted to visuals. I loved drawing, comics, and videos, and I've had so many visual influences over the years that it's tough for me to pinpoint only a few. I would like to tell you that there was a particular painting by Picasso, for instance, that inspired me so much that it clearly led me to where I am today, or at least pointed me in a certain direction, but that isn't the case. To be honest, in my house there was a print of Picasso's *Guernica*, but I just wouldn't regard that as an important influence, although I liked it a lot. Other things had a much stronger influence on me.

Paperkut magazine © Taobot

Something I enjoyed very much was being outside, exploring the world with my friends, and skateboarding, which I did on a daily basis for years. Looking back, I tried many different sports, but skateboarding stuck. I guess it gave me the chance to be creative and try new tricks all the time because it had no fixed set of rules. In addition, I could go skating whenever I wanted on my own or with a whole bunch of people, which gave me the freedom to explore my surroundings and learn from them. You'll often hear that if you do some kind of sport, you also adopt parts of its lifestyle, and this is especially true for skate-boarding. I was influenced by deck graphics, magazine ads, videos, and graffiti culture. During that time, I tried painting, graffiti, and airbrush art—sometimes even on gaming consoles.

© Vans

Rancid, "...*And Out Come the Wolves*", © Epitaph 1995

Although I never properly learned to play an instrument, another strong influence for me was music, mainly punk, metal, electronica, and a little hip hop. Some of my best friends still are musicians, and I love to just hang out with them, listening to their music, flipping through magazines, and having controversial discussions about all sorts of weird topics. Later through my interest in urban landscapes, I explored other disciplines such as architecture, fashion design, and photography.

And as I mentioned, throughout my youth, my family had all these computers and other technical gadgets in the house. Still, I never got that deep into coding, but because I grew up surrounded by technology, I dealt with it on a regular basis and would design birthday cards on 9-needle printers and play with early graphic design applications on screens that were way too small. Eventually in the late 1990s, I started to create basic websites to earn a few bucks after school, but I couldn't really relate to the early text-based environments.

OFFF 2003, The Jelly Bellys live video © Taobot

My biggest problem was that I needed some sort of visual feedback. You could have told me that the Web would be an amazing breakthrough for business applications or whatever, and I could even imagine this, but it didn't interest me especially. What I couldn't imagine was that there would be a time when I would love to work with this medium—when working on the Web would become much, much more than a job after school. I struggled to find a discipline or profession in which I could combine my various interests anyway. Having so many influences to combine wasn't easy, because I didn't want to lose a single one from the mix. It was at this time that I was introduced to Flash, which was at version 3.

It's certainly not as if I was overwhelmed with all the capabilities of the tool. When I first used Flash I had no idea of all it was capable of—I just had fun playing around and creating small animations. After the next version of Flash (version 4), endless hours of research, and a few small projects, I got a better feel for Flash and understood it offered me a way to combine my various interests. Surfing the Web while looking at all the emerging Flash resources and experimental sites like yugop.com, I saw a creative community that I hadn't experienced in that form before. I always appreciated what people like John Maeda did with C++ or other coding languages, but like I said, I just couldn't find a way into that code-eating command-line style of programming. Through ActionScript (which seemed to be an enabler rather than a stumbling block to programming) and through the visual feedback the Flash authoring tool provided, I was finally able to connect the right and left sides of my brain.

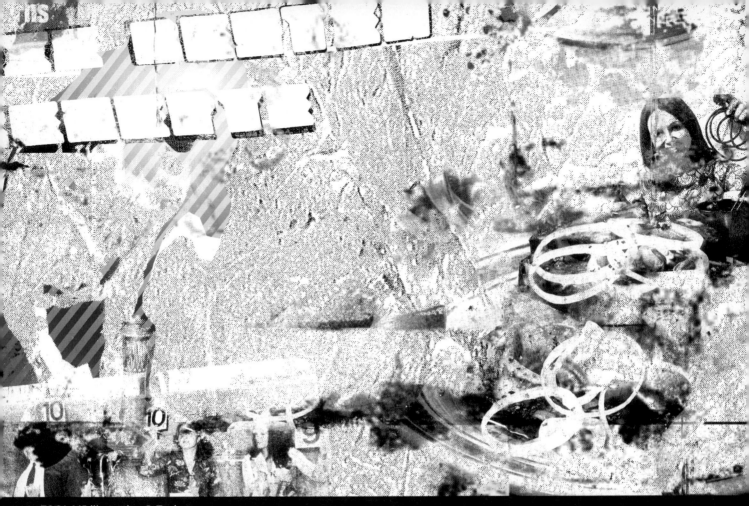

TOCA ME illustration © Taobot

Flash evolved, and so did I—at least I like to think I did. Sometimes I get asked that dreaded question, Do you consider yourself a designer or a developer? From my background, you might be able to guess that I don't know, don't care, and don't consider this very important anyway. I like to try out many things from various disciplines, and Flash gave me the option to combine most of my interests. I believe no human being stays the same over time. Skills, interests, and surroundings are constantly changing. This is good, by the way; the world would be pretty boring otherwise. For example, I've been working in graphic, motion, and 3D design in parallel with studying various information systems topics such as Java, SQL, math, or economics—that's just the way I tick. Of course, it's worth pointing out that I wasn't equally successful in every field I tried out!

In my opinion, it's more important to have some sort of restless passion for everything you do. If I work on a project, I put my heart into it, thus I'm not easily satisfied. Many people concentrate on being excellent in one field, and if they're happy with that, it's absolutely fantastic. What I learned, though, by collaborating with so many motivated individuals from diverse fields is that whatever you do, you should be open to new ideas and methods. There will always be people around you with different interests and skills. I've never evolved by ignoring these; rather, I've grown by respecting different opinions, learning from them, and embracing new influences.

" FLASH EVOLVED, AND SO DID I "

Sceyelines magazine graphic © Taobot

Tutorials overview

The files you'll work on in this chapter relate to multiple aspects of Flash, which is why I selected them. They incorporate graphic design, animation, interaction, ActionScript, a little math, and one of my favorite mediums: sound. You'll work on two files so you can see how to reuse and enhance code in multiple situations, which leads to slightly different results.

I based the first experiment on the SWFs I created for a recent project commissioned by 3deluxe. I'd like to thank Sascha Koeth (www.sascha-koeth.de) and 3deluxe (www.3deluxe.de) for giving me permission to use some of their fabulous 3D renderings as a source. In addition, I'd like to thank my friend Marcelo Baldin (www.combustion.ws) for creating the original sound for this chapter's files.

To enable you to better understand and follow the process of what I tried to achieve through these experiments, I'll discuss the ideas behind the files briefly. 3deluxe designed a music club and restaurant, the Cocoon Club, in Frankfurt, Germany, for the recording label Cocoon, which is run by the godfather of techno, Sven Väth.

3deluxe commissioned me to work on Flash files for the project. The idea was that users could reach certain parts of the website by interacting with it. The navigation would disappear, and emotional worlds of graphics and sounds would come into being.

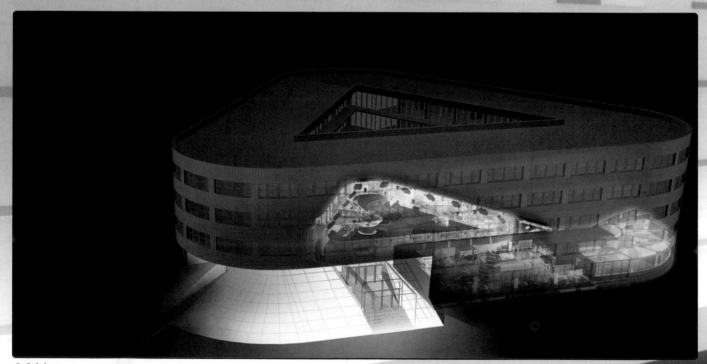

© 3deluxe

As you can imagine, a major factor in this project was sound, as this was what the Cocoon Club would be all about. Another factor was that no real images of the club were to be used, because the site launched before the official opening of the club, and also because the site was supposed to reflect emotional, abstract worlds of sound in certain areas. Thus, only subtle parts of graphics of the interior architecture and 3D renderings by 3deluxe were used to build these worlds. The desired effect was that people who came to the club would be able to recognize some of the graphics they saw on the website as the club's interior architecture. In addition, lighting was an important factor that was used to emphasize the club's interior architecture. So these graphics were combined with lighting and figurative elements out of nature to create the mood of emotional worlds in Flash.

cocoonclub.net website © 3deluxe

© 3deluxe

A little math

To get started, you need to understand a few basic math and sound concepts, which you'll use in the projects. Don't panic— I'll try to explain the math part of it as intuitively as I can, and even if you aren't able to understand a formula completely, this shouldn't prevent you from following the tutorials. I just want to give you a rough idea of what's going on and why you'll use certain code constructs later on. Later, you'll fake a little 3D with really simple trigonometric functions. You'll mainly use sine and cosine to achieve the effect of swinging and rotation, so I'll cover those concepts here.

Some of you might remember the **unit circle** from school. It's a circle with a radius around the origin of the coordinate system. If you draw a straight line from the origin until it intersects the circle, the line will always have a length of 1.

Now assume you draw a straight line from the origin at an angle of 60 degrees, to the upper right of the circle. In the context of the resulting triangle, this line is referred to as the **hypotenuse**.

The dashed line of the triangle at the opposite side of the y-axis represents the sine or length of that dashed line in the unit circle, which in this case is 0.866. This line is called the **opposite** because it's located at the opposite side of the triangle to the angle. The dashed line on the x-axis represents the cosine or length of the triangle's adjacent line in the unit circle, which in this case is 0.5. Predictably, this line is called the **adjacent**.

If you now rotate the hypotenuse line to, say, 90 degrees, the sine of the line will be 1 and the cosine will be 0. This is because the line has a length of 1 and it lies completely on the y-axis. Rotating the line further to 180 degrees means the line is located on the x-axis, and the sine is 0 and the cosine is –1. So if you rotate the line continuously around the circle, the sine and cosine will have values between 1 and –1, where the sine is 1 or –1 when the cosine is 0, and vice versa. If you like, just imagine the sine and cosine as being two functions that map a line on the y- and x-axes, although my math teacher would probably punish me for simplifying it that way.

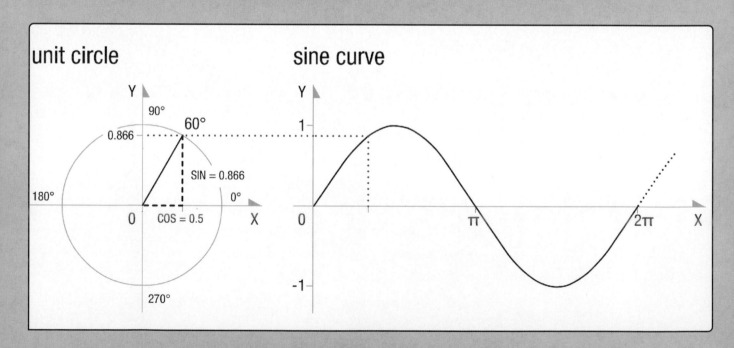

Please stay with me a little longer—we'll be done with the math part soon and then move on to Flash!

An angle in the unit circle can be expressed in degrees or in **radians** (i.e., by how much it goes around on the outer of the unit circle). The complete unit circle has an outer length of 2 Pi (≈ 2 x 3.14), so the mapping of the sine and cosine onto the axis takes place between 0 and 2 Pi. This basically means that if you draw the sine and cosine in a coordinate system, both curves will look like waves, as you can see in the preceding diagram. If you begin with the angle set to 0 and move once around the circle to 360 degrees, the sine starts at 0 and goes up to 1, then down to –1 and back to 0 in a range of 2 Pi or 360 degrees. The cosine does the same "swing," but it starts at 1 and goes back to 1. It's worth taking another look at the previous paragraph to understand why the sine starts at 0 and the cosine starts at 1, and the implications this can have when you use the functions.

Up until now, you should have kept in mind that the sine and cosine are functions that map a line on the y- or x-axis, and that the functions look like swinging waves. This is what you'll need to remember later on.

Let's move on to another concept that you're going to use to model sound waves. If you add two base frequencies (in terms of sound) or two functions (in terms of math), the sum will look like the overlay of both.

That's it for the math part! Remember that you don't need to know every detail about sine and cosine—you'll get an intuitive feeling for what you need to do once you start working on the Flash project in the next exercise.

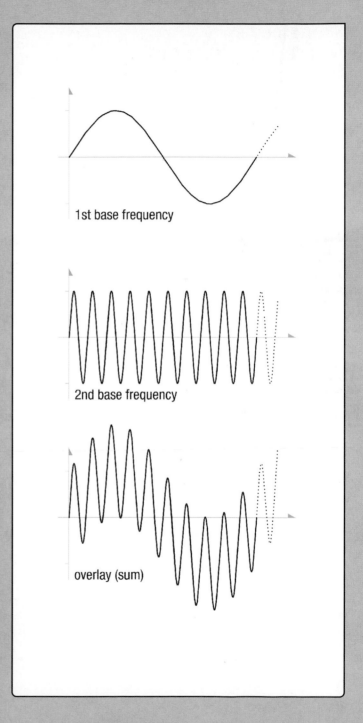

1st base frequency

2nd base frequency

overlay (sum)

Sound pollen

To start, please open the `sound_pollen_start.fla` file from the CD. If you like, also open `sound_pollen_final.swf` to take a look at the effect you're going to create. In this final file, a flower opens on a coordinate system and releases pollen that then moves around the blossom, plays a sound, and interacts with the mouse.

> *I recommend copying this chapter's entire folder from the CD to your local hard drive before you start working.*

Once you open the file you'll see five layers on the stage: script, grid, flower, coordinates, and background. The script layer holds all the ActionScript code for this project. I already put a `grid_mc` movie clip made out of lines onto the grid layer. This movie clip forms a sort of coordinate system together with `coordinateSystem_mc` from the coordinates layer. You won't use it for anything other than having a visual pseudo-coordinate system in the first experiment, so it's just a graphical enhancement on the stage at this point.

> *Keep in mind that whenever you do mathematical calculations or place something on the stage, your reference coordinate system will always be the main timeline, which has its origin at the upper-left corner of the stage. It's also worth noting that the y-axis in Flash points downward, unlike in the Cartesian coordinate system you know from school in which the y-axis points upward.*

I also put a rectangle with a radial fill that covers the whole stage onto the background layer. The flower layer is empty, so you'll work on that next.

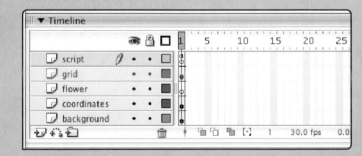

You'll find three flower FLVs of different types on the CD and also a flower in QuickTime format. If you want to try out different compression settings on your own, you can import the QuickTime movie. Otherwise, just import `flower_high_q.flv`, which I created by using the Flash Video Exporter in Adobe After Effects.

1. Create a new movie clip, name it `flower`, and import the video into it. The Import dialog box will ask you whether Flash should automatically insert the required frames for the video into the timeline, so click the Yes button.

2. Back on the main timeline, drag an instance of the `flower` movie clip onto the flower layer on the stage and give it the instance name `flower_mc`. Also set its X and Y values to 200.

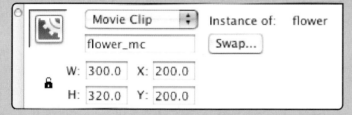

3. Now that you've placed all your movie clips on the stage, let's move on to the scripting part. Select the script layer and open the ActionScript editor.

As you'll notice I'm using suffixes such a `_mc` to trigger **code hints**. I do this first of all because I'm lazy and I can select my functions via the pop-up menu. Also, it helps me to identify the types of variables within my script, and I can keep my code organized that way.

4. The first line of code will set the variable `range` to 90. `range` is the number of different sine and cosine values you want to create. Next, you'll initialize two arrays, `sinusStorage_array` and `cosinusStorage_array`, with `range` number of entries.

You'll store the sine and cosine values in the arrays so you won't need to recalculate them every frame during the runtime of the movie.

```
// ::::::::::::::::::::::::::::::::::::::::::::::
// by Danny Franzreb - http://www.taobot.com
// ::::::::::::::::::::::::::::::::::::::::::::::
range = 90;

sinusStorage_array = new Array(range);
cosinusStorage_array = new Array(range);
```

5. Since you already initialized the arrays, you can now go ahead and fill them with values using a `for` loop. You'll want to run once around the unit circle in 90 steps while storing the sine and cosine values for each step in your arrays. In other words, you want to create one full sine- and cosine-swinging wave. The factor `i/range` represents the percentage value of the current loop. You multiply this by the outer length of the unit circle 2 * `Math.PI` to get your current position on it, and then you calculate the sine and cosine values through the use of the `Math` object.

```
for(var i = 0; i < range; i++){

  var r = (i / range) * 2 * Math.PI;
  sinusStorage_array[i] = Math.sin(r);
  cosinusStorage_array[i] = Math.cos(r);
}
```

6. Next, you define a constructor function that will store coordinates with two properties: an x-coordinate and a y-coordinate.

```
Coordinate = function(x, y){
  this.x = x;
  this.y = y;
};
```

7. You just created the `Coordinate` object, so let's use it right away. The `origin` variable is located at the center of the blossom, because that will be the origin from which the pollen spreads out. If you'd like to see the blossom, please refer to `sound_pollen_final.swf` or go inside the `flower_mc` movie clip and play it to the end.

```
origin = new Coordinate(383, 319);
```

origin in the blossom's center

8. At this point, let's take care of the pollen. You need an `Array` to store references to your pollen movie clips. In addition, you set the size of the pollen to 1, its color to a light yellow (0xFFFFCC), and the initial alpha to 80.

```
pollen_array = new Array();

pollenSize = 1;
pollenColor = "0xFFFFCC";
pollenAlpha = 80;
// ==================================
```

Now you need to create two empty movie clips that will act as containers for your sound loops. Since you want to control two sounds individually in the timeline through the `setVolume` function of the `Sound` object, you have to attach these sounds to two different movie clips. This is because if `setVolume` is tied to a movie clip or a main timeline, `setVolume` affects all sounds in that movie clip or timeline.

9. There's a really neat new function in Flash MX 2004 called `getNextHighestDepth` that returns the next available depth that renders above all current movie clips within a movie clip. Please note that you can simply replace this function by integers if you want to export to the Flash 6 player. Your first movie clip, `flowerSound_mc`, will act as a container for the loop that's supposed to play once the mouse gets close to the pollen.

```
var nextDepth = this.getNextHighestDepth();

this.createEmptyMovieClip
➥ ("flowerSound_mc", nextDepth);
```

10. A new `Sound` object is created in `flowerSound_mc`, and the target of the `Sound` object should also be `flowerSound_mc`. That's why you pass it to the function. `flower_sound` now controls all sounds nested within `flowerSound_mc`.

```
flowerSound_mc.flower_sound = new
➥ Sound(flowerSound_mc);
```

11. To connect a sound loop to the `flower_sound` object, you're going to import `flower_loop.wav` into the Library. Please set the linkage identifier of the file in the Library to `flower_loop` by selecting Export for ActionScript and making sure Export in first frame is selected as well. Then attach `flower_loop` from the Library to the `Sound` object.

```
flowerSound_mc.flower_sound.attachSound
➥ ("flower_loop");
```

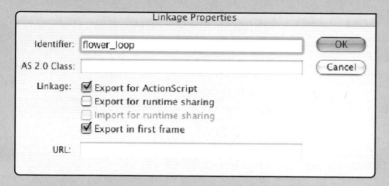

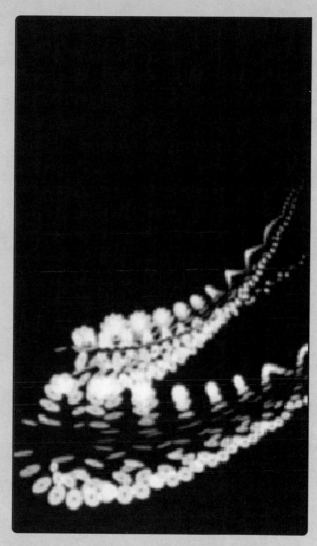

12. You start the sound loop at the beginning, so the **offset** is 0, which is the first argument. The sound should loop during the entire time the SWF plays. Unfortunately, there's no other way in Flash to tell a sound to loop endlessly other than to set the loop value to a high integer. So by the second argument, you tell a 5-second sound to loop 100,000 times, for instance. This is about 8,333 minutes or 138 hours, which should do the job. In addition, you set the **volume** of the flower sound loop to 0 because it's supposed to loop loudly only once the mouse gets close to the pollen.

```
flowerSound_mc.flower_sound.start(0, 100000);
flowerSound_mc.flower_sound.setVolume(0);
```

13. Next, you need to create the second empty movie clip and Sound object for the background loop. The only major difference between this loop and the previous one is that you work with other identifiers and variable names. Repeat steps 9 through 12 and substitute flower with background.

```
nextDepth = this.getNextHighestDepth();

this.createEmptyMovieClip("backgroundSound_mc", nextDepth);

backgroundSound_mc.background_sound = new Sound(backgroundSound_mc);
backgroundSound_mc.background_sound.attachSound("background_loop");
backgroundSound_mc.background_sound.start(0, 100000);
```

14. This loop will also be present when the mouse is far away from the pollen; therefore, you set the volume to 100 and don't touch it anymore. By the way, the standard value for volume is 100, so you don't really need to set that explicitly.

```
backgroundSound_mc.background_sound.setVolume(100);
// ===================================================
```

15. At this point, you're able to move on and build the function `createPollen` that you'll later call to initiate a single grain of pollen. The function takes a few arguments: `clip_mc` is the clip that you attach the grain of pollen to, `pollenOrigin` is the place where you create the grain of pollen, and `pollenPos` represents the pollen's final destination. Both parameters will be passed to the function as `Coordinate` objects. `pollenSize`, `pollenColor`, and `pollenAlpha` are self-explanatory: here you'll pass the variables you set earlier to the function. In the function, you create an empty movie clip inside `clip_mc` and store a reference to that movie clip in `ref_mc`. Please note that some of the functions are fairly long. I advise you to open and study the `sound_pollen_final.fla` file—it's a valuable learning resource.

```
function createPollen(clip_mc, pollenOrigin,
➥ pollenPos, pollenSize, pollenColor, pollenAlpha){
  var nextDepth = clip_mc.getNextHighestDepth();
  clip_mc.createEmptyMovieClip("pollen" +
  ➥ nextDepth, nextDepth);
  var ref_mc = clip_mc["pollen" + nextDepth];
```

You use the keyword `var` so that objects not needed after the function is executed can be released from memory. For the same reason, you attach only references to other functions to the event handlers inside your function. If you had created inner functions within your function, this would have forced memory management to keep the outer function and its variables in memory, even though you don't need them after you've initialized the pollen. This would result in wasted memory.

16. Back to the initializing process, you set the `ref_mc._x` and `ref_mc._y` positions to `pollenOrigin`, and store its final position in `pos`. Then you set the line style of `ref_mc` to the values that you passed to the function, and draw a line from **(0,0)** to **(1,1)** to the center of `ref_mc`. This dot represents the first grain of pollen. Next, you draw two more lines somewhere at a maximum of 40 pixels x and y away from the center, and `Math.random() * 80 - 40` returns a value between +40 and −40. You also modify the alpha value of the lines in a range of +10 to −10 from the original `pollenAlpha` to have three dots inside your `ref_mc` that look slightly different. You might wonder why you don't create a movie clip for every dot you draw. This is simply because of performance issues. Whenever I refer to **pollen** here, I actually mean the pollen movie clip with three dots in it that represent the drawn pollen.

```
ref_mc._x = pollenOrigin.x;
ref_mc._y = pollenOrigin.y;
ref_mc.pos = pollenPos;

ref_mc.lineStyle(pollenSize, pollenColor,
➡ pollenAlpha);
ref_mc.lineTo(1, 1);

for(var i = 0; i< 2; i++){
   var alp = Math.random() * (pollenAlpha-10) + 10;
   ref_mc.lineStyle(pollenSize, pollenColor, alp);
   var x = Math.round(Math.random() * 80 - 40);
   var y = Math.round(Math.random() * 80 - 40);
   ref_mc.moveTo(x, y);
   rcf_mc.lineTo(x+1, y+1);
}
```

17. A count variable will control the current sine value that you use to get the pollen swinging. Each grain of pollen should start to swing at a slightly different position on the sine wave, but not throughout the whole wave. Thus, they swing only a little out of sync.

```
ref_mc.count = Math.floor(Math.random() *
➡ clip_mc.range / 2);
```

18. Remember the sine curve again for a moment. `count` will run continually through that wave, and by adding these sine values to the x and y positions of the pollen, the pollen will swing, in this case +10 to −10 in the x direction and −2 to +2 in the y direction. `tempPosX` and `tempPosY` will store the first final position of the pollen. This is the position where you want to move the pollen from its origin.

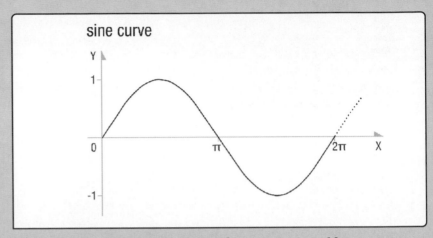

```
ref_mc.tempPosX = ref_mc.pos.x + clip_mc.sinusStorage_array[ref_mc.count] * 10;
ref_mc.tempPosY = ref_mc.pos.y - clip_mc.sinusStorage_array[ref_mc.count] * 2;
```

19. The `movePollenToPos` function will take care of moving the pollen to its final position. You attach it to the `onEnterFrame` event so it's executed each frame. After that, you return the reference to your pollen clip and exit the function.

```
ref_mc.onEnterFrame = movePollenToPos;

   return ref_mc;
}
// ============================================================
```

20. Next, you'll write the function `movePollenToPos`, which controls the movement of the pollen to its final position. First, you calculate the x and y distances to the pollen's final position. If these absolute distances are smaller than 1, you attach the `movePollen` function to `onEnterFrame`. Otherwise, you move the pollen a little closer to its final position.

```
movePollenToPos = function(){

   this.xDist = this.tempPosX - this._x;
   this.yDist = this.tempPosY - this._y;

   if(Math.abs(this.xDist) < 1 && Math.abs(this.yDist) < 1){

      this.onEnterFrame = movePollen;
   }else{
      this._x += this.xDist / 10;
      this._y += this.yDist / 10;
   }
};
// ============================================================
```

21. Now you can work on the `movePollen` function, which moves a single grain of pollen once it has reached its final position. First, you calculate the x and y distances between the pollen and the mouse, and with the help of the Pythagorean theorem ($a^2 + b^2 = c^2$), you calculate the pollen's absolute distance to the mouse. If the distance is smaller than 1, you set it to 1. You don't want to divide by values smaller than 1, because this could lead to huge (nearly infinite) numbers if the value you divide by is very small.

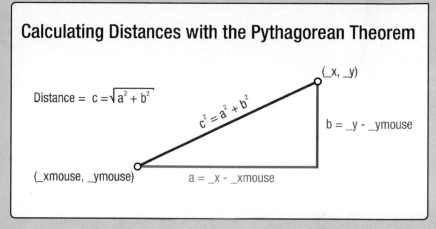

Calculating Distances with the Pythagorean Theorem

$$\text{Distance} = c = \sqrt{a^2 + b^2}$$

$$c^2 = a^2 + b^2$$

$(\_x, \_y)$

$b = \_y - \_ymouse$

$(\_xmouse, \_ymouse)$

$a = \_x - \_xmouse$

```
movePollen = function(){

    this.xDistMouse = this._x - this._parent._xmouse;
    this.yDistMouse = this._y - this._parent._ymouse;
    this.distMouse = Math.sqrt(Math.pow(this.xDistMouse, 2) + Math.pow(this.yDistMouse, 2) );

    if(Math.abs(this.distMouse) < 1){
        this.distMouse = 1;
    }
```

22. The maximum distance from the mouse to a point on the stage is 1,000 (the square root of Stage.width² + Stage.height²; in this case the square root of 800² + 600²), so `distMouse` will never be larger than 1,000, and normally it will be much smaller. `xDistMouse` and `yDistMouse` will therefore also be multiplied by a fixed number of 1,000 because you work with `powMouse`. You use `distMouse` to the power of 2 instead of a linear function, so the effect gets much stronger when the mouse is close to the pollen and is nearly nonexistent when the mouse is far away

```
    this.xAdd = this.xDistMouse * 1000;
    this.yAdd = this.yDistMouse * 1000;
    this.powMouse = Math.pow(this.distMouse, 2);
```

The next step is a bit tricky. You calculate a `controller` variable that you'll use to control the size of your movie clips. Why choose 200,000 as a value to be divided by `powMouse` for this? The straightforward explanation is that there's a huge value in the denominator, so you need a pretty big value in the numerator as well to get rather small results for the `controller` variable. The more complicated mathematical explanation is that you don't want the pollen to change size before the mouse gets close to it. For example, say you want the pollen grains to change size once the mouse gets into a range of 100 pixels, and you have a normal size of 20 (if the value calculated by `controller` is less, an `if` statement takes care of this), so once the mouse is within 100 pixels, `controller` should grow. This leads to the following formula:

```
20 = value / Math.pow(range, 2);

range is 100 so:

20 = value / 10000

Or: value = 20 * 10000

Hence: value = 200000
```

23. With this in mind, you apply your calculated value to the **scale** of your movie clip, which will always be between 20% and 100%.

```
this.controller = 200000 / this.powMouse;

  if(this.controller < 20){
    this.controller = 20;
  }else if(this.controller > 100){
    this.controller = 100;
  }

  this._xscale = this._yscale =
➡ this.controller;
```

You'll use several concepts now at once to move the pollen:

- `(this.pos.x - this._x) / 2` will make the pollen move to its normal position, if it isn't already there.

- `(xAdd / powMouse)`, the value I explained earlier, is added to the position of the movie clip, which leads to the pollen evading the mouse.

- `clip_mc.sinusStorage[this.count]` controls the pseudo 3D-wave movement of the pollen multiplied by 10 for a larger wave.

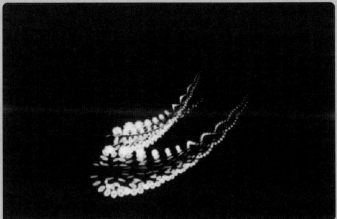

24. All the same concepts are used for calculating the _y
value of the movie clip:

```
this._x += (this.pos.x - this._x) / 2 + (this.xAdd / this.powMouse) +
➡ this._parent.sinusStorage_array [this.count] * 10;
this._y += (this.pos.y - this._y) / 2 + (this.yAdd / this.powMouse) -
➡ this._parent.sinusStorage_array[this.count] * 2;
```

25. The only thing that's left to do inside the movePollen
function is keep track of the current value of the sine
wave. As I said before, count keeps track of where you
are in the sine array. Once it reaches the end, you'll start
again at the beginning of the array.

```
if(this.count < this._parent.range-1){
    this.count++;
}else{
    this.count = 0;
}

};
// ============================================================
```

26. Without further delay, you can now initiate your pollen, so take a look at the `initPollen` function. You'll pass it an argument, `clip_mc`, which is the movie clip where you want your pollen to be initiated—in this case, on the main timeline. Then you create 80 pollen movie clips and determine their final positions. As you know, `origin` represents the center of the blossom. For x, the second value `i/3` basically says "Every time you go up, go `i/3` to the right." For example, for `i = 30`, that would be 10 pixels to the right in the thirtieth iteration, and the third part is supposed to add a random placement `1.2*i` in both directions of the x-axis. For y, `i*1.4` basically says "Every time you go up, go 1.4 pixels up instead of only 1," and then you add a random placement. After that, you put the calculated values into a new `Coordinate` object and pass your variables to the `createPollen` function. One more thing you need to do is store a reference to the created pollen in `pollen_array` and attach the `controlSound` function to the `onEnterFrame` event of `clip_mc`.

```
initPollen = function(clip_mc){

   for(var i=0; i<80; i++){

      var x = clip_mc.origin.x + i/3 + Math.random() * 2.4*i - 1.2*i;
      var y = clip_mc.origin.y - i*1.4 + Math.random() * -i;
      var pollenPos = new Coordinate(x, y);

      var pollen = createPollen(clip_mc, clip_mc.origin, pollenPos, clip_mc.pollenSize,
      ➥ clip_mc.pollenColor, clip_mc.pollenAlpha);

      clip_mc.pollen_array.push(pollen);
   }

clip_mc.onEnterFrame = controlSound;
};
```

27. With the controlSound function, you want to control the volume of flower_loop, so you again use the Pythagorean theorem to calculate the distance from the mouse to the center of the pollen. Note that you set the center 50 pixels above origin. In addition, you make use of the controller variable this time to determine and set the volume of flower_sound. Although it would be possible to do so, you don't allow values above 100 or below 0 for volume, because you don't want any distorted sound.

```
controlSound = function(){

  this.xDistMouse = this.origin.x - this._xmouse;
  this.yDistMouse = (this.origin.y - 50) - this._ymouse;
  this.distMouse = Math.sqrt(Math.pow(this.xDistMouse, 2) + Math.pow(this.yDistMouse, 2));

  this.controller = 200000 / Math.pow(this.distMouse, 2)

  if(this.controller < 1){
    this.flowerSound_mc.flower_sound.setVolume(0);
  }else if(this.controller > 100){
    this.flowerSound_mc.flower_sound.setVolume(100);
  }else{
    this.flowerSound_mc.flower_sound.setVolume(this.controller);
  }
```

28. Now you want a part of the pollen to blink depending on the distance to the mouse, and you know `controller` is a good indicator for that. Since you can't make more pollen than you have on stage blink, you check whether `controller` is greater than the number of pollen grains before starting the `for` loop. Inside the loop, you modify the alpha of randomly selected pollen a little, which leads to that blinking effect. The alpha value also depends a little on the distance to the mouse: the closer the pollen grains are to the mouse, the brighter they are.

```
this.len = this.pollen_array.length;
if(this.controller >= this.len){
  this.controller = this.len;
}

for(var i=0; i<this.controller; i++){

  this.arrIndex = Math.floor(Math.random() * this.len);

  this.pollen_array[this.arrIndex]._alpha = Math.random() * 60 + this.controller/5;
}
};
// ================================================================
```

29. You're nearly done with your first experiment now! The only thing left to do is write a function that checks whether `flower_mc` has played to the end, or, in other words, if the flower has opened. You then stop the video, call the `initPollen` function with your main timeline as an argument, and off the pollen goes.

```
flower_mc.onEnterFrame = function(){
  if(this._currentframe == this._totalframes){
    this.stop();
    initPollen(this._parent);
    this.onEnterFrame = undefined;
  }
};
// ================================================================
```

30. Save your file and export the movie to see the result. I wrote some additional ideas and comments in the source code of sound_pollen_final.fla that are intended to help you experiment further with the script.

FlashAmp

For the second experiment, you're going to use a tool called **FlashAmp 2 Pro**, which is able to extract sound information out of tracks and save it into arrays you can use in Flash. You're mostly interested in the **amplitude** of a sound, which represents the changing pattern of loudness that occurs over the duration of the sound, but FlashAmp 2 Pro is able to extract much more information than that, so I advise you to play around with the demo version on the book's CD.

Since the demo is only able to output arrays with a length of 10, I've already processed the sound loops you're going to use, which is actually very easy to do in FlashAmp. You just need to set the frame rate of your movie, input file, and output folder. (For advanced settings, please refer to the FlashAmp user guide.) What happens here is that FlashAmp goes through one of the loops from beginning to end and stores its current amplitude value in an array 30 times per second, which is the frame rate of the movie. These amplitude values range from 0 to 100, where 100 represents the loudest point of the sound. I named the arrays amp_array0 to amp_array7 and saved them to an external ActionScript file, ampArrays.as. If you'd like to take a look at the AS file, Flash MX 2004 Professional users can see the AS file inside of Flash, and Flash MX 2004 Standard users will have to open the AS file in Dreamweaver or a third-party text editor such as Notepad.

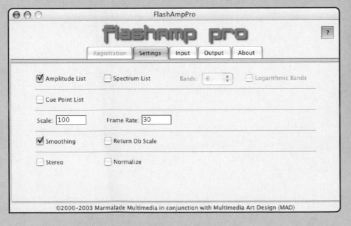

Sound waves

The second experiment is based on the concepts you learned in the sound pollen exercise. I'd like to show how you can use some of the concepts that you've just learned to achieve totally different effects by modifying the source code. You'll work with a new file from now on, so please open sound_waves_start.fla. If you like, you can also open sound_waves_final.fla and use it as a reference.

Once you open sound_waves_start.fla, you'll notice that exactly the same objects are on the stage as in the sound pollen exercise. This time you'll create waves of sound. Each wave is supposed to represent a different sound, and it should also react to that sound. Moving a wave up and down with the drag handle at the end of the wave controls the volume. Moving a wave left and right controls the pan of the attached sound. In this way, you're able to mix your own tracks by interacting with the piece.

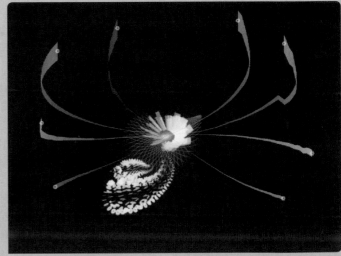

1. Import `sound_loop_00.wav` to `sound_loop_07.wav` from the `sound_loops` folder into the Library and set their linkage identifiers to `loop0` to `loop7`.

2. It's essential to have at least some sort of order in your Library so you can find things with ease when it contains a few hundred objects. To this end, put the sound loops into a subfolder named sound loops. I put three more new objects into the Library for you: `wave.circleBack`, `wave.circleFront`, and `wave`. The movie clips `wave.circleBack` and `wave.circleFront` both sit inside the wave movie clip, which acts as the drag handle. Thus, the wave movie clip also has a linkage identifier named wave so you can access it via ActionScript later on.

If you look at the ActionScript code of the final version, you'll spot lines that you'll recognize from the previous experiment. I won't talk about these again; rather, I'll concentrate on the new sections.

3. In the ActionScript editor, set the quality of the SWF to medium (this setting depends on the speed of your machine) and include your previously saved amplitude arrays file. Make sure your `ampArrays.as` file is in the same folder as your FLA file.

```
_quality = "MEDIUM";

#include "ampArrays.as"
```

4. Next, you'll insert some code you should be familiar with by now:

```
range = 90;

sinusStorage_array = new Array(range);
cosinusStorage_array = new Array(range);

for(var i = 0; i < range; i++){

  var r = (i / range) * 2 * Math.PI;
```

```
  sinusStorage_array[i] = Math.sin(r);
  cosinusStorage_array[i] = Math.cos(r);
}
```

5. You won't use a class here to store coordinates; just store the blossom's center in two variables.

```
centerX = 383;
centerY = 319;
```

6. The next new lines of code build an object and store values of `grid_mc` in it, which you'll later use as a background for your sound waves.

```
musicBack = new Object();
musicBack.left = grid_mc._x;
musicBack.right = grid_mc._x +
➥ grid_mc._width;
musicBack.top = grid_mc._y;
musicBack.bottom = grid_mc._y +
➥ grid_mc._height;
musicBack.wide = grid_mc._width;
musicBack.high = grid_mc._height;
```

7. You also store the different colors for each wave in an array and set `waveLength` to 20. This means that one wave will have 20 segments.

```
colors_array = new Array("0xFF99FF",
➥ "0xFF33FF", "0xCC99CC", "0xCC33CC",
➥ "0xEEF3F7", "0xAAD4FE", "0xAFC5DC",
➥ "0x8AC4FF");

waveLength = 20;
// ======================================
```

8. Again, you write a function to initiate the object `createWave`, and this time you attach the movie clip `wave` from the Library to `clip_mc`. I put a circle graphic inside that wave clip, which will act as the dragger. Then you store variables that you passed to the function and set `waveDirection` to −1 (I'll come back to that variable in step 19). You also place the wave at a random position on `clip_mc.musicBack` (your `grid_mc`) and attach one of the loops from the Library to the movie clip.

Drag handle

Next, you'll have a look at the functions and references that you attach to the various event handlers at the end of this function.

```
createWave = function(clip_mc, waveId, waveLength, waveColor, amp_array){

    var nextDepth = clip_mc.getNextHighestDepth();
    clip_mc.attachMovie("wave", "wave_mc" + nextDepth, nextDepth);
    var ref_mc =   clip_mc["wave_mc" + nextDepth];
    ref_mc.waveLength = waveLength;
    ref_mc.waveColor = waveColor;
    ref_mc.amp_array = amp_array;
    ref_mc.wave_array = new Array();
    ref_mc.waveDirection = -1;

    ref_mc._x = clip_mc.musicBack.left + clip_mc.musicBack.wide * Math.random();
    ref_mc._y = clip_mc.musicBack.top + clip_mc.musicBack.high * Math.random();
    ref_mc.count = Math.floor(Math.random() * clip_mc.range / 2);

    ref_mc.loop_sound = new Sound(ref_mc);
    ref_mc.loop_sound.attachSound("loop" + waveId);
    ref_mc.loop_sound.start(0, 100000);

    ref_mc.calculateVolAndPan = calculateVolAndPan;

    ref_mc.calculateVolAndPan();

    ref_mc.segment = segment;

    ref_mc.onPress = startDragging;

    ref_mc.onRelease = ref_mc.onReleaseOutside = stopDragging;

    ref_mc.onMouseMove = updateDragging;

    ref_mc.onEnterFrame = drawWave;

    return ref_mc;
};
// ================================================================
```

9. `segment` is a function that you use to draw your wave segments with. All segments together form the wave. This function is straightforward: it connects four points and fills the segment with a color and an alpha value.

```
segment = function(x1, y1, x2, y2, x3,
➡ y3, x4, y4, alpha, col){

  this.beginFill(col, alpha);
  this.moveTo(x1, y1);
  this.lineTo(x3, y3);
  this.lineTo(x4, y4);
  this.lineTo(x2, y2);
  this.lineTo(x1, y1);
};
// ===============================
```

10. `startDragging` and `stopDragging` are attached to the `onPress` and `onRelease` events of the movie clips. They set the `dragged` variable that you'll use to check whether this specific movie clip is currently dragged.

```
startDragging = function(){
  this.dragged = true;
};

stopDragging = function(){
  this.dragged = false;
};
```

11. `updateDragging` checks if a movie clip is dragged every time the mouse moves, and it recalculates its volume and pan if this is the case.

```
updateDragging = function(){
  if(this.dragged){
    this.calculateVolAndPan();
  }
};
// ===============================
```

12. calculateVolAndPan basically does what its name indicates. It considers the total size of the musicBack object and the position of the drag handler of the wave on musicBack as a base for its calculations.

```
calculateVolAndPan = function(){
  this.vol = 100 * (1 - (this._y - this._parent.musicBack.top) /
  ➥ this._parent.musicBack.high);
  this.pan = 200 * ((this._x - this._parent.musicBack.left) /
  ➥ this._parent.musicBack.wide) - 100;

  if(this.vol > 100){
    this.vol = 100;
  }else if(this.vol < 0){
    this.vol = 0;
  }

  if(this.pan > 100){
    this.pan = 100;
  }else if(this.pan < -100){
    this.pan = -100;
  }

  this.loop_sound.setPan(this.pan);
  this.loop_sound.setVolume(this.vol);
};
// ============================================================
```

13. Now we come to the most interesting part of this script: the drawWave function. First, you check if this movie clip is currently dragged and, if so, move it according to the mouse. Then you determine its distance to the mouse. If the distance is smaller than 20, you move the movie clip in the direction of the mouse, so it's a little easier to catch the wave with the mouse. If you feel that it's still hard to catch the wave in the end, you can increase this value.

```
drawWave = function(){
  if(this.dragged){
    this._x = this._parent._xmouse;
    this._y = this._parent._ymouse;
  }

  this.xDistMouse = this._parent._xmouse - this._x;
  this.yDistMouse = this._parent._ymouse - this._y;
  this.distMouse = Math.sqrt(Math.pow(this.xDistMouse, 2) +
  ➥ Math.pow(this.yDistMouse, 2));
  if(this.distMouse < 20){
    this._x += this.xDistMouse / 3;
    this._y += this.yDistMouse / 3;
  }
```

14. In soundPos you store the position of the current sound loop. You therefore use the position property of the Sound object, which returns the position in milliseconds. In addition, you divide this value by 1,000 to get seconds, and then multiply that by the frame rate of the movie to get the position at the current frame. Remember that FlashAmp produced 30 values per second. With this variable, you're now able to address amp_array with your saved amplitude values and store the amplitude for the current position of the sound in amp.

```
this.soundPos = Math.floor(this.loop_sound.position/1000*30);
this.amp = this.amp_array[this.soundPos];
```

15. The head of the wave should swing only if the movie clip isn't dragged, so you need to check that before making it swing with your sine array (this is similar to what you did in the sound pollen exercise).

```
if(!this.dragged){
    this._x += this._parent.sinusStorage_array[this.count] * 3;
    this._y += this._parent.sinusStorage_array[this.count] * 1;
}
```

16. Next, you let the whole wave swing and react to the sound. You attach a value to the end of wave_array that consists of sinusStorage_array[this.count]*100, this.amp/10, and this.vol/10. There's a **base frequency** of the sine wave overlaid by your **amplitude wave** and vertically stretched by the **current volume**. Please refer to the "A little math" section of this chapter for an illustration of the overlaid frequencies effect. The following illustration shows volume stretching. If wave_array is longer than the number of segments, you remove the first value from the array, so the wave travels through all segments.

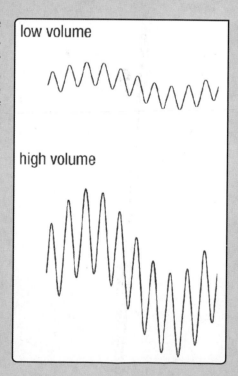

low volume

high volume

```
this.wave_array.unshift(this._parent.sinusStorage
➡ _array[this.count]*100 + this.amp/10 * this.vol/10);

  if(this.wave_array.length > this.waveLength){
    this.wave_array.pop();
  }
  this.len = this.wave_array.length;
```

17. The wave's center is `this._x` and `this._y` away from the blossom's center. This is because the flower's origin is (0, 0) and the wave's origin is that of the movie clip (`this._x`, `this._y`). The drag handler is located in the origin of the wave. To let the wave know where its center would be located if it still was at (0,0), you just need to subtract the wave's coordinates from the center of the flower's coordinates.

```
this.centerX = this._parent.centerX - this._x;
this.centerY = this._parent.centerY - this._y;
```

18. `wave_array[0]` tells you the y-coordinate of the first segment you draw. You'll store this to later draw the first segment in the origin of the movie clip and not above it. `segmentWidth` will depend on the volume of the loop. The louder the sound is, the longer the wave will be. You set the x values for your first segment to 0 because it's supposed to start in the origin of the wave. The two y values also depend on the volume; this means you'll get a larger diameter or height if the sound is louder.

```
this.diff = this.wave_array[0];

    this.segmentWidth = this.vol/2;

    this.x1 = this.x2 = 0;
    this.y1 = this.vol/4;
    this.y2 = -this.vol/4;
```

19. `waveDirection` is based on the width of the stage and takes values from –1 to 1. Essentially it tells the wave the direction it should draw the curve to. If the wave is on the left side of the stage, it should curve to the left, which means –1, and vice versa. As a test, you can comment out the entire `if` clause in the final file. You already set `waveDirection` to –1 when you initiated the wave, so since you don't update `waveDirection` anymore, the wave should now always curve to the left independent of where it's located on the stage.

```
if(this._x <= this._parent.centerX){
    this.waveDirection = -1 + (this._x/this._parent.centerX);
}else{
    this.waveDirection = (this._x - this._parent.centerX)
    ➡ /(Stage.width - this._parent.centerX);
}
```

20. Next, you'll prepare your movie clip by clearing anything drawn on it in previous frames and starting the loop you'll use for drawing the updated wave. The loop is started at 1, not 0, because you already set the first x and y values outside of it.

```
    this.clear();
    this.moveTo(0, 0);

    for(var i = 1; i < this.waveLength; i++){
```

21. `free` plays a major role in bending the wave toward the center of the blossom. Set the `free` variable to a static value of 1 for the moment, and export the SWF to get a feel for what would happen without your calculation. Now bring back the equation. What happens is that you calculate a percentage value from slightly below 1 to 0, which expresses how much freedom your segment has. A few lines below that, you mix the segment's coordinates with the blossom's coordinates, so if `free` is close to 1, the segment's coordinates predominate, and if `free` is close to 0, the blossom's coordinates predominate and the wave bends toward the blossom. `segmentHeight` will also decrease with `free`.

```
this.free = (this.waveLength - i - 1) / (this.waveLength - 1);
this.segmentHeight = this.free * this.vol/4;
```

22. In each loop you need to store the values of the previous loop as starting points for your current segment and to calculate the end points. The width of a segment is calculated by multiplying `segmentWidth` by the current loop index `i` and `waveDirection`, which is bigger at the sides of the stage. For the height determination, `wave_array[i]` will act as the y-coordinate and `segmentHeight` will act as the diameter. By subtracting `diff`, you draw your wave relative to the first segment, because this is supposed to be in the center of the movie clip, as I mentioned.

```
this.x3 = this.x1;
this.y3 = this.y1;
this.x4 = this.x2;
this.y4 = this.y2;

this.x1 = this.segmentWidth * i * this.waveDirection;
this.y1 = this.wave_array[i] + this.segmentHeight - this.diff;
this.x2 = this.x1;
this.y2 = this.wave_array[i] - this.segmentHeight - this.diff;
```

23. It's now time to mix your coordinates with the coordinates of the blossom. As I mentioned, `free` determines which one will predominate. The values of ±0.5 for `y1` and `y2` are there so you have a minimum vertical wave-size of 1.

```
this.x1 = (this.x1 * this.free + this.centerX * (1 - this.free));
this.y1 = 0.5 + (this.y1 * this.free + this.centerY * (1 - this.free));
this.x2 = this.x1;
this.y2 = -0.5 + (this.y2 * this.free + this.centerY * (1 - this.free));
```

24. Now you can draw the segment. `free` is also used here for the variable alpha value of the segment. By checking `i`, you ensure that the wave animates at the beginning of the movie. The illustration opposite shows how the segment function will draw one segment of the wave.

```
if(i < this.len){
        this.segment(this.x1, this.y1, this.x2,
        ➡ this.y2, this.x3, this.y3, this.x4,
        ➡ this.y4, (this.free*40 + 30),
        ➡ this.waveColor);
    }
}
```

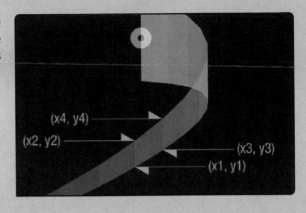

25. The last step after the loop is to update the `count` variable that keeps track of where you are in the sine wave. (Refer to the "Sound pollen" section for a detailed description of this.)

```
if(this.count < this._parent.range-1){
    this.count++;
}else{
    this.count = 0;
}
};
// ================================================================
```

Again, you initiate the waves once the flower animation has stopped playing. Inside the `for` loop, `i` acts as an identifier for your sound loops and amplitude arrays.

```
flower_mc.onEnterFrame  = function(){
    if(this._currentframe == this._totalframes){
        this.stop();
        this.onEnterFrame = undefined;
        for(var i = 0; i < 8; i++){
            createWave(this._parent, i, this._parent.waveLength,
            ➡ this._parent.colors_array[i], this._parent["amp_array" + i]);
        }
    }
};
```

Now you can export the file and take a look at the final effect. You'll find the sound files on the CD, so there's plenty of room for additional experimentation. It's always a good starting point to play with the files and modify just some of the variables to achieve different effects. Within the FLA files, I added a few comments and also suggested some modifications that you can try out, so please have a look at the source files for additional information.

Summary

As you've probably noticed through working with me during this chapter, I'm not really able to decide what I like best in Flash because there are so many interesting things to explore. You have some interactivity, visual effects, scripting, and sound in this chapter's experiments. I believe that what makes a great project is bringing all of these things together. The process of connecting different components of the various disciplines determines to a great degree the success of your work.

Whether you do that all on your own or you collaborate with other people to accomplish your goals depends on quite a few factors, and it's ultimately up to you. What's important in the end is that you stay open to new influences, never stop learning, and put your heart into what you do.

Through this chapter's explorations, I hope you've not only learned some concepts that you can use in your projects, but also enjoyed the experiments themselves. Thanks, it was a pleasure!

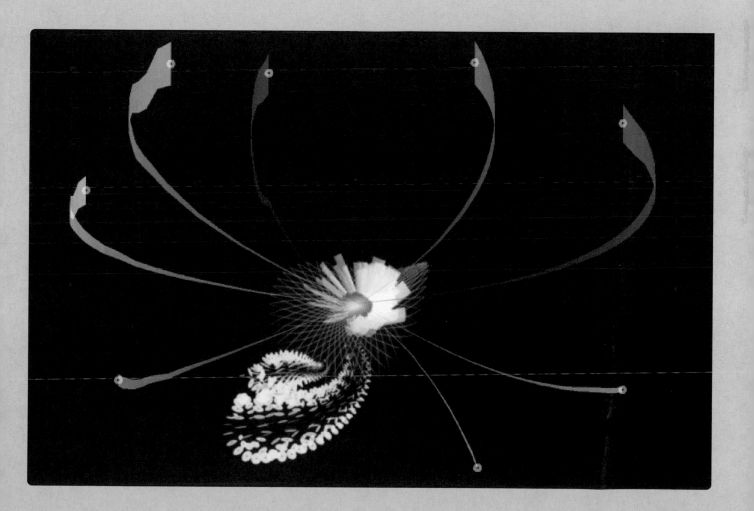

INDEX

1-59059-303-0 $29.99 [US]

1-59059-305-7 $34.99 [US]

1-59059-308-1 $34.99 [US]

1-59059-336-7 $34.99 [US]

1-59059-210-7 $34.99 [US]

EXPERIENCE THE DESIGNER TO DESIGNER™ DIFFERENCE

1-59059-306-5 $34.99 [US]

1-59059-238-7 $24.99 [US]

1-59059-149-6 $24.99 [US]

1-59059-224-7 $39.99 [US]

1-59059-221-2 $39.99 [US]

1-59059-236-0 $39.99 [US]

1-59059-372-3 $39.99 [US]

1-59059-262-X $49.99 [US]

1-59059-304-9 $49.99 [US]

1-59059-309-X $49.99 [US]

1-59059-399-5 $44.99 [US]

1-59059-110-0 $49.99 [US]

friendsof

DESIGNER TO DESIGNER™

an Apress® company

1-59059-231-X $39.99 [US]

1-59059-408-8 $34.99 [US]

1-59059-355-3 $39.99 [US]

1-59059-381-2 $29.99 [US]

1-59059-409-6 $39.99 [US]

friendsofed.com/forums

Join the friends of ED forums to find out more about our books, the technologies that we publish on, or to get a helping hand on a challenging project. Designer to Designer™ is what it's all about: the friends of ED community sharing ideas and helping each other out. In the friends of ED forums you'll find a wide range of topics to discuss, so look around, find a forum, and dive right in!

Books and Information
Chat about friends of ED books, gossip about the community, tell us some bad jokes!

Flash
Design issues, ActionScript, dynamic content: gotoAndPost!

Web design
Front-end frustrations, back-end blight: share your problems and your knowledge.

Site check
Show off your work, or find inspiration.

Digital Imagery
Photoshop, Fireworks, Illustrator, Paint Shop Pro: let's create some eye candy!

ArchivED
An archive of all those old questions and answers.

HOW TO PARTICIPATE

Go to the friends of ED Forums at **www.friendsofed.com/forums**.

Visit **www.friendsofed.com** to get the latest on books, community gossip, and some of the slickest sites online today

friendsof ™

DESIGNER TO DESIGNER™

an Apress® company

License Agreement (Single-User Products)

THIS IS A LEGAL AGREEMENT BETWEEN YOU, THE END USER, AND APRESS. BY OPENING THE SEALED DISK PACKAGE, YOU ARE AGREEING TO BE BOUND BY THE TERMS OF THIS AGREEMENT. IF YOU DO NOT AGREE TO THE TERMS OF THIS AGREEMENT, PROMPTLY RETURN THE UNOPENED DISK PACKAGE AND THE ACCOMPANYING ITEMS (INCLUDING WRITTEN MATERIALS AND BINDERS AND OTHER CONTAINERS) TO THE PLACE YOU OBTAINED THEM FOR A FULL REFUND.

APRESS SOFTWARE LICENSE

1. GRANT OF LICENSE. Apress grants you the right to use one copy of this enclosed Apress software program (the "SOFTWARE") on a single terminal connected to a single computer (e.g., with a single CPU). You may not network the SOFTWARE or otherwise use it on more than one computer or computer terminal at the same time.

2. COPYRIGHT. The SOFTWARE copyright is owned by Apress and is protected by United States copyright laws and international treaty provisions. No part of the SOFTWARE may be reproduced or transmitted in any form or by any means, electronic or mechanical, including photocopying, recording, or by any information storage or retrieval system, without prior written permission. You must treat the SOFTWARE like any other copyrighted material (e.g., a book or musical recording) except that you may either (a) make one copy of the SOFTWARE solely for backup or archival purposes, or (b) transfer the SOFTWARE to a single hard disk, provided you keep the original solely for backup or archival purposes. You may not copy the written material accompanying the SOFTWARE.

3. OTHER RESTRICTIONS. You may not rent or lease the SOFTWARE, but you may transfer the SOFTWARE and accompanying written materials on a permanent basis provided you retain no copies and the recipient agrees to the terms of this Agreement. You may not reverse engineer, decompile, or disassemble the SOFTWARE. If SOFTWARE is an update, any transfer must include the update and all prior versions.

4. By breaking the seal on the disk package, you agree to the terms and conditions printed in the Apress License Agreement. If you do not agree with the terms, simply return this book with the still-sealed CD package to the place of purchase for a refund.

DISCLAIMER OF WARRANTY

NO WARRANTIES. Apress disclaims all warranties, either express or implied, including, but not limited to, implied warranties of merchantability and fitness for a particular purpose, with respect to the SOFTWARE and the accompanying written materials. The software and any related documentation is provided "as is." You may have other rights, which vary from state to state.

NO LIABILITIES FOR CONSEQUENTIAL DAMAGES. In no event shall be liable for any damages whatsoever (including, without limitation, damages from loss of business profits, business interruption, loss of business information, or other pecuniary loss) arising out of the use or inability to use this Apress product, even if Apress has been advised of the possibility of such damages. Because some states do not allow the exclusion or limitation of liability for consequential or incidental damages, the above limitation may not apply to you.

U.S. GOVERNMENT RESTRICTED RIGHTS

The SOFTWARE and documentation are provided with RESTRICTED RIGHTS. Use, duplication, or disclosure by the Government is subject to restriction as set forth in subparagraph (c) (1) (ii) of The Rights in Technical Data and Computer Software clause at 52.227-7013. Contractor/manufacturer is Apress, 2560 Ninth Street, Suite 219, Berkeley, California, 94710.

This Agreement is governed by the laws of the State of California.

Should you have any questions concerning this Agreement, or if you wish to contact Apress for any reason, please write to Apress, 2560 Ninth Street, Suite 219, Berkeley, California, 94710.